331.12
PRO
2002

3 6480 000070211

Occupational Projections and Training Data

2002-03 Edition

U.S. Department of Labor
Elaine L. Chao, Secretary

Bureau of Labor Statistics
Lois Orr, Acting Commissioner

January 2002

Bulletin 2542

W9-BML-618

For sale by the Superintendent of Documents, U.S. Government Printing Office
Internet: bookstore.gpo.gov Phone: toll free (866) 512-1800; DC area (202) 512-1800
Fax: (202) 512-2250 Mail: Stop SSOP, Washington, DC 20402-0001

ISBN 0-16-051115-1

Preface

This statistical and research supplement to the 2002-03 *Occupational Outlook Handbook* presents detailed, comprehensive statistics used in preparing the *Handbook*. It also discusses how the data are prepared and other topics—information that is valuable to training officials, education planners, vocational and employment counselors, jobseekers, and others interested in occupational information. Each topic is addressed in a separate chapter. This edition of the supplement is the 16th in a series dating back to 1971.

Chapter I discusses the incorporation of the 2000 Standard Occupational Classification (SOC) system into the national employment projections. This system eventually will be used by all Federal agencies for collecting and distributing occupational information. Incorporating the SOC system, however, created several challenges including—preparing an occupational directory, adjusting Occupational Employment Statistics survey data, and distributing 1990 Census of Population based 2000 CPS employment data to national employment matrix occupations.

Chapter II presents detailed information about all occupations in the national employment matrix. In addition to statistics on employment and employment changes, growth rates, job openings, and self-employed workers, table 2 includes rankings, from very low to very high, for a number of variables. It also identifies the most significant source of postsecondary education or training for each occupation. This table provides the user with a comprehensive picture of a specific occupation and makes it easier to compare the attributes of different occupations. The data used in preparing table 2 are available electronically for those who want to array them differently for analytical purposes.

Changes in industry employment and in the utilization of an occupation within an industry affect occupational employment. Chapter III presents information about the factors driving these changes.

The concept of replacement needs often is confusing. Chapter IV explains what the data on replacement needs represent, and describes how they were prepared. Projected replacement rates and estimates of replacement needs for 2000-10 also are presented.

Finally, data from the National Center for Education Statistics on completions of institutional education and training programs by field of study appear in chapter V.

In all cases, national data are provided. Data for States and local areas may be obtained from sources identified in the appendix.

Jill Auyer, Doug Braddock, Jeff Gruenert, Henry Kasper, T. Alan Lacey, Roger Moncarz, Azure Reaser, Erik Savisaar, Terry Schau, Lynn Shniper, Tiffany Stringer, and Carolyn Veneri prepared this bulletin. Theresa Cosca, Supervisory Economist, Division of Occupational Outlook, and Alan Eck, Manager, Occupational Outlook Studies, supervised its preparation under the direction of Mike Pilot, Chief, Division of Occupational Outlook. For further information about material contained in this bulletin, please call the Chief, Division of Occupational Outlook, at (202) 691-5703.

Material in this publication is in the public domain and, with appropriate credit, may be reproduced without permission. This information is available to sensory impaired individuals upon request. Voice phone: (202) 691-5200; Federal Relay Service: 1-800-877-8339.

Information on the Internet

The Office of Occupational Statistics and Employment Projections maintains the "Employment Projections" home page on the BLS Internet site (**http://stats.bls.gov/emp/**). It provides access to electronic copies of the *Occupational Outlook Handbook, Career Guide to Industries,* and *Occupational Outlook Quarterly*; articles from the November 2001 *Monthly Labor Review* describing the 2000-10 projections in detail; frequently requested tables; and many other items of interest to users of industry and occupation employment projections. The "Employment Projections" home page also provides access to two online searchable databases. The first permits searches of data on occupational employment, job openings, earnings, training, and other information from this publication; the second provides access to detailed employment data that make up the 2000-10 national employment matrix.

Contents

Chapter I. 2000-10 Occupational Projections Incorporate the 2000 Standard Occupational Classification System

The Bureau of Labor Statistics (BLS) has produced occupational projections biennially as part of its Occupational Outlook program for more than 50 years. Students and individuals seeking a job change use the information to evaluate career choices. Counselors and training program planners also find extensive use for expected job opportunity information. The most recent, the 2000-10 projections, are discussed in detail in the November, 2001 edition of the *Monthly Labor Review*. These projections also serve as the source for information presented in the 2002-03 editions of the widely used career guidance publications, *Occupational Outlook Handbook* and *Career Guide to Industries*. Public access to the projections and related materials from the BLS Internet site, which accounts for about half of all visits to the site, testifies to the popularity of the information. Occupational projections for 2000-10 differ from those in the past in one major aspect, however—they incorporate the 2000 Standard Occupational Classification (SOC) system.

The 2000 SOC system revises the 1980 SOC system, the first structure designed to ensure that Federal agencies collected and distributed consistent occupational information. The promise of the 1980 system did not become reality, however, because different occupational classifications remained in use during the 1990's.

Concerned that occupational data collected in Federal Government surveys were difficult to compare because they frequently used different classification systems, and that the occupations might not adequately reflect the work performed in the changing work systems of the "new economy," the U.S. Office of Management and Budget chartered the Standard Occupation Classification Revision Policy Committee (SOC Committee) in 1994. The SOC Committee's efforts resulted in the 2000 SOC system.[1] The SOC eventually will be used by all Federal agencies collecting occupational information.

In 1999, the Occupational Employment Statistics (OES) survey, a major data source for preparing occupational projections, became the first BLS program to adopt the 2000 SOC. Conversion to the new SOC for the 2000-10 projections was prompted by the availability of 2000 SOC system-based 1999 OES survey employment and earnings data. Adopting the 2000 SOC system into the 2000-10 projections, however, presented challenges, as described below.

Background

BLS occupational projections use an employment matrix as a tool for analyzing occupation utilization within industries, as well as for projecting occupational employment. An initial step for each projection cycle entails defining the base-year employment matrix structure. Occupations define rows, while class of worker categories—self-employed; unpaid family; and wage and salary workers, by industry—define columns. Once defined, three matrixes use the same matrix structure.

Data on self-employed worker employment; unpaid family worker employment; and wage and salary worker employment by industry from a variety of sources fill the cells of the base-year matrix. Employment in the matrix measures jobs, not individuals, because individuals may be employed by more than one firm.

Self-employed and unpaid family worker employment comes from the Current Population Survey (CPS).[2] The CPS is a monthly survey of about 50,000 households conducted for BLS by the U.S. Census Bureau. It collects class of worker, industry, and occupation information about the primary job of all employed persons age 16 and over. Second job information also is collected for one-quarter of the sample each month and combined with primary job occupational employment estimates to estimate self-employed and unpaid family worker jobs.

Wage and salary industry employment estimates, by occupation, are derived by multiplying the proportion of wage and salary occupational employment in the industry by base-year total wage and salary industry employment. For most industries, OES survey data identify occupational distributions and Current Employment Statistics (CES) data provide the industry total employment information.[3] Both collect information from establishments.

Total base-year employment for an occupation is the sum of employment in a row across all columns—the combination of self-employed, unpaid family, and wage and salary workers.

The second matrix, the change-factor matrix, uses the same structure as the base-year employment matrix and presents estimates of changes in utilization of wage and salary workers, by occupation, within industries. System

---

[1] See Chester Levine, Laurie Salmon, and Daniel H. Weinberg, "Revising the Standard Occupation Classification System," *Monthly Labor Review*, May 1999, pp. 36-45.

[2] Extensive information about the concepts and methodology used in the CPS is available at: **http://www.bls.census.gov/cps/cpsmain.htm**

[3] The OES surveys about 400,000 establishments each year, one-third of the sample, to collect occupational wage and salary employment and wage data. Surveying the entire sample takes three years. Detailed information about the OES survey is available at:
http://stats.bls.gov/oes/2000/oestec2000.htm
CES wage and salary employment data comes from a monthly sample of about 300,000 establishments. For more information, visit:
http://stats.bls.gov/ces/home.htm

analysts, for example, would be expected to become a greater proportion of an industry's employment as the number of applications for computer use continue to increase. The change factor multiplied by the base-year wage and salary occupational distribution determines occupational distribution in the projected year.

Preparing the projected-year employment matrix is the last step in the projection process. Projected-year wage and salary employment for an industry multiplied by the projected-year occupational distribution yields projected-year wage and salary occupational employment for the industry. Occupational employment for self-employed and unpaid family workers is projected separately using time series analytical techniques, and is combined in the matrix with projected wage and salary occupational employment. In the end, total projected-year occupational employment is the sum of employment in a row across all columns—the sum of self-employed, unpaid family, and wage and salary workers.

Since their inception over 30 years ago, national employment matrixes incorporated industry-by-occupation wage and salary employment information from three different occupational classification systems or data sources. The industry and occupation classification systems from the 1960 and 1970 Censuses of Population, which provided industry-by-occupation employment patterns based on the responses of individuals, initially determined the base-year matrix structures. Similarities between the two census classification systems simplified the transition between the 1960 and 1970 decennial census data.

The OES survey-based industry-by-occupation employment data adopted for use with the 1980-90 projections constituted the second major occupational structure and data source used in the national employment matrix. The OES survey occupation structure, with some exceptions, classified occupations according to the principles of the newly created 1980 Standard Occupational Classification system, and generally was consistent with the 1970 and 1980 census occupational classification systems. Large differences in employment for identical occupations occurred, however, because the OES survey obtained information from employers while the censuses relied on the responses of individuals. While some additional occupations were added, and some changes to industry coverage occurred that affected occupational consistency, BLS used the 1980 SOC based OES structure with only minor adjustments through the 1998-2008 occupational projections.

The 2000-10 occupational projections incorporate a third occupational classification system—the 2000 Standard Occupational Classification system—that also results in major differences in occupational employment between the OES survey and data based on the 1990 census occupational classification system. In this case, the differences result not from a change in a data source, but from the change in the classification system used in obtaining the data.

Incorporating the 2000 SOC into the 2000 national employment matrix

Incorporating the 2000 SOC system was the primary goal of efforts to restructure the national employment matrix. Establishing the broadest employment coverage possible, however, remained a secondary goal. The 2000 matrix occupational structure achieved both goals, a task that required identifying and accounting for all valid 2000 SOC occupations, and identifying data sources for occupations and industries not covered by the 1999 OES survey.

While occupations define the rows in the matrix, several types of occupations exist in the final structure.[4] (See table 1.)

- Summary occupations (202) combine employment information for detailed—"line item" or "rollup"—occupations.

- Line item occupations (668) possess the greatest level of published occupation detail in the matrix, have a one-to-one relationship with OES survey occupation data, and display 2000 and projected 2010 employment estimates.

- Rollup occupations (27) possess the greatest level of published occupation detail in the matrix, present data from two or more collapsed or current occupations, and display 2000 and projected 2010 employment estimates.

- Collapsed occupations (43) possess only base-year employment; they are combined to create rollup occupations. Base-year employment estimates are suppressed and are retained for internal use only, because of confidentiality or data concerns. Employment is not projected for these occupations.

- Current occupations (59) possess only base-year employment; they are combined to create rollup occupations. Base-year employment may be published, but employment is not projected because historical or other data about these occupations are not available.

Full implementation of the SOC system in the national employment matrix fell just short of complete success at the most detailed occupational level. Of the 695 detailed occupations—those individual occupations identified as line item or rollup occupation types in table 1—654 are consistent with a 2000 SOC occupation. Residual occupa-

---

[4] A fifth occupation type, excluded occupations (134), was used for accounting purposes in preparing the 2000 matrix occupation directory but is not included in table 1 because occupations in this category have no data associated with them. Exclude occupations generally are OES survey occupations used to collect specific details about occupational employment—for example, research activities in the education services industry. OES survey staff does not release employment data for these occupations. In some cases—for example, the detailed medical specialty occupations within physicians and surgeons—OES survey data were not used. These occupations also were categorized as exclude occupations.

tions—the "all other..." occupation category used to classify a number of occupations within a specific group—accounted for most of those not consistent with the SOC. The treatment of residual occupations in the OES survey explains much of the inconsistencies, and is discussed later in this chapter.

Complete consistency exists between the 2000 national employment matrix and the 22 SOC major occupation groups and the 10 intermediate aggregation group levels (excluding SOC military occupations, which are not covered in the matrix).

Class-of-worker categories define the columns, the other dimension of the national employment matrix. All classes of workers are included among the columns for self-employed workers; unpaid family workers; and wage and salary workers, by industry. Industry employment information is available only for wage and salary workers.

Consistent with providing a broad measure, the national employment matrix estimates jobs, not individuals, as individuals may hold several jobs with different employers.[5] The class-of-worker structure of the matrix columns is identical to that used with the 1998-2008 projections. As the following shows, the OES survey contributes occupational distribution information for wage and salary workers in 256 of the 262 industries, by far the largest source of occupational information. In addition, OES survey staff recode Office of Personnel Management (OPM) and the United States Postal Service (USPS) occupational employment data to the 2000 SOC structure for use in the national employment matrix.

Class of worker category	Number of columns	Data source
Total	270	
Self-employed, primary job	*1*	*CPS*
Self-employed, secondary job	*1*	*CPS*
Unpaid family worker, primary job	*1*	*CPS*
Unpaid family worker, secondary job	*1*	*CPS*
Wage and salary worker, primary job, agriculture, forestry, fishing, and private household	*4*	*CPS*
Wage and salary worker, secondary job, agriculture, forestry, fishing, and private household	*4*	*CPS*
Wage and salary workers, Federal Government	*1*	*OPM*
Wage and salary workers, United States Postal Service	*1*	*USPS*
Wage and salary workers, other industries	*256*	*OES*

Challenges in incorporating the 2000 SOC system

Implementation of the SOC system for collecting data in the 1999 OES survey—the major source of industry by occupation employment and earnings—precipitated an assessment as to whether those SOC based data should be incorporated into the 2000-10 occupational projections and related products. The fact that the 1999 data constituted information from only one-third of the full OES survey sample raised quality issues.[6] Continuing to use 1998 industry-by-occupation employment patterns based on an obsolete occupational classification system caused concern that the occupations in 2000-10 projections would be inconsistent with those displayed with the 2000 OES survey data and cause unnecessary confusion among data users. Being able to use more recent occupational earnings data became another argument in favor of using the 2000 SOC-based OES data.

On balance, the advantages prompted the decision to use the 1999 OES survey data for preparing the 2000-10 projections. Implementing the decision, however, created several challenges including: Preparing an occupational directory, adjusting the data, and distributing 1990 Census of Population-based 2000 CPS employment data to national employment matrix occupations.

Preparing the 2000-10 occupation directory. The 2000-10 occupation directory defines the occupation structure for the 2000-10 projections; it establishes the occupations appearing in the rows of the matrix. While generally consistent with the 2000 SOC system structure at the detailed occupation level, and completely consistent at the major occupation group level, differences from the 2000 SOC structure occur for several reasons.

Alphabetical versus numerical code listing. The SOC system structures occupations using six-digit numerical codes. In the SOC system, occupation titles appear in numeric code sequence. While those who constructed the SOC system wished to produce a numeric list of occupation titles that would coincide with an alphabetical list, their efforts were not completely successful. BLS uses the 2000 SOC codes to identify occupations, but the codes do not appear in tables presenting the occupational projections. To assist users in locating occupational information, BLS lists occupations alphabetically within SOC major occupation groups in the occupation directory—for example, table 1 displays 11-9010 Agricultural managers before 11-1011 Chief executives.

Non-SOC occupation coverage. In an effort to reduce the number of residual occupations listed on the survey forms, the OES survey in some cases combined residual occupations from different broad occupational groups. For exam-

---

[5] Current Population Survey (CPS) data on more than 2 million secondary jobs were included in the 1998-2008 occupational projections. See "Chapter I. New Secondary Job Employment Data," *Occupational Projections and Training Needs*, Bulletin 2521 (Bureau of Labor Statistics, May 2000), pp. 1-4.

[6] The OES survey collects data in all industries from one-third of the full sample each year over a 3-year cycle. OES survey methods are described in "Appendix B. Survey Methods and Reliability of the 1999 Occupational Employment Statistics Estimates" in *Occupational Employment and Wages, 1999*, Bulletin 1545 (Bureau of Labor Statistics, September 2001), pp. 175-184.

ple, the OES survey combined the SOC occupations 11-9039 Education administrators, all other, and 11-9199 Managers, all other into the survey occupation 11-9199 All other managers. Although the survey occupation was associated with a valid SOC code, the data collected represented two SOC occupations. To be assigned a valid SOC occupation code in the 2000 matrix directory, an occupation must represent a single SOC occupation and must represent employment data for all classes of workers and industries. Because the OES survey occupation 11-9199 All other managers consists of two SOC occupations, it is judged not to be a valid SOC occupation for inclusion in the 2000 matrix directory and is assigned the non-SOC code 11-1198. The title All other managers differs from the SOC title and is retained.

In another case, the OES survey occupation 11-9011 Farm, ranch, and other agricultural managers provided employment information for wage and salary workers only in the agricultural services industry. Because of its limited employment coverage, the OES survey occupation data for Farm, ranch, and other agricultural managers were assigned the matrix occupation code 11-9012, a non-SOC code. To expand coverage, CPS employment data for Farm, ranch, and other agricultural managers in industries other than agricultural services were obtained and assigned to another matrix occupation with the non-SOC code 11-9013. Achieving consistency between the 2000 national employment matrix and the SOC system for Farm, ranch, and other agricultural managers required combining data for the two non-SOC occupations into a third occupation and using the valid SOC code 11-9011. Base- and projected-year employment are distributed only for the rollup occupation 11-9011 Farm, ranch, and other agricultural managers.

Examination of each occupation in the 2000 matrix determined whether consistency with a single SOC occupation exists and comprehensive employment data are represented. Matrix occupations that are assigned a SOC system code met both criteria.

Adjusting the data. Examination of the 1999 OES survey results data identified differences in employment levels between non-SOC 1998 OES survey occupations and 2000 SOC based OES survey occupations with like definitions that could not be explained. Because the 1999 data represent only one-third of the total OES survey sample, large sampling errors could explain the differences.[7] To increase the sample size, the analysts who developed the 2000 national employment matrix data used 2000 interim OES survey data that represent about 50 percent of the full OES survey sample.

Although delaying preparation of the final data, the processing of information from an expanded sample was not a complicating factor. Dealing with the impact of the OES survey's occupational structure, recoding of OPM and USPS employment data by OES staff, and deciding whether to use the "enhancement" adjustment process provided greater challenges.

[7] Ibid.

Impact of OES survey structure. As discussed earlier, the OES survey structure at times resulted in the collection of information for "All other…" residual occupations that was inconsistent with the SOC structure. Significant employment for some occupations could not be identified as a result. The undercount for physicians' and surgeons' employment (148,000, or more than 25 percent of their wage and salary employment) created the greatest concern because of the occupation's prominence, the potential uses of the data, and the availability of other employment data with different estimates that might raise questions about the credibility of BLS estimates.

The 2002-03 edition of *Occupational Outlook Handbook* is intended to provide total employment information for all physicians and surgeons, as well as for specific specialties. In the past, American Medical Association data were used to distribute employment among medical specialties. Under the 2000 SOC structure, this information could be collected for detailed occupations and aggregated to the broad occupation 29-1060 Physicians and surgeons, as follows:

> 29-1060 Physicians and surgeons
> 29-1061 Anesthesiologists
> 29-1062 Family and general practitioners
> 29-1063 Internists, general
> 29-1064 Obstetricians and gynecologists
> 29-1065 Pediatricians, general
> 29-1066 Psychiatrists
> 29-1067 Surgeons
> 29-1069 Physicians and surgeons, all other

The problem with the OES survey data for 29-1060 Physicians and surgeons exists because the employment data for SOC occupation 29-1069 Physicians and surgeons, all other are not collected separately. Rather, they are collected in the OES residual occupation 29-1199 All other health diagnosing and treating practitioners, along with two other occupations. The OES survey code 29-1199 is a valid SOC code but, as shown below, contains employment data for more than one SOC occupation and is not consistent with the SOC occupation definition.

OES Survey code and title	Component SOC occupation code and title
29-1199 All other health diagnosing and treating practitioners	29-1069 Physician and surgeons all other
	29-1129 Therapists, all other
	29-1199 Health diagnosing and treating practitioners, all other.

The survey structure precludes estimating employment for detailed SOC occupation 29-1069 Physician and surgeons, all other. The structure thus precludes estimating total employment for the SOC broad occupation group, 29-1060 Physicians and surgeons that includes the "all other" occupation category.

To calculate 2000 employment for 29-1060 Physicians and surgeons, the occupation's 1998 percent employment distribution in each industry was substituted for the 2000 employment distribution of the detailed SOC physician and surgeon occupation data captured by the 1999 OES survey. Physician and surgeon employment estimates in 2000 were developed by applying the 1998 occupation distribution, by industry, to 2000 industry employment. Any revisions intended to maintain industry employment as a result of increases to total Physician and surgeon employment were made by reducing employment in the residual occupations.

Occupation employment distribution patterns, by industry, from the 1999 OES survey also were replaced with 1998 OES survey patterns for education administrators and biological scientists. For these occupations also, industry employment estimates were maintained by adjusting appropriate residual occupation employment.

OES staff recoding of OPM and USPS occupational data. OPM and USPS provide OES staff occupational employment data using occupational codes and occupation titles unique to their organizations. The OES staff recodes the OPM and USPS occupational data to SOC occupations. Review of the recoded OPM and USPS occupational data by staff preparing the occupational projections revealed deficiencies—for example, all Federal computer specialist employment was categorized into only 3 of the 9 SOC computer specialist occupations. Recommended changes to the distribution of OPM and USPS occupation data to SOC-based Federal occupational employment were incorporated, and significantly changed employment patterns.

Initial OES coded Federal Government information technology occupations

15-1021 *Computer programmers*
15-1011 *Computer and information specialists, research*
15-1051 *Computer systems analysts*

Adjusted OES coded Federal Government information technology occupations

15-1011 *Computer and information scientists, research*
15-1021 *Computer programmers*
15-1031 *Computer software engineers, applications*
15-1032 *Computer software engineers, systems software*
15-1041 *Computer support specialists*
15-1051 *Computer systems analysts*
15-1061 *Data base administrators*
15-1071 *Network and computer systems administrators*
15-1081 *Network systems and data communications analysts*
15-1099 *All other computer specialists*

As noted above, the distribution of employment in information technology was widened from three to nine occupations. Distributions for some technician, clerical, and transportation occupations also were revised.

Should the "enhancement" procedure be used? As part of the 1998-2008 and other projections series, employment in the base-year wage and salary matrix was augmented—or "enhanced"—in industry and occupation cells not covered by the OES survey using 1990 Census of Population em-

ployment data. Only OES occupation and industry cells with definitions judged to exactly match those used in the Census of Population could receive employment. The enhancement process moves OES survey-based wage and salary employment from residual occupations to detailed occupations in each industry identified by the 1990 census data. The incorporation of the SOC introduced a new occupational classification system that would complicate identifying comparable occupations. The increased difficulty of matching occupations was one of several factors causing use of the enhancement procedure to be questioned. Others issues requiring investigation were the relevancy of 10-year-old data and the expanded industry coverage of the OES survey.

To assess their relevance, 1995-99 CPS microdata were tabulated to identify employment for the same industry-occupation cells as those from the 1990 census data that were used to enhance the 1998 employment matrix. Both the CPS and census data for the same industry-occupation cells produced the same employment estimate—2.5 million. Employment from the CPS, however, appeared in 1,643 industry-occupation cells, far fewer than the 3,808 from the census data. The smaller number of cells in the CPS could reflect better industry-occupation coding, the result of responses having been obtained by CPS interviewers rather than simply being provided by individuals completing a form. At the least, the results suggested there may be a lot of "noise" in the 1990 census data.

Examining the impact of expanded OES survey industry coverage was complicated by the need to identify comparable occupations. OES survey data for 64 comparable occupations in the industry-occupation cells used in the enhancement procedure, however, provided higher employment estimates than the 1990 Census data—389,000 versus 319,000—testifying to better OES survey industry coverage.

Because of concerns about occupational comparability and 1990 data relevancy, as well as indications of better OES survey industry coverage, the enhancement procedure was not used in preparing 2000 base-year employment estimates.

Distributing 2000 CPS employment data to SOC occupations. In addition to the major contribution of 2000 SOC-based OES survey data, the national employment matrix depends on 2000 CPS employment data for estimates of the numbers of self-employed, unpaid family workers, and wage and salary workers in some industries. Other CPS data are used in estimating replacement needs and demographic characteristics. CPS data, however, use the 1990 Census of Population classification system. Developing a "crosswalk" to convert 2000 CPS employment estimates to the 2000 national employment matrix structure provided yet another challenge in adopting the 2000 SOC and in preparing the 2000 base-year matrix. Actually, several occupational crosswalks—1990 Census of Population to 2000 Census of Population, 2000 Census of Population to 2000 SOC, and 2000 SOC to 2000 national employment matrix—were needed. Because the latter two generally are consistent with the 2000 SOC, their construction was not difficult. The same cannot be said about converting 1990 Census of Population-based occupational employment data to a 2000 Census of Population basis. As the following indicates, the process used was tedious and subjective.

Distributing 1990 census occupation employment among 2000 census occupations draws on two U.S. Census Bureau crosswalks. For the first, the SOC Revision Policy Committee staff took the job titles associated with each 1990 census occupation and distributed them among the 2000 census occupations. After distribution, the job titles associated with the 1990 occupation are associated with one, two, or more 2000 census occupations. Because the number of job titles associated with each 1990 occupation is known, and the number going to each 2000 occupation is known, the proportion going to each 2000 job title can be calculated.

Distributing employment using the distribution of job titles possessed the inherent weakness that the job title distribution assigns each title the same weight. For example, two job titles associated with a 1990 census occupation assigned to different 2000 census occupations would distribute 1990 employment equally. In reality, however, one title could account for 10 percent of the 1990 occupation's employment and the other, for 90 percent. As a result, the employment distribution would be incorrect.

A second Census Bureau crosswalk—the recode crosswalk—sought to address the question of distributing employment directly by recoding occupational responses for 100,000 individuals in the 1990 census to the 2000 census occupational classification system. Weights assigned to individual respondents were used to distribute 1990 occupation employment to the 2000 occupation.

The two files then were merged and sorted so that each 1990 occupation displayed matches to a 2000 occupation based on:

- A match appearing both in the 1990 census response recode and job title assignment files.
- A match appearing only in the 1990 census response recode file.
- A match appearing only in the job title assignment file.

Applying several rules reduced the number of 2000 occupations available for review and simplified evaluation of 1990 occupation employment distribution.

1. A 1990 occupation could be distributed only to 2000 occupations appearing in both the recode and title distribution crosswalks.

2. When the title distribution crosswalk identified 100 percent of all 1990 titles belonging to one 2000 occupation, that 2000 occupation received 100 percent of 1990 employment.

3. When only one 2000 occupation appeared on both the recode and title crosswalks but neither crosswalk distributed 100 percent of the 1990 occupation employment to the single 2000 occupation, that 2000 occupation still would receive 100 percent of 1990 employment.

4. When 1990 occupations had multiple 2000 occupations eligible to receive employment, subjective judgments about the recode and title crosswalk distributions determined which were preferable. If the recode crosswalk identified one 2000 occupation to receive far more employment than any in the title crosswalk, the recode distribution, which reflected the impact of weighted employment data, usually was selected. In general, if two or more 2000 occupations on either the recode or title crosswalk accounted for more than 80 percent of the distribution, those occupations, and their distributions scaled to 100 percent, received the 1990 employment.

Until detailed 2000 SOC system based occupational information becomes available from the 2000 Census of Population or the CPS, a crosswalk will be needed to convert existing data.

Future changes

Many of the problems encountered in incorporating the 2000 SOC into the 2000 national employment matrix resulted from the structure of the OES survey. In the 2001 survey, data will be collected for all detailed 2000 SOC occupations. Residual "All other..." occupations will not be listed on the survey forms. Respondents will add information to identify occupations not listed on the survey form. State analysts will recode the employer entries to SOC occupations. In theory, data will be collected and processed in accordance with the 2000 SOC structure. The results should be available by the end of 2002.

Beginning in January 2003, CPS occupational data will be developed using the 2000 Census of Population occupational classification system, which closely resembles the 2000 SOC. Detailed 2000 Census of Population occupational employment data also should be available in 2003.

Table 1. National employment matrix occupational directory, 2000

Matrix code	Valid SOC Code?	Matrix occupation title	Occupation Type	Matrix code	Valid SOC Code?	Matrix occupation title	Occupation Type
00-0000	NO	Total, all occupations	Summary	13-1090	NO	Human resources, training, and labor relations specialists	Summary
11-1300	NO	Management, business, and financial occupations	Summary	13-1072	YES	Compensation, benefits, and job analysis specialists	Line item
11-0000	YES	Management occupations	Summary	13-1071	YES	Employment, recruitment, and placement specialists	Line item
11-3011	YES	Administrative services managers	Line item	13-1073	YES	Training and development specialists	Line item
11-2000	YES	Advertising, marketing, promotions, public relations, and sales managers	Summary	13-1111	YES	Management analysts	Line item
11-2011	YES	Advertising and promotions managers	Line item	13-1121	YES	Meeting and convention planners	Line item
11-2020	YES	Marketing and sales managers	Summary	13-1198	NO	All other business operations specialists	Line item
11-2021	YES	Marketing managers	Line item	13-2000	YES	Financial specialists	Summary
11-2022	YES	Sales managers	Line item	13-2011	YES	Accountants and auditors	Line item
11-2031	YES	Public relations managers	Line item	13-2021	YES	Appraisers and assessors of real estate	Line Item
11-9010	YES	Agricultural managers	Summary	13-2031	YES	Budget analysts	Line item
11-9011	YES	Farm, ranch, and other agricultural managers	Rollup	13-2041	YES	Credit analysts	Line item
11-9013	NO	Farm, ranch, and other agricultural managers (SIC 07)	Collapsed	13-2051	YES	Financial analysts	Line item
11-9014	NO	Farm, ranch, and other agricultural managers (SIC 01,02)	Collapsed	13-2061	YES	Financial examiners	Line item
				13-2053	YES	Insurance underwriters	Line Item
11-9012	YES	Farmers and ranchers	Line item	13-2070	YES	Loan counselors and officers	Summary
11-1011	YES	Chief executives	Line item	13-2071	YES	Loan counselors	Line Item
11-3021	YES	Computer and information systems managers	Line item	13-2072	YES	Loan officers	Line item
				13-2052	YES	Personal financial advisors	Line Item
11-9021	YES	Construction managers	Line item	13-2081	YES	Tax examiners, collectors, and revenue agents	Line Item
11-9030	YES	Education administrators	Line item				
11-9041	YES	Engineering managers	Line item	13-2082	YES	Tax preparers	Line Item
11-3031	YES	Financial managers	Line item	13-2099	YES	All other financial specialists	Line item
11-9051	YES	Food service managers	Line item	14-0000	NO	Professional and related occupations	Summary
11-9061	YES	Funeral directors	Line item	15-0000	YES	Computer and mathematical occupations	Summary
11-9071	YES	Gaming managers	Line item	15-1000	YES	Computer specialists	Summary
11-1021	YES	General and operations managers	Line item	15-1021	YES	Computer programmers	Line Item
11-3040	YES	Human resources managers	Line item	15-1100	NO	Computer scientists and systems analysts	Summary
11-3051	YES	Industrial production managers	Line item				
11-1031	YES	Legislators	Line item	15-1011	YES	Computer and information scientists, research	Line Item
11-9081	YES	Lodging managers	Line item	15-1051	YES	Computer systems analysts	Line Item
11-9111	YES	Medical and health services managers	Line item	15-1030	YES	Computer software engineers	Summary
11-9121	YES	Natural sciences managers	Line item	15-1031	YES	Computer software engineers, applications	Line Item
11-9131	YES	Postmasters and mail superintendents	Line item				
11-9141	YES	Property, real estate, and community association managers	Line item	15-1032	YES	Computer software engineers, systems software	Line Item
11-3061	YES	Purchasing managers	Line item	15-1041	YES	Computer support specialists	Line Item
11-9151	YES	Social and community service managers	Line item	15-1061	YES	Database administrators	Line Item
11-3071	YES	Transportation, storage, and distribution managers	Line item	15-1071	YES	Network and computer systems administrators	Line Item
11-9198	NO	All other managers	Line item	15-1081	YES	Network systems and data communications analysts	Line item
13-0000	YES	Business and financial operations occupations	Summary				
13-1000	YES	Business operations specialists	Summary	15-1099	YES	All other computer specialists	Line item
13-1011	YES	Agents and business managers of artists, performers, and athletes	Line item	15-2000	YES	Mathematical science occupations	Summary
				15-2100	NO	Mathematical scientists and technicians	Summary
13-1020	YES	Buyers and purchasing agents	Summary	15-2011	YES	Actuaries	Line Item
13-1021	YES	Purchasing agents and buyers, farm products	Line item	15-2021	YES	Mathematicians	Line Item
13-1023	YES	Purchasing agents, except wholesale, retail, and farm products	Line item	15-2031	YES	Operations research analysts	Line Item
				15-2041	YES	Statisticians	Line item
13-1022	YES	Wholesale and retail buyers, except farm products	Line item	15-2090	YES	Miscellaneous mathematical science occupations	Rollup
13-1030	YES	Claims adjusters, appraisers, examiners, and investigators	Summary	15-2091	YES	Mathematical technicians	Collapsed
				15-2099	YES	Mathematical scientists, all other	Collapsed
13-1031	YES	Claims adjusters, examiners, and investigators	Line item	17-0000	YES	Architecture and engineering occupations	Summary
13-1032	YES	Insurance appraisers, auto damage	Line item	17-1000	YES	Architects, surveyors, and cartographers	Summary
13-1041	YES	Compliance officers, except agriculture, construction, health and safety, and transportation	Line item	17-1010	YES	Architects, except naval	Summary
				17-1011	YES	Architects, except landscape and naval	Line item
13-1051	YES	Cost estimators	Line item	17-1012	YES	Landscape architects	Line item
13-1061	YES	Emergency management specialists	Line item	17-1020	YES	Surveyors, cartographers, and photogrammetrists	Summary

Matrix code	Valid SOC Code?	Matrix occupation title	Occupation Type	Matrix code	Valid SOC Code?	Matrix occupation title	Occupation Type
17-1021	YES	Cartographers and photogrammetrists	Line item	19-2041	YES	Environmental scientists and specialists, including health	Line item
17-1022	YES	Surveyors	Line item	19-2042	YES	Geoscientists, except hydrologists and geographers	Line item
17-1099	NO	All other architects, surveyors, and cartographers	Line item	19-2043	YES	Hydrologists	Line item
17-2000	YES	Engineers Summary		19-2099	YES	All other physical scientists	Line item
17-2011	YES	Aerospace engineers	Line item	19-3000	YES	Social scientists and related occupations	Summary
17-2021	YES	Agricultural engineers	Line item	19-3011	YES	Economists	Line item
17-2031	YES	Biomedical engineers	Line item	19-3020	YES	Market and survey researchers	Summary
17-2041	YES	Chemical engineers	Line item	19-3021	YES	Market research analysts	Line item
17-2051	YES	Civil engineers	Line item	19-3022	YES	Survey researchers	Line item
17-2061	YES	Computer hardware engineers	Line item	19-3060	NO	Psychologists	Rollup
17-2070	YES	Electrical and electronics engineers	Summary	19-3031	YES	Clinical, counseling, and school psychologists	Collapsed
17-2071	YES	Electrical engineers	Line item	19-3032	YES	Industrial-organizational psychologists	Collapsed
17-2072	YES	Electronics engineers, except computer	Line item	19-3097	NO	Social scientists, other	Rollup
17-2081	YES	Environmental engineers	Line item	19-3091	YES	Anthropologists and archeologists	Current
17-2110	YES	Industrial engineers, including health and safety	Summary	19-3092	YES	Geographers	Current
17-2111	YES	Health and safety engineers, except mining safety engineers and inspectors	Line item	19-3093	YES	Historians	Current
				19-3094	YES	Political scientists	Current
17-2112	YES	Industrial engineers	Line item	19-3041	YES	Sociologists	Current
17-2121	YES	Marine engineers and naval architects	Line item	19-3051	YES	Urban and regional planners	Line item
17-2131	YES	Materials engineers	Line item	19-3098	NO	All other social scientists and related workers	Line item
17-2141	YES	Mechanical engineers	Line item	19-4000	YES	Life, physical, and social science technicians	Summary
17-2151	YES	Mining and geological engineers, including mining safety engineers	Line item	19-4011	YES	Agricultural and food science technicians	Line item
17-2161	YES	Nuclear engineers	Line item	19-4021	YES	Biological technicians	Line item
17-2171	YES	Petroleum engineers	Line item	19-4031	YES	Chemical technicians	Line item
17-2199	YES	All other engineers	Line item	19-4041	YES	Geological and petroleum technicians	Line item
17-3000	YES	Drafters, engineering, and mapping technicians	Summary	19-4051	YES	Nuclear technicians	Line item
17-3040	NO	Drafters	Summary	19-4080	NO	Other life, physical, and social science technicians	Summary
17-3011	YES	Architectural and civil drafters	Line item	19-4091	YES	Environmental science and protection technicians, including health	Line item
17-3012	YES	Electrical and electronics drafters	Line item	19-4092	YES	Forensic science technicians	Line item
17-3013	YES	Mechanical drafters	Line item	19-4093	YES	Forest and conservation technicians	Line item
17-3050	NO	Engineering technicians, except drafters	Summary	19-4099	YES	All other life, physical, and social science technicians	Line item
17-3021	YES	Aerospace engineering and operations technicians	Line item	21-0000	YES	Community and social services occupations	Summary
17-3022	YES	Civil engineering technicians	Line item	21-1030	NO	Counselors	Summary
17-3023	YES	Electrical and electronic engineering technicians	Line item	21-1012	YES	Educational, vocational, and school counselors	Line item
17-3024	YES	Electro-mechanical technicians	Line item	21-1013	YES	Marriage and family therapists	Line item
17-3025	YES	Environmental engineering technicians	Line item	21-1014	YES	Mental health counselors	Line item
17-3026	YES	Industrial engineering technicians	Line item	21-1015	YES	Rehabilitation counselors	Line item
17-3027	YES	Mechanical engineering technicians	Line item	21-1011	YES	Substance abuse and behavioral disorder counselors	Line item
17-3031	YES	Surveying and mapping technicians	Line item	21-1050	NO	Miscellaneous community and social service specialists	Summary
17-3099	NO	All other drafters, engineering, and mapping technicians	Line item	21-1091	YES	Health educators	Line item
19-0000	YES	Life, physical, and social science occupations	Summary	21-1092	YES	Probation officers and correctional treatment specialists	Line item
19-1000	YES	Life scientists	Summary	21-1093	YES	Social and human service assistants	Line item
19-1010	YES	Agricultural and food scientists	Line item	21-2050	NO	Religious workers	Summary
19-1020	YES	Biological scientists	Line item	21-2011	YES	Clergy	Line item
19-1030	YES	Conservation scientists and foresters	Summary	21-2021	YES	Directors, religious activities and education	Line item
19-1031	YES	Conservation scientists	Line item	21-1040	NO	Social workers	Summary
19-1032	YES	Foresters	Line item	21-1021	YES	Child, family, and school social workers	Line item
19-1040	YES	Medical scientists	Rollup	21-1022	YES	Medical and public health social workers	Line item
19-1041	YES	Epidemiologists	Current	21-1023	YES	Mental health and substance abuse social workers	Line item
19-1042	YES	Medical scientists, except epidemiologists	Current	21-9099	NO	All other counselors, social, and religious workers	Line item
19-1060	NO	All other life scientists	Line item	23-0000	YES	Legal occupations	Summary
19-2000	YES	Physical scientists	Summary	23-1020	YES	Judges, magistrates, and other judicial workers	Summary
19-2010	YES	Astronomers and physicists	Rollup	23-1021	YES	Administrative law judges, adjudicators, and hearing officers	Line item
19-2011	YES	Astronomers	Current				
19-2012	YES	Physicists	Current				
19-2021	YES	Atmospheric and space scientists	Line item				
19-2030	YES	Chemists and materials scientists	Summary				
19-2031	YES	Chemists	Line item				
19-2032	YES	Materials scientists	Line item				
19-2050	NO	Environmental scientists and geoscientists	Summary				

Table 1. National employment matrix occupational directory, 2000—Continued

Matrix code	Valid SOC Code?	Matrix occupation title	Occupation Type	Matrix code	Valid SOC Code?	Matrix occupation title	Occupation Type
23-1022	YES	Arbitrators, mediators, and conciliators	Line item	25-2011	YES	Preschool teachers, except special education	Line item
23-1023	YES	Judges, magistrate judges, and magistrates	Line item	25-2012	YES	Kindergarten teachers, except special education	Line item
23-1011	YES	Lawyers	Line item				
23-2011	YES	Paralegals and legal assistants	Line item	25-2020	YES	Elementary and middle school teachers	Summary
23-2080	NO	Miscellaneous legal support workers	Summary	25-2021	YES	Elementary school teachers, except special education	Line item
23-2091	YES	Court reporters	Line item				
23-2092	YES	Law clerks	Line item	25-2022	YES	Middle school teachers, except special and vocational education	Line item
23-2093	YES	Title examiners, abstractors, and searchers	Line item	25-2023	YES	Vocational education teachers, middle school	Line item
23-9099	NO	All other legal and related workers	Line item				
25-0000	YES	Education, training, and library occupations	Summary	25-2030	YES	Secondary school teachers	Summary
25-1000	YES	Postsecondary teachers	Rollup	25-2031	YES	Secondary school teachers, except special and vocational education	Line item
25-1041	YES	Agricultural sciences teachers, postsecondary	Current	25-2032	YES	Vocational education teachers, secondary school	Line item
25-1061	YES	Anthropology and archeology teachers, postsecondary	Current				
25-1031	YES	Architecture teachers, postsecondary	Current	25-2040	YES	Special education teachers	Summary
25-1062	YES	Area, ethnic, and cultural studies teachers, postsecondary	Current	25-2041	YES	Special education teachers, preschool, kindergarten, and elementary school	Line item
25-1121	YES	Art, drama, and music teachers, postsecondary	Current	25-2042	YES	Special education teachers, middle school	Line item
25-1051	YES	Atmospheric, earth, marine, and space sciences teachers, postsecondary	Current	25-2043	YES	Special education teachers, secondary school	Line item
25-1042	YES	Biological science teachers, postsecondary	Current	25-3000	YES	Other teachers and instructors	Summary
25-1011	YES	Business teachers, postsecondary	Current	25-3011	YES	Adult literacy, remedial education, and GED teachers and instructors	Line item
25-1052	YES	Chemistry teachers, postsecondary	Current				
25-1122	YES	Communications teachers, postsecondary	Current	25-3021	YES	Self-enrichment education teachers	Line item
25-1021	YES	Computer science teachers, postsecondary	Current	25-3999	NO	All other teachers, primary, secondary, and adult	Line item
25-1111	YES	Criminal justice and law enforcement teachers, postsecondary	Current	25-4100	NO	Library, museum, training, and other education occupations	Summary
25-1063	YES	Economics teachers, postsecondary	Current	25-4010	YES	Archivists, curators, and museum technicians	Line item
25-1081	YES	Education teachers, postsecondary	Current				
25-1032	YES	Engineering teachers, postsecondary	Current	25-4021	YES	Librarians	Line item
25-1123	YES	English language and literature teachers, postsecondary	Current	25-4031	YES	Library technicians	Line item
				25-9041	YES	Teacher assistants	Line item
25-1053	YES	Environmental science teachers, postsecondary	Current	25-9100	NO	Other education, training, library, and museum workers	Summary
25-1124	YES	Foreign language and literature teachers, postsecondary	Current	25-9011	YES	Audio-visual collections specialists	Line item
				25-9021	YES	Farm and home management advisors	Line item
25-1043	YES	Forestry and conservation science teachers, postsecondary	Current	25-9031	YES	Instructional coordinators	Line item
25-1064	YES	Geography teachers, postsecondary	Current	25-9199	NO	All other library, museum, training, and other education workers	Line item
25-1191	YES	Graduate teaching assistants	Current				
25-1071	YES	Health specialties teachers, postsecondary	Current	27-0000	YES	Arts, design, entertainment, sports, and media occupations	Summary
25-1125	YES	History teachers, postsecondary	Current	27-1000	YES	Art and design occupations	Summary
25-1192	YES	Home economics teachers, postsecondary	Current	27-1110	NO	Artists and related workers	Summary
25-1112	YES	Law teachers, postsecondary	Current	27-1011	YES	Art directors	Line item
25-1082	YES	Library science teachers, postsecondary	Current	27-1013	YES	Fine artists, including painters, sculptors, and illustrators	Line item
25-1022	YES	Mathematical science teachers, postsecondary	Current	27-1014	YES	Multi-media artists and animators	Line item
				27-1120	NO	Designers	Summary
25-1072	YES	Nursing instructors and teachers, postsecondary	Current	27-1021	YES	Commercial and industrial designers	Line item
25-1126	YES	Philosophy and religion teachers, postsecondary	Current	27-1022	YES	Fashion designers	Line item
				27-1023	YES	Floral designers	Line item
25-1054	YES	Physics teachers, postsecondary	Current	27-1024	YES	Graphic designers	Line item
25-1065	YES	Political science teachers, postsecondary	Current	27-1025	YES	Interior designers	Line item
25-1066	YES	Psychology teachers, postsecondary	Current	27-1026	YES	Merchandise displayers and window trimmers	Line item
25-1193	YES	Recreation and fitness studies teachers, postsecondary	Current	27-1027	YES	Set and exhibit designers	Line item
25-1113	YES	Social work teachers, postsecondary	Current	27-1099	NO	All other art and design workers	Line item
25-1067	YES	Sociology teachers, postsecondary	Current	27-2000	YES	Entertainers and performers, sports and related occupations	Summary
25-1194	YES	Vocational education teachers, postsecondary	Current	27-2010	YES	Actors, producers, and directors	Summary
25-1198	NO	All other postsecondary teachers	Current	27-2011	YES	Actors	Line item
25-2000	YES	Primary, secondary, and special education teachers	Summary	27-2012	YES	Producers and directors	Line item
25-2010	YES	Preschool and kindergarten teachers	Summary	27-2020	YES	Athletes, coaches, umpires, and related workers	Summary

Table 1. National employment matrix occupational directory, 2000—Continued

Matrix code	Valid SOC Code?	Matrix occupation title	Occupation Type	Matrix code	Valid SOC Code?	Matrix occupation title	Occupation Type
27-2021	YES	Athletes and sports competitors	Line item	29-2010	YES	Clinical laboratory technologists and technicians	Summary
27-2022	YES	Coaches and scouts	Line item	29-2011	YES	Medical and clinical laboratory technologists	Line item
27-2023	YES	Umpires, referees, and other sports officials	Line item	29-2012	YES	Medical and clinical laboratory technicians	Line item
27-2030	YES	Dancers and choreographers	Summary	29-2021	YES	Dental hygienists	Line item
27-2031	YES	Dancers	Line item	29-2030	YES	Diagnostic related technologists and technicians	Summary
27-2032	YES	Choreographers	Line item	29-2031	YES	Cardiovascular technologists and technicians	Line item
27-2040	YES	Musicians, singers, and related workers	Summary	29-2032	YES	Diagnostic medical sonographers	Line item
27-2041	YES	Music directors and composers	Line item	29-2033	YES	Nuclear medicine technologists	Line item
27-2042	YES	Musicians and singers	Line item	29-2034	YES	Radiologic technologists and technicians	Line item
27-2099	YES	All other entertainers and performers, sports and related workers	Line item	29-2041	YES	Emergency medical technicians and paramedics	Line item
27-3000	YES	Media and communication occupations	Summary	29-2050	YES	Health diagnosing and treating practitioner support technicians	Summary
27-3010	YES	Announcers	Line item	29-2051	YES	Dietetic technicians	Line item
27-3020	YES	News analysts, reporters, and correspondents	Line item	29-2052	YES	Pharmacy technicians	Line item
27-3031	YES	Public relations specialists	Line item	29-2053	YES	Psychiatric technicians	Line item
27-3040	YES	Writers and editors	Summary	29-2054	YES	Respiratory therapy technicians	Line item
27-3041	YES	Editors	Line item	29-2055	YES	Surgical technologists	Line item
27-3042	YES	Technical writers	Line item	29-2056	YES	Veterinary technologists and technicians	Line item
27-3043	YES	Writers and authors	Line item	29-2061	YES	Licensed practical and licensed vocational nurses	Line item
27-3090	YES	Miscellaneous media and communications workers	Summary	29-2071	YES	Medical records and health information technicians	Line item
27-3091	YES	Interpreters and translators	Line item	29-2081	YES	Opticians, dispensing	Line item
27-3099	YES	All other media and communication workers	Line item	29-9100	NO	Other health practitioners and technical workers	Summary
27-4000	YES	Media and communication equipment occupations	Summary	29-9091	YES	Athletic trainers	Line item
27-4010	YES	Broadcast and sound engineering technicians and radio operators	Summary	29-9010	YES	Occupational health and safety specialists and technicians	Line item
27-4011	YES	Audio and video equipment technicians	Line item	29-2091	YES	Orthotists and prosthetists	Line item
27-4012	YES	Broadcast technicians	Line item	29-9198	NO	All other health practitioners and technical workers	Line item
27-4013	YES	Radio operators	Line item	32-0000	NO	Service occupations	Summary
27-4014	YES	Sound engineering technicians	Line item	31-0000	YES	Healthcare support occupations	Summary
27-4021	YES	Photographers	Line item	31-9091	YES	Dental assistants	Line item
27-4030	YES	Television, video, and motion picture camera operators and editors	Summary	31-9011	YES	Massage therapists	Line item
27-4031	YES	Camera operators, television, video, and motion picture	Line item	31-1010	YES	Nursing, psychiatric, and home health aides	Summary
27-4032	YES	Film and video editors	Line item	31-1011	YES	Home health aides	Line item
27-4099	YES	All other media and communication equipment workers	Line item	31-1012	YES	Nursing aides, orderlies, and attendants	Line item
29-0000	YES	Healthcare practitioners and technical occupations	Summary	31-1013	YES	Psychiatric aides	Line item
29-1000	YES	Health diagnosing and treating practitioners	Summary	31-2010	YES	Occupational therapist assistants, and aides	Summary
29-1011	YES	Chiropractors	Line item	31-2011	YES	Occupational therapist assistants	Line item
29-1020	YES	Dentists	Line item	31-2012	YES	Occupational therapist aides	Line item
29-1031	YES	Dietitians and nutritionists	Line item	31-2020	YES	Physical therapist assistants and aides	Summary
29-1041	YES	Optometrists	Line item	31-2021	YES	Physical therapist assistants	Line item
29-1051	YES	Pharmacists	Line item	31-2022	YES	Physical therapist aides	Line item
29-1060	YES	Physicians and surgeons	Line item	31-9080	NO	Medical assistants and other healthcare support occupations	Summary
29-1071	YES	Physician assistants	Line item	31-9092	YES	Medical assistants	Line item
29-1081	YES	Podiatrists	Line item	31-9093	YES	Medical equipment preparers	Line item
29-1111	YES	Registered nurses	Line item	31-9094	YES	Medical transcriptionists	Line item
29-1210	NO	Therapists	Summary	31-9095	YES	Pharmacy aides	Line item
29-1121	YES	Audiologists	Line item	31-9096	YES	Veterinary assistants and laboratory animal caretakers	Line item
29-1122	YES	Occupational therapists	Line item	31-9099	YES	All other healthcare support workers	Line item
29-1123	YES	Physical therapists	Line item	33-0000	YES	Protective service occupations	Summary
29-1124	YES	Radiation therapists	Line item	33-1000	YES	First-line supervisors/managers, protective service workers	Summary
29-1125	YES	Recreational therapists	Line item	33-1011	YES	First-line supervisors/managers of correctional officers	Line item
29-1126	YES	Respiratory therapists	Line item	33-1021	YES	First-line supervisors/managers of fire fighting and prevention workers	Line item
29-1127	YES	Speech-language pathologists	Line item				
29-1131	YES	Veterinarians	Line item				
29-1198	NO	All other health diagnosing and treating practitioners	Line item				
29-2100	NO	Other health professionals and technicians	Summary				

Table 1. National employment matrix occupational directory, 2000—Continued

Matrix code	Valid SOC Code?	Matrix occupation title	Occupation Type	Matrix code	Valid SOC Code?	Matrix occupation title	Occupation Type
33-1012	YES	First-line supervisors/managers of police and detectives	Line item	37-1012	YES	First-line supervisors/managers of landscaping, lawn service, and groundskeeping workers	Line item
33-1099	YES	First-line supervisors/managers of protective service workers, except police, fire and corrections	Line item	37-2100	NO	Building cleaning workers	Summary
33-2011	YES	Fire fighters	Line item	37-2011	YES	Janitors and cleaners, except maids and housekeeping cleaners	Line item
33-2020	YES	Fire inspectors	Rollup	37-2012	YES	Maids and housekeeping cleaners	Rollup
33-2021	YES	Fire inspectors and investigators	Current	37-2101	NO	Cleaners and servants, private household	Current
33-2022	YES	Forest fire inspectors and prevention specialists	Current	37-2102	NO	Housekeepers and butlers, private household	Current
33-3000	YES	Law enforcement workers	Summary	37-2103	NO	Maids and housekeeping cleaners, except private household	Current
33-3010	YES	Bailiffs, correctional officers, and jailers	Summary	37-3100	NO	Grounds maintenance workers	Summary
33-3011	YES	Bailiffs	Line item	37-3011	YES	Landscaping and groundskeeping workers	Line item
33-3012	YES	Correctional officers and jailers	Line item	37-3012	YES	Pesticide handlers, sprayers, and applicators, vegetation	Line item
33-3021	YES	Detectives and criminal investigators	Line item	37-3013	YES	Tree trimmers and pruners	Line item
33-3031	YES	Fish and game wardens	Line item	37-2021	YES	Pest control workers	Line item
33-3041	YES	Parking enforcement workers	Line item	37-9099	NO	All other building and grounds cleaning and maintenance workers	Line item
33-3051	YES	Police and sheriff's patrol officers	Line item	39-0000	YES	Personal care and service occupations	Summary
33-3052	YES	Transit and railroad police	Line item	39-1021	YES	First-line supervisors/managers of personal service workers	Line item
33-9000	YES	Other protective service workers	Summary	39-2000	YES	Animal care and service workers	Summary
33-9011	YES	Animal control workers	Line item	39-2011	YES	Animal trainers	Line item
33-9091	YES	Crossing guards	Line item	39-2021	YES	Nonfarm animal caretakers	Line item
33-9021	YES	Private detectives and investigators	Line item	39-9011	YES	Child care workers	Rollup
33-9030	YES	Security guards and gaming surveillance officers	Summary	39-9012	NO	Child care workers, private household	Current
33-9031	YES	Gaming surveillance officers and gaming investigators	Line item	39-9013	NO	Child care workers, except private household	Current
33-9032	YES	Security guards	Line item	39-3100	NO	Entertainment attendants and related workers	Summary
33-9095	NO	All other protective service workers	Line item	39-3021	YES	Motion picture projectionists	Line item
35-0000	YES	Food preparation and serving related occupations	Summary	39-3031	YES	Ushers, lobby attendants, and ticket takers	Line item
35-1000	YES	Supervisors, food preparation and serving workers	Summary	39-3080	NO	Miscellaneous entertainment attendants and related workers	Summary
35-1011	YES	Chefs and head cooks	Line item	39-3091	YES	Amusement and recreation attendants	Line item
35-1012	YES	First-line supervisors/managers of food preparation and serving workers	Line item	39-3088	NO	Costume, locker room, and other attendants	Rollup
35-2100	NO	Cooks and food preparation workers	Summary	39-3092	YES	Costume attendants	Collapsed
35-2200	NO	Cooks	Summary	39-3093	YES	Locker room, coatroom, and dressing room attendants	Collapsed
35-2011	YES	Cooks, fast food	Line item	39-4000	YES	Funeral service workers	Summary
35-2012	YES	Cooks, institution and cafeteria	Line item	39-4011	YES	Embalmers	Line item
35-2013	YES	Cooks, private household	Line item	39-1200	NO	Gaming occupations	Summary
35-2014	YES	Cooks, restaurant	Line item	39-1010	YES	First-line supervisors/managers, gaming workers	Summary
35-2015	YES	Cooks, short order	Line item	39-1011	YES	Gaming supervisors	Line item
35-2021	YES	Food preparation workers	Line item	39-1012	YES	Slot key persons	Summary
35-3000	YES	Food and beverage serving workers	Summary	39-3012	YES	Gaming and sports book writers and runners	Line item
35-3011	YES	Bartenders	Line item	39-3011	YES	Gaming dealers	Line item
35-3021	YES	Combined food preparation and serving workers, including fast food	Line item	39-3199	NO	All other gaming service workers	Line item
35-3022	YES	Counter attendants, cafeteria, food concession, and coffee shop	Line item	39-5000	YES	Personal appearance workers	Summary
35-3041	YES	Food servers, nonrestaurant	Line item	39-5011	YES	Barbers	Line item
35-3031	YES	Waiters and waitresses	Line item	39-5012	YES	Hairdressers, hairstylists, and cosmetologists	Line item
35-9000	YES	Other food preparation and serving related workers	Summary	39-5090	YES	Miscellaneous personal appearance workers	Summary
35-9011	YES	Dining room and cafeteria attendants and bartender helpers	Line item	39-5092	YES	Manicurists and pedicurists	Line item
35-9021	YES	Dishwashers	Line item	39-5093	YES	Shampooers	Line item
35-9031	YES	Hosts and hostesses, restaurant, lounge, and coffee shop	Line item	39-5094	YES	Skin care specialists	Line item
35-9098	NO	All other food preparation and serving related workers	Line item	39-9021	YES	Personal and home care aides	Line item
37-0000	YES	Building and grounds cleaning and maintenance occupations	Summary	39-9030	YES	Recreation and fitness workers	Summary
37-1000	YES	Supervisors, building and grounds cleaning and maintenance workers	Summary	39-9031	YES	Fitness trainers and aerobics instructors	Line item
				39-9032	YES	Recreation workers	Line item
37-1011	YES	First-line supervisors/managers of housekeeping and janitorial workers	Line item	39-9041	YES	Residential advisors	Line item

Matrix code	Valid SOC Code?	Matrix occupation title	Occupation Type	Matrix code	Valid SOC Code?	Matrix occupation title	Occupation Type
39-6000	YES	Transportation, tourism, and lodging attendants	Summary	43-3051	YES	Payroll and timekeeping clerks	Line item
39-6010	YES	Baggage porters, bellhops, and concierges	Summary	43-3061	YES	Procurement clerks	Line item
39-6011	YES	Baggage porters and bellhops	Line item	43-3071	YES	Tellers	Line item
39-6012	YES	Concierges	Line item	43-4000	YES	Information and record clerks	Summary
39-6020	YES	Tour and travel guides	Rollup	43-4011	YES	Brokerage clerks	Line item
39-6021	YES	Tour guides and escorts	Current	43-4021	YES	Correspondence clerks	Line item
39-6022	YES	Travel guides	Current	43-4031	YES	Court, municipal, and license clerks	Line item
39-6030	YES	Transportation attendants	Summary	43-4041	YES	Credit authorizers, checkers, and clerks	Line item
39-6031	YES	Flight attendants	Line item	43-4051	YES	Customer service representatives	Line item
39-6032	YES	Transportation attendants, except flight attendants and baggage porters	Line item	43-4061	YES	Eligibility interviewers, government programs	Line item
39-9098	NO	All other personal care and service workers	Rollup	43-4071	YES	File clerks	Line item
39-5091	YES	Makeup artists, theatrical and performance	Collapsed	43-4081	YES	Hotel, motel, and resort desk clerks	Line item
39-9099	YES	Personal care and service workers, all other	Collapsed	43-4161	YES	Human resources assistants, except payroll and timekeeping	Line item
41-0000	YES	Sales and related occupations	Summary	43-4111	YES	Interviewers, except eligibility and loan	Line item
41-3011	YES	Advertising sales agents	Line item	43-4121	YES	Library assistants, clerical	Line item
41-2010	YES	Cashiers	Summary	43-4131	YES	Loan interviewers and clerks	Line item
41-2011	YES	Cashiers, except gaming	Line item	43-4141	YES	New accounts clerks	Line item
41-2012	YES	Gaming change persons and booth cashiers	Line item	43-4151	YES	Order clerks	Line item
41-2021	YES	Counter and rental clerks	Line item	43-4171	YES	Receptionists and information clerks	Line item
41-9091	YES	Door-to-door sales workers, news and street vendors, and related workers	Line item	43-4181	YES	Reservation and transportation ticket agents and travel clerks	Line item
41-3021	YES	Insurance sales agents	Line item	43-4999	NO	All other financial, information, and record clerks	Line item
41-9010	YES	Models, demonstrators, and product promoters	Summary	43-5000	YES	Material recording, scheduling, dispatching, and distributing occupations	Summary
41-9011	YES	Demonstrators and product promoters	Line item	43-5011	YES	Cargo and freight agents	Line item
41-9012	YES	Models	Line item	43-5021	YES	Couriers and Messengers	Line item
41-2022	YES	Parts salespersons	Line item	43-5030	YES	Dispatchers	Summary
41-9020	YES	Real estate brokers and sales agents	Summary	43-5032	YES	Dispatchers, except police, fire, and ambulance	Line item
41-9021	YES	Real estate brokers	Line item	43-5031	YES	Police, fire, and ambulance dispatchers	Line item
41-9022	YES	Real estate sales agents	Line item	43-5041	YES	Meter readers, utilities	Line item
41-2031	YES	Retail salespersons	Line item	43-5050	YES	Postal service workers	Summary
41-9031	YES	Sales engineers	Line item	43-5051	YES	Postal service clerks	Line item
41-4010	YES	Sales representatives, wholesale and manufacturing	Summary	43-5052	YES	Postal service mail carriers	Line item
41-4011	YES	Sales representatives, wholesale and manufacturing, technical and scientific products	Line item	43-5053	YES	Postal service mail sorters, processors, and processing machine operators	Line item
41-4012	YES	Sales representatives, wholesale and manufacturing, except technical and scientific products	Line item	43-5061	YES	Production, planning, and expediting clerks	Line item
				43-5071	YES	Shipping, receiving, and traffic clerks	Line item
41-3031	YES	Securities, commodities, and financial services sales agents	Line item	43-5081	YES	Stock clerks and order fillers	Line item
41-1000	YES	Supervisors, sales workers	Summary	43-5111	YES	Weighers, measurers, checkers, and samplers, recordkeeping	Line item
41-1011	YES	First-line supervisors/managers of retail sales workers	Line item	43-5199	NO	All other material recording, scheduling, dispatching, and distributing workers	Line item
41-1012	YES	First-line supervisors/managers of non-retail sales workers	Line item	43-8000	NO	Secretaries, administrative assistants, and other office support occupations	Summary
41-9041	YES	Telemarketers	Line item	43-9011	YES	Computer operators	Line item
41-3041	YES	Travel agents	Line item	43-9020	YES	Data entry and information processing workers	Summary
41-9098	NO	All other sales and related workers	Line item	43-9021	YES	Data entry keyers	Line item
43-0000	YES	Office and administrative support occupations	Summary	43-9022	YES	Word processors and typists	Line item
43-1011	YES	First-line supervisors/managers of office and administrative support workers	Line item	43-9031	YES	Desktop publishers	Line item
43-2000	YES	Communications equipment operators	Summary	43-9041	YES	Insurance claims and policy processing clerks	Line item
43-2011	YES	Switchboard operators, including answering service	Line item	43-9051	YES	Mail clerks and mail machine operators, except postal service	Line item
43-2021	YES	Telephone operators	Line item	43-9061	YES	Office clerks, general	Line item
43-2099	YES	All other communications equipment operators	Line item	43-9071	YES	Office machine operators, except computer	Line item
43-7000	NO	Financial, information, and record clerks	Summary	43-9081	YES	Proofreaders and copy markers	Line item
43-3000	YES	Financial clerks	Summary	43-6010	YES	Secretaries and administrative assistants	Summary
43-3011	YES	Bill and account collectors	Line item	43-6011	YES	Executive secretaries and administrative assistants	Line item
43-3021	YES	Billing and posting clerks and machine operators	Line item	43-6012	YES	Legal secretaries	Line item
43-3031	YES	Bookkeeping, accounting, and auditing clerks	Line item	43-6013	YES	Medical secretaries	Line item
43-3041	YES	Gaming cage workers	Line item	43-6014	YES	Secretaries, except legal, medical, and executive	Line item

Table 1. National employment matrix occupational directory, 2000—Continued

Matrix code	Valid SOC Code?	Matrix occupation title	Occupation Type
43-9111	YES	Statistical assistants	Line item
43-9999	NO	All other secretaries, administrative assistants, and other office support workers	Line item
45-0000	YES	Farming, fishing, and forestry occupations	Summary
45-1010	YES	First-line supervisors/managers/contractors of farming, fishing, and forestry workers	Rollup
45-1011	YES	First-line supervisors/managers of farming, fishing, and forestry workers	Collapsed
45-1012	YES	Farm labor contractors	Collapsed
45-2100	NO	Agricultural workers	Summary
45-2011	YES	Agricultural inspectors	Line item
45-2080	NO	Farmworkers	Rollup
45-2094	NO	Farmworkers, agricultural production	Current
45-2092	YES	Farmworkers and laborers, crop, nursery, and greenhouse	Current
45-2093	YES	Farmworkers, farm and ranch animals	Current
45-2041	YES	Graders and sorters, agricultural products	Line item
45-3500	NO	Fishers and fishing vessel operators	Rollup
45-3031	NO	Captains and other officers, fishing vessels	Collapsed
45-3011	YES	Fishers and related fishing workers	Collapsed
45-4100	NO	Forest, conservation, and logging workers	Summary
45-4011	YES	Forest and conservation workers	Line item
45-4030	NO	Logging workers	Summary
45-4021	YES	Fallers	Line item
45-4022	YES	Logging equipment operators	Line item
45-4023	YES	Log graders and scalers	Line item
45-9100	NO	All other farming, fishing, and forestry workers	Rollup
45-2091	YES	Agricultural equipment operators	Collapsed
45-2021	YES	Animal breeders	Collapsed
45-9099	NO	All other farming, fishing, and forestry workers	Collapsed
47-0000	YES	Construction and extraction occupations	Summary
47-1011	YES	First-line supervisors/managers of construction trades and extraction workers	Line item
47-2000	YES	Construction trades and related workers	Summary
47-2011	YES	Boilermakers	Line item
47-2020	YES	Brickmasons, blockmasons, and stonemasons	Summary
47-2021	YES	Brickmasons and blockmasons	Line item
47-2022	YES	Stonemasons	Line item
47-2031	YES	Carpenters	Line item
47-2040	YES	Carpet, floor, and tile installers and finishers	Summary
47-2041	YES	Carpet installers	Line item
47-2042	YES	Floor layers, except carpet, wood, and hard tiles	Line item
47-2043	YES	Floor sanders and finishers	Line item
47-2044	YES	Tile and marble setters	Line item
47-2050	YES	Cement masons, concrete finishers, and terrazzo workers	Line item
47-2053	YES	Terrazzo workers and finishers	Line item
47-2061	YES	Construction laborers	Line item
47-2070	YES	Construction equipment operators	Summary
47-2073	YES	Operating engineers and other construction equipment operators	Line item
47-2071	YES	Paving, surfacing, and tamping equipment operators	Line item
47-2072	YES	Pile-driver operators	Line item
47-2080	YES	Drywall installers, ceiling tile installers, and tapers	Summary
47-2081	YES	Drywall and ceiling tile installers	Line item
47-2082	YES	Tapers	Line item
47-2111	YES	Electricians	Line item
47-2121	YES	Glaziers	Line item
47-2130	YES	Insulation workers	Line item
47-2141	YES	Painters, construction and maintenance	Line item
47-2142	YES	Paperhangers	Line item
47-2150	YES	Pipelayers, plumbers, pipefitters, and steamfitters	Summary
47-2151	YES	Pipelayers	Line item
47-2152	YES	Plumbers, pipefitters, and steamfitters	Line item
47-2161	YES	Plasterers and stucco masons	Line item
47-2171	YES	Reinforcing iron and rebar workers	Line item
47-2181	YES	Roofers	Line item
47-2211	YES	Sheet metal workers	Line item
47-2221	YES	Structural iron and steel workers	Summary
47-3011	YES	Helpers—Brickmasons, blockmasons, stonemasons, and tile and marble setters	Line item
47-3012	YES	Helpers—Carpenters	Line item
47-3013	YES	Helpers—Electricians	Line item
47-3014	YES	Helpers—Painters, paperhangers, plasterers, and stucco masons	Line item
47-3015	YES	Helpers—Pipelayers, plumbers, pipefitters, and steamfitters	Line item
47-3016	YES	Helpers—Roofers	Line item
47-3019	YES	All other helpers, construction trades	Line item
47-4000	YES	Other construction and related workers	Summary
47-4011	YES	Construction and building inspectors	Line item
47-4021	YES	Elevator installers and repairers	Line item
47-4031	YES	Fence erectors	Line item
47-4041	YES	Hazardous materials removal workers	Line item
47-4051	YES	Highway maintenance workers	Line item
47-4061	YES	Rail-track laying and maintenance equipment operators	Line item
47-4071	YES	Septic tank servicers and sewer pipe cleaners	Line item
47-4095	NO	All other construction and related workers	Rollup
47-4091	YES	Segmental pavers	Collapsed
47-4999	NO	All other construction trades and related workers	Collapsed
47-5000	YES	Extraction workers	Summary
47-5010	YES	Derrick, rotary drill, and service unit operators, oil, gas, and mining	Summary
47-5011	YES	Derrick operators, oil and gas	Line item
47-5013	YES	Service unit operators, oil, gas, and mining	Line item
47-5021	YES	Earth drillers, except oil and gas	Line item
47-5031	YES	Explosives workers, ordnance handling experts, and blasters	Line item
47-5081	YES	Helpers—Extraction workers	Line item
47-5040	YES	Mining machine operators	Summary
47-5041	YES	Continuous mining machine operators	Line item
47-5038	NO	Miscellaneous mining machine operators	Rollup
47-5042	YES	Mine cutting and channeling machine operators	Collapsed
47-5049	YES	All other mining machine operators	Collapsed
47-5071	YES	Roustabouts, oil and gas	Line item
47-5068	NO	All other extraction workers	Rollup
47-5051	YES	Rock splitters, quarry	Collapsed
47-5061	YES	Roof bolters, mining	Collapsed
47-5099	YES	Extraction workers, all other	Collapsed
49-0000	YES	Installation, maintenance, and repair occupations	Summary
49-1011	YES	First-line supervisors/managers of mechanics, installers, and repairers	Line item
49-2000	YES	Electrical and electronic equipment mechanics, installers, and repairers	Summary
49-2091	YES	Avionics technicians	Line item
49-2011	YES	Computer, automated teller, and office machine repairers	Line item
49-2092	YES	Electric motor, power tool, and related repairers	Line item
49-2093	YES	Electrical and electronics installers and repairers, transportation equipment	Line item

Table 1. National employment matrix occupational directory, 2000—Continued

Matrix code	Valid SOC Code?	Matrix occupation title	Occupation Type
49-2080	NO	Electrical and electronics repairers, industrial and utility	Summary
49-2094	YES	Electrical and electronics repairers, commercial and industrial equipment	Line item
49-2095	YES	Electrical and electronics repairers, powerhouse, substation, and relay	Line item
49-2096	YES	Electronic equipment installers and repairers, motor vehicles	Line item
49-2097	YES	Electronic home entertainment equipment installers and repairers	Line item
49-2020	YES	Radio and telecommunications equipment installers and repairers	Summary
49-2021	YES	Radio mechanics	Line item
49-2022	YES	Telecommunications equipment installers and repairers, except line installers	Line item
49-2098	YES	Security and fire alarm systems installers	Line item
49-2099	NO	All other electrical and electronic equipment mechanics, installers, and repairers	Line item
49-3000	YES	Vehicle and mobile equipment mechanics, installers, and repairers	Summary
49-3011	YES	Aircraft mechanics and service technicians	Line item
49-3021	YES	Automotive body and related repairers	Line item
49-3022	YES	Automotive glass installers and repairers	Line item
49-3023	YES	Automotive service technicians and mechanics	Line item
49-3031	YES	Bus and truck mechanics and diesel engine specialists	Line item
49-3040	YES	Heavy vehicle and mobile equipment service technicians and mechanics	Summary
49-3041	YES	Farm equipment mechanics	Line item
49-3042	YES	Mobile heavy equipment mechanics, except engines	Line item
49-3043	YES	Rail car repairers	Line item
49-3050	YES	Small engine mechanics	Summary
49-3051	YES	Motorboat mechanics	Line item
49-3052	YES	Motorcycle mechanics	Line item
49-3053	YES	Outdoor power equipment and other small engine mechanics	Line item
49-3080	NO	Miscellaneous vehicle and mobile equipment mechanics, installers, and repairers	Summary
49-3091	YES	Bicycle repairers	Line item
49-3092	YES	Recreational vehicle service technicians	Line item
49-3093	YES	Tire repairers and changers	Line item
49-3099	NO	All other vehicle and mobile equipment mechanics, installers, and repairers	Line item
49-9000	YES	Other installation, maintenance, and repair occupations	Summary
49-9091	YES	Coin, vending, and amusement machine servicers and repairers	Line item
49-9010	YES	Control and valve installers and repairers	Summary
49-9012	YES	Control and valve installers and repairers, except mechanical door	Line item
49-9011	YES	Mechanical door repairers	Line item
49-9021	YES	Heating, air conditioning, and refrigeration mechanics and installers	Line item
49-9098	YES	Helpers--Installation, maintenance, and repair workers	Line item
49-9031	YES	Home appliance repairers	Line item
49-9041	YES	Industrial machinery mechanics	Line item
49-9050	YES	Line installers and repairers	Summary
49-9051	YES	Electrical power-line installers and repairers	Line item
49-9052	YES	Telecommunications line installers and repairers	Line item
49-9094	YES	Locksmiths and safe repairers	Line item
49-9042	YES	Maintenance and repair workers, general	Line item
49-9043	YES	Maintenance workers, machinery	Line item

Matrix code	Valid SOC Code?	Matrix occupation title	Occupation Type
49-9095	YES	Manufactured building and mobile home installers	Line item
49-9044	YES	Millwrights	Line item
49-9060	YES	Precision instrument and equipment repairers	Summary
49-9061	YES	Camera and photographic equipment repairers	Line item
49-9062	YES	Medical equipment repairers	Line item
49-9063	YES	Musical instrument repairers and tuners	Line item
49-9064	YES	Watch repairers	Line item
49-9069	YES	All other precision instrument and equipment repairers	Line item
49-9096	YES	Riggers	Line item
49-9088	NO	All other installation, maintenance, and repair workers	Rollup
49-9092	YES	Commercial divers	Current
49-9093	YES	Fabric menders, except garment	Current
49-9045	YES	Refractory materials repairers, except brickmasons	Current
49-9097	YES	Signal and track switch repairers	Current
49-9099	YES	Installation, maintenance, and repair workers, all other	Current
51-0000	YES	Production occupations	Summary
51-1011	YES	First-line supervisors/managers of production and operating workers	Line item
51-2000	YES	Assemblers and fabricators	Summary
51-2011	YES	Aircraft structure, surfaces, rigging, and systems assemblers	Line item
51-2020	YES	Electrical, electronics, and electromechanical assemblers	Summary
51-2021	YES	Coil winders, tapers, and finishers	Line item
51-2022	YES	Electrical and electronic equipment assemblers	Line item
51-2023	YES	Electromechanical equipment assemblers	Line item
51-2031	YES	Engine and other machine assemblers	Line item
51-2041	YES	Structural metal fabricators and fitters	Line item
51-2090	YES	Miscellaneous assemblers and fabricators	Summary
51-2091	YES	Fiberglass laminators and fabricators	Line item
51-2092	YES	Team assemblers	Line item
51-2093	YES	Timing device assemblers, adjusters, and calibrators	Line item
51-2099	YES	All other assemblers and fabricators	Line item
51-3000	YES	Food processing occupations	Summary
51-3011	YES	Bakers	Line item
51-3020	YES	Butchers and other meat, poultry, and fish processing workers	Summary
51-3021	YES	Butchers and meat cutters	Line item
51-3022	YES	Meat, poultry, and fish cutters and trimmers	Line item
51-3023	YES	Slaughterers and meat packers	Line item
51-3091	YES	Food and tobacco roasting, baking, and drying machine operators and tenders	Line item
51-3092	YES	Food batchmakers	Line item
51-3093	YES	Food cooking machine operators and tenders	Line item
51-3099	NO	All other food processing workers	Line item
51-4000	YES	Metal workers and plastic workers	Summary
51-4010	YES	Computer control programmers and operators	Summary
51-4011	YES	Computer-controlled machine tool operators, metal and plastic	Line item
51-4012	YES	Numerical tool and process control programmers	Line item
51-4031	YES	Cutting, punching, and press machine setters, operators, and tenders, metal and plastic	Line item
51-4032	YES	Drilling and boring machine tool setters, operators, and tenders, metal and plastic	Line item

Table 1. National employment matrix occupational directory, 2000—Continued

Matrix code	Valid SOC Code?	Matrix occupation title	Occupation Type
51-4021	YES	Extruding and drawing machine setters, operators, and tenders, metal and plastic	Line item
51-4022	YES	Forging machine setters, operators, and tenders, metal and plastic	Line item
51-4033	YES	Grinding, lapping, polishing, and buffing machine tool setters, operators, and tenders, metal and plastic	Line item
51-4191	YES	Heat treating equipment setters, operators, and tenders, metal and plastic	Line item
51-4034	YES	Lathe and turning machine tool setters, operators, and tenders, metal and plastic	Line item
51-4192	YES	Lay-out workers, metal and plastic	Line item
51-4041	YES	Machinists	Line item
51-4050	YES	Metal furnace and kiln operators and tenders	Summary
51-4051	YES	Metal-refining furnace operators and tenders	Line item
51-4052	YES	Pourers and casters, metal	Line item
51-4035	YES	Milling and planing machine setters, operators, and tenders, metal and plastic	Line item
51-4060	YES	Model makers and patternmakers, metal and plastic	Summary
51-4061	YES	Model makers, metal and plastic	Line item
51-4062	YES	Patternmakers, metal and plastic	Line item
51-4090	NO	Molders and molding machine setters, operators, and tenders, metal and plastic	Summary
51-4071	YES	Foundry mold and coremakers	Line item
51-4072	YES	Molding, coremaking, and casting machine setters, operators, and tenders, metal and plastic	Line item
51-4081	YES	Multiple machine tool setters, operators, and tenders, metal and plastic	Line item
51-4193	YES	Plating and coating machine setters, operators, and tenders, metal and plastic	Line item
51-4023	YES	Rolling machine setters, operators, and tenders, metal and plastic	Line item
51-4111	YES	Tool and die makers	Line item
51-4194	YES	Tool grinders, filers, and sharpeners	Line item
51-4120	YES	Welding, soldering, and brazing workers	Summary
51-4121	YES	Welders, cutters, solderers, and brazers	Line item
51-4122	YES	Welding, soldering, and brazing machine setters, operators, and tenders	Line item
51-4199	YES	All other metal workers and plastic workers	Line item
51-8000	YES	Plant and system operators	Summary
51-8010	YES	Power plant operators, distributors, and dispatchers	Summary
51-8011	YES	Nuclear power reactor operators	Line item
51-8012	YES	Power distributors and dispatchers	Line item
51-8013	YES	Power plant operators	Line item
51-8021	YES	Stationary engineers and boiler operators	Line item
51-8031	YES	Water and liquid waste treatment plant and system operators	Line item
51-8090	YES	Miscellaneous plant and system operators	Summary
51-8091	YES	Chemical plant and system operators	Line item
51-8092	YES	Gas plant operators	Line item
51-8093	YES	Petroleum pump system operators, refinery operators, and gaugers	Line item
51-8099	YES	All other plant and system operators	Line item
51-5000	YES	Printing occupations	Summary
51-5010	YES	Bookbinders and bindery workers	Summary
51-5011	YES	Bindery workers	Line item
51-5012	YES	Bookbinders	Line item
51-5021	YES	Job printers	Line item
51-5022	YES	Prepress technicians and workers	Line item
51-5023	YES	Printing machine operators	Line item
51-5099	NO	All other printing workers	Line item
51-6000	YES	Textile, apparel, and furnishings occupations	Summary
51-6091	YES	Extruding and forming machine setters, operators, and tenders, synthetic and glass fibers	Line item
51-6092	YES	Fabric and apparel patternmakers	Line item
51-6011	YES	Laundry and dry-cleaning workers	Line item
51-6021	YES	Pressers, textile, garment, and related materials	Rollup
51-6022	NO	Launderers and ironers, private household	Collapsed
51-6023	NO	Pressers, textile, garment, and related materials, except private household	Collapsed
51-6031	YES	Sewing machine operators	Line item
51-6041	YES	Shoe and leather workers and repairers	Line item
51-6042	YES	Shoe machine operators and tenders	Line item
51-6050	YES	Tailors, dressmakers, and sewers	Summary
51-6051	YES	Sewers, hand	Line item
51-6061	YES	Textile bleaching and dyeing machine operators and tenders	Line item
51-6062	YES	Textile cutting machine setters, operators, and tenders	Line item
51-6063	YES	Textile knitting and weaving machine setters, operators, and tenders	Line item
51-6064	YES	Textile winding, twisting, and drawing out machine setters, operators, and tenders	Line item
51-6093	YES	Upholsterers	Line item
51-6099	YES	All other textile, apparel, and furnishings workers	Line item
51-7000	YES	Woodworkers	Summary
51-7011	YES	Cabinetmakers and bench carpenters	Line item
51-7021	YES	Furniture finishers	Line item
51-7030	YES	Model makers and patternmakers, wood	Rollup
51-7031	YES	Model makers, wood	Current
51-7032	YES	Patternmakers, wood	Current
51-7041	YES	Sawing machine setters, operators, and tenders, wood	Line item
51-7042	YES	Woodworking machine setters, operators, and tenders, except sawing	Line item
51-7099	YES	All other woodworkers	Line item
51-9000	YES	Other production occupations	Summary
51-9191	YES	Cementing and gluing machine operators and tenders	Line item
51-9010	YES	Chemical processing machine setters, operators, and tenders	Summary
51-9011	YES	Chemical equipment operators and tenders	Line item
51-9012	YES	Separating, filtering, clarifying, precipitating, and still machine setters, operators, and tenders	Line item
51-9192	YES	Cleaning, washing, and metal pickling equipment operators and tenders	Line item
51-9193	YES	Cooling and freezing equipment operators and tenders	Line item
51-9020	YES	Crushing, grinding, polishing, mixing, and blending workers	Summary
51-9021	YES	Crushing, grinding, and polishing machine setters, operators, and tenders	Line item
51-9022	YES	Grinding and polishing workers, hand	Line item
51-9023	YES	Mixing and blending machine setters, operators, and tenders	Line item
51-9030	YES	Cutting workers	Summary
51-9031	YES	Cutters and trimmers, hand	Line item
51-9032	YES	Cutting and slicing machine setters, operators, and tenders	Line item

Table 1. National employment matrix occupational directory, 2000—Continued

Matrix code	Valid SOC Code?	Matrix occupation title	Occupation Type	Matrix code	Valid SOC Code?	Matrix occupation title	Occupation Type
51-9041	YES	Extruding, forming, pressing, and compacting machine setters, operators, and tenders	Line item	53-3022	YES	Bus drivers, school	Line item
				53-3021	YES	Bus drivers, transit and intercity	Line item
51-9051	YES	Furnace, kiln, oven, drier, and kettle operators and tenders	Line item	53-3030	YES	Driver/sales workers and truck drivers	Summary
				53-3031	YES	Driver/sales workers	Line item
51-9198	YES	Helpers--Production workers	Line item	53-3032	YES	Truck drivers, heavy and tractor-trailer	Line item
51-9061	YES	Inspectors, testers, sorters, samplers, and weighers	Line item	53-3033	YES	Truck drivers, light or delivery services	Line item
				53-3041	YES	Taxi drivers and chauffeurs	Line item
51-9071	YES	Jewelers and precious stone and metal workers	Line item	53-3099	YES	All other motor vehicle operators	Line item
				53-4000	YES	Rail transportation occupations	Rollup
51-9080	YES	Medical, dental, and ophthalmic laboratory workers	Summary	53-4011	YES	Locomotive engineers	Collapsed
				53-4012	YES	Locomotive firers	Collapsed
51-9081	YES	Dental laboratory technicians	Line item	53-4021	YES	Railroad brake, signal, and switch operators	Line item
51-9082	YES	Medical appliance technicians	Line item	53-4013	YES	Rail yard engineers, dinkey operators, and hostlers	Line item
51-9195	YES	Molders, shapers, and casters, except metal and plastic	Line item	53-4098	NO	All other rail transportation workers	Rollup
51-9111	YES	Packaging and filling machine operators and tenders	Line item	53-4041	YES	Subway and streetcar operators	Collapsed
				53-4099	YES	Rail transportation workers, all other	Collapsed
51-9120	YES	Painting workers	Summary	53-5000	YES	Water transportation occupations	Summary
51-9121	YES	Coating, painting, and spraying machine setters, operators, and tenders	Line item	53-5011	YES	Sailors and marine oilers	Line item
				53-5020	YES	Ship and boat captains and operators	Rollup
				53-5021	YES	Captains, mates, and pilots of water vessels	Current
51-9122	YES	Painters, transportation equipment	Line item	53-5022	YES	Motorboat operators	Current
51-9123	YES	Painting, coating, and decorating workers	Line item	53-5031	YES	Ship engineers	Line item
51-9196	YES	Paper goods machine setters, operators, and tenders	Line item	53-5099	NO	All other water transportation workers	Line item
				53-6000	YES	Related transportation occupations	Summary
51-9130	YES	Photographic process workers and processing machine operators	Summary	53-6011	YES	Bridge and lock tenders	Line item
				53-6021	YES	Parking lot attendants	Line item
51-9131	YES	Photographic process workers	Line item	53-6031	YES	Service station attendants	Line item
51-9141	YES	Semiconductor processors	Line item	53-6041	YES	Traffic technicians	Line item
51-9197	YES	Tire builders	Line item	53-6051	YES	Transportation inspectors	Line item
51-9199	YES	All other production workers	Line item	53-6099	YES	All other related transportation workers	Line item
53-0000	YES	Transportation and material moving occupations	Summary	53-7000	YES	Material moving occupations	Summary
				53-7061	YES	Cleaners of vehicles and equipment	Line item
53-1000	YES	Supervisors, transportation and material moving workers	Summary	53-7011	YES	Conveyor operators and tenders	Line item
				53-7021	YES	Crane and tower operators	Line item
53-1011	YES	Aircraft cargo handling supervisors	Line item	53-7032	YES	Excavating and loading machine and dragline operators	Line item
53-1021	YES	First-line supervisors/managers of helpers, laborers, and material movers, hand	Line item	53-7051	YES	Industrial truck and tractor operators	Line item
53-1031	YES	First-line supervisors/managers of transportation and material-moving machine and vehicle operators	Line item	53-7062	YES	Laborers and freight, stock, and material movers, hand	Line item
				53-7063	YES	Machine feeders and offbearers	Line item
53-2000	YES	Air transportation occupations	Summary	53-7064	YES	Packers and packagers, hand	Line item
53-2010	YES	Aircraft pilots and flight engineers	Summary	53-7070	YES	Pumping station operators	Summary
53-2011	YES	Airline pilots, copilots, and flight engineers	Line item	53-7071	YES	Gas compressor and gas pumping station operators	Line item
53-2012	YES	Commercial pilots	Line item	53-7072	YES	Pump operators, except wellhead pumpers	Line item
53-2020	YES	Air traffic controllers and airfield operations specialists	Summary	53-7073	YES	Wellhead pumpers	Line item
				53-7081	YES	Refuse and recyclable material collectors	Line item
53-2021	YES	Air traffic controllers	Line item	53-7121	YES	Tank car, truck, and ship loaders	Line item
53-2022	YES	Airfield operations specialists	Line item	53-7098	NO	All other material moving workers	Rollup
53-2099	NO	All other air transportation workers	Line item	53-7031	YES	Dredge operators	Collapsed
53-3000	YES	Motor vehicle operators	Summary	53-7033	YES	Loading machine operators, underground mining	Collapsed
53-3011	YES	Ambulance drivers and attendants, except emergency medical technicians	Line item	53-7111	YES	Shuttle car operators	Collapsed
53-3020	YES	Bus drivers	Summary	53-7199	YES	Material moving workers, all other	Collapsed

16

Chapter II. Selected Occupational Data, 2000 and Projected 2010

Every other year, the Bureau of Labor Statistics updates data on current and projected employment, annual average job openings, and other characteristics for all national employment matrix occupations to ensure that the information is current. These data are distributed in a variety of formats and publications, ranging from the detailed discussion and tables in the *Monthly Labor Review* (November 2001) to the brief text and graphic presentations in the *Occupational Outlook Quarterly* (winter edition, 2001-02). In addition, the searchable National Employment Matrix and Occupational Employment, Training, and Earnings Internet sites display the data. The data also underlie the job outlook information published in the *Occupational Outlook Handbook.*

Table 2 displays data on 2000 and projected 2010 employment, employment change, self-employment, annual average job openings, and other characteristics for all national employment matrix occupations. Also presented are quartile rankings designating the relative magnitude of data for each detailed occupation. As a result, readers using table 2 can obtain specific data about several variables for any occupation and can use the rankings to determine how information for a specific occupation compares with that for other occupations.

In some cases, 2000 OES survey employment data for two or more occupations were combined into a single national employment matrix occupation because confidentiality or reliability concerns determined 2000 employment for those individual occupations should not be released. In other cases, reliable 2000 employment was available but research required to prepare a projection could not be completed. Base year employment for these occupations, termed "collapsed" and "current" occupations respectively, was combined to create occupations unique to the national employment matrix—"rollup" occupations (see table 1).

Employment was projected for the "rollup" occupations, not for their components. Because employment for "current" occupations was not projected, these occupations do not appear in table 2. Information about the number currently employed in an occupation, however, is valuable for providing a measure of the occupation's significance in the labor market. Table 3 provides that measure: It displays 2000 employment for "current" occupations that supplements information in table 2.

Data presented

Information about each variable's data source and potential use is presented below. The Occupational Employment Statistics (OES) survey and the Current Population Survey (CPS) provide almost all of the employment data used in developing the 2000-10 projections. These surveys also are the sources of other statistical information contained in table 2.

Occupational data from the OES survey are not entirely comparable with those from the CPS because of differences in occupational classification systems and in concepts and methods used in the two surveys. Information about worker characteristics from the CPS is applied to matrix occupations based on judgments identifying the most comparable CPS occupations. Comparisons based on CPS occupations with fewer than 50,000 workers in 2000 and some other occupations for which the data appeared unreliable were excluded; data for CPS proxy occupations were substituted. Where possible, larger, closely related CPS occupations were chosen as proxies for the excluded occupations. When a detailed occupation could not be identified, a summary occupational group was used.

Rankings for data categories identify the relative magnitude of variables in terms of the distribution of employment. For example, to rank the projected percent change in employment, data on 2000 employment and projected 2000-10 percent change in employment were assembled for each occupation. Each occupation's employment as a percent of 2000 total employment was calculated. The occupations were sorted by employment change in descending order and the cumulative percent of 2000 employment for each was determined. Occupations within the group accounting for less than 25 percent of total employment are designated "VH" for a very high growth rate. Similarly, occupations sorted by descending order of employment change accounting for 25 to 50 percent of employment are "H" (high); 50 to 75 percent, "L" (low); and 75 to 100 percent, "VL" (very low). Occupations were sorted by other data elements, and rankings were determined in the same manner.

Employment, 2000 and 2010. (Source: Bureau of Labor Statistics, national employment matrixes for 2000 and 2010.) Employment information is a useful starting point for assessing opportunities because large occupations usually have more openings than do small ones, regardless of growth or replacement rates. The data include jobs in all industries. Wage and salary, self-employed, and unpaid family workers are included.

Employment change, 2000-10, numeric. (Source: Bureau

of Labor Statistics, national employment matrixes for 2000 and 2010.) Information on numerical change provides an absolute measure of projected job gains or losses.

Employment change, 2000-10, percent. (Source: Bureau of Labor Statistics, national employment matrixes for 2000 and 2010.) The percent change in employment measures the rate of change. A rapidly growing occupation usually indicates favorable prospects for employment. Moreover, the high demand for workers in a rapidly growing occupation improves their chances for advancement and mobility. Modest employment growth in a large occupation can result in many more job openings than does rapid employment growth in a small occupation.

Percent self-employed, 2000. (Source: Bureau of Labor Statistics, national employment matrixes for 2000 and 2010.) Individuals who are interested in creating and managing their own business may find it important to know the percentage of self-employed workers in an occupation. This percentage is calculated from CPS data on unincorporated self-employed persons in their primary or secondary job who are included in matrix employment data. The unincorporated self-employed work for earnings or fees in their own business and, unlike self-employed persons in businesses that are incorporated, do not receive a wage or salary.

Job openings due to growth and total replacement needs, 2000-10. (Source: Bureau of Labor Statistics, this publication.) These data provide the broadest measure of job opportunities and identify the total number of additional employees needed annually in an occupation. The number of openings due to growth is calculated using data on increases in occupational employment from national employment matrixes for 2000-10. If employment declines, job openings due to growth are zero. Estimates of total replacement needs encompass replacement of workers at all experience levels who leave their jobs to work in another occupation, stop working because of retirement or other reasons, or die. Total replacement needs reflect the normal movements in the labor force. Total replacement needs are calculated from 1999-2000 CPS data, and are described in chapter IV. Data from CPS proxy occupations are used to estimate replacement needs for some matrix occupations.

Job openings due to growth and to net replacement needs, 2000-10. (Source: Bureau of Labor Statistics, this publication.) These data indicate the number of new workers needed annually in an occupation and, if training is required, measure minimum training needs. The number of openings due to growth is calculated using data on increases in occupational employment from national employment matrixes for 2000-10. If employment declines, job openings due to growth are zero. Net replacement job openings typically are due to experienced workers leaving the occupation or the labor force. Net replacement needs

are calculated from CPS data and are described in chapter IV. Data from CPS proxy occupations are used to estimate replacement needs for some matrix occupations.

Median annual earnings, 2000. (Source: 2000 OES survey for most occupations. Estimates developed from 2000 CPS data provide information for occupations not covered by the OES survey, such as farmers and ranchers; fishers and fishing vessel operators; and cooks, private household.) Table 2 presents median annual earnings of workers in different occupations.

Unemployment rate. (Source: Average of 1998-2000 CPS data.) Some occupations are more susceptible to factors that result in unemployment: Seasonality, fluctuations in economic conditions, and individual business failures. A high unemployment rate indicates that individuals in a given occupation are more likely to become unemployed than are those in occupations with a low rate. Data from CPS proxy occupations are used to estimate unemployment rates for some matrix occupations.

Percent part time. (Source: Average of 1998-2000 CPS data.) Persons who prefer part-time work may want to know the proportion of employees in an occupation who work fewer than 35 hours per week. Data from CPS proxy occupations are used to estimate the proportion of part-time workers for some matrix occupations.

Most significant source of postsecondary education or training. (Source: Bureau of Labor Statistics.) BLS uses eleven categories to describe all types of postsecondary education or training. Occupation analysts assign a single category that best describes the education or training needed by most workers to become fully qualified. While individuals with different levels of education or training can enter most occupations, a single category is needed to facilitate analysis of current employment, employment growth, earnings, or other characteristics.

The categories can be used as an initial reference for assessing what postsecondary education or training may be preferable. Since qualification generally can be accomplished in several ways, however, the categories should not be viewed as an absolute standard. Reviewing the "Training, other qualifications, and advancement" material in the *Occupational Outlook Handbook* can help determine if alternatives exist. In most occupations, alternatives do exist. For example, a significant number of computer systems analysts have acquired the qualifying skills but do not have a bachelor's degree—the postsecondary education category designated for the occupation. Such insights are available from the *Handbook*.

Based on analysis of the occupation's most significant source of postsecondary education or training, occupations are classified into 1 of 11 categories listed below, according to these principles:

- An occupation is placed into the category that best describes the education or training that most workers need in order to become fully qualified.

- Postsecondary awards, if generally needed for entry into the occupation, take precedence over work-related training, even though additional skills or experience may be needed for a worker to become fully qualified.

- The length of time that an average worker generally needs to become fully qualified through a combination of on-the-job training and experience is used to categorize occupations in which a postsecondary award generally is not needed for entry.

Postsecondary awards

First professional degree. Completion of the degree usually requires at least 3 years of full-time academic study beyond a bachelor's degree. The first professional degree is the minimum preparation required for entry into several professions, including law, medicine, and dentistry.

Doctoral degree. Completion of a Ph.D. or other doctoral degree usually requires at least 3 years of full-time academic work beyond the bachelor's degree.

Master's degree. Completion of the degree usually requires 1 or 2 years of full-time academic study beyond a bachelor's degree.

Bachelor's or higher degree, plus work experience. Most occupations in this category are management occupations. All require experience in a related nonmanagement position for which a bachelor's or higher degree is usually required. Jobs usually are filled with experienced staff who are promoted into a management position, such as engineers who advance to engineering manager.

Bachelor's degree. Completion of the degree generally requires at least 4 years, but not more than 5 years, of full-time academic study beyond high school.

Associate degree. Completion of the degree usually requires at least 2 years of full-time academic study beyond high school.

Postsecondary vocational awards. Programs lead to a certificate or other award but not a degree. Some programs last only a few weeks, while others may last more than a year. Occupations in this category include some that require only the completion of a training program and some that require individuals to pass a licensing exam after completion of the program before they can work.

Work-related training

Work experience in a related occupation. Many occupations requiring work experience are first-line supervisors/managers of service, sales and related, production, or other occupations, or are other types of managers.

Long-term on-the-job training. More than 12 months of on-the-job training or combined work experience and formal classroom instruction are needed for workers to develop the skills to become fully qualified. This category includes formal or informal apprenticeships that may last up to 5 years. Long-term on-the-job training also includes intensive occupation-specific, employer-sponsored programs that workers must successfully complete. These include fire and police academies and schools for air traffic controllers and flight attendants. In other occupations—insurance sales and securities sales, for example—trainees take formal courses, often provided at the jobsite, to prepare for the required licensing exams. Individuals undergoing training usually are considered employed in the occupation. Also included in this category is the development of natural ability—such as that possessed by musicians, athletes, actors, and other entertainers—that must be cultivated over several years, frequently in a nonwork setting.

Moderate-term on-the-job training. Skills needed to be fully qualified can be acquired during 1 to 12 months of combined on-the-job experience and informal training.

Short-term on-the-job training. Skills needed to be fully qualified can be acquired during a short demonstration of job duties or during 1 month or less of on-the-job experience or instruction.

Once again, the categories identify the postsecondary education or training used by most individuals in an occupation to become fully qualified. They can and do not describe all paths and are not intended to indicate the educational attainment required to be hired.

Using ranked information

Table 2 consolidates 2000 and 2010 projected employment data, and also provides comparisons of occupational data. It ranks information about current and projected employment, projected job openings, earnings, unemployment rates, and the proportion of part-time workers. Except for the unemployment and part-time categories, a high ranking indicates a favorable assessment. A high ranking for the unemployment rate is considered undesirable. Unemployment rates in construction occupations, however, are inflated by characteristics of the industry that make comparisons misleading. For example, construction workers typically experience periods of unemployment after completing a project and before starting work on a new project.

The ranking for the part-time category also should not be used routinely in assessing the desirability of employment because the assessment depends on the perspective of the user. For example, high school students might consider a large proportion of part-time work desirable because they normally prefer not to work full time. A recent college graduate or anyone seeking full-time employment might reach the opposite conclusion. (Text continues on page 57.)

(Numbers in thousands)

2000 national employment matrix occupation	Employment		Employment change, 2000-10				Per-cent self-emp-loyed, 2000	Annual average job openings due to growth and total replacement needs, 2000-10	
			Numeric		Percent				
	2000	2010	Number	Rank	Number	Rank		Number	Rank
Total, all occupations	145,594	167,754	22,160	-	15.2	-	7.9	23,198	-
Management, business, and financial occupations	15,519	17,635	2,115	-	13.6	-	18.3	1,790	-
Management occupations	10,564	11,834	1,270	-	12.0	-	22.9	1,192	-
Administrative services managers	362	436	74	H	20.4	VH	.0	38	L
Advertising, marketing, promotions, public relations, and sales managers	707	936	229	-	32.4	-	1.7	68	-
Advertising and promotions managers	100	135	34	L	34.3	VH	.0	10	VL
Marketing and sales managers	533	701	168	-	31.5	-	1.8	49	-
Marketing managers	190	246	55	L	29.1	VH	2.2	17	VL
Sales managers	343	455	112	H	32.8	VH	1.6	32	L
Public relations managers	74	101	27	L	36.3	VH	3.1	9	VL
Agricultural managers	1,462	1,144	-318	-	-21.7	-	86.1	160	-
Farm, ranch, and other agricultural managers[1]	169	179	10	VL	6.0	VL	5.4	15	VL
Farmers and ranchers[1]	1,294	965	-328	VL	-25.4	VL	96.7	146	H
Chief executives	547	641	94	H	17.2	H	.0	57	L
Computer and information systems managers	313	463	150	H	47.9	VH	11.8	43	L
Construction managers	308	358	50	L	16.3	H	24.4	31	L
Education administrators	453	513	61	L	13.4	L	8.7	41	L
Engineering managers	282	305	23	L	8.0	VL	13.2	26	VL
Financial managers	658	780	122	H	18.5	H	6.7	65	L
Food service managers	465	535	70	L	15.0	H	33.8	62	L
Funeral directors	32	32	1	VL	3.0	VL	19.3	3	VL
Gaming managers	4	5	1	VL	30.0	VH	.0	1	VL
General and operations managers	2,398	2,761	363	VH	15.2	H	3.9	272	H
Human resources managers	219	246	28	L	12.7	L	.0	17	VL
Industrial production managers	255	271	16	L	6.2	VL	19.7	23	VL
Legislators	54	61	7	VL	12.7	L	.0	6	VL
Lodging managers	68	75	6	VL	9.3	L	51.5	9	VL
Medical and health services managers	250	330	81	H	32.3	VH	6.8	35	L
Natural sciences managers	42	45	3	VL	7.6	VL	.0	4	VL
Postmasters and mail superintendents	25	26	1	VL	2.5	VL	.0	2	VL
Property, real estate, and community association managers	270	331	61	L	22.7	VH	47.7	30	L
Purchasing managers	132	125	-7	VL	-5.5	VL	.0	17	VL
Social and community service managers	128	160	32	L	24.8	VH	23.5	16	VL
Transportation, storage, and distribution managers	149	179	30	L	20.2	VH	21.9	16	VL
All other managers	981	1,074	93	H	9.5	L	36.6	106	H
Business and financial operations occupations	4,956	5,801	845	-	17.1	-	8.6	608	-
Business operations specialists	2,841	3,320	479	-	16.8	-	8.2	344	-
Agents and business managers of artists, performers, and athletes	17	22	5	VL	27.9	VH	63.7	2	VL
Buyers and purchasing agents	404	424	20	-	4.8	-	4.4	47	-
Purchasing agents and buyers, farm products	20	23	3	VL	16.8	H	5.2	2	VL
Purchasing agents, except wholesale, retail, and farm products	237	266	29	L	12.3	L	1.1	26	VL
Wholesale and retail buyers, except farm products	148	135	-13	VL	-8.7	VL	9.6	18	VL
Claims adjusters, appraisers, examiners, and investigators	207	238	31	-	15.0	-	2.2	28	-
Claims adjusters, examiners, and investigators	194	223	29	L	15.1	H	2.3	26	VL
Insurance appraisers, auto damage	13	15	2	VL	14.3	H	.0	2	VL
Compliance officers, except agriculture, construction, health and safety, and transportation[1]	140	152	12	VL	8.9	L	.0	11	VL
Cost estimators	211	246	35	L	16.5	H	6.7	31	L
Emergency management specialists	10	12	2	VL	18.1	H	.0	2	VL
Human resources, training, and labor relations specialists	490	578	88	-	18.0	-	4.3	56	-
Compensation, benefits, and job analysis specialists ...	87	100	14	VL	15.7	H	4.3	10	VL
Employment, recruitment, and placement specialists ...	199	234	35	L	17.6	H	4.4	23	VL
Training and development specialists	204	244	40	L	19.4	H	4.4	24	VL

[1] One or more Current Population Survey (CPS) proxy occupations are used to estimate CPS based data.
[2] Bachelor's degree or higher, plus work experience.
[3] Work experience in a related occupation.

NOTE: Rankings are based on employment in all detailed occupations in the National Employment Matrix. For details, see "Data presented" section of text. Codes for describing the ranked variables are: VH = Very high, H = High, L = Low, VL = Very low, and n. a. = data not available. A dash indicates data are not applicable.

Table 2. Occupational employment and job openings data, 2000-10, and worker characteristics, 2000

(Numbers in thousands)

Annual average job openings due to growth and net replacement needs, 2000-10		Median annual earnings		Ranking of:		Most significant source of postsecondary education or training	2000 national employment matrix occupation
Number	Rank	Dollars	Rank	Unemployment rate	Percent part-time		
5,793	-	-	-	-	-	-	**Total, all occupations**
511	-	-	-	-	-	-	**Management, business, and financial occupations**
333	-	-	-	-	-	-	Management occupations
13	L	47,080	VH	VL	VL	Bachelor's plus experience[2]	Administrative services managers
							Advertising, marketing, promotions, public relations, and sales managers
33	-	-	-	-	-	-	Advertising, marketing, promotions, public relations, and sales managers
5	VL	53,360	VH	L	VL	Bachelor's plus experience[2]	Advertising and promotions managers
24	-	-	-	-	-	-	Marketing and sales managers
8	L	71,240	VH	L	VL	Bachelor's plus experience[2]	Marketing managers
16	L	68,520	VH	L	VL	Bachelor's plus experience[2]	Sales managers
4	VL	54,540	VH	L	VL	Bachelor's plus experience[2]	Public relations managers
10	-	-	-	-	-	-	Agricultural managers
3	VL	38,400	H	VL	L	Bachelor's plus experience[2]	Farm, ranch, and other agricultural managers[1]
7	VL	n.a.	H	VL	H	Long-term on-the-job	Farmers and ranchers[1]
27	H	113,810	VH	VL	L	Bachelor's plus experience[2]	Chief executives
20	L	78,830	VH	VL	VL	Bachelor's plus experience[2]	Computer and information systems managers
10	L	58,250	VH	VL	VL	Bachelor's degree	Construction managers
18	L	58,054	VH	VL	L	Bachelor's plus experience[2]	Education administrators
7	VL	84,070	VH	VL	VL	Bachelor's plus experience[2]	Engineering managers
22	L	67,020	VH	VL	VL	Bachelor's plus experience[2]	Financial managers
12	L	31,720	H	L	L	Related work experience[3]	Food service managers
1	VL	41,110	VH	VL	L	Associate degree	Funeral directors
0	VL	53,380	VH	L	L	Bachelor's plus experience[2]	Gaming managers
77	VH	61,160	VH	VL	VL	Bachelor's plus experience[2]	General and operations managers
7	VL	59,000	VH	L	VL	Bachelor's plus experience[2]	Human resources managers
6	VL	61,660	VH	VL	VL	Bachelor's degree	Industrial production managers
2	VL	14,110	VL	VL	VL	Bachelor's plus experience[2]	Legislators
1	VL	30,770	H	L	L	Related work experience[3]	Lodging managers
12	L	56,370	VH	L	L	Bachelor's plus experience[2]	Medical and health services managers
1	VL	75,880	VH	VL	VL	Bachelor's plus experience[2]	Natural sciences managers
0	VL	44,260	VH	VL	VL	Related work experience[3]	Postmasters and mail superintendents
11	L	36,020	H	L	H	Bachelor's degree	Property, real estate, and community association managers
4	VL	53,030	VH	VL	VL	Bachelor's plus experience[2]	Purchasing managers
6	VL	39,130	H	L	L	Bachelor's degree	Social and community service managers
5	VL	54,230	VH	VL	VL	Related work experience[3]	Transportation, storage, and distribution managers
27	H	60,500	VH	VL	VL	Related work experience[3]	All other managers
178	-	-	-	-	-	-	Business and financial operations occupations
105	-	-	-	-	-	-	Business operations specialists
							Agents and business managers of artists, performers, and athletes
1	VL	57,040	VH	L	H	Bachelor's plus experience[2]	Agents and business managers of artists, performers, and athletes
13	-	-	-	-	-	-	Buyers and purchasing agents
1	VL	37,560	H	VL	L	Related work experience[3]	Purchasing agents and buyers, farm products
8	L	41,370	VH	L	VL	Bachelor's degree	Purchasing agents, except wholesale, retail, and farm products
4	VL	37,200	H	L	H	Bachelor's degree	Wholesale and retail buyers, except farm products
5	-	-	-	-	-	-	Claims adjusters, appraisers, examiners, and investigators
5	VL	41,080	VH	VL	VL	Long-term on-the-job	Claims adjusters, examiners, and investigators
0	VL	40,000	VH	VL	L	Long-term on-the-job	Insurance appraisers, auto damage
							Compliance officers, except agriculture, construction, health and safety, and transportation[1]
5	VL	40,910	VH	VL	VL	Long-term on-the-job	Compliance officers, except agriculture, construction, health and safety, and transportation[1]
8	L	45,800	VH	VL	L	Bachelor's degree	Cost estimators
0	VL	39,210	H	L	L	Related work experience[3]	Emergency management specialists
18	-	-	-	-	-	-	Human resources, training, and labor relations specialists
3	VL	41,660	VH	L	L	Bachelor's degree	Compensation, benefits, and job analysis specialists
7	VL	36,480	H	L	L	Bachelor's degree	Employment, recruitment, and placement specialists
8	L	40,830	VH	L	L	Bachelor's degree	Training and development specialists

[1] One or more Current Population Survey (CPS) proxy occupations are used to estimate CPS based data.
[2] Bachelor's degree or higher, plus work experience.
[3] Work experience in a related occupation.

NOTE: Rankings are based on employment in all detailed occupations in the National Employment Matrix. For details, see "Data presented" section of text. Codes for describing the ranked variables are: VH = Very high, H = High, L = Low, VL = Very low, and n. a. = data not available. A dash indicates data are not applicable.

(Numbers in thousands)

2000 national employment matrix occupation	Employment		Employment change, 2000-10				Percent self-employed, 2000	Annual average job openings due to growth and total replacement needs, 2000-10	
			Numeric		Percent				
	2000	2010	Number	Rank	Number	Rank		Number	Rank
Management analysts	501	646	145	H	28.9	VH	32.5	64	L
Meeting and convention planners	34	42	8	VL	23.3	VH	5.2	4	VL
All other business operations specialists	827	960	133	H	16.1	H	>0	100	H
Financial specialists	2,115	2,481	367	-	17.3	-	9.1	266	-
Accountants and auditors	976	1,157	181	VH	18.5	H	12.2	119	H
Appraisers and assessors of real estate	57	67	10	VL	18.0	H	2.3	7	VL
Budget analysts	70	80	10	VL	14.6	H	7.2	9	VL
Credit analysts	60	70	10	VL	16.0	H	.0	8	VL
Financial analysts	145	182	37	L	25.5	VH	.0	23	VL
Financial examiners	25	27	3	VL	10.2	L	.0	3	VL
Insurance underwriters	107	109	2	VL	2.0	VL	.0	11	VL
Loan counselors and officers	265	281	16	-	6.1	-	9.7	33	-
Loan counselors	29	33	5	VL	16.0	H	9.0	4	VL
Loan officers	236	248	12	VL	4.9	VL	9.8	29	L
Personal financial advisors	94	126	32	L	34.0	VH	29.3	16	VL
Tax examiners, collectors, and revenue agents	79	86	7	VL	8.3	VL	.0	7	VL
Tax preparers	69	81	12	VL	17.4	H	16.7	9	VL
All other financial specialists	169	216	47	L	28.0	VH	1.3	25	VL
Professional and related occupations	26,758	33,709	6,952	-	26.0	-	7.1	3,201	-
Computer and mathematical occupations	2,993	4,988	1,996	-	66.7	-	5.2	420	-
Computer specialists	2,903	4,894	1,991	-	68.6	-	5.3	411	-
Computer programmers	585	680	95	H	16.2	H	3.8	45	L
Computer scientists and systems analysts	459	729	269	-	58.6	-	10.3	63	-
Computer and information scientists, research	28	39	11	VL	40.3	VH	9.7	3	VL
Computer systems analysts	431	689	258	VH	59.7	VH	10.3	60	L
Computer software engineers	697	1,361	664	-	95.4	-	7.0	118	-
Computer software engineers, applications	380	760	380	VH	100.0	VH	7.5	66	L
Computer software engineers, systems software	317	601	284	VH	89.7	VH	6.5	52	L
Computer support specialists	506	996	490	VH	97.0	VH	1.9	89	L
Database administrators	106	176	70	L	65.9	VH	1.7	15	VL
Network and computer systems administrators	229	416	187	VH	81.9	VH	.9	37	L
Network systems and data communications analysts	119	211	92	H	77.5	VH	1.7	19	VL
All other computer specialists	203	326	123	H	60.7	VH	10.0	28	VL
Mathematical science occupations	89	95	5	-	5.7	-	.0	8	-
Mathematical scientists and technicians	85	90	5	-	5.9	-	.0	8	-
Actuaries	14	15	1	VL	5.4	VL	.0	1	VL
Mathematicians	4	4	0	VL	-1.9	VL	.0	0	VL
Operations research analysts	47	51	4	VL	8.0	VL	.0	5	VL
Statisticians	19	20	0	VL	2.3	VL	.0	2	VL
Miscellaneous mathematical science occupations	5	5	0	VL	2.7	VL	.0	0	VL
Architecture and engineering occupations	2,605	2,930	325	-	12.5	-	4.2	198	-
Architects, surveyors, and cartographers	196	229	33	-	17.1	-	19.0	13	-
Architects, except naval	124	150	26	-	20.7	-	27.7	7	-
Architects, except landscape and naval	102	121	19	L	18.5	H	28.1	6	VL
Landscape architects	22	29	7	VL	31.1	VH	25.8	2	VL
Surveyors, cartographers, and photogrammetrists	65	71	6	-	9.2	-	3.9	9	-
Cartographers and photogrammetrists	7	8	1	VL	18.5	H	.0	1	VL
Surveyors	58	63	5	VL	8.1	VL	4.3	8	VL
All other architects, surveyors, and cartographers	6	8	2	VL	28.5	VH	4.9	1	VL
Engineers	1,465	1,603	138	-	9.4	-	2.9	79	-
Aerospace engineers	50	57	7	VL	13.9	L	.0	3	VL
Agricultural engineers	2	3	0	VL	14.8	H	.0	0	VL
Biomedical engineers	7	9	2	VL	31.4	VH	20.0	1	VL
Chemical engineers	33	34	1	VL	4.1	VL	.0	2	VL
Civil engineers	232	256	24	L	10.2	L	5.2	7	VL
Computer hardware engineers	60	75	15	L	24.9	VH	2.5	5	VL

[1] One or more Current Population Survey (CPS) proxy occupations are used to estimate CPS based data.
[2] Bachelor's degree or higher, plus work experience.
[3] Work experience in a related occupation.

NOTE: Rankings are based on employment in all detailed occupations in the National Employment Matrix. For details, see "Data presented" section of text. Codes for describing the ranked variables are: VH = Very high, H = High, L = Low, VL = Very low, and n. a. = data not available. A dash indicates data are not applicable.

Table 2. Occupational employment and job openings data, 2000-10, and worker characteristics, 2000 — Continued

(Numbers in thousands)

Annual average job openings due to growth and net replacement needs, 2000-10		Median annual earnings		Ranking of:		Most significant source of postsecondary education or training	2000 national employment matrix occupation
				Unemploy-ment rate	Percent part-time		
Number	Rank	Dollars	Rank				
19	L	55,040	VH	L	H	Bachelor's plus experience[2]	Management analysts
1	VL	35,540	H	L	L	Bachelor's degree	Meeting and convention planners
34	H	47,120	VH	L	L	Bachelor's degree	All other business operations specialists
73	-	-	-	-	-	-	Financial specialists
33	H	43,500	VH	VL	L	Bachelor's degree	Accountants and auditors
3	VL	38,300	H	VL	VL	Postsecondary vocational award	Appraisers and assessors of real estate
2	VL	48,370	VH	VL	L	Bachelor's degree	Budget analysts
2	VL	40,180	VH	VL	L	Bachelor's degree	Credit analysts
6	VL	52,420	VH	VL	L	Bachelor's degree	Financial analysts
1	VL	53,060	VH	VL	L	Bachelor's degree	Financial examiners
2	VL	43,150	VH	VL	VL	Bachelor's degree	Insurance underwriters
7	-	-	-	-	-	-	Loan counselors and officers
1	VL	32,160	H	VL	L	Bachelor's degree	Loan counselors
6	VL	41,420	VH	VL	L	Bachelor's degree	Loan officers
4	VL	55,320	VH	VL	L	Bachelor's degree	Personal financial advisors
3	VL	40,180	VH	VL	VL	Bachelor's degree	Tax examiners, collectors, and revenue agents
3	VL	25,580	L	VL	L	Moderate-term on-the-job	Tax preparers
8	L	41,470	VH	VL	L	Bachelor's degree	All other financial specialists
1,216	-	-	-	-	-	-	Professional and related occupations
228	-	-	-	-	-	-	Computer and mathematical occupations
226	-	-	-	-	-	-	Computer specialists
22	L	57,590	VH	VL	L	Bachelor's degree	Computer programmers
31	-	-	-	-	-	-	Computer scientists and systems analysts
1	VL	70,590	VH	VL	VL	Doctoral degree	Computer and information scientists, research
30	H	59,330	VH	VL	VL	Bachelor's degree	Computer systems analysts
71	-	-	-	-	-	-	Computer software engineers
41	H	67,670	VH	VL	VL	Bachelor's degree	Computer software engineers, applications
31	H	69,530	VH	VL	VL	Bachelor's degree	Computer software engineers, systems software
51	VH	36,460	H	VL	VL	Associate degree	Computer support specialists
7	VL	51,990	VH	VL	VL	Bachelor's degree	Database administrators
20	L	51,280	VH	VL	VL	Bachelor's degree	Network and computer systems administrators
10	L	54,510	VH	VL	VL	Bachelor's degree	Network systems and data communications analysts
14	L	50,590	VH	VL	VL	Postsecondary vocational award	All other computer specialists
3	-	-	-	-	-	-	Mathematical science occupations
2	-	-	-	-	-	-	Mathematical scientists and technicians
0	VL	66,590	VH	VL	H	Bachelor's plus experience[2]	Actuaries
0	VL	68,640	VH	VL	VL	Master's degree	Mathematicians
2	VL	53,420	VH	VL	VL	Master's degree	Operations research analysts
0	VL	51,990	VH	VL	L	Master's degree	Statisticians
0	VL	52,430	VH	VL	L	Master's degree	Miscellaneous mathematical science occupations
87	-	-	-	-	-	-	Architecture and engineering occupations
6	-	-	-	-	-	-	Architects, surveyors, and cartographers
3	-	-	-	-	-	-	Architects, except naval
2	VL	52,510	VH	VL	VL	Bachelor's degree	Architects, except landscape and naval
1	VL	43,540	VH	VL	VL	Bachelor's degree	Landscape architects
3	-	-	-	-	-	-	Surveyors, cartographers, and photogrammetrists
0	VL	39,410	H	H	L	Bachelor's degree	Cartographers and photogrammetrists
2	VL	36,700	H	H	L	Bachelor's degree	Surveyors
0	VL	40,290	VH	VL	VL	Bachelor's degree	All other architects, surveyors, and cartographers
43	-	-	-	-	-	-	Engineers
2	VL	67,930	VH	VL	VL	Bachelor's degree	Aerospace engineers
0	VL	55,850	VH	VL	VL	Bachelor's degree	Agricultural engineers
0	VL	57,480	VH	VL	VL	Bachelor's degree	Biomedical engineers
1	VL	65,960	VH	VL	VL	Bachelor's degree	Chemical engineers
6	VL	55,740	VH	VL	VL	Bachelor's degree	Civil engineers
2	VL	67,300	VH	VL	VL	Bachelor's degree	Computer hardware engineers

[1] One or more Current Population Survey (CPS) proxy occupations are used to estimate CPS based data.
[2] Bachelor's degree or higher, plus work experience.
[3] Work experience in a related occupation.

NOTE: Rankings are based on employment in all detailed occupations in the National Employment Matrix. For details, see "Data presented" section of text. Codes for describing the ranked variables are: VH = Very high, H = High, L = Low, VL = Very low, and n. a. = data not available. A dash indicates data are not applicable.

2000 national employment matrix occupation	Employment		Employment change, 2000-10				Percent self-employed, 2000	Annual average job openings due to growth and total replacement needs, 2000-10	
			Numeric		Percent				
	2000	2010	Number	Rank	Number	Rank		Number	Rank
Electrical and electronics engineers	288	319	31	-	10.9	-	2.9	17	-
Electrical engineers	157	175	18	L	11.3	L	3.1	9	VL
Electronics engineers, except computer	130	144	14	VL	10.4	L	2.7	8	VL
Environmental engineers	52	66	14	VL	26.0	VH	2.8	5	VL
Industrial engineers, including health and safety	198	210	12	-	5.9	-	.0	14	-
Health and safety engineers, except mining safety engineers and inspectors	44	49	5	VL	10.9	L	.0	3	VL
Industrial engineers	154	161	7	VL	4.5	VL	.0	10	VL
Marine engineers and naval architects	5	5	0	VL	2.1	VL	.0	0	VL
Materials engineers	33	35	2	VL	5.3	VL	.0	2	VL
Mechanical engineers	221	251	29	L	13.1	L	3.2	10	VL
Mining and geological engineers, including mining safety engineers	6	6	0	VL	-1.3	VL	.0	0	VL
Nuclear engineers	14	14	0	VL	1.8	VL	.0	1	VL
Petroleum engineers	9	8	-1	VL	-7.2	VL	.0	0	VL
All other engineers	253	254	1	VL	.4	VL	4.3	16	VL
Drafters, engineering, and mapping technicians	944	1,098	154	-	16.3	-	3.1	111	-
Drafters	213	255	42	-	19.5	-	4.7	30	-
Architectural and civil drafters	102	123	21	L	20.8	VH	4.6	14	VL
Electrical and electronics drafters	41	51	10	VL	23.3	VH	4.9	6	VL
Mechanical drafters	70	81	11	VL	15.4	H	4.7	9	VL
Engineering technicians, except drafters	519	582	62	-	12.0	-	2.1	55	-
Aerospace engineering and operations technicians[1]	21	22	1	VL	5.6	VL	.0	2	VL
Civil engineering technicians[1]	94	105	11	VL	11.9	L	2.5	10	VL
Electrical and electronic engineering technicians[1]	233	258	25	L	10.8	L	2.7	24	VL
Electro-mechanical technicians[1]	43	50	6	VL	14.5	H	.0	5	VL
Environmental engineering technicians[1]	18	24	5	VL	29.1	VH	.0	2	VL
Industrial engineering technicians[1]	52	57	5	VL	10.1	L	2.1	5	VL
Mechanical engineering technicians[1]	58	66	8	VL	13.9	L	2.1	6	VL
Surveying and mapping technicians[1]	55	70	14	VL	25.3	VH	4.7	9	VL
All other drafters, engineering, and mapping technicians[1]	156	192	36	L	23.2	VH	3.9	19	VL
Life, physical, and social science occupations	1,164	1,386	223	-	19.1	-	10.6	140	-
Life scientists	184	218	33	-	18.1	-	7.0	15	-
Agricultural and food scientists	17	19	2	VL	8.8	L	23.1	1	VL
Biological scientists	73	88	15	L	21.0	VH	8.0	7	VL
Conservation scientists and foresters	29	31	2	-	7.7	-	3.3	2	-
Conservation scientists	16	18	1	VL	8.3	VL	3.2	1	VL
Foresters	12	13	1	VL	7.0	VL	3.4	1	VL
Medical scientists	37	47	10	VL	26.5	VH	5.7	3	VL
All other life scientists	28	33	4	VL	15.9	H	.0	2	VL
Physical scientists	239	283	44	-	18.3	-	2.9	21	-
Astronomers and physicists	10	11	1	VL	10.5	L	.0	1	VL
Atmospheric and space scientists	7	8	1	VL	17.1	H	.0	1	VL
Chemists and materials scientists	92	110	18	-	19.2	-	1.9	8	-
Chemists	84	100	16	L	19.1	H	2.0	8	VL
Materials scientists	8	9	2	VL	19.8	H	.0	1	VL
Environmental scientists and geoscientists	97	118	21	-	21.5	-	4.1	9	-
Environmental scientists and specialists, including health	64	78	14	L	22.3	VH	4.5	6	VL
Geoscientists, except hydrologists and geographers	25	30	5	VL	18.1	H	4.4	2	VL
Hydrologists	8	10	2	VL	25.7	VH	.0	1	VL
All other physical scientists[1]	33	36	3	VL	9.4	L	3.8	3	VL
Social scientists and related occupations	410	492	82	-	20.1	-	23.9	56	-
Economists	22	26	4	VL	18.5	H	33.2	4	VL
Market and survey researchers	113	142	30	-	26.4	-	11.6	20	-
Market research analysts	90	112	22	L	24.4	VH	10.9	16	VL
Survey researchers	23	30	8	VL	34.5	VH	14.1	4	VL

[1] One or more Current Population Survey (CPS) proxy occupations are used to estimate CPS based data.
[2] Bachelor's degree or higher, plus work experience.
[3] Work experience in a related occupation.

NOTE: Rankings are based on employment in all detailed occupations in the National Employment Matrix. For details, see "Data presented" section of text. Codes for describing the ranked variables are: VH = Very high, H = High, L = Low, VL = Very low, and n. a. = data not available. A dash indicates data are not applicable.

(Numbers in thousands)

Annual average job openings due to growth and net replacement needs, 2000-10		Median annual earnings		Ranking of:		Most significant source of postsecondary education or training	2000 national employment matrix occupation
Number	Rank	Dollars	Rank	Unemployment rate	Percent part-time		
8	-	-	-	-	-	-	Electrical and electronics engineers
5	VL	64,910	VH	L	VL	Bachelor's degree	Electrical engineers
4	VL	64,830	VH	L	VL	Bachelor's degree	Electronics engineers, except computer
2	VL	57,780	VH	VL	VL	Bachelor's degree	Environmental engineers
4	-	-	-	-	-	-	Industrial engineers, including health and safety
1	VL	54,630	VH	L	VL	Bachelor's degree	Health and safety engineers, except mining safety engineers and inspectors
3	VL	58,580	VH	L	VL	Bachelor's degree	Industrial engineers
0	VL	60,890	VH	H	VL	Bachelor's degree	Marine engineers and naval architects
1	VL	59,100	VH	VL	VL	Bachelor's degree	Materials engineers
9	L	58,710	VH	VL	VL	Bachelor's degree	Mechanical engineers
0	VL	60,820	VH	VL	VL	Bachelor's degree	Mining and geological engineers, including mining safety engineers
0	VL	79,360	VH	VL	VL	Bachelor's degree	Nuclear engineers
0	VL	78,910	VH	VL	VL	Bachelor's degree	Petroleum engineers
5	VL	66,070	VH	VL	VL	Bachelor's degree	All other engineers
38	-	-	-	-	-	-	Drafters, engineering, and mapping technicians
11	-	-	-	-	-	-	Drafters
5	VL	35,220	H	L	L	Postsecondary vocational award	Architectural and civil drafters
2	VL	38,210	H	L	L	Postsecondary vocational award	Electrical and electronics drafters
3	VL	37,840	H	L	L	Postsecondary vocational award	Mechanical drafters
17	-	-	-	-	-	-	Engineering technicians, except drafters
1	VL	48,600	VH	L	L	Associate degree	Aerospace engineering and operations technicians[1]
3	VL	35,990	H	L	L	Associate degree	Civil engineering technicians[1]
7	VL	40,020	VH	L	L	Associate degree	Electrical and electronic engineering technicians[1]
2	VL	36,150	H	L	L	Associate degree	Electro-mechanical technicians[1]
1	VL	34,000	H	L	L	Associate degree	Environmental engineering technicians[1]
2	VL	40,910	VH	L	L	Associate degree	Industrial engineering technicians[1]
2	VL	39,570	H	L	L	Associate degree	Mechanical engineering technicians[1]
3	VL	28,030	H	H	VL	Moderate-term on-the-job	Surveying and mapping technicians[1]
7	VL	41,710	VH	L	L	Associate degree	All other drafters, engineering, and mapping technicians[1]
56	-	-	-	-	-	-	Life, physical, and social science occupations
9	-	-	-	-	-	-	Life scientists
1	VL	52,160	VH	VL	L	Bachelor's degree	Agricultural and food scientists
4	VL	49,239	VH	VL	L	Doctoral degree	Biological scientists
1	-	-	-	-	-	-	Conservation scientists and foresters
1	VL	47,140	VH	L	L	Bachelor's degree	Conservation scientists
0	VL	43,640	VH	L	L	Bachelor's degree	Foresters
2	VL	57,196	VH	VL	L	Doctoral degree	Medical scientists
1	VL	41,630	VH	VL	L	Bachelor's degree	All other life scientists
12	-	-	-	-	-	-	Physical scientists
0	VL	82,535	VH	VL	L	Doctoral degree	Astronomers and physicists
0	VL	58,510	VH	VL	L	Bachelor's degree	Atmospheric and space scientists
5	-	-	-	-	-	-	Chemists and materials scientists
4	VL	50,080	VH	VL	VL	Bachelor's degree	Chemists
0	VL	60,620	VH	VL	VL	Bachelor's degree	Materials scientists
5	-	-	-	-	-	-	Environmental scientists and geoscientists
3	VL	44,180	VH	VL	VL	Bachelor's degree	Environmental scientists and specialists, including health
1	VL	56,230	VH	VL	VL	Bachelor's degree	Geoscientists, except hydrologists and geographers
0	VL	55,410	VH	VL	VL	Bachelor's degree	Hydrologists
2	VL	61,590	VH	L	H	Bachelor's degree	All other physical scientists[1]
18	-	-	-	-	-	-	Social scientists and related occupations
1	VL	64,830	VH	VL	L	Bachelor's degree	Economists
5	-	-	-	-	-	-	Market and survey researchers
4	VL	51,190	VH	VL	L	Bachelor's degree	Market research analysts
1	VL	26,200	H	VL	L	Bachelor's degree	Survey researchers

[1] One or more Current Population Survey (CPS) proxy occupations are used to estimate CPS based data.
[2] Bachelor's degree or higher, plus work experience.
[3] Work experience in a related occupation.

NOTE: Rankings are based on employment in all detailed occupations in the National Employment Matrix. For details, see "Data presented" section of text. Codes for describing the ranked variables are: VH = Very high, H = High, L = Low, VL = Very low, and n. a. = data not available. A dash indicates data are not applicable.

Table 2. Occupational employment and job openings data, 2000-10, and worker characteristics, 2000 — Continued

(Numbers in thousands)

2000 national employment matrix occupation	Employment		Employment change, 2000-10				Per-cent self-emp-loyed, 2000	Annual average job openings due to growth and total replacement needs, 2000-10	
			Numeric		Percent				
	2000	2010	Number	Rank	Number	Rank		Number	Rank
Psychologists	182	214	33	L	18.1	H	41.4	21	VL
Social scientists, other[1]	15	17	3	VL	17.2	H	.0	2	VL
Urban and regional planners[1]	30	35	5	VL	16.4	H	.0	4	VL
All other social scientists and related workers[1]	49	58	8	VL	17.1	H	5.4	6	VL
Life, physical, and social science technicians	330	393	63	-	19.0	-	1.6	57	-
Agricultural and food science technicians	18	20	3	VL	15.2	H	.0	3	VL
Biological technicians	41	52	11	VL	26.4	VH	.0	8	VL
Chemical technicians[1]	73	84	11	VL	15.0	H	.0	14	VL
Geological and petroleum technicians[1]	10	11	1	VL	6.5	VL	.0	2	VL
Nuclear technicians	3	4	1	VL	20.7	VH	.0	0	VL
Other life, physical, and social science technicians	184	221	37	-	20.0	-	2.8	24	-
Environmental science and protection technicians, including health[1]	27	34	7	VL	24.5	VH	3.7	4	VL
Forensic science technicians[1]	6	7	1	VL	13.0	L	.0	1	VL
Forest and conservation technicians[1]	18	19	1	VL	3.2	VL	.0	2	VL
All other life, physical, and social science technicians[1]	133	161	29	L	21.7	VH	3.2	17	VL
Community and social services occupations	1,869	2,398	529	-	28.3	-	2.2	273	-
Counselors	465	585	120	-	25.8	-	3.5	63	-
Educational, vocational, and school counselors	205	257	52	L	25.3	VH	3.8	28	VL
Marriage and family therapists	21	27	6	VL	29.9	VH	.0	3	VL
Mental health counselors	67	82	15	L	21.7	VH	3.8	9	VL
Rehabilitation counselors	110	136	26	L	23.6	VH	3.4	15	VL
Substance abuse and behavioral disorder counselors	61	82	21	L	35.0	VH	3.8	9	VL
Miscellaneous community and social service specialists	398	575	177	-	44.5	-	.8	83	-
Health educators[1]	43	53	10	VL	23.5	VH	.0	8	VL
Probation officers and correctional treatment specialists[1]	84	105	20	L	23.8	VH	.6	16	VL
Social and human service assistants[1]	271	418	147	H	54.2	VH	1.0	59	L
Religious workers	293	338	45	-	15.4	-	.0	30	-
Clergy	171	197	26	L	15.0	H	.0	14	VL
Directors, religious activities and education	121	141	19	L	15.9	H	.0	25	VL
Social workers	468	609	141	-	30.1	-	2.3	73	-
Child, family, and school social workers	281	357	76	H	26.9	VH	2.3	43	L
Medical and public health social workers	104	136	33	L	31.6	VH	2.5	16	VL
Mental health and substance abuse social workers	83	116	33	L	39.1	VH	2.2	14	VL
All other counselors, social, and religious workers[1]	244	290	46	L	18.8	H	4.7	38	L
Legal occupations	1,119	1,335	216	-	19.3	-	19.8	102	-
Judges, magistrates, and other judicial workers	43	44	2	-	3.8	-	.0	4	-
Administrative law judges, adjudicators, and hearing officers[1]	14	14	0	VL	1.1	VL	.0	1	VL
Arbitrators, mediators, and conciliators[1]	4	6	1	VL	27.2	VH	.0	1	VL
Judges, magistrate judges, and magistrates[1]	24	24	0	VL	1.1	VL	.0	2	VL
Lawyers	681	803	123	H	18.0	H	28.3	47	L
Paralegals and legal assistants	188	251	62	L	33.2	VH	3.5	29	L
Miscellaneous legal support workers	98	106	8	-	7.7	-	11.6	11	-
Court reporters	18	21	3	VL	16.2	H	13.2	2	VL
Law clerks	31	35	4	VL	13.2	L	11.5	4	VL
Title examiners, abstractors, and searchers	48	49	0	VL	1.0	VL	11.1	5	VL
All other legal and related workers	109	131	22	L	20.2	VH	10.1	13	VL
Education, training, and library occupations	8,260	9,831	1,571	-	19.0	-	2.3	1,100	-
Postsecondary teachers[1]	1,344	1,659	315	VH	23.5	VH	2.4	216	H
Primary, secondary, and special education teachers	4,284	4,995	711	-	16.6	-	.2	443	-
Preschool and kindergarten teachers	597	707	110	-	18.4	-	1.7	89	-
Preschool teachers, except special education	423	507	85	H	20.0	VH	1.6	64	L
Kindergarten teachers, except special education	175	200	25	L	14.5	H	1.8	25	VL
Elementary and middle school teachers	2,122	2,381	260	-	12.2	-	.0	225	-
Elementary school teachers, except special education	1,532	1,734	202	VH	13.2	L	.0	164	H

[1] One or more Current Population Survey (CPS) proxy occupations are used to estimate CPS based data.
[2] Bachelor's degree or higher, plus work experience.
[3] Work experience in a related occupation.

NOTE: Rankings are based on employment in all detailed occupations in the National Employment Matrix. For details, see "Data presented" section of text. Codes for describing the ranked variables are: VH = Very high, H = High, L = Low, VL = Very low, and n. a. = data not available. A dash indicates data are not applicable.

(Numbers in thousands)

Annual average job openings due to growth and net replacement needs, 2000-10		Median annual earnings		Ranking of:		Most significant source of postsecondary education or training	2000 national employment matrix occupation
Number	Rank	Dollars	Rank	Unemployment rate	Percent part-time		
8	L	48,596	VH	VL	H	Master's degree	Psychologists
1	VL	48,330	VH	VL	H	Master's degree	Social scientists, other[1]
1	VL	46,500	VH	VL	VL	Master's degree	Urban and regional planners[1]
2	VL	48,070	VH	VL	H	Master's degree	All other social scientists and related workers[1]
16	-	-	-	-	-	-	Life, physical, and social science technicians
1	VL	27,080	H	L	H	Associate degree	Agricultural and food science technicians
2	VL	31,540	H	L	H	Associate degree	Biological technicians
3	VL	35,450	H	L	VL	Associate degree	Chemical technicians[1]
0	VL	36,490	H	L	H	Associate degree	Geological and petroleum technicians[1]
0	VL	59,160	VH	VL	VL	Associate degree	Nuclear technicians
10	-	-	-	-	-	-	Other life, physical, and social science technicians
2	VL	33,830	H	L	H	Associate degree	Environmental science and protection technicians, including health[1]
0	VL	37,520	H	L	H	Associate degree	Forensic science technicians[1]
1	VL	29,580	H	L	H	Associate degree	Forest and conservation technicians[1]
8	L	30,300	H	L	H	Associate degree	All other life, physical, and social science technicians[1]
85	-	-	-	-	-	-	Community and social services occupations
22	-	-	-	-	-	-	Counselors
9	L	42,110	VH	VL	L	Master's degree	Educational, vocational, and school counselors
1	VL	34,660	H	VL	L	Master's degree	Marriage and family therapists
3	VL	27,570	H	VL	L	Master's degree	Mental health counselors
5	VL	24,450	L	VL	L	Master's degree	Rehabilitation counselors
3	VL	28,510	H	VL	L	Master's degree	Substance abuse and behavioral disorder counselors
24	-	-	-	-	-	-	Miscellaneous community and social service specialists
2	VL	33,860	H	L	L	Master's degree	Health educators[1]
3	VL	38,150	H	L	L	Bachelor's degree	Probation officers and correctional treatment specialists[1]
19	L	22,330	L	L	L	Moderate-term on-the-job	Social and human service assistants[1]
11	-	-	-	-	-	-	Religious workers
7	VL	31,760	H	VL	L	First professional degree	Clergy
4	VL	27,000	H	VL	VH	Bachelor's degree	Directors, religious activities and education
19	-	-	-	-	-	-	Social workers
11	L	31,470	H	L	L	Bachelor's degree	Child, family, and school social workers
4	VL	34,790	H	L	L	Bachelor's degree	Medical and public health social workers
4	VL	30,170	H	L	L	Master's degree	Mental health and substance abuse social workers
9	L	30,410	H	L	L	Bachelor's degree	All other counselors, social, and religious workers[1]
30	-	-	-	-	-	-	Legal occupations
1	-	-	-	-	-	-	Judges, magistrates, and other judicial workers
0	VL	61,240	VH	VL	VL	Bachelor's plus experience[2]	Administrative law judges, adjudicators, and hearing officers[1]
0	VL	43,060	VH	VL	VL	Bachelor's plus experience[2]	Arbitrators, mediators, and conciliators[1]
1	VL	86,760	VH	VL	VL	Bachelor's plus experience[2]	Judges, magistrate judges, and magistrates[1]
17	L	88,280	VH	VL	L	First professional degree	Lawyers
7	VL	35,360	H	L	L	Associate degree	Paralegals and legal assistants
2	-	-	-	-	-	-	Miscellaneous legal support workers
0	VL	39,660	H	L	L	Postsecondary vocational award	Court reporters
1	VL	28,510	H	L	L	Bachelor's degree	Law clerks
0	VL	29,950	H	L	L	Moderate-term on-the-job	Title examiners, abstractors, and searchers
3	VL	36,130	H	L	L	Bachelor's degree	All other legal and related workers
336	-	-	-	-	-	-	Education, training, and library occupations
68	VH	46,330	VH	L	VH	Doctoral degree	Postsecondary teachers[1]
166	-	-	-	-	-	-	Primary, secondary, and special education teachers
18	-	-	-	-	-	-	Preschool and kindergarten teachers
14	L	17,810	VL	L	VH	Bachelor's degree	Preschool teachers, except special education
5	VL	37,610	H	L	VH	Bachelor's degree	Kindergarten teachers, except special education
74	-	-	-	-	-	-	Elementary and middle school teachers
55	VH	39,700	VH	VL	L	Bachelor's degree	Elementary school teachers, except special education

[1] One or more Current Population Survey (CPS) proxy occupations are used to estimate CPS based data.
[2] Bachelor's degree or higher, plus work experience.
[3] Work experience in a related occupation.

NOTE: Rankings are based on employment in all detailed occupations in the National Employment Matrix. For details, see "Data presented" section of text. Codes for describing the ranked variables are: VH = Very high, H = High, L = Low, VL = Very low, and n. a. = data not available. A dash indicates data are not applicable.

Table 2. Occupational employment and job openings data, 2000-10, and worker characteristics, 2000 — Continued

(Numbers in thousands)

2000 national employment matrix occupation	Employment		Employment change, 2000-10				Percent self-employed, 2000	Annual average job openings due to growth and total replacement needs, 2000-10	
			Numeric		Percent				
	2000	2010	Number	Rank	Number	Rank		Number	Rank
Middle school teachers, except special and vocational education	570	625	55	L	9.6	L	.0	59	L
Vocational education teachers, middle school	20	22	3	VL	13.1	L	.0	2	VL
Secondary school teachers	1,113	1,314	201	-	18.1	-	.0	87	-
Secondary school teachers, except special and vocational education	1,004	1,190	187	VH	18.6	H	.0	79	L
Vocational education teachers, secondary school	109	123	15	L	13.4	L	.0	8	VL
Special education teachers	453	592	140	-	30.9	-	.0	43	-
Special education teachers, preschool, kindergarten, and elementary school	234	320	86	H	36.8	VH	.0	24	VL
Special education teachers, middle school	96	119	23	L	24.4	VH	.0	8	VL
Special education teachers, secondary school	123	153	30	L	24.6	VH	.0	11	VL
Other teachers and instructors	901	1,076	175	-	19.4	-	16.0	183	-
Adult literacy, remedial education, and GED teachers and instructors	67	80	13	VL	19.4	H	20.3	14	VL
Self-enrichment education teachers	186	220	34	L	18.5	H	16.1	38	L
All other teachers, primary, secondary, and adult	648	776	128	H	19.7	H	15.5	132	H
Library, museum, training, and other education occupations	1,731	2,101	370	-	21.4	-	.1	324	-
Archivists, curators, and museum technicians[1]	21	24	3	VL	11.9	L	9.5	1	VL
Librarians	149	160	10	VL	7.0	VL	.0	7	VL
Library technicians	109	130	21	L	19.5	H	.0	31	L
Teacher assistants	1,262	1,562	301	VH	23.9	VH	.0	286	VH
Other education, training, library, and museum workers	190	225	35	-	18.2	-	.2	40	-
Audio-visual collections specialists	11	13	2	VL	13.6	L	.0	2	VL
Farm and home management advisors	11	11	1	VL	6.1	VL	.0	2	VL
Instructional coordinators	81	101	20	L	25.0	VH	.0	17	VL
All other library, museum, training, and other education workers	87	99	12	VL	14.0	L	.4	18	VL
Arts, design, entertainment, sports, and media occupations	2,371	2,864	493	-	20.8	-	32.3	383	-
Art and design occupations	750	903	153	-	20.3	-	41.0	121	-
Artists and related workers	147	176	29	-	20.0	-	56.6	21	-
Art directors[1]	47	56	10	VL	21.1	VH	54.4	7	VL
Fine artists, including painters, sculptors, and illustrators[1]	31	35	4	VL	13.4	L	56.7	4	VL
Multi-media artists and animators[1]	69	85	15	L	22.2	VH	58.0	10	VL
Designers	492	596	104	-	21.2	-	31.8	83	-
Commercial and industrial designers	50	62	12	VL	23.8	VH	37.8	9	VL
Fashion designers	16	19	3	VL	20.3	VH	29.4	3	VL
Floral designers	102	118	15	L	14.9	H	28.6	17	VL
Graphic designers	190	241	51	L	26.7	VH	31.1	33	L
Interior designers	46	54	8	VL	17.4	H	32.1	8	VL
Merchandise displayers and window trimmers	76	88	12	VL	15.9	H	33.5	12	VL
Set and exhibit designers	12	15	3	VL	27.0	VH	34.3	2	VL
All other art and design workers[1]	112	130	19	L	16.8	H	61.4	17	VL
Entertainers and performers, sports and related occupations	626	763	136	-	21.8	-	31.7	128	-
Actors, producers, and directors	158	200	42	-	26.9	-	.0	35	-
Actors	99	126	26	L	26.7	VH	36.8	23	VL
Producers and directors[1]	58	74	16	L	27.1	VH	21.9	13	VL
Athletes, coaches, umpires, and related workers	129	153	24	-	18.7	-	29.8	27	-
Athletes and sports competitors	18	22	4	VL	22.5	VH	27.2	4	VL
Coaches and scouts	99	117	17	L	17.6	H	30.0	21	VL
Umpires, referees, and other sports officials	11	14	3	VL	22.7	VH	32.2	2	VL
Dancers and choreographers	26	30	4	-	16.3	-	11.6	4	-
Dancers[1]	15	18	3	VL	17.3	H	11.4	3	VL
Choreographers[1]	11	12	2	VL	14.9	H	12.0	2	VL
Musicians, singers, and related workers	240	285	45	-	18.7	-	40.9	46	-
Music directors and composers	50	56	6	VL	13.1	L	23.7	9	VL
Musicians and singers	191	229	38	L	20.1	VH	45.4	37	L

[1] One or more Current Population Survey (CPS) proxy occupations are used to estimate CPS based data.
[2] Bachelor's degree or higher, plus work experience.
[3] Work experience in a related occupation.

NOTE: Rankings are based on employment in all detailed occupations in the National Employment Matrix. For details, see "Data presented" section of text. Codes for describing the ranked variables are: VH = Very high, H = High, L = Low, VL = Very low, and n. a. = data not available. A dash indicates data are not applicable.

28

(Numbers in thousands)

Annual average job openings due to growth and net replacement needs, 2000-10		Median annual earnings		Ranking of:		Most significant source of postsecondary education or training	2000 national employment matrix occupation
Number	Rank	Dollars	Rank	Unemployment rate	Percent part-time		
18	L	39,750	VH	VL	L	Bachelor's degree	Middle school teachers, except special and vocational education
1	VL	39,330	H	VL	L	Bachelor's degree	Vocational education teachers, middle school
54	-	-	-	-	-	-	Secondary school teachers
49	H	40,870	VH	VL	L	Bachelor's degree	Secondary school teachers, except special and vocational education
5	VL	42,080	VH	VL	L	Bachelor's degree	Vocational education teachers, secondary school
20	-	-	-	-	-	-	Special education teachers
12	L	40,880	VH	VL	L	Bachelor's degree	Special education teachers, preschool, kindergarten, and elementary school
4	VL	38,600	H	VL	L	Bachelor's degree	Special education teachers, middle school
5	VL	41,290	VH	VL	L	Bachelor's degree	Special education teachers, secondary school
27	-	-	-	-	-	-	Other teachers and instructors
2	VL	33,540	H	L	VH	Bachelor's degree	Adult literacy, remedial education, and GED teachers and instructors
5	VL	27,960	H	L	VH	Related work experience[3]	Self-enrichment education teachers
19	L	28,640	H	L	VH	Bachelor's degree	All other teachers, primary, secondary, and adult
74	-	-	-	-	-	-	Library, museum, training, and other education occupations
1	VL	33,080	H	VL	H	Master's degree	Archivists, curators, and museum technicians[1]
4	VL	41,700	VH	VL	H	Master's degree	Librarians
7	VL	23,170	L	L	VH	Short-term on-the-job	Library technicians
56	VH	17,350	VL	L	VH	Short-term on-the-job	Teacher assistants
6	-	-	-	-	-	-	Other education, training, library, and museum workers
0	VL	33,290	H	L	VH	Moderate-term on-the-job	Audio-visual collections specialists
0	VL	36,290	H	L	VH	Bachelor's degree	Farm and home management advisors
3	VL	44,230	VH	L	VH	Master's degree	Instructional coordinators
2	VL	24,870	L	L	VH	Bachelor's degree	All other library, museum, training, and other education workers
95	-	-	-	-	-	-	Arts, design, entertainment, sports, and media occupations
25	-	-	-	-	-	-	Art and design occupations
6	-	-	-	-	-	-	Artists and related workers
2	VL	56,880	VH	L	H	Bachelor's plus experience[2]	Art directors[1]
1	VL	31,190	H	L	H	Long-term on-the-job	Fine artists, including painters, sculptors, and illustrators[1]
3	VL	41,130	VH	L	H	Bachelor's degree	Multi-media artists and animators[1]
15	-	-	-	-	-	-	Designers
2	VL	48,780	VH	L	H	Bachelor's degree	Commercial and industrial designers
0	VL	48,530	VH	L	H	Bachelor's degree	Fashion designers
3	VL	18,360	VL	L	H	Moderate-term on-the-job	Floral designers
7	VL	34,570	H	L	H	Bachelor's degree	Graphic designers
1	VL	36,540	H	L	H	Bachelor's degree	Interior designers
2	VL	20,930	L	L	H	Moderate-term on-the-job	Merchandise displayers and window trimmers
0	VL	31,440	H	L	H	Bachelor's degree	Set and exhibit designers
4	VL	33,190	H	L	H	Bachelor's degree	All other art and design workers[1]
26	-	-	-	-	-	-	Entertainers and performers, sports and related occupations
7	VL	-	-	-	-	-	Actors, producers, and directors
5	VL	25,920	H	VH	L	Long-term on-the-job	Actors
3	VL	41,030	VH	VH	L	Bachelor's plus experience[2]	Producers and directors[1]
5	-	-	-	-	-	-	Athletes, coaches, umpires, and related workers
1	VL	32,700	H	L	VH	Long-term on-the-job	Athletes and sports competitors
4	VL	28,020	H	L	VH	Long-term on-the-job	Coaches and scouts
0	VL	18,540	L	L	VH	Long-term on-the-job	Umpires, referees, and other sports officials
1	-	-	-	-	-	-	Dancers and choreographers
1	VL	22,470	L	H	VH	Long-term on-the-job	Dancers[1]
0	VL	27,010	H	H	VH	Related work experience[3]	Choreographers[1]
9	-	-	-	-	-	-	Musicians, singers, and related workers
2	VL	31,510	H	H	VH	Bachelor's plus experience[2]	Music directors and composers
7	VL	36,740	H	H	VH	Long-term on-the-job	Musicians and singers

[1] One or more Current Population Survey (CPS) proxy occupations are used to estimate CPS based data.
[2] Bachelor's degree or higher, plus work experience.
[3] Work experience in a related occupation.

NOTE: Rankings are based on employment in all detailed occupations in the National Employment Matrix. For details, see "Data presented" section of text. Codes for describing the ranked variables are: VH = Very high, H = High, L = Low, VL = Very low, and n. a. = data not available. A dash indicates data are not applicable.

(Numbers in thousands)

2000 national employment matrix occupation	Employment		Employment change, 2000-10				Per-cent self-emp-loyed, 2000	Annual average job openings due to growth and total replacement needs, 2000-10	
			Numeric		Percent				
	2000	2010	Number	Rank	Number	Rank		Number	Rank
All other entertainers and performers, sports and related workers[1]	74	95	21	L	28.3	VH	12.9	13	VL
Media and communication occupations	703	856	153	-	21.8	-	24.5	102	-
Announcers	71	68	-4	VL	-5.5	VL	28.0	4	VL
News analysts, reporters and correspondents	78	80	2	VL	2.8	VL	15.4	10	VL
Public relations specialists	137	186	49	L	36.1	VH	6.3	24	VL
Writers and editors	305	385	80	-	26.3	-	36.6	45	-
Editors	122	149	27	L	22.6	VH	16.5	17	VL
Technical writers	57	74	17	L	29.6	VH	17.9	7	VL
Writers and authors	126	162	36	L	28.4	VH	64.6	22	VL
Miscellaneous media and communications workers	112	137	25	-	22.4	-	17.5	19	-
Interpreters and translators[1]	22	27	5	VL	23.8	VH	21.5	4	VL
All other media and communication workers[1]	90	110	20	L	22.1	VH	16.5	15	VL
Media and communication equipment occupations	291	342	51	-	17.5	-	29.9	32	-
Broadcast and sound engineering technicians and radio operators	87	99	12	-	14.0	-	7.5	8	-
Audio and video equipment technicians[1]	37	43	6	VL	16.8	H	10.7	4	VL
Broadcast technicians[1]	36	40	4	VL	10.2	L	7.2	3	VL
Radio operators[1]	3	3	0	VL	6.2	VL	.0	0	VL
Sound engineering technicians[1]	11	13	2	VL	19.0	H	.0	1	VL
Photographers	131	153	22	L	17.0	H	51.9	15	VL
Television, video, and motion picture camera operators and editors	43	53	11	-	25.8	-	26.4	5	-
Camera operators, television, video, and motion picture	27	33	7	VL	25.8	VH	24.4	3	VL
Film and video editors	16	20	4	VL	25.8	VH	29.7	2	VL
All other media and communication equipment workers[1]	31	36	6	VL	18.1	H	4.2	2	VL
Healthcare practitioners and technical occupations	6,379	7,978	1,599	-	25.1	-	4.7	603	-
Health diagnosing and treating practitioners	3,921	4,888	966	-	24.6	-	7.3	330	-
Chiropractors	50	62	12	VL	23.4	VH	67.4	3	VL
Dentists	152	161	9	VL	5.7	VL	41.1	7	VL
Dietitians and nutritionists	49	56	7	VL	15.2	H	11.4	6	VL
Optometrists	31	37	6	VL	18.7	H	.0	2	VL
Pharmacists	217	270	53	L	24.3	VH	2.8	26	VL
Physicians and surgeons	598	705	107	H	17.9	H	16.6	38	L
Physician assistants	58	89	31	L	53.5	VH	.0	8	VL
Podiatrists	18	20	3	VL	14.2	L	22.5	1	VL
Registered nurses	2,194	2,755	561	VH	25.6	VH	1.1	196	H
Therapists	439	584	145	-	33.2	-	5.1	34	-
Audiologists[1]	13	19	6	VL	44.7	VH	5.0	1	VL
Occupational therapists	78	105	27	L	33.9	VH	5.4	6	VL
Physical therapists[1]	132	176	44	L	33.3	VH	9.2	10	VL
Radiation therapists	16	19	4	VL	22.8	VH	.0	1	VL
Recreational therapists[1]	29	32	2	VL	8.6	L	3.9	2	VL
Respiratory therapists	83	112	29	L	34.8	VH	.0	7	VL
Speech-language pathologists[1]	88	122	34	L	39.2	VH	5.0	7	VL
Veterinarians	59	77	19	L	31.8	VH	27.5	4	VL
All other health diagnosing and treating practitioners	57	71	14	VL	24.8	VH	8.1	4	VL
Other health professionals and technicians	2,457	3,090	633	-	25.7	-	.5	293	-
Clinical laboratory technologists and technicians	295	348	53	-	18.0	-	.7	44	-
Medical and clinical laboratory technologists	148	174	25	L	17.0	H	.7	22	VL
Medical and clinical laboratory technicians	147	175	28	L	19.0	H	.7	22	VL
Dental hygienists	147	201	54	L	37.1	VH	.7	10	VL
Diagnostic related technologists and technicians	257	322	65	-	25.2	-	.0	26	-
Cardiovascular technologists and technicians	39	52	14	VL	34.9	VH	.0	4	VL
Diagnostic medical sonographers	33	41	9	VL	26.1	VH	.0	3	VL
Nuclear medicine technologists	18	22	4	VL	22.4	VH	.0	2	VL

[1] One or more Current Population Survey (CPS) proxy occupations are used to estimate CPS based data.
[2] Bachelor's degree or higher, plus work experience.
[3] Work experience in a related occupation.

NOTE: Rankings are based on employment in all detailed occupations in the National Employment Matrix. For details, see "Data presented" section of text. Codes for describing the ranked variables are: VH = Very high, H = High, L = Low, VL = Very low, and n. a. = data not available. A dash indicates data are not applicable.

Table 2. Occupational employment and job openings data, 2000-10, and worker characteristics, 2000 — Continued

(Numbers in thousands)

Annual average job openings due to growth and net replacement needs, 2000-10		Median annual earnings		Ranking of:		Most significant source of postsecondary education or training	2000 national employment matrix occupation
Number	Rank	Dollars	Rank	Unemployment rate	Percent part-time		
4	VL	29,620	H	H	VH	Long-term on-the-job	All other entertainers and performers, sports and related workers[1]
32	-	-	-	-	-	-	Media and communication occupations
1	VL	19,800	L	H	VH	Long-term on-the-job	Announcers
3	VL	29,110	H	L	L	Long-term on-the-job	News analysts, reporters and correspondents
7	VL	39,580	H	L	L	Bachelor's degree	Public relations specialists
16	-	-	-	-	-		Writers and editors
7	VL	39,370	H	L	L	Bachelor's degree	Editors
3	VL	47,790	VH	H	L	Bachelor's degree	Technical writers
6	VL	42,270	VH	L	H	Bachelor's degree	Writers and authors
5	-	-	-	-	-		Miscellaneous media and communications workers
1	VL	31,110	H	H	VH	Long-term on-the-job	Interpreters and translators[1]
4	VL	37,810	H	H	VH	Long-term on-the-job	All other media and communication workers[1]
12	-	-	-	-	-	-	Media and communication equipment occupations
4	-	-	-	-	-	-	Broadcast and sound engineering technicians and radio operators
2	VL	30,310	H	L	L	Long-term on-the-job	Audio and video equipment technicians[1]
1	VL	26,950	H	L	L	Postsecondary vocational award	Broadcast technicians[1]
0	VL	29,260	H	L	L	Long-term on-the-job	Radio operators[1]
1	VL	39,480	H	L	L	Postsecondary vocational award	Sound engineering technicians[1]
5	VL	22,300	L	H	H	Long-term on-the-job	Photographers
2	-	-	-	-	-	-	Television, video, and motion picture camera operators and editors
1	VL	27,870	H	H	H	Moderate-term on-the-job	Camera operators, television, video, and motion picture
1	VL	34,160	H	H	H	Bachelor's degree	Film and video editors
2	VL	34,190	H	L	L	Moderate-term on-the-job	All other media and communication equipment workers[1]
300	-	-	-	-	-	-	Healthcare practitioners and technical occupations
177	-	-	-	-	-	-	Health diagnosing and treating practitioners
2	VL	67,030	VH	VL	H	First professional degree	Chiropractors
4	VL	129,030	VH	VL	H	First professional degree	Dentists
2	VL	38,450	H	L	H	Bachelor's degree	Dietitians and nutritionists
1	VL	82,860	VH	VL	H	First professional degree	Optometrists
12	L	70,950	VH	VL	L	First professional degree	Pharmacists
20	L	138,400	VH	VL	L	First professional degree	Physicians and surgeons
4	VL	61,910	VH	VL	H	Bachelor's degree	Physician assistants
1	VL	107,560	VH	VL	H	First professional degree	Podiatrists
100	VH	44,840	VH	VL	H	Associate degree	Registered nurses
25	-	-	-	-	-	-	Therapists
1	VL	44,830	VH	VL	H	Master's degree	Audiologists[1]
5	VL	49,450	VH	L	VH	Bachelor's degree	Occupational therapists
8	L	54,810	VH	VL	H	Master's degree	Physical therapists[1]
1	VL	47,470	VH	VL	H	Associate degree	Radiation therapists
1	VL	28,650	H	VL	H	Bachelor's degree	Recreational therapists[1]
5	VL	37,680	H	VL	H	Associate degree	Respiratory therapists
6	VL	46,640	VH	VL	H	Master's degree	Speech-language pathologists[1]
3	VL	60,910	VH	VL	L	First professional degree	Veterinarians
3	VL	48,380	VH	VL	H	First professional degree	All other health diagnosing and treating practitioners
122	-	-	-	-	-	-	Other health professionals and technicians
12	-	-	-	-	-	-	Clinical laboratory technologists and technicians
6	VL	40,510	VH	L	H	Bachelor's degree	Medical and clinical laboratory technologists
6	VL	27,540	H	L	H	Associate degree	Medical and clinical laboratory technicians
8	L	51,330	VH	VL	VH	Associate degree	Dental hygienists
12	-	-	-	-	-	-	Diagnostic related technologists and technicians
2	VL	33,350	H	VL	H	Associate degree	Cardiovascular technologists and technicians
2	VL	44,820	VH	VL	H	Associate degree	Diagnostic medical sonographers
1	VL	44,130	VH	VL	H	Associate degree	Nuclear medicine technologists

[1] One or more Current Population Survey (CPS) proxy occupations are used to estimate CPS based data.
[2] Bachelor's degree or higher, plus work experience.
[3] Work experience in a related occupation.

NOTE: Rankings are based on employment in all detailed occupations in the National Employment Matrix. For details, see "Data presented" section of text. Codes for describing the ranked variables are: VH = Very high, H = High, L = Low, VL = Very low, and n. a. = data not available. A dash indicates data are not applicable.

(Numbers in thousands)

2000 national employment matrix occupation	Employment		Employment change, 2000-10				Per-cent self-emp-loyed, 2000	Annual average job openings due to growth and total replacement needs, 2000-10	
			Numeric		Percent				
	2000	2010	Number	Rank	Number	Rank		Number	Rank
Radiologic technologists and technicians	167	206	39	L	23.1	VH	.0	17	VL
Emergency medical technicians and paramedics	172	226	54	L	31.3	VH	.0	25	VL
Health diagnosing and treating practitioner support technicians	417	551	134	-	32.2	-	.0	61	-
Dietetic technicians	26	33	7	VL	27.6	VH	.0	4	VL
Pharmacy technicians	190	259	69	L	36.4	VH	.0	29	L
Psychiatric technicians	54	59	5	VL	8.5	L	.0	7	VL
Respiratory therapy technicians	27	36	9	VL	34.6	VH	.0	4	VL
Surgical technologists	71	96	25	L	34.7	VH	.0	11	VL
Veterinary technologists and technicians	49	69	19	L	39.3	VH	.0	8	VL
Licensed practical and licensed vocational nurses	700	842	142	H	20.3	VH	.2	72	L
Medical records and health information technicians[1]	136	202	66	L	49.0	VH	.0	21	VL
Opticians, dispensing	68	81	13	VL	19.0	H	8.8	3	VL
Other health practitioners and technical workers	266	317	50	-	19.0	-	.2	27	-
Athletic trainers	15	17	3	VL	18.5	H	.0	2	VL
Occupational health and safety specialists and technicians	35	40	5	VL	15.0	H	.0	5	VL
Orthotists and prosthetists	5	6	1	VL	17.3	H	.0	1	VL
All other health practitioners and technical workers[1]	212	253	42	L	19.7	H	.2	21	VL
Service occupations	26,075	31,163	5,088	-	19.5	-	6.4	6,112	-
Healthcare support occupations	3,196	4,264	1,067	-	33.4	-	3.0	665	-
Dental assistants	247	339	92	H	37.2	VH	.0	25	VL
Massage therapists	34	45	10	VL	30.4	VH	20.8	8	VL
Nursing, psychiatric, and home health aides	2,053	2,676	623	-	30.4	-	3.5	462	-
Home health aides	615	907	291	VH	47.3	VH	3.5	149	H
Nursing aides, orderlies, and attendants	1,373	1,697	323	VH	23.5	VH	3.6	300	VH
Psychiatric aides	65	73	9	VL	13.2	L	3.0	13	VL
Occupational therapist assistants and aides	25	35	10	-	41.5	-	.0	6	-
Occupational therapist assistants	17	23	7	VL	39.7	VH	.0	4	VL
Occupational therapist aides	9	12	4	VL	45.2	VH	.0	2	VL
Physical therapist assistants and aides	80	116	36	-	45.5	-	.0	20	-
Physical therapist assistants	44	64	20	L	44.8	VH	.0	11	VL
Physical therapist aides	36	53	17	L	46.3	VH	.0	9	VL
Medical assistants and other healthcare support occupations	757	1,052	295	-	39.0	-	2.1	143	-
Medical assistants	329	516	187	VH	57.0	VH	1.9	68	L
Medical equipment preparers	33	39	6	VL	18.2	H	.0	6	VL
Medical transcriptionists	102	132	30	L	29.8	VH	2.1	18	VL
Pharmacy aides	57	68	11	VL	19.5	H	.0	10	VL
Veterinary assistants and laboratory animal caretakers	55	77	22	L	39.8	VH	2.1	10	VL
All other healthcare support workers	181	219	38	L	21.1	VH	3.5	31	L
Protective service occupations	3,087	3,896	809	-	26.2	-	.5	470	-
First-line supervisors/managers, protective service workers	273	319	46	-	16.7	-	.0	27	-
First-line supervisors/managers of correctional officers	30	38	9	VL	29.6	VH	.0	4	VL
First-line supervisors/managers of fire fighting and prevention workers[1]	62	66	4	VL	7.2	VL	.0	6	VL
First-line supervisors/managers of police and detectives	121	136	16	L	13.1	L	.0	11	VL
First-line supervisors/managers of protective service workers, except police, fire and corrections[1]	61	78	17	L	27.1	VH	.0	7	VL
Fire fighters	258	280	23	L	8.9	L	.0	14	VL
Fire inspectors[1]	13	15	2	VL	15.1	H	.0	1	VL
Law enforcement workers	1,150	1,445	295	-	25.6	-	.0	86	-
Bailiffs, correctional officers, and jailers	427	563	136	-	31.8	-	.0	44	-
Bailiffs[1]	14	15	2	VL	12.5	L	.0	1	VL
Correctional officers and jailers[1]	414	548	134	H	32.4	VH	.0	43	L
Detectives and criminal investigators	93	108	15	L	16.4	H	.0	5	VL
Fish and game wardens[1]	8	9	1	VL	11.4	L	.0	0	VL

[1] One or more Current Population Survey (CPS) proxy occupations are used to estimate CPS based data.
[2] Bachelor's degree or higher, plus work experience.
[3] Work experience in a related occupation.

NOTE: Rankings are based on employment in all detailed occupations in the National Employment Matrix. For details, see "Data presented" section of text. Codes for describing the ranked variables are: VH = Very high, H = High, L = Low, VL = Very low, and n. a. = data not available. A dash indicates data are not applicable.

Table 2. Occupational employment and job openings data, 2000-10, and worker characteristics, 2000 — Continued

(Numbers in thousands)

Annual average job openings due to growth and net replacement needs, 2000-10		Median annual earnings		Ranking of:		Most significant source of postsecondary education or training	2000 national employment matrix occupation
				Unemploy-ment rate	Per-cent part-time		
Number	Rank	Dollars	Rank				
8	L	36,000	H	VL	H	Associate degree	Radiologic technologists and technicians
10	L	22,460	L	L	H	Postsecondary vocational award	Emergency medical technicians and paramedics
24	-	-	-	-	-	-	Health diagnosing and treating practitioner support technicians
1	VL	21,340	L	L	H	Moderate-term on-the-job	Dietetic technicians
12	L	20,650	L	L	H	Moderate-term on-the-job	Pharmacy technicians
2	VL	24,420	L	L	H	Postsecondary vocational award	Psychiatric technicians
2	VL	32,860	H	L	H	Postsecondary vocational award	Respiratory therapy technicians
4	VL	29,020	H	L	H	Postsecondary vocational award	Surgical technologists
3	VL	21,640	L	L	H	Associate degree	Veterinary technologists and technicians
32	H	29,440	H	L	H	Postsecondary vocational award	Licensed practical and licensed vocational nurses
10	L	22,750	L	L	L	Associate degree	Medical records and health information technicians[1]
3	VL	24,430	L	L	H	Long-term on-the-job	Opticians, dispensing
12	-	-	-	-	-	-	Other health practitioners and technical workers
1	VL	32,080	H	L	H	Bachelor's degree	Athletic trainers
1	VL	42,750	VH	L	H	Bachelor's degree	Occupational health and safety specialists and technicians
0	VL	45,740	VH	L	H	Bachelor's degree	Orthotists and prosthetists
10	L	30,370	H	L	H	Associate degree	All other health practitioners and technical workers[1]
1,350	-	-	-	-	-	-	**Service occupations**
161	-	-	-	-	-	-	Healthcare support occupations
14	L	25,970	H	VL	VH	Moderate-term on-the-job	Dental assistants
2	VL	27,190	H	H	VH	Postsecondary vocational award	Massage therapists
88	-	-	-	-	-	-	Nursing, psychiatric, and home health aides
37	H	17,120	VL	H	H	Short-term on-the-job	Home health aides
50	VH	18,500	L	H	H	Short-term on-the-job	Nursing aides, orderlies, and attendants
2	VL	21,740	L	H	H	Short-term on-the-job	Psychiatric aides
2	-	-	-	-	-	-	Occupational therapist assistants and aides
1	VL	34,340	H	H	VH	Associate degree	Occupational therapist assistants
1	VL	20,710	L	H	VH	Short-term on-the-job	Occupational therapist aides
6	-	-	-	-	-	-	Physical therapist assistants and aides
3	VL	33,870	H	H	VH	Associate degree	Physical therapist assistants
3	VL	19,670	L	H	VH	Short-term on-the-job	Physical therapist aides
50	-	-	-	-	-	-	Medical assistants and other healthcare support occupations
27	H	23,000	L	L	H	Moderate-term on-the-job	Medical assistants
1	VL	21,140	L	L	H	Short-term on-the-job	Medical equipment preparers
6	VL	25,270	L	L	H	Postsecondary vocational award	Medical transcriptionists
3	VL	17,720	VL	L	H	Short-term on-the-job	Pharmacy aides
4	VL	16,640	VL	L	H	Short-term on-the-job	Veterinary assistants and laboratory animal caretakers
9	L	21,960	L	L	H	Short-term on-the-job	All other healthcare support workers
168	-	-	-	-	-	-	Protective service occupations
12	-	-	-	-	-	-	First-line supervisors/managers, protective service workers
1	VL	41,880	VH	L	VL	Related work experience[3]	First-line supervisors/managers of correctional officers
2	VL	51,990	VH	L	VL	Related work experience[3]	First-line supervisors/managers of fire fighting and prevention workers[1]
5	VL	57,210	VH	VL	VL	Related work experience[3]	First-line supervisors/managers of police and detectives
4	VL	31,010	H	L	VL	Related work experience[3]	First-line supervisors/managers of protective service workers, except police, fire and corrections[1]
9	L	34,170	H	VL	VL	Long-term on-the-job	Fire fighters
1	VL	40,793	VH	VH	VL	Related work experience[3]	Fire inspectors[1]
55	-	-	-	-	-	-	Law enforcement workers
24	-	-	-	-	-	-	Bailiffs, correctional officers, and jailers
1	VL	31,180	H	VL	VL	Moderate-term on-the-job	Bailiffs[1]
23	L	31,170	H	VL	VL	Moderate-term on-the-job	Correctional officers and jailers[1]
4	VL	48,870	VH	VL	VL	Related work experience[3]	Detectives and criminal investigators
0	VL	39,950	VH	VL	VL	Long-term on-the-job	Fish and game wardens[1]

[1] One or more Current Population Survey (CPS) proxy occupations are used to estimate CPS based data.

[2] Bachelor's degree or higher, plus work experience.

[3] Work experience in a related occupation.

NOTE: Rankings are based on employment in all detailed occupations in the National Employment Matrix. For details, see "Data presented" section of text. Codes for describing the ranked variables are: VH = Very high, H = High, L = Low, VL = Very low, and n. a. = data not available. A dash indicates data are not applicable.

Table 2. Occupational employment and job openings data, 2000-10, and worker characteristics, 2000 — Continued

(Numbers in thousands)

2000 national employment matrix occupation	Employment		Employment change, 2000-10				Per-cent self-emp-loyed, 2000	Annual average job openings due to growth and total replacement needs, 2000-10	
			Numeric		Percent				
	2000	2010	Number	Rank	Number	Rank		Number	Rank
Parking enforcement workers[1]	9	10	1	VL	13.2	L	.0	0	VL
Police and sheriff's patrol officers[1]	607	748	141	H	23.2	VH	.0	35	L
Transit and railroad police	6	7	1	VL	16.5	H	.0	0	VL
Other protective service workers	1,394	1,837	443	-	31.8	-	1.2	391	-
Animal control workers	9	10	1	VL	12.8	L	.0	4	VL
Crossing guards[1]	74	81	6	VL	8.7	L	.0	19	VL
Private detectives and investigators	39	48	9	VL	23.5	VH	39.3	10	VL
Security guards and gaming surveillance officers	1,117	1,509	393	-	35.2	-	1.4	284	-
Gaming surveillance officers and gaming investigators[1]	11	13	2	VL	16.8	H	.0	3	VL
Security guards[1]	1,106	1,497	391	VH	35.4	VH	1.4	281	VH
All other protective service workers	156	190	34	L	21.7	VH	.6	75	L
Food preparation and serving related occupations	10,140	11,717	1,577	-	15.6	-	1.2	3,052	-
Supervisors, food preparation and serving workers	788	882	95	-	12.1	-	5.0	182	-
Chefs and head cooks	139	151	12	VL	9.0	L	1.3	36	L
First-line supervisors/managers of food preparation and serving workers	649	731	83	H	12.7	L	5.7	145	H
Cooks and food preparation workers	2,709	3,041	333	-	12.3	-	1.1	695	-
Cooks	1,864	2,054	190	-	10.2	-	1.4	461	-
Cooks, fast food[1]	522	518	-4	VL	-.7	VL	1.2	124	H
Cooks, institution and cafeteria[1]	465	500	35	L	7.6	VL	1.5	114	H
Cooks, private household[1]	5	4	-1	VL	-18.0	VL	.0	1	VL
Cooks, restaurant[1]	668	813	145	H	21.7	VH	1.5	173	H
Cooks, short order[1]	205	219	14	VL	6.8	VL	1.2	50	L
Food preparation workers	844	988	143	H	16.9	H	.5	245	H
Food and beverage serving workers	5,201	6,384	1,182	-	22.7	-	.3	1,777	-
Bartenders	387	439	52	L	13.4	L	1.3	89	L
Combined food preparation and serving workers, including fast food	2,206	2,879	673	VH	30.5	VH	.1	804	VH
Counter attendants, cafeteria, food concession, and coffee shop	421	482	61	L	14.4	H	.6	222	H
Food servers, nonrestaurant	205	238	34	L	16.4	H	.2	88	L
Waiters and waitresses	1,983	2,347	364	VH	18.3	H	.2	632	VH
Other food preparation and serving related workers	1,442	1,410	-33	-	-2.3	-	2.3	482	-
Dining room and cafeteria attendants and bartender helpers	431	402	-29	VL	-6.7	VL	.6	161	H
Dishwashers	525	483	-42	VL	-8.0	VL	.2	156	H
Hosts and hostesses, restaurant, lounge, and coffee shop	343	388	45	L	13.0	L	7.9	89	L
All other food preparation and serving related workers	143	137	-7	VL	-4.6	VL	1.9	43	L
Building and grounds cleaning and maintenance occupations	5,549	6,328	779	-	14.0	-	7.4	1,209	-
Supervisors, building and grounds cleaning and maintenance workers	378	441	63	-	16.7	-	16.4	34	-
First-line supervisors/managers of housekeeping and janitorial workers	219	250	31	L	14.2	L	.8	21	VL
First-line supervisors/managers of landscaping, lawn service, and groundskeeping workers	159	191	32	L	20.1	VH	37.8	13	VL
Building cleaning workers	3,981	4,381	400	-	10.1	-	4.7	892	-
Janitors and cleaners, except maids and housekeeping cleaners	2,348	2,665	317	VH	13.5	L	4.7	538	VH
Maids and housekeeping cleaners[1]	1,633	1,716	83	H	5.1	VL	.0	354	VH
Grounds maintenance workers	973	1,245	272	-	27.9	-	12.9	237	-
Landscaping and groundskeeping workers	894	1,154	260	VH	29.0	VH	12.8	218	H
Pesticide handlers, sprayers, and applicators, vegetation	27	30	4	VL	13.6	L	13.5	6	VL
Tree trimmers and pruners	52	61	8	VL	16.3	H	14.2	12	VL
Pest control workers[1]	58	71	13	VL	22.1	VH	14.0	8	VL
All other building and grounds cleaning and maintenance workers	159	190	31	L	19.6	H	16.4	37	L

[1] One or more Current Population Survey (CPS) proxy occupations are used to estimate CPS based data.
[2] Bachelor's degree or higher, plus work experience.
[3] Work experience in a related occupation.

NOTE: Rankings are based on employment in all detailed occupations in the National Employment Matrix. For details, see "Data presented" section of text. Codes for describing the ranked variables are: VH = Very high, H = High, L = Low, VL = Very low, and n. a. = data not available. A dash indicates data are not applicable.

(Numbers in thousands)

Annual average job openings due to growth and net replacement needs, 2000-10		Median annual earnings		Ranking of:		Most significant source of postsecondary education or training	2000 national employment matrix occupation
Number	Rank	Dollars	Rank	Unemployment rate	Percent part-time		
0	VL	25,740	L	VL	VL	Short-term on-the-job	Parking enforcement workers[1]
27	H	39,790	VH	VL	VL	Long-term on-the-job	Police and sheriff's patrol officers[1]
0	VL	40,370	VH	VL	VL	Long-term on-the-job	Transit and railroad police
91	-	-	-	-	-	-	Other protective service workers
1	VL	23,000	L	H	VH	Moderate-term on-the-job	Animal control workers
3	VL	17,400	VL	H	VH	Short-term on-the-job	Crossing guards[1]
2	VL	26,750	H	VH	H	Related work experience[3]	Private detectives and investigators
70	-	-	-	-	-	-	Security guards and gaming surveillance officers
0	VL	21,220	L	VH	H	Moderate-term on-the-job	Gaming surveillance officers and gaming investigators[1]
69	VH	17,570	VL	VH	H	Short-term on-the-job	Security guards[1]
15	L	20,300	L	H	VH	Short-term on-the-job	All other protective service workers
626	-	-	-	-	-	-	Food preparation and serving related occupations
30	-	-	-	-	-	-	Supervisors, food preparation and serving workers
6	VL	25,110	L	VH	VH	Postsecondary vocational award	Chefs and head cooks
25	H	22,680	L	H	H	Related work experience[3]	First-line supervisors/managers of food preparation and serving workers
119	-	-	-	-	-	-	Cooks and food preparation workers
72	-	-	-	-	-	-	Cooks
15	L	13,590	VL	VH	VH	Short-term on-the-job	Cooks, fast food[1]
17	L	17,090	VL	VH	VH	Long-term on-the-job	Cooks, institution and cafeteria[1]
0	VL	n.a.	VL	VH	VH	Long-term on-the-job	Cooks, private household[1]
34	H	18,140	VL	VH	VH	Long-term on-the-job	Cooks, restaurant[1]
7	VL	15,700	VL	VH	VH	Short-term on-the-job	Cooks, short order[1]
47	H	15,360	VL	VH	VH	Short-term on-the-job	Food preparation workers
422	-	-	-	-	-	-	Food and beverage serving workers
20	L	14,270	VL	H	VH	Short-term on-the-job	Bartenders
202	VH	13,550	VL	VH	VH	Short-term on-the-job	Combined food preparation and serving workers, including fast food
39	H	13,970	VL	VH	VH	Short-term on-the-job	Counter attendants, cafeteria, food concession, and coffee shop
12	L	14,710	VL	VH	VH	Short-term on-the-job	Food servers, nonrestaurant
148	VH	13,350	VL	VH	VH	Short-term on-the-job	Waiters and waitresses
54	-	-	-	-	-	-	Other food preparation and serving related workers
14	L	13,580	VL	VH	VH	Short-term on-the-job	Dining room and cafeteria attendants and bartender helpers
20	L	13,920	VL	VH	VH	Short-term on-the-job	Dishwashers
15	L	14,450	VL	H	VH	Short-term on-the-job	Hosts and hostesses, restaurant, lounge, and coffee shop
5	VL	15,090	VL	VH	VH	Short-term on-the-job	All other food preparation and serving related workers
191	-	-	-	-	-	-	Building and grounds cleaning and maintenance occupations
13	-	-	-	-	-	-	Supervisors, building and grounds cleaning and maintenance workers
9	L	25,760	L	H	L	Related work experience[3]	First-line supervisors/managers of housekeeping and janitorial workers
4	VL	30,580	H	H	L	Related work experience[3]	First-line supervisors/managers of landscaping, lawn service, and groundskeeping workers
118	-	-	-	-	-	-	Building cleaning workers
74	VH	17,180	VL	VH	H	Short-term on-the-job	Janitors and cleaners, except maids and housekeeping cleaners
44	H	15,410	VL	VH	VH	Short-term on-the-job	Maids and housekeeping cleaners[1]
52	-	-	-	-	-	-	Grounds maintenance workers
48	H	18,300	VL	VH	H	Short-term on-the-job	Landscaping and groundskeeping workers
1	VL	23,100	L	VH	H	Moderate-term on-the-job	Pesticide handlers, sprayers, and applicators, vegetation
2	VL	23,730	L	VH	H	Short-term on-the-job	Tree trimmers and pruners
2	VL	22,150	L	H	VL	Moderate-term on-the-job	Pest control workers[1]
6	VL	20,010	L	VH	H	Short-term on-the-job	All other building and grounds cleaning and maintenance workers

[1] One or more Current Population Survey (CPS) proxy occupations are used to estimate CPS based data.
[2] Bachelor's degree or higher, plus work experience.
[3] Work experience in a related occupation.

NOTE: Rankings are based on employment in all detailed occupations in the National Employment Matrix. For details, see "Data presented" section of text. Codes for describing the ranked variables are: VH = Very high, H = High, L = Low, VL = Very low, and n. a. = data not available. A dash indicates data are not applicable.

(Numbers in thousands)

2000 national employment matrix occupation	Employment		Employment change, 2000-10				Per-cent self-emp-loyed, 2000	Annual average job openings due to growth and total replacement needs, 2000-10	
			Numeric		Percent				
	2000	2010	Number	Rank	Number	Rank		Number	Rank
Personal care and service occupations	4,103	4,959	856	-	20.9	-	24.8	888	-
First-line supervisors/managers of personal service workers	125	144	19	L	15.1	H	31.1	10	VL
Animal care and service workers	145	176	31	-	21.2	-	31.6	25	-
Animal trainers[1]	15	17	3	VL	18.4	H	58.5	2	VL
Nonfarm animal caretakers	131	159	28	L	21.6	VH	28.6	23	VL
Child care workers	1,193	1,319	127	H	10.6	L	39.4	382	VH
Entertainment attendants and related workers	344	421	77	-	22.5	-	1.7	109	-
Motion picture projectionists[1]	11	8	-3	VL	-27.0	VL	.0	2	VL
Ushers, lobby attendants, and ticket takers[1]	112	124	12	VL	11.0	L	.0	27	VL
Miscellaneous entertainment attendants and related workers	221	289	68	-	30.9	-	2.7	76	-
Amusement and recreation attendants	197	260	64	L	32.4	VH	3.0	68	L
Costume, locker room, and other attendants	24	28	5	VL	19·1	H	.0	8	VL
Funeral service workers	33	38	5	-	13.8	-	.0	7	-
Embalmers	7	7	0	VL	-.6	VL	.0	1	VL
Funeral attendants	26	31	5	VL	17.8	H	.0	6	VL
Gaming occupations	167	211	44	-	26.5	-	.0	52	-
First-line supervisors/managers, gaming workers	46	55	9	-	20.0	-	.0	4	-
Gaming supervisors	31	37	6	VL	18.4	H	.0	3	VL
Slot key persons	14	18	3	VL	23.3	VH	.0	1	VL
Gaming services workers	100	131	31	-	31.1	-	.0	35	-
Gaming and sports book writers and runners	12	15	3	VL	21.6	VH	.0	4	VL
Gaming dealers	88	116	28	L	32.4	VH	.0	31	L
All other gaming service workers	21	25	4	VL	18.7	H	.0	7	VL
Personal appearance workers	790	880	90	-	11.4	-	49.9	99	-
Barbers	73	64	-8	VL	-11.5	VL	80.6	3	VL
Hairdressers, hairstylists, and cosmetologists	636	718	82	H	13.0	L	48.5	86	L
Miscellaneous personal appearance workers	81	97	16	-	19.8	-	33.1	12	-
Manicurists and pedicurists	40	51	11	VL	26.5	VH	32.1	6	VL
Shampooers	20	22	3	VL	13.2	L	37.7	3	VL
Skin care specialists	21	24	3	VL	13.3	L	30.7	3	VL
Personal and home care aides[1]	414	672	258	VH	62.5	VH	1.5	110	H
Recreation and fitness workers	427	545	118	-	27.6	-	6.1	63	-
Fitness trainers and aerobics instructors	158	222	64	L	40.3	VH	5.7	25	VL
Recreation workers	269	323	54	L	20.1	VH	6.4	37	L
Residential advisors	44	55	11	VL	24.0	VH	.0	10	VL
Transportation, tourism, and lodging attendants	259	300	41	-	15.7	-	2.9	37	-
Baggage porters, bellhops, and concierges	68	78	9	-	13.4	-	2.0	17	-
Baggage porters and bellhops[1]	51	57	6	VL	12.6	L	2.7	12	VL
Concierges[1]	18	20	3	VL	15.7	H	.0	4	VL
Tour and travel guides[1]	44	48	4	VL	9.5	L	13.9	10	VL
Transportation attendants	147	174	27	-	18.6	-	.0	12	-
Flight attendants[1]	124	147	23	L	18.4	H	.0	10	VL
Transportation attendants, except flight attendants and baggage porters[1]	23	27	5	VL	20.0	VH	.0	2	VL
All other personal care and service workers	163	198	35	L	21.7	VH	14.4	31	L
Sales and related occupations	15,513	17,365	1,852	-	11.9	-	13.3	2,979	-
Advertising sales agents	155	196	41	L	26.3	VH	3.9	29	L
Cashiers	3,363	3,851	488	-	14.5	-	.4	1,186	-
Cashiers, except gaming	3,325	3,799	474	VH	14.2	L	.4	1,172	VH
Gaming change persons and booth cashiers	38	52	14	VL	36.1	VH	.0	14	VL
Counter and rental clerks	423	506	82	H	19.4	H	2.4	159	H
Door-to-door sales workers, news and street vendors, and related workers	166	156	-10	VL	-6.2	VL	79.9	42	L
Insurance sales agents	378	390	13	VL	3.3	VL	33.7	44	L
Models, demonstrators, and product promoters	121	152	30	-	24.9	-	5.6	38	-

[1] One or more Current Population Survey (CPS) proxy occupations are used to estimate CPS based data.
[2] Bachelor's degree or higher, plus work experience.
[3] Work experience in a related occupation.

NOTE: Rankings are based on employment in all detailed occupations in the National Employment Matrix. For details, see "Data presented" section of text. Codes for describing the ranked variables are: VH = Very high, H = High, L = Low, VL = Very low, and n. a. = data not available. A dash indicates data are not applicable.

36

(Numbers in thousands)

Annual average job openings due to growth and net replacement needs, 2000-10		Median annual earnings		Ranking of:		Most significant source of postsecondary education or training	2000 national employment matrix occupation
Number	Rank	Dollars	Rank	Unemployment rate	Percent part-time		
205	-	-	-	-	-	-	Personal care and service occupations
5	VL	27,160	H	L	H	Related work experience[3]	First-line supervisors/managers of personal service workers
6	-	-	-	-	-	-	Animal care and service workers
1	VL	21,930	L	H	VH	Moderate-term on-the-job	Animal trainers[1]
6	VL	15,960	VL	H	VH	Short-term on-the-job	Nonfarm animal caretakers
53	VH	15,460	VL	H	VH	Short-term on-the-job	Child care workers
25	-	-	-	-	-	-	Entertainment attendants and related workers
0	VL	14,720	VL	VH	VH	Short-term on-the-job	Motion picture projectionists[1]
10	L	13,740	VL	VH	VH	Short-term on-the-job	Ushers, lobby attendants, and ticket takers[1]
14	-	-	-	-	-	-	Miscellaneous entertainment attendants and related workers
13	L	13,980	VL	VH	VH	Short-term on-the-job	Amusement and recreation attendants
1	VL	17,085	VL	VH	VH	Short-term on-the-job	Costume, locker room, and other attendants
1	-	-	-	-	-	-	Funeral service workers
0	VL	32,870	H	H	VH	Postsecondary vocational award	Embalmers
1	VL	16,930	VL	H	VH	Short-term on-the-job	Funeral attendants
10	-	-	-	-	-	-	Gaming occupations
2	-	-	-	-	-	-	First-line supervisors/managers, gaming workers
1	VL	37,900	H	L	H	Postsecondary vocational award	Gaming supervisors
1	VL	21,620	L	VL	H	Postsecondary vocational award	Slot key persons
7	-	-	-	-	-	-	Gaming services workers
1	VL	17,100	VL	VH	VH	Postsecondary vocational award	Gaming and sports book writers and runners
6	VL	13,330	VL	VH	VH	Postsecondary vocational award	Gaming dealers
1	VL	18,540	L	VH	VH	Moderate-term on-the-job	All other gaming service workers
29	-	-	-	-	-	-	Personal appearance workers
2	VL	17,740	VL	L	H	Postsecondary vocational award	Barbers
24	L	17,660	VL	L	VH	Postsecondary vocational award	Hairdressers, hairstylists, and cosmetologists
4	-	-	-	-	-	-	Miscellaneous personal appearance workers
2	VL	15,440	VL	L	VH	Postsecondary vocational award	Manicurists and pedicurists
1	VL	13,690	VL	L	VH	Short-term on-the-job	Shampooers
1	VL	20,080	L	L	VH	Postsecondary vocational award	Skin care specialists
32	H	15,600	VL	H	VH	Short-term on-the-job	Personal and home care aides[1]
21	-	-	-	-	-	-	Recreation and fitness workers
10	L	22,790	L	L	VH	Postsecondary vocational award	Fitness trainers and aerobics instructors
11	L	17,130	VL	L	VH	Bachelor's degree	Recreation workers
2	VL	20,060	L	H	VH	Moderate-term on-the-job	Residential advisors
13	-	18,770	-	-	-	-	Transportation, tourism, and lodging attendants
3	-	-	-	-	-	-	Baggage porters, bellhops, and concierges
2	VL	16,210	VL	H	H	Short-term on-the-job	Baggage porters and bellhops[1]
1	VL	20,210	L	H	H	Related work experience[3]	Concierges[1]
2	VL	18,677	L	VH	VH	Moderate-term on-the-job	Tour and travel guides[1]
8	-	-	-	-	-	-	Transportation attendants
7	VL	38,820	H	VL	VH	Long-term on-the-job	Flight attendants[1]
1	VL	17,630	VL	VL	VH	Short-term on-the-job	Transportation attendants, except flight attendants and baggage porters[1]
7	VL	17,522	VL	L	VH	Short-term on-the-job	All other personal care and service workers
671	-	-	-	-	-	-	**Sales and related occupations**
7	VL	35,850	H	L	L	Moderate-term on-the-job	Advertising sales agents
201	-	-	-	-	-	-	Cashiers
198	VH	14,460	VL	VH	VH	Short-term on-the-job	Cashiers, except gaming
3	VL	18,280	VL	VH	VH	Short-term on-the-job	Gaming change persons and booth cashiers
27	H	16,370	VL	VH	VH	Short-term on-the-job	Counter and rental clerks
4	VL	24,050	L	VH	VH	Short-term on-the-job	Door-to-door sales workers, news and street vendors, and related workers
11	L	38,750	H	VL	L	Bachelor's degree	Insurance sales agents
7	-	-	-	-	-	-	Models, demonstrators, and product promoters

[1] One or more Current Population Survey (CPS) proxy occupations are used to estimate CPS based data.
[2] Bachelor's degree or higher, plus work experience.
[3] Work experience in a related occupation.

NOTE: Rankings are based on employment in all detailed occupations in the National Employment Matrix. For details, see "Data presented" section of text. Codes for describing the ranked variables are: VH = Very high, H = High, L = Low, VL = Very low, and n. a. = data not available. A dash indicates data are not applicable.

2000 national employment matrix occupation	Employment		Employment change, 2000-10				Per-cent self-emp-loyed, 2000	Annual average job openings due to growth and total replacement needs, 2000-10	
			Numeric		Percent				
	2000	2010	Number	Rank	Number	Rank		Number	Rank
Demonstrators and product promoters	118	147	29	L	24.9	VH	5.5	37	L
Models	4	5	1	VL	26.0	VH	8.1	1	VL
Parts salespersons	260	248	-12	VL	-4.4	VL	.8	21	VL
Real estate brokers and sales agents	432	473	41	-	9.5	-	68.1	40	-
Real estate brokers	93	102	9	VL	9.6	L	63.1	9	VL
Real estate sales agents	339	371	32	L	9.5	L	69.4	31	L
Retail salespersons	4,109	4,619	510	VH	12.4	L	4.1	1,175	VH
Sales engineers[1]	85	100	15	L	17.7	H	.0	6	VL
Sales representatives, wholesale and manufacturing	1,821	1,932	111	-	6.1	-	5.4	121	-
Sales representatives, wholesale and manufacturing, technical and scientific products[1]	396	426	30	L	7.5	VL	5.2	27	VL
Sales representatives, wholesale and manufacturing, except technical and scientific products[1]	1,425	1,507	82	H	5.7	VL	5.5	94	L
Securities, commodities, and financial services sales agents	367	449	82	H	22.3	VH	24.5	64	L
Supervisors, sales workers	2,504	2,697	193	-	7.7	-	36.6	267	-
First-line supervisors/managers of retail sales workers	2,072	2,240	168	H	8.1	VL	38.7	223	H
First-line supervisors/managers of non-retail sales workers	432	457	25	L	5.8	VL	27.0	43	L
Telemarketers	572	699	127	H	22.2	VH	17.3	158	H
Travel agents	135	139	4	VL	3.2	VL	7.3	23	VL
All other sales and related workers[1]	621	758	137	H	22.0	VH	13.8	113	H
Office and administrative support occupations	23,882	26,053	2,171	-	9.1	-	1.8	4,411	-
First-line supervisors/managers of office and administrative support workers[1]	1,392	1,522	130	H	9.4	L	.0	159	H
Communications equipment operators	339	273	-65	-	-19.3	-	.0	63	-
Switchboard operators, including answering service[1]	259	218	-41	VL	-15.7	VL	.0	48	L
Telephone operators	54	35	-19	VL	-35.3	VL	.0	10	VL
All other communications equipment operators[1]	26	20	-6	VL	-21.8	VL	.0	5	VL
Financial, information, and record clerks	9,006	10,178	1,172	-	13.0	-	2.8	1,896	-
Financial clerks	3,696	3,821	126	-	3.4	-	5.6	597	-
Bill and account collectors	400	502	101	H	25.3	VH	.6	81	L
Billing and posting clerks and machine operators[1]	506	549	43	L	8.5	L	.3	73	L
Bookkeeping, accounting, and auditing clerks	1,991	2,030	39	L	2.0	VL	10.1	302	VH
Gaming cage workers	22	27	6	VL	25.2	VH	.0	8	VL
Payroll and timekeeping clerks	201	206	5	VL	2.3	VL	1.4	26	VL
Procurement clerks	76	67	-9	VL	-12.2	VL	.0	13	VL
Tellers	499	440	-59	VL	-11.8	VL	.0	98	H
Information and record clerks	5,099	6,105	1,006	-	19.7	-	.7	1,243	-
Brokerage clerks	70	69	-1	VL	-1.4	VL	.0	7	VL
Correspondence clerks[1]	38	42	3	VL	9.1	L	.0	6	VL
Court, municipal, and license clerks	105	117	13	VL	12.0	L	.0	15	VL
Credit authorizers, checkers, and clerks	86	90	4	VL	4.1	VL	.0	18	VL
Customer service representatives	1,946	2,577	631	VH	32.4	VH	.2	422	VH
Eligibility interviewers, government programs[1]	117	106	-11	VL	-9.3	VL	.0	13	VL
File clerks	288	314	26	L	9.1	L	1.7	81	L
Hotel, motel, and resort desk clerks	177	236	59	L	33.4	VH	.0	79	L
Human resources assistants, except payroll and timekeeping[1]	177	211	34	L	19.3	H	.0	28	VL
Interviewers, except eligibility and loan	154	205	51	L	33.4	VH	.0	58	L
Library assistants, clerical	98	118	19	L	19.7	H	.0	28	VL
Loan interviewers and clerks	139	101	-38	VL	-27.6	VL	.0	25	VL
New accounts clerks	87	89	2	VL	2.7	VL	.0	30	L
Order clerks[1]	348	277	-71	VL	-20.4	VL	.0	49	L
Receptionists and information clerks	1,078	1,334	256	VH	23.7	VH	1.3	294	VH
Reservation and transportation ticket agents and travel clerks	191	219	28	L	14.5	H	5.0	42	L

[1] One or more Current Population Survey (CPS) proxy occupations are used to estimate CPS based data.
[2] Bachelor's degree or higher, plus work experience.
[3] Work experience in a related occupation.

NOTE: Rankings are based on employment in all detailed occupations in the National Employment Matrix. For details, see "Data presented" section of text. Codes for describing the ranked variables are: VH = Very high, H = High, L = Low, VL = Very low, and n. a. = data not available. A dash indicates data are not applicable.

Annual average job openings due to growth and net replacement needs, 2000-10		Median annual earnings		Ranking of:		Most significant source of postsecondary education or training	2000 national employment matrix occupation
Number	Rank	Dollars	Rank	Unem-ploy-ment rate	Per-cent part-time		
7	VL	19,770	L	VH	VH	Moderate-term on-the-job	Demonstrators and product promoters
0	VL	19,080	L	VH	VH	Moderate-term on-the-job	Models
8	L	22,570	L	L	L	Moderate-term on-the-job	Parts salespersons
12	-	-	-	-	-	-	Real estate brokers and sales agents
2	VL	47,690	VH	VL	H	Related work experience[3]	Real estate brokers
9	L	27,640	H	VL	H	Postsecondary vocational award	Real estate sales agents
207	VH	16,670	VL	VH	VH	Short-term on-the-job	Retail salespersons
4	VL	56,520	VH	VL	VL	Bachelor's degree	Sales engineers[1]
61	-	-	-	-	-	-	Sales representatives, wholesale and manufacturing
14	L	52,620	VH	L	L	Moderate-term on-the-job	Sales representatives, wholesale and manufacturing, technical and scientific products[1]
47	H	40,340	VH	L	L	Moderate-term on-the-job	Sales representatives, wholesale and manufacturing, except technical and scientific products[1]
11	L	56,080	VH	L	L	Bachelor's degree	Securities, commodities, and financial services sales agents
56	-	-	-	-	-	-	Supervisors, sales workers
47	H	27,510	H	VL	L	Related work experience[3]	First-line supervisors/managers of retail sales workers
9	L	48,960	VH	VL	L	Related work experience[3]	First-line supervisors/managers of non-retail sales workers
24	H	18,840	L	VH	VH	Short-term on-the-job	Telemarketers
4	VL	25,150	L	L	H	Postsecondary vocational award	Travel agents
27	H	29,840	H	H	H	Moderate-term on-the-job	All other sales and related workers[1]
767	-	-	-	-	-	-	**Office and administrative support occupations**
40	H	36,420	H	VL	VL	Related work experience[3]	First-line supervisors/managers of office and administrative support workers[1]
10	-	-	-	-	-	-	Communications equipment operators
8	L	20,210	L	VH	H	Short-term on-the-job	Switchboard operators, including answering service[1]
2	VL	27,990	H	VH	H	Short-term on-the-job	Telephone operators
1	VL	30,220	H	VL	H	Short-term on-the-job	All other communications equipment operators[1]
324	-	-	-	-	-	-	Financial, information, and record clerks
112	-	-	-	-	-	-	Financial clerks
20	L	25,310	L	L	L	Short-term on-the-job	Bill and account collectors
17	L	24,560	L	H	H	Short-term on-the-job	Billing and posting clerks and machine operators[1]
42	H	25,670	L	L	VH	Moderate-term on-the-job	Bookkeeping, accounting, and auditing clerks
2	VL	20,790	L	VH	VH	Short-term on-the-job	Gaming cage workers
6	VL	27,180	H	L	L	Short-term on-the-job	Payroll and timekeeping clerks
2	VL	27,720	H	H	L	Short-term on-the-job	Procurement clerks
24	H	19,170	L	L	VH	Short-term on-the-job	Tellers
205	-	-	-	-	-	-	Information and record clerks
1	VL	31,060	H	L	L	Moderate-term on-the-job	Brokerage clerks
1	VL	24,150	L	L	L	Short-term on-the-job	Correspondence clerks[1]
3	VL	26,150	H	L	H	Short-term on-the-job	Court, municipal, and license clerks
1	VL	24,570	L	L	L	Short-term on-the-job	Credit authorizers, checkers, and clerks
80	VH	24,600	L	H	H	Moderate-term on-the-job	Customer service representatives
3	VL	28,380	H	VL	VL	Moderate-term on-the-job	Eligibility interviewers, government programs[1]
12	L	18,700	L	H	VH	Short-term on-the-job	File clerks
14	L	16,380	VL	H	H	Short-term on-the-job	Hotel, motel, and resort desk clerks
7	VL	28,340	H	VL	L	Short-term on-the-job	Human resources assistants, except payroll and timekeeping[1]
8	L	20,840	L	VH	VH	Short-term on-the-job	Interviewers, except eligibility and loan
6	VL	17,980	VL	L	VH	Short-term on-the-job	Library assistants, clerical
1	VL	26,410	H	L	H	Short-term on-the-job	Loan interviewers and clerks
2	VL	23,090	L	VH	VH	Related work experience[3]	New accounts clerks
7	VL	23,620	L	H	L	Short-term on-the-job	Order clerks[1]
49	H	20,040	L	H	VH	Short-term on-the-job	Receptionists and information clerks
8	L	22,620	L	L	H	Short-term on-the-job	Reservation and transportation ticket agents and travel clerks

[1] One or more Current Population Survey (CPS) proxy occupations are used to estimate CPS based data.
[2] Bachelor's degree or higher, plus work experience.
[3] Work experience in a related occupation.

NOTE: Rankings are based on employment in all detailed occupations in the National Employment Matrix. For details, see "Data presented" section of text. Codes for describing the ranked variables are: VH = Very high, H = High, L = Low, VL = Very low, and n. a. = data not available. A dash indicates data are not applicable.

(Numbers in thousands)

2000 national employment matrix occupation	Employment		Employment change, 2000-10				Per-cent self-emp-loyed, 2000	Annual average job openings due to growth and total replacement needs, 2000-10	
	2000	2010	Numeric		Percent				
			Number	Rank	Number	Rank		Number	Rank
All other financial, information, and record clerks	211	252	41	L	19.3	H	3.1	27	VL
Material recording, scheduling, dispatching, and distributing occupations	4,238	4,579	341	-	8.1	-	.4	766	-
Cargo and freight agents	60	65	5	VL	8.3	VL	.0	9	VL
Couriers and messengers	141	135	-5	VL	-3.9	VL	5.7	37	L
Dispatchers	254	304	50	-	19.6	-	.0	17	-
Dispatchers, except police, fire, and ambulance[1]	168	206	37	L	22.2	VH	.0	12	VL
Police, fire, and ambulance dispatchers[1]	86	98	12	VL	14.5	H	.0	5	VL
Meter readers, utilities[1]	49	36	-13	VL	-26.0	VL	.0	8	VL
Postal service workers	688	683	-5	-	-.7	-	.0	29	-
Postal service clerks	74	76	2	VL	2.4	VL	.0	3	VL
Postal service mail carriers[1]	324	332	8	VL	2.4	VL	.0	14	VL
Postal service mail sorters, processors, and processing machine operators	289	275	-14	VL	-4.9	VL	.0	12	VL
Production, planning, and expediting clerks[1]	332	391	60	L	17.9	H	.9	42	L
Shipping, receiving, and traffic clerks	890	973	83	H	9.3	L	.2	141	H
Stock clerks and order fillers[1]	1,679	1,821	142	H	8.5	L	.2	481	VH
Weighers, measurers, checkers, and samplers, recordkeeping[1]	83	98	15	L	17.9	H	.0	14	VL
All other material recording, scheduling, dispatching, and distributing workers[1]	63	73	10	VL	15.5	H	.5	18	VL
Secretaries, administrative assistants, and other office support occupations	8,908	9,500	592	-	6.6	-	1.9	1,484	-
Computer operators[1]	194	161	-33	VL	-17.1	VL	2.1	31	L
Data entry and information processing workers	806	774	-32	-	-3.9	-	3.6	138	-
Data entry keyers	509	534	25	L	4.9	VL	1.7	93	L
Word processors and typists	297	240	-57	VL	-19.1	VL	6.8	47	L
Desktop publishers	38	63	25	L	66.7	VH	2.6	7	VL
Insurance claims and policy processing clerks[1]	289	231	-58	VL	-20.2	VL	.0	35	L
Mail clerks and mail machine operators, except postal service[1]	188	207	19	L	9.9	L	.0	24	VL
Office clerks, general	2,705	3,135	430	VH	15.9	H	.5	719	VH
Office machine operators, except computer[1]	84	68	-16	VL	-18.8	VL	.0	18	VL
Proofreaders and copy markers[1]	35	33	-2	VL	-5.5	VL	13.7	7	VL
Secretaries and administrative assistants	3,902	4,167	265	-	6.8	-	2.2	528	-
Executive secretaries and administrative assistants	1,445	1,612	167	H	11.5	L	2.3	202	H
Legal secretaries	279	336	57	L	20.3	VH	2.5	41	L
Medical secretaries	314	373	60	L	19.0	H	2.0	46	L
Secretaries, except legal, medical, and executive	1,864	1,846	-18	VL	-1.0	VL	2.2	239	H
Statistical assistants	21	22	0	VL	2.1	VL	.0	2	VL
All other secretaries, administrative assistants, and other office support workers[1]	645	639	-6	VL	-.9	VL	4.6	89	L
Farming, fishing, and forestry occupations	1,429	1,480	51	-	3.6	-	8.8	273	-
First-line supervisors/managers/contractors of farming, fishing, and forestry workers[1]	100	113	13	VL	13.0	L	28.8	10	VL
Agricultural workers	987	1,024	37	-	3.7	-	2.1	206	-
Agricultural inspectors[1]	15	16	1	VL	6.6	VL	.0	2	VL
Farmworkers[1]	909	939	30	L	3.3	VL	2.3	195	H
Graders and sorters, agricultural products[1]	63	69	6	VL	9.1	L	.0	13	VL
Fishers and fishing vessel operators[1]	53	46	-6	VL	-12.2	VL	63.3	5	VL
Forest, conservation, and logging workers	90	88	-2	-	-1.8	-	22.3	15	-
Forest and conservation workers[1]	21	22	1	VL	3.9	VL	18.9	4	VL
Logging workers	69	66	-2	-	-3.5	-	23.3	11	-
Fallers	13	12	-1	VL	-8.7	VL	23.3	2	VL
Logging equipment operators	47	46	-1	VL	-2.0	VL	23.4	7	VL
Log graders and scalers	8	8	0	VL	-4.0	VL	22.8	1	VL

[1] One or more Current Population Survey (CPS) proxy occupations are used to estimate CPS based data.
[2] Bachelor's degree or higher, plus work experience.
[3] Work experience in a related occupation.

NOTE: Rankings are based on employment in all detailed occupations in the National Employment Matrix. For details, see "Data presented" section of text. Codes for describing the ranked variables are: VH = Very high, H = High, L = Low, VL = Very low, and n. a. = data not available. A dash indicates data are not applicable.

(Numbers in thousands)

Annual average job openings due to growth and net replacement needs, 2000-10		Median annual earnings		Ranking of:		Most significant source of postsecondary education or training	2000 national employment matrix occupation
Number	Rank	Dollars	Rank	Unemployment rate	Percent part-time		
7	VL	25,200	L	L	L	Short-term on-the-job	All other financial, information, and record clerks
							Material recording, scheduling, dispatching, and distributing occupations
153	-	-	-	-	-	-	
2	VL	28,560	H	H	L	Moderate-term on-the-job	Cargo and freight agents
4	VL	18,630	L	H	VH	Short-term on-the-job	Couriers and messengers
9	-	-	-	-	-	-	Dispatchers
7	VL	28,410	H	L	L	Moderate-term on-the-job	Dispatchers, except police, fire, and ambulance[1]
3	VL	25,750	L	L	L	Moderate-term on-the-job	Police, fire, and ambulance dispatchers[1]
1	VL	27,710	H	VL	VL	Short-term on-the-job	Meter readers, utilities[1]
19	-	-	-	-	-	-	Postal service workers
2	VL	39,010	H	L	VL	Short-term on-the-job	Postal service clerks
11	L	38,420	H	VL	L	Short-term on-the-job	Postal service mail carriers[1]
							Postal service mail sorters, processors, and processing machine operators
6	VL	32,080	H	L	VL	Short-term on-the-job	
12	L	30,590	H	L	L	Short-term on-the-job	Production, planning, and expediting clerks[1]
26	H	21,880	L	H	L	Short-term on-the-job	Shipping, receiving, and traffic clerks
74	VH	18,210	VL	VH	VH	Short-term on-the-job	Stock clerks and order fillers[1]
3	VL	23,640	L	H	H	Short-term on-the-job	Weighers, measurers, checkers, and samplers, recordkeeping[1]
3	VL	24,260	L	VH	VL	Short-term on-the-job	All other material recording, scheduling, dispatching, and distributing workers[1]
240	-	-	-	-	-	-	Secretaries, administrative assistants, and other office support occupations
3	VL	27,670	H	L	L	Moderate-term on-the-job	Computer operators[1]
17	-	-	-	-	-	-	Data entry and information processing workers
11	L	21,300	L	H	H	Moderate-term on-the-job	Data entry keyers
6	VL	24,710	L	H	H	Moderate-term on-the-job	Word processors and typists
3	VL	30,600	H	L	L	Postsecondary vocational award	Desktop publishers
5	VL	28,010	H	L	L	Moderate-term on-the-job	Insurance claims and policy processing clerks[1]
7	VL	19,840	L	H	H	Short-term on-the-job	Mail clerks and mail machine operators, except postal service[1]
95	VH	21,130	L	H	H	Short-term on-the-job	Office clerks, general
3	VL	20,790	L	VH	H	Short-term on-the-job	Office machine operators, except computer[1]
1	VL	22,390	L	VH	VH	Short-term on-the-job	Proofreaders and copy markers[1]
95	-	-	-	-	-	-	Secretaries and administrative assistants
41	H	31,090	H	L	H	Moderate-term on-the-job	Executive secretaries and administrative assistants
10	L	34,740	H	L	H	Postsecondary vocational award	Legal secretaries
11	L	23,430	L	L	H	Postsecondary vocational award	Medical secretaries
32	H	23,870	L	L	H	Moderate-term on-the-job	Secretaries, except legal, medical, and executive
0	VL	27,870	H	VL	L	Moderate-term on-the-job	Statistical assistants
10	L	26,880	H	L	H	Short-term on-the-job	All other secretaries, administrative assistants, and other office support workers[1]
49	-	-	-	-	-	-	**Farming, fishing, and forestry occupations**
							First-line supervisors/managers/contractors of farming, fishing, and forestry workers[1]
2	VL	26,172	H	H	L	Related work experience[3]	
36	-	-	-	-	-	-	Agricultural workers
0	VL	28,590	H	VL	VL	Related work experience[3]	Agricultural inspectors[1]
33	H	14,102	VL	VH	H	Short-term on-the-job	Farmworkers[1]
2	VL	14,790	VL	VH	L	Related work experience[3]	Graders and sorters, agricultural products[1]
2	VL	n.a.	H	VH	L	Short-term on-the-job	Fishers and fishing vessel operators[1]
2	-	-	-	-	-	-	Forest, conservation, and logging workers
1	VL	18,650	L	VH	L	Moderate-term on-the-job	Forest and conservation workers[1]
1	-	-	-	-	-	-	Logging workers
0	VL	25,650	L	VH	L	Moderate-term on-the-job	Fallers
1	VL	25,100	L	VH	L	Moderate-term on-the-job	Logging equipment operators
0	VL	27,190	H	VH	L	Moderate-term on-the-job	Log graders and scalers

[1] One or more Current Population Survey (CPS) proxy occupations are used to estimate CPS based data.
[2] Bachelor's degree or higher, plus work experience.
[3] Work experience in a related occupation.

NOTE: Rankings are based on employment in all detailed occupations in the National Employment Matrix. For details, see "Data presented" section of text. Codes for describing the ranked variables are: VH = Very high, H = High, L = Low, VL = Very low, and n. a. = data not available. A dash indicates data are not applicable.

(Numbers in thousands)

2000 national employment matrix occupation	Employment		Employment change, 2000-10				Percent self-employed, 2000	Annual average job openings due to growth and total replacement needs, 2000-10	
			Numeric		Percent				
	2000	2010	Number	Rank	Number	Rank		Number	Rank
All other farming, fishing, and forestry workers[1]	199	209	10	VL	4.9	VL	10.9	40	L
Construction and extraction occupations	**7,451**	**8,439**	**989**	**-**	**13.3**	**-**	**17.6**	**1,111**	**-**
First-line supervisors/managers of construction trades and extraction workers[1]	792	923	131	H	16.5	H	37.4	56	L
Construction trades and related workers	6,466	7,328	862	-	13.3	-	15.6	1,050	-
Boilermakers[1]	27	28	1	VL	2.1	VL	6.2	2	VL
Brickmasons, blockmasons, and stonemasons	158	179	21	-	13.2	-	28.1	22	-
Brickmasons and blockmasons[1]	144	162	18	L	12.5	L	28.3	20	VL
Stonemasons[1]	14	17	3	VL	20.8	VH	26.1	2	VL
Carpenters[1]	1,204	1,302	98	H	8.2	VL	28.6	171	H
Carpet, floor, and tile installers and finishers	167	189	22	-	13.2	-	48.4	17	-
Carpet installers	76	84	8	VL	10.5	L	48.5	7	VL
Floor layers, except carpet, wood, and hard tiles	23	27	4	VL	15.8	H	47.5	2	VL
Floor sanders and finishers	14	16	2	VL	14.7	H	45.6	1	VL
Tile and marble setters	54	62	8	VL	15.6	H	49.4	5	VL
Cement masons, concrete finishers, and terrazzo workers	166	171	5	-	3.0	-	6.0	4	-
Cement masons and concrete finishers	162	167	5	VL	3.0	VL	6.1	4	VL
Terrazzo workers and finishers	3	4	0	VL	2.0	VL	.0	0	VL
Construction laborers	791	926	135	H	17.0	H	.0	249	H
Construction equipment operators	416	450	34	-	8.1	-	5.6	35	-
Operating engineers and other construction equipment operators[1]	357	382	25	L	6.9	VL	6.6	28	VL
Paving, surfacing, and tamping equipment operators[1]	55	63	8	VL	15.5	H	.0	7	VL
Pile-driver operators	4	5	1	VL	14.0	L	.0	1	VL
Drywall installers, ceiling tile installers, and tapers	188	205	17	-	9.1	-	20.4	26	-
Drywall and ceiling tile installers	143	157	13	VL	9.4	L	20.4	20	VL
Tapers	44	48	4	VL	8.3	VL	20.7	6	VL
Electricians[1]	698	819	120	H	17.3	H	8.0	78	L
Glaziers[1]	49	56	7	VL	14.8	H	2.1	7	VL
Insulation workers	53	60	7	VL	13.6	L	.0	13	VL
Painters, construction and maintenance	491	585	94	H	19.1	H	46.5	76	L
Paperhangers[1]	27	32	5	VL	20.2	VH	60.2	4	VL
Pipelayers, plumbers, pipefitters, and steamfitters	568	627	59	-	10.4	-	13.5	61	-
Pipelayers[1]	65	73	8	VL	11.9	L	13.4	7	VL
Plumbers, pipefitters, and steamfitters[1]	503	554	51	L	10.2	L	13.5	54	L
Plasterers and stucco masons[1]	54	61	6	VL	11.9	L	16.8	7	VL
Reinforcing iron and rebar workers	27	32	5	VL	17.5	H	.0	4	VL
Roofers	158	188	31	L	19.4	H	27.5	41	L
Sheet metal workers[1]	224	276	51	L	23.0	VH	1.0	19	VL
Structural iron and steel workers	84	99	15	L	18.4	H	2.5	13	VL
Helpers, construction trades	450	510	60	-	13.3	-	.5	113	-
Helpers-brickmasons, blockmasons, stonemasons, and tile and marble setters	58	66	8	VL	14.1	L	.5	15	VL
Helpers-carpenters	101	108	7	VL	6.6	VL	.5	25	VL
Helpers-electricians	114	129	15	L	13.3	L	.4	29	VL
Helpers-painters, paperhangers, plasterers, and stucco masons	27	30	3	VL	12.9	L	.6	7	VL
Helpers-pipelayers, plumbers, pipefitters, and steamfitters	86	96	10	VL	11.5	L	.5	21	VL
Helpers-roofers	23	28	5	VL	19.3	H	.6	6	VL
All other helpers, construction trades	41	53	12	VL	29.1	VH	.7	11	VL
Other construction and related workers	465	534	69	-	14.8	-	6.0	82	-
Construction and building inspectors	75	86	11	VL	15.0	H	6.2	3	VL
Elevator installers and repairers[1]	23	27	4	VL	17.2	H	.0	3	VL
Fence erectors	29	30	1	VL	4.6	VL	22.0	5	VL
Hazardous materials removal workers	37	49	12	VL	32.8	VH	.0	10	VL

[1] One or more Current Population Survey (CPS) proxy occupations are used to estimate CPS based data.
[2] Bachelor's degree or higher, plus work experience.
[3] Work experience in a related occupation.

NOTE: Rankings are based on employment in all detailed occupations in the National Employment Matrix. For details, see "Data presented" section of text. Codes for describing the ranked variables are: VH = Very high, H = High, L = Low, VL = Very low, and n. a. = data not available. A dash indicates data are not applicable.

(Numbers in thousands)

Annual average job openings due to growth and net replacement needs, 2000-10		Median annual earnings		Ranking of:		Most significant source of postsecondary education or training	2000 national employment matrix occupation
Number	Rank	Dollars	Rank	Unemployment rate	Percent part-time		
7	VL	18,462	VL	VH	H	Moderate-term on-the-job	All other farming, fishing, and forestry workers[1]
247	-	-	-	-	-		**Construction and extraction occupations**
31	H	44,790	VH	L	VL	Related work experience[3]	First-line supervisors/managers of construction trades and extraction workers[1]
209	-	-	-	-	-	-	Construction trades and related workers
1	VL	37,020	H	VH	VL	Long-term on-the-job	Boilermakers[1]
5	-	-	-	-	-		Brickmasons, blockmasons, and stonemasons
4	VL	40,280	VH	VH	L	Long-term on-the-job	Brickmasons and blockmasons[1]
1	VL	31,150	H	VH	L	Long-term on-the-job	Stonemasons[1]
30	H	32,640	H	H	VL	Long-term on-the-job	Carpenters[1]
5	-	-	-	-	-		Carpet, floor, and tile installers and finishers
2	VL	30,070	H	H	L	Moderate-term on-the-job	Carpet installers
1	VL	30,810	H	H	L	Moderate-term on-the-job	Floor layers, except carpet, wood, and hard tiles
0	VL	27,390	H	H	L	Moderate-term on-the-job	Floor sanders and finishers
2	VL	34,290	H	H	L	Long-term on-the-job	Tile and marble setters
2	-	-	-	-	-		Cement masons, concrete finishers, and terrazzo workers
2	VL	28,070	H	VH	VL	Long-term on-the-job	Cement masons and concrete finishers
0	VL	31,320	H	VH	VL	Long-term on-the-job	Terrazzo workers and finishers
21	L	23,200	L	VH	L	Moderate-term on-the-job	Construction laborers
12	-	-	-	-	-		**Construction equipment operators**
10	L	33,250	H	VH	VL	Moderate-term on-the-job	Operating engineers and other construction equipment operators[1]
2	VL	26,780	H	VH	VL	Moderate-term on-the-job	Paving, surfacing, and tamping equipment operators[1]
0	VL	41,290	VH	VH	VL	Moderate-term on-the-job	Pile-driver operators
4	-	-	-	-	-		Drywall installers, ceiling tile installers, and tapers
3	VL	32,870	H	VH	L	Moderate-term on-the-job	Drywall and ceiling tile installers
1	VL	37,050	H	VH	L	Moderate-term on-the-job	Tapers
25	H	40,120	VH	L	VL	Long-term on-the-job	Electricians[1]
2	VL	29,780	H	VL	VL	Long-term on-the-job	Glaziers[1]
2	VL	27,130	H	VH	VL	Moderate-term on-the-job	Insulation workers
18	L	27,250	H	VH	L	Moderate-term on-the-job	Painters, construction and maintenance
1	VL	31,880	H	L	H	Moderate-term on-the-job	Paperhangers[1]
15	-	-	-	-	-		Pipelayers, plumbers, pipefitters, and steamfitters
2	VL	27,450	H	H	VL	Moderate-term on-the-job	Pipelayers[1]
13	L	37,840	H	H	VL	Long-term on-the-job	Plumbers, pipefitters, and steamfitters[1]
2	VL	33,290	H	VH	L	Long-term on-the-job	Plasterers and stucco masons[1]
1	VL	34,900	H	VH	VL	Long-term on-the-job	Reinforcing iron and rebar workers
7	VL	29,030	H	VH	L	Moderate-term on-the-job	Roofers
10	L	31,850	H	H	VL	Moderate-term on-the-job	Sheet metal workers[1]
2	VL	37,270	H	VH	VL	Long-term on-the-job	Structural iron and steel workers
28	-	-	-	-	-		**Helpers, construction trades**
4	VL	22,780	L	VH	L	Short-term on-the-job	Helpers-brickmasons, blockmasons, stonemasons, and tile and marble setters
6	VL	20,610	L	VH	L	Short-term on-the-job	Helpers-carpenters
7	VL	21,370	L	VH	L	Short-term on-the-job	Helpers-electricians
2	VL	19,290	L	VH	L	Short-term on-the-job	Helpers-painters, paperhangers, plasterers, and stucco masons
5	VL	21,240	L	VH	L	Short-term on-the-job	Helpers-pipelayers, plumbers, pipefitters, and steamfitters
2	VL	19,440	L	VH	L	Short-term on-the-job	Helpers-roofers
3	VL	19,460	L	VH	L	Short-term on-the-job	All other helpers, construction trades
16	-	26,180	-	-	-		**Other construction and related workers**
3	VL	38,750	H	VL	VL	Related work experience[3]	Construction and building inspectors
1	VL	47,380	VH	VL	VL	Long-term on-the-job	Elevator installers and repairers[1]
1	VL	21,900	L	VH	VL	Moderate-term on-the-job	Fence erectors
2	VL	28,520	H	VH	VL	Moderate-term on-the-job	Hazardous materials removal workers

[1] One or more Current Population Survey (CPS) proxy occupations are used to estimate CPS based data.
[2] Bachelor's degree or higher, plus work experience.
[3] Work experience in a related occupation.

NOTE: Rankings are based on employment in all detailed occupations in the National Employment Matrix. For details, see "Data presented" section of text. Codes for describing the ranked variables are: VH = Very high, H = High, L = Low, VL = Very low, and n. a. = data not available. A dash indicates data are not applicable.

2000 national employment matrix occupation	Employment		Employment change, 2000-10				Per-cent self-emp-loyed, 2000	Annual average job openings due to growth and total replacement needs, 2000-10	
			Numeric		Percent				
	2000	2010	Number	Rank	Number	Rank		Number	Rank
Highway maintenance workers	151	159	8	VL	5.2	VL	6.3	32	L
Rail-track laying and maintenance equipment operators	12	9	-3	VL	-26.1	VL	.0	3	VL
Septic tank servicers and sewer pipe cleaners	15	18	3	VL	16.5	H	.0	4	VL
All other construction and related workers	123	156	33	L	26.7	VH	5.8	24	VL
Extraction workers	193	189	-4	-	-2.1	-	2.3	16	-
Derrick, rotary drill, and service unit operators, oil, gas, and mining	45	44	-2	-	-3.5	-	.0	3	-
Derrick operators, oil and gas[1]	16	16	0	VL	.1	VL	.0	1	VL
Rotary drill operators, oil and gas[1]	18	17	-1	VL	-8.0	VL	.0	1	VL
Service unit operators, oil, gas, and mining[1]	11	11	0	VL	-1.2	VL	.0	1	VL
Earth drillers, except oil and gas[1]	24	27	3	VL	12.6	L	18.4	3	VL
Explosives workers, ordnance handling experts, and blasters[1]	5	5	0	VL	1.9	VL	.0	0	VL
Helpers-Extraction workers[1]	37	38	1	VL	2.4	VL	.0	6	VL
Mining machine operators	22	19	-3	-	-12.9	-	.0	1	-
Continuous mining machine operators[1]	10	8	-1	VL	-13.4	VL	.0	1	VL
Miscellaneous mining machine operators[1]	12	11	-2	VL	-12.5	VL	.0	1	VL
Roustabouts, oil and gas[1]	41	40	-2	VL	-4.2	VL	.0	3	VL
All other extraction workers[1]	19	17	-2	VL	-10.7	VL	.0	1	VL
Installation, maintenance, and repair occupations	5,820	6,482	662	-	11.4	-	7.5	603	-
First-line supervisors/managers of mechanics, installers, and repairers[1]	442	513	71	H	16.0	H	3.7	46	L
Electrical and electronic equipment mechanics, installers, and repairers	683	726	43	-	6.3	-	7.4	72	-
Avionics technicians	16	17	2	VL	9.8	L	.0	2	VL
Computer, automated teller, and office machine repairers	172	197	24	L	14.2	L	14.8	26	VL
Electric motor, power tool, and related repairers	37	40	3	VL	7.9	VL	11.3	4	VL
Electrical and electronics installers and repairers, transportation equipment	14	15	2	VL	13.6	L	.0	2	VL
Electrical and electronics repairers, industrial and utility	108	116	8	-	7.3	-	.0	13	-
Electrical and electronics repairers, commercial and industrial equipment	90	98	8	VL	9.2	L	.0	11	VL
Electrical and electronics repairers, powerhouse, substation, and relay	18	18	0	VL	-2.3	VL	.0	2	VL
Electronic equipment installers and repairers, motor vehicles	13	15	2	VL	15.6	H	.0	1	VL
Electronic home entertainment equipment installers and repairers	37	30	-7	VL	-17.9	VL	16.8	4	VL
Radio and telecommunications equipment installers and repairers	196	188	-7	-	-3.8	-	6.0	10	-
Radio mechanics[1]	7	5	-2	VL	-24.2	VL	.0	0	VL
Telecommunications equipment installers and repairers, except line installers[1]	189	183	-6	VL	-3.1	VL	6.2	9	VL
Security and fire alarm systems installers	44	54	10	VL	23.4	VH	6.4	5	VL
All other electrical and electronic equipment mechanics, installers, and repairers[1]	48	54	6	VL	13.4	L	.7	3	VL
Vehicle and mobile equipment mechanics, installers, and repairers	1,931	2,218	286	-	14.8	-	11.3	235	-
Aircraft mechanics and service technicians[1]	158	184	26	L	16.7	H	1.8	13	VL
Automotive body and related repairers	199	219	20	L	10.2	L	13.4	20	VL
Automotive glass installers and repairers	22	24	2	VL	10.5	L	6.5	2	VL
Automotive service technicians and mechanics[1]	840	991	151	H	18.0	H	17.9	119	H
Bus and truck mechanics and diesel engine specialists	285	326	40	L	14.2	L	3.9	24	VL
Heavy vehicle and mobile equipment service technicians and mechanics	185	203	17	-	9.4	-	3.6	18	-
Farm equipment mechanics[1]	41	42	0	VL	.9	VL	4.1	4	VL
Mobile heavy equipment mechanics, except engines[1]	130	148	18	L	14.0	L	3.6	13	VL
Rail car repairers[1]	14	13	-1	VL	-7.6	VL	1.8	1	VL

[1] One or more Current Population Survey (CPS) proxy occupations are used to estimate CPS based data.
[2] Bachelor's degree or higher, plus work experience.
[3] Work experience in a related occupation.

NOTE: Rankings are based on employment in all detailed occupations in the National Employment Matrix. For details, see "Data presented" section of text. Codes for describing the ranked variables are: VH = Very high, H = High, L = Low, VL = Very low, and n. a. = data not available. A dash indicates data are not applicable.

(Numbers in thousands)

Annual average job openings due to growth and net replacement needs, 2000-10		Median annual earnings		Ranking of:		Most significant source of postsecondary education or training	2000 national employment matrix occupation
Number	Rank	Dollars	Rank	Unemployment rate	Percent part-time		
3	VL	26,660	H	VH	L	Moderate-term on-the-job	Highway maintenance workers
0	VL	31,060	H	VH	L	Moderate-term on-the-job	Rail-track laying and maintenance equipment operators
1	VL	27,080	H	VH	L	Moderate-term on-the-job	Septic tank servicers and sewer pipe cleaners
5	VL	26,145	H	VH	VL	Moderate-term on-the-job	All other construction and related workers
7	-	-	-	-	-	-	Extraction workers
							Derrick, rotary drill, and service unit operators, oil, gas, and mining
2	-			-	VL		Derrick operators, oil and gas[1]
1	VL	25,810	H	H	VL	Moderate-term on-the-job	Rotary drill operators, oil and gas[1]
1	VL	30,860	H	H	VL	Moderate-term on-the-job	Service unit operators, oil, gas, and mining[1]
0	VL	25,220	L	H	VL	Moderate-term on-the-job	Earth drillers, except oil and gas[1]
1	VL	30,530	H	H	VL	Moderate-term on-the-job	Explosives workers, ordnance handling experts, and blasters[1]
0	VL	32,950	H	H	VL	Moderate-term on-the-job	Helpers-Extraction workers[1]
2	VL	22,850	L	H	VL	Short-term on-the-job	Mining machine operators
1	-	-	-	-	-	-	Continuous mining machine operators[1]
0	VL	32,530	H	H	VL	Moderate-term on-the-job	Miscellaneous mining machine operators[1]
0	VL	36,420	H	H	VL	Moderate-term on-the-job	Roustabouts, oil and gas[1]
1	VL	20,450	L	H	VL	Moderate-term on-the-job	All other extraction workers[1]
1	VL	27,250	H	VH	VL	Moderate-term on-the-job	
194	-	-	-	-	-	-	**Installation, maintenance, and repair occupations**
19	L	44,250	VH	VL	VL	Related work experience[3]	First-line supervisors/managers of mechanics, installers, and repairers[1]
18	-	-	-	-	-	-	Electrical and electronic equipment mechanics, installers, and repairers
0	VL	41,300	VH	L	VL	Postsecondary vocational award	Avionics technicians
4	VL	31,380	H	L	L	Postsecondary vocational award	Computer, automated teller, and office machine repairers
1	VL	32,860	H	VL	VL	Postsecondary vocational award	Electric motor, power tool, and related repairers
0	VL	35,210	H	L	VL	Postsecondary vocational award	Electrical and electronics installers and repairers, transportation equipment
3	-	-	-	-	-	-	Electrical and electronics repairers, industrial and utility
3	VL	36,910	H	L	VL	Postsecondary vocational award	Electrical and electronics repairers, commercial and industrial equipment
0	VL	48,540	VH	L	VL	Postsecondary vocational award	Electrical and electronics repairers, powerhouse, substation, and relay
0	VL	25,080	L	VL	VL	Postsecondary vocational award	Electronic equipment installers and repairers, motor vehicles
1	VL	26,450	H	L	VL	Postsecondary vocational award	Electronic home entertainment equipment installers and repairers
4	-	-	-	-	-	-	Radio and telecommunications equipment installers and repairers
0	VL	32,990	H	VL	VL	Postsecondary vocational award	Radio mechanics[1]
4	VL	44,030	VH	VL	VL	Postsecondary vocational award	Telecommunications equipment installers and repairers, except line installers[1]
2	VL	30,490	H	L	VL	Postsecondary vocational award	Security and fire alarm systems installers
2	VL	33,220	H	VL	VL	Postsecondary vocational award	All other electrical and electronic equipment mechanics, installers, and repairers[1]
78	-	-	-	-	-	-	Vehicle and mobile equipment mechanics, installers, and repairers
6	VL	40,550	VH	VL	VL	Postsecondary vocational award	Aircraft mechanics and service technicians[1]
7	VL	31,190	H	H	VL	Long-term on-the-job	Automotive body and related repairers
1	VL	25,920	H	H	VL	Long-term on-the-job	Automotive glass installers and repairers
35	H	28,490	H	H	VL	Postsecondary vocational award	Automotive service technicians and mechanics[1]
11	L	32,350	H	L	VL	Postsecondary vocational award	Bus and truck mechanics and diesel engine specialists
7	-	-	-	-	-	-	Heavy vehicle and mobile equipment service technicians and mechanics
1	VL	25,760	H	L	VL	Postsecondary vocational award	Farm equipment mechanics[1]
5	VL	33,950	H	L	VL	Postsecondary vocational award	Mobile heavy equipment mechanics, except engines[1]
0	VL	33,670	H	L	VL	Long-term on-the-job	Rail car repairers[1]

[1] One or more Current Population Survey (CPS) proxy occupations are used to estimate CPS based data.
[2] Bachelor's degree or higher, plus work experience.
[3] Work experience in a related occupation.

NOTE: Rankings are based on employment in all detailed occupations in the National Employment Matrix. For details, see "Data presented" section of text. Codes for describing the ranked variables are: VH = Very high, H = High, L = Low, VL = Very low, and n. a. = data not available. A dash indicates data are not applicable.

2000 national employment matrix occupation	Employment		Employment change, 2000-10				Per-cent self-emp-loyed, 2000	Annual average job openings due to growth and total replacement needs, 2000-10	
			Numeric		Percent				
	2000	2010	Number	Rank	Number	Rank		Number	Rank
Small engine mechanics	73	79	6	-	8.6	-	23.6	15	-
Motorboat mechanics	25	27	2	VL	9.0	L	22.5	5	VL
Motorcycle mechanics	14	16	1	VL	8.6	L	24.0	3	VL
Outdoor power equipment and other small engine mechanics	33	36	3	VL	8.2	VL	24.4	7	VL
Miscellaneous vehicle and mobile equipment mechanics, installers, and repairers	170	192	22	-	13.2	-	1.0	53	-
Bicycle repairers	9	10	2	VL	17.7	H	.0	3	VL
Recreational vehicle service technicians	12	15	3	VL	25.4	VH	.0	4	VL
Tire repairers and changers	89	95	6	VL	6.8	VL	.0	27	VL
All other vehicle and mobile equipment mechanics, installers, and repairers	60	72	12	VL	19.6	H	2.7	19	VL
Other installation, maintenance, and repair occupations	2,764	3,026	262	-	9.5	-	5.4	238	-
Coin, vending, and amusement machine servicers and repairers	37	44	7	VL	18.5	H	6.4	5	VL
Control and valve installers and repairers	46	48	2	-	5.2	-	.0	5	-
Control and valve installers and repairers, except mechanical door[1]	34	35	1	VL	2.7	VL	.0	4	VL
Mechanical door repairers[1]	11	13	1	VL	12.7	L	.0	1	VL
Heating, air conditioning, and refrigeration mechanics and installers	243	297	54	L	22.3	VH	20.0	26	VL
Helpers-Installation, maintenance, and repair workers[1]	145	172	27	L	18.5	H	.0	37	L
Home appliance repairers[1]	43	46	3	VL	6.2	VL	23.5	6	VL
Industrial machinery mechanics	198	205	7	VL	3.4	VL	9.0	8	VL
Line installers and repairers	263	317	54	-	20.7	-	.6	18	-
Electrical power-line installers and repairers	99	108	9	VL	9.3	L	.0	5	VL
Telecommunications line installers and repairers[1]	164	209	45	L	27.6	VH	1.0	13	VL
Locksmiths and safe repairers[1]	23	25	2	VL	8.7	L	43.3	3	VL
Maintenance and repair workers, general	1,251	1,310	59	L	4.7	VL	.4	109	H
Maintenance workers, machinery[1]	114	120	7	VL	5.8	VL	.0	5	VL
Manufactured building and mobile home installers	17	20	3	VL	19.1	H	15.9	2	VL
Millwrights	72	75	3	VL	3.9	VL	.0	8	VL
Precision instrument and equipment repairers	63	69	6	-	9.7	-	27.1	7	-
Camera and photographic equipment repairers[1]	7	7	0	VL	-2.1	VL	28.3	1	VL
Medical equipment repairers[1]	28	33	4	VL	14.9	H	27.2	3	VL
Musical instrument repairers and tuners[1]	7	8	1	VL	9.4	L	24.3	1	VL
Watch repairers[1]	5	6	0	VL	6.2	VL	28.2	1	VL
All other precision instrument and equipment repairers[1]	15	16	1	VL	6.8	VL	27.0	2	VL
Riggers	20	22	2	VL	10.1	L	10.3	2	VL
All other installation, maintenance, and repair workers	228	254	26	L	11.5	L	13.8	19	VL
Production occupations	13,060	13,811	750	-	5.7	-	2.7	2,002	-
First-line supervisors/managers of production and operating workers	819	827	9	VL	1.0	VL	3.6	72	L
Assemblers and fabricators	2,653	2,824	171	-	6.5	-	1.3	519	-
Aircraft structure, surfaces, rigging, and systems assemblers[1]	20	23	3	VL	14.2	L	.0	2	VL
Electrical, electronics, and electromechanical assemblers	508	492	-16	-	-3.1	-	>0	90	-
Coil winders, tapers, and finishers	56	61	5	VL	8.2	VL	.2	10	VL
Electrical and electronic equipment assemblers	379	355	-24	VL	-6.3	VL	.0	66	L
Electromechanical equipment assemblers	73	76	3	VL	4.5	VL	.0	13	VL
Engine and other machine assemblers[1]	67	72	5	VL	7.1	VL	.0	11	VL
Structural metal fabricators and fitters	101	120	20	L	19.5	H	.0	22	VL
Miscellaneous assemblers and fabricators	1,957	2,117	160	-	8.2	-	1.8	396	-
Fiberglass laminators and fabricators[1]	48	53	5	VL	11.4	L	.0	10	VL
Team assemblers[1]	1,458	1,545	87	H	5.9	VL	1.6	292	VH
Timing device assemblers, adjusters, and calibrators[1]	12	12	0	VL	2.5	VL	.0	2	VL
All other assemblers and fabricators[1]	439	507	68	L	15.4	H	2.5	92	L

[1] One or more Current Population Survey (CPS) proxy occupations are used to estimate CPS based data.
[2] Bachelor's degree or higher, plus work experience.
[3] Work experience in a related occupation.

NOTE: Rankings are based on employment in all detailed occupations in the National Employment Matrix. For details, see "Data presented" section of text. Codes for describing the ranked variables are: VH = Very high, H = High, L = Low, VL = Very low, and n. a. = data not available. A dash indicates data are not applicable.

Table 2. Occupational employment and job openings data, 2000-10, and worker characteristics, 2000 — Continued

(Numbers in thousands)

Annual average job openings due to growth and net replacement needs, 2000-10		Median annual earnings		Ranking of:		Most significant source of postsecondary education or training	2000 national employment matrix occupation
Number	Rank	Dollars	Rank	Unemployment rate	Percent part-time		
2	-	-	-	-	-	-	Small engine mechanics
1	VL	26,660	H	L	L	Long-term on-the-job	Motorboat mechanics
0	VL	25,100	L	L	L	Long-term on-the-job	Motorcycle mechanics
1	VL	23,780	L	L	L	Moderate-term on-the-job	Outdoor power equipment and other small engine mechanics
9	-	-	-	-	-	-	Miscellaneous vehicle and mobile equipment mechanics, installers, and repairers
0	VL	18,030	VL	H	H	Moderate-term on-the-job	Bicycle repairers
1	VL	25,370	L	H	H	Long-term on-the-job	Recreational vehicle service technicians
4	VL	18,750	L	H	H	Short-term on-the-job	Tire repairers and changers
3	VL	32,750	H	L	L	Moderate-term on-the-job	All other vehicle and mobile equipment mechanics, installers, and repairers
80	-	32,620	-	-	-	-	Other installation, maintenance, and repair occupations
1	VL	25,660	L	VL	VL	Moderate-term on-the-job	Coin, vending, and amusement machine servicers and repairers
2	-	-	-	-	-	-	Control and valve installers and repairers
1	VL	41,330	VH	VL	VL	Moderate-term on-the-job	Control and valve installers and repairers, except mechanical door[1]
1	VL	28,630	H	VL	VL	Moderate-term on-the-job	Mechanical door repairers[1]
8	L	32,770	H	L	VL	Long-term on-the-job	Heating, air conditioning, and refrigeration mechanics and installers
10	L	20,750	L	H	H	Short-term on-the-job	Helpers-Installation, maintenance, and repair workers[1]
1	VL	28,860	H	L	VL	Long-term on-the-job	Home appliance repairers[1]
6	VL	35,980	H	L	VL	Long-term on-the-job	Industrial machinery mechanics
12	-	-	-	-	-	-	Line installers and repairers
4	VL	45,780	VH	L	VL	Long-term on-the-job	Electrical power-line installers and repairers
8	L	38,110	H	VL	VL	Long-term on-the-job	Telecommunications line installers and repairers[1]
1	VL	27,490	H	L	L	Moderate-term on-the-job	Locksmiths and safe repairers[1]
22	L	27,850	H	H	VL	Long-term on-the-job	Maintenance and repair workers, general
4	VL	30,970	H	H	VL	Long-term on-the-job	Maintenance workers, machinery[1]
1	VL	21,700	L	L	L	Moderate-term on-the-job	Manufactured building and mobile home installers
2	VL	40,210	VH	H	VL	Long-term on-the-job	Millwrights
2	-	-	-	-	-	-	Precision instrument and equipment repairers
0	VL	28,990	H	L	L	Moderate-term on-the-job	Camera and photographic equipment repairers[1]
1	VL	35,340	H	L	L	Moderate-term on-the-job	Medical equipment repairers[1]
0	VL	31,410	H	L	L	Long-term on-the-job	Musical instrument repairers and tuners[1]
0	VL	25,130	L	L	L	Long-term on-the-job	Watch repairers[1]
0	VL	41,320	VH	L	L	Long-term on-the-job	All other precision instrument and equipment repairers[1]
1	VL	32,080	H	L	L	Short-term on-the-job	Riggers
7	VL	32,437	H	L	VL	Moderate-term on-the-job	All other installation, maintenance, and repair workers
393	-	-	-	-	-	-	**Production occupations**
22	L	40,330	VH	VL	VL	Related work experience[3]	First-line supervisors/managers of production and operating workers
70	-	-	-	-	-	-	Assemblers and fabricators
1	VL	40,850	VH	L	VL	Long-term on-the-job	Aircraft structure, surfaces, rigging, and systems assemblers[1]
14	-	-	-	-	-	-	Electrical, electronics, and electromechanical assemblers
2	VL	20,320	L	H	VL	Short-term on-the-job	Coil winders, tapers, and finishers
10	L	21,450	L	H	VL	Short-term on-the-job	Electrical and electronic equipment assemblers
2	VL	23,210	L	H	VL	Short-term on-the-job	Electromechanical equipment assemblers
2	VL	28,010	H	H	VL	Short-term on-the-job	Engine and other machine assemblers[1]
4	VL	27,280	H	H	L	Moderate-term on-the-job	Structural metal fabricators and fitters
50	-	-	-	-	-	-	Miscellaneous assemblers and fabricators
1	VL	22,510	L	H	VL	Moderate-term on-the-job	Fiberglass laminators and fabricators[1]
34	H	21,470	L	H	VL	Moderate-term on-the-job	Team assemblers[1]
0	VL	22,420	L	H	VL	Moderate-term on-the-job	Timing device assemblers, adjusters, and calibrators[1]
14	L	21,020	L	H	VL	Moderate-term on-the-job	All other assemblers and fabricators[1]

[1] One or more Current Population Survey (CPS) proxy occupations are used to estimate CPS based data.
[2] Bachelor's degree or higher, plus work experience.
[3] Work experience in a related occupation.

NOTE: Rankings are based on employment in all detailed occupations in the National Employment Matrix. For details, see "Data presented" section of text. Codes for describing the ranked variables are: VH = Very high, H = High, L = Low, VL = Very low, and n. a. = data not available. A dash indicates data are not applicable.

2000 national employment matrix occupation	Employment		Employment change, 2000-10				Percent self-employed, 2000	Annual average job openings due to growth and total replacement needs, 2000-10	
			Numeric		Percent				
	2000	2010	Number	Rank	Number	Rank		Number	Rank
Food processing occupations	760	783	23	-	3.0	-	1.7	103	-
Bakers	160	187	27	L	16.8	H	4.4	28	VL
Butchers and other meat, poultry, and fish processing workers	411	415	5	-	1.2	-	1.4	47	-
Butchers and meat cutters[1]	141	128	-13	VL	-8.9	VL	1.3	16	VL
Meat, poultry, and fish cutters and trimmers[1]	148	162	14	VL	9.5	L	1.5	18	VL
Slaughterers and meat packers[1]	122	125	3	VL	2.6	VL	1.3	14	VL
Food and tobacco roasting, baking, and drying machine operators and tenders[1]	18	17	-2	VL	-9.0	VL	.0	3	VL
Food batchmakers[1]	66	67	1	VL	1.4	VL	.0	9	VL
Food cooking machine operators and tenders	37	37	0	VL	.6	VL	.0	7	VL
All other food processing workers[1]	69	61	-8	VL	-11.6	VL	.0	9	VL
Metal workers and plastic workers	2,907	3,156	249	-	8.6	-	1.4	355	-
Computer control programmers and operators	186	222	36	-	19.3	-	.0	21	-
Computer-controlled machine tool operators, metal and plastic[1]	162	194	32	L	19.7	H	.0	19	VL
Numerical tool and process control programmers[1]	24	28	4	VL	16.6	H	.0	3	VL
Cutting, punching, and press machine setters, operators, and tenders, metal and plastic[1]	372	357	-15	VL	-4.0	VL	.0	35	L
Drilling and boring machine tool setters, operators, and tenders, metal and plastic[1]	71	68	-3	VL	-4.5	VL	.0	8	VL
Extruding and drawing machine setters, operators, and tenders, metal and plastic[1]	126	143	17	L	13.5	L	.0	24	VL
Forging machine setters, operators, and tenders, metal and plastic[1]	54	59	5	VL	9.1	L	.0	6	VL
Grinding, lapping, polishing, and buffing machine tool setters, operators, and tenders, metal and plastic[1]	145	156	11	VL	7.3	VL	.0	27	VL
Heat treating equipment setters, operators, and tenders, metal and plastic[1]	43	49	6	VL	13.4	L	.0	10	VL
Lathe and turning machine tool setters, operators, and tenders, metal and plastic[1]	84	78	-6	VL	-7.4	VL	.0	12	VL
Lay-out workers, metal and plastic[1]	18	17	-1	VL	-6.0	VL	.0	1	VL
Machinists[1]	430	469	39	L	9.1	L	1.4	32	L
Metal furnace and kiln operators and tenders	40	43	3	-	7.2	-	.0	6	-
Metal-refining furnace operators and tenders[1]	24	26	2	VL	7.4	VL	.0	4	VL
Pourers and casters, metal[1]	16	18	1	VL	6.9	VL	.0	2	VL
Milling and planing machine setters, operators, and tenders, metal and plastic[1]	34	32	-2	VL	-6.7	VL	.0	4	VL
Model makers and patternmakers, metal and plastic	19	18	-1	-	-5.6	-	2.3	2	-
Model makers, metal and plastic[1]	11	10	0	VL	-3.2	VL	4.2	1	VL
Patternmakers, metal and plastic[1]	9	8	-1	VL	-8.4	VL	.0	1	VL
Molders and molding machine setters, operators, and tenders, metal and plastic	235	252	17	-	7.0	-	.0	53	-
Foundry mold and coremakers[1]	59	59	-1	VL	-1.2	VL	.0	13	VL
Molding, coremaking, and casting machine setters, operators, and tenders, metal and plastic[1]	176	193	17	L	9.8	L	.0	40	L
Multiple machine tool setters, operators, and tenders, metal and plastic	105	121	15	L	14.7	H	.0	22	VL
Plating and coating machine setters, operators, and tenders, metal and plastic[1]	65	72	7	VL	10.2	L	.0	15	VL
Rolling machine setters, operators, and tenders, metal and plastic[1]	49	50	1	VL	1.4	VL	.0	6	VL
Tool and die makers[1]	130	132	3	VL	2.2	VL	1.6	6	VL
Tool grinders, filers, and sharpeners[1]	29	27	-2	VL	-7.7	VL	3.5	2	VL
Welding, soldering, and brazing workers	521	618	97	-	18.7	-	5.8	70	-
Welders, cutters, solderers, and brazers[1]	446	532	86	H	19.3	H	5.8	60	L
Welding, soldering, and brazing machine setters, operators, and tenders[1]	74	86	11	VL	15.1	H	5.9	10	VL

[1] One or more Current Population Survey (CPS) proxy occupations are used to estimate CPS based data.
[2] Bachelor's degree or higher, plus work experience.
[3] Work experience in a related occupation.

NOTE: Rankings are based on employment in all detailed occupations in the National Employment Matrix. For details, see "Data presented" section of text. Codes for describing the ranked variables are: VH = Very high, H = High, L = Low, VL = Very low, and n. a. = data not available. A dash indicates data are not applicable.

Annual average job openings due to growth and net replacement needs, 2000-10		Median annual earnings		Ranking of:		Most significant source of postsecondary education or training	2000 national employment matrix occupation
Number	Rank	Dollars	Rank	Unemployment rate	Percent part-time		
21	-	-	-	-	-	-	Food processing occupations
5	VL	19,710	L	H	H	Long-term on-the-job	Bakers
							Butchers and other meat, poultry, and fish processing
12	-	-	-	-	-	-	workers
3	VL	24,120	L	H	L	Long-term on-the-job	Butchers and meat cutters[1]
5	VL	16,760	VL	H	L	Short-term on-the-job	Meat, poultry, and fish cutters and trimmers[1]
3	VL	19,410	L	H	L	Moderate-term on-the-job	Slaughterers and meat packers[1]
							Food and tobacco roasting, baking, and drying machine
0	VL	22,690	L	VH	H	Short-term on-the-job	operators and tenders[1]
2	VL	20,990	L	H	L	Short-term on-the-job	Food batchmakers[1]
1	VL	20,630	L	L	VL	Short-term on-the-job	Food cooking machine operators and tenders
2	VL	18,170	VL	VH	H	Short-term on-the-job	All other food processing workers[1]
99	-	-	-	-	-	-	Metal workers and plastic workers
10	-	-	-	-	-	-	Computer control programmers and operators
							Computer-controlled machine tool operators, metal and
9	L	27,400	H	VL	VL	Long-term on-the-job	plastic[1]
1	VL	36,810	H	VL	VL	Long-term on-the-job	Numerical tool and process control programmers[1]
							Cutting, punching, and press machine setters, operators, and
7	VL	22,940	L	H	VL	Moderate-term on-the-job	tenders, metal and plastic[1]
							Drilling and boring machine tool setters, operators, and
2	VL	25,470	L	H	VL	Moderate-term on-the-job	tenders, metal and plastic[1]
							Extruding and drawing machine setters, operators, and
4	VL	24,260	L	H	VL	Moderate-term on-the-job	tenders, metal and plastic[1]
							Forging machine setters, operators, and tenders, metal and
2	VL	25,190	L	VL	L	Moderate-term on-the-job	plastic[1]
							Grinding, lapping, polishing, and buffing machine tool setters,
5	VL	24,360	L	H	VL	Moderate-term on-the-job	operators, and tenders, metal and plastic[1]
							Heat treating equipment setters, operators, and tenders,
1	VL	26,290	H	VL	VL	Moderate-term on-the-job	metal and plastic[1]
							Lathe and turning machine tool setters, operators, and
3	VL	28,640	H	L	VL	Moderate-term on-the-job	tenders, metal and plastic[1]
0	VL	29,680	H	VH	VL	Moderate-term on-the-job	Lay-out workers, metal and plastic[1]
13	L	30,740	H	L	VL	Long-term on-the-job	Machinists[1]
1	-	-	-	-	-	-	Metal furnace and kiln operators and tenders
1	VL	28,030	H	L	VL	Moderate-term on-the-job	Metal-refining furnace operators and tenders[1]
1	VL	26,360	H	L	VL	Moderate-term on-the-job	Pourers and casters, metal[1]
							Milling and planing machine setters, operators, and tenders,
1	VL	27,570	H	VH	VL	Moderate-term on-the-job	metal and plastic[1]
1	-	-	-	-	-	-	Model makers and patternmakers, metal and plastic
0	VL	33,420	H	VL	L	Moderate-term on-the-job	Model makers, metal and plastic[1]
0	VL	30,850	H	VL	L	Moderate-term on-the-job	Patternmakers, metal and plastic[1]
							Molders and molding machine setters, operators, and
7	-	-	-	-	-	-	tenders, metal and plastic
1	VL	24,710	L	H	VL	Moderate-term on-the-job	Foundry mold and coremakers[1]
							Molding, coremaking, and casting machine setters,
5	VL	21,620	L	H	VL	Moderate-term on-the-job	operators, and tenders, metal and plastic[1]
							Multiple machine tool setters, operators, and tenders, metal
3	VL	26,960	H	H	L	Moderate-term on-the-job	and plastic
							Plating and coating machine setters, operators, and tenders,
2	VL	23,360	L	VH	VL	Moderate-term on-the-job	metal and plastic[1]
							Rolling machine setters, operators, and tenders, metal and
2	VL	26,740	H	H	VL	Moderate-term on-the-job	plastic[1]
4	VL	41,110	VH	L	VL	Long-term on-the-job	Tool and die makers[1]
1	VL	27,510	H	H	L	Moderate-term on-the-job	Tool grinders, filers, and sharpeners[1]
24	-	-	-	-	-	-	Welding, soldering, and brazing workers
21	L	27,300	H	H	VL	Postsecondary vocational award	Welders, cutters, solderers, and brazers[1]
							Welding, soldering, and brazing machine setters,
3	VL	27,220	H	H	VL	Moderate-term on-the-job	operators, and tenders[1]

[1] One or more Current Population Survey (CPS) proxy occupations are used to estimate CPS based data.
[2] Bachelor's degree or higher, plus work experience.
[3] Work experience in a related occupation.

NOTE: Rankings are based on employment in all detailed occupations in the National Employment Matrix. For details, see "Data presented" section of text. Codes for describing the ranked variables are: VH = Very high, H = High, L = Low, VL = Very low, and n. a. = data not available. A dash indicates data are not applicable.

(Numbers in thousands)

2000 national employment matrix occupation	Employment		Employment change, 2000-10				Per-cent self-emp-loyed, 2000	Annual average job openings due to growth and total replacement needs, 2000-10	
			Numeric		Percent				
	2000	2010	Number	Rank	Number	Rank		Number	Rank
All other metal workers and plastic workers[1]	150	174	25	L	16.4	H	1.1	23	VL
Plant and system operators	368	384	16	-	4.4	-	.0	29	-
Power plant operators, distributors, and dispatchers	55	55	0	-	-.4	-	.0	4	-
Nuclear power reactor operators[1]	4	4	0	VL	-3.4	VL	.0	0	VL
Power distributors and dispatchers[1]	15	14	-1	VL	-5.1	VL	.0	1	VL
Power plant operators[1]	36	37	1	VL	1.8	VL	.0	3	VL
Stationary engineers and boiler operators[1]	57	56	-1	VL	-1.3	VL	.0	4	VL
Water and liquid waste treatment plant and system operators[1]	88	104	16	L	18.1	H	.0	8	VL
Miscellaneous plant and system operators	167	168	1	-	.6	-	.0	12	-
Chemical plant and system operators[1]	71	69	-2	VL	-3.3	VL	.0	5	VL
Gas plant operators[1]	12	11	-1	VL	-6.3	VL	.0	1	VL
Petroleum pump system operators, refinery operators, and gaugers[1]	35	34	-1	VL	-4.1	VL	.0	2	VL
All other plant and system operators[1]	49	54	6	VL	11.4	L	.0	4	VL
Printing occupations	534	543	8	-	1.6	-	1.7	62	-
Bookbinders and bindery workers	115	124	9	-	7.4	-	.0	15	-
Bindery workers[1]	105	113	8	VL	7.3	VL	.0	14	VL
Bookbinders[1]	10	10	1	VL	8.2	VL	.0	1	VL
Job printers	56	59	4	VL	6.4	VL	5.9	6	VL
Prepress technicians and workers[1]	107	90	-17	VL	-15.6	VL	.2	12	VL
Printing machine operators[1]	222	234	12	VL	5.5	VL	2.6	25	VL
All other printing workers[1]	34	35	1	VL	2.0	VL	.0	4	VL
Textile, apparel, and furnishings occupations	1,317	1,285	-32	-	-2.4	-	7.0	275	-
Extruding and forming machine setters, operators, and tenders, synthetic and glass fibers[1]	41	44	2	VL	5.7	VL	.0	6	VL
Fabric and apparel patternmakers[1]	15	14	-1	VL	-5.4	VL	.0	2	VL
Laundry and dry-cleaning workers[1]	236	263	27	L	11.4	L	7.3	64	L
Pressers, textile, garment, and related materials[1]	110	112	2	VL	1.7	VL	3.5	19	VL
Sewing machine operators	399	348	-51	VL	-12.9	VL	2.8	81	L
Shoe and leather workers and repairers[1]	19	15	-4	VL	-21.4	VL	26.8	3	VL
Shoe machine operators and tenders[1]	9	4	-5	VL	-53.6	VL	.0	2	VL
Tailors, dressmakers, and sewers	101	91	-9	-	-9.3	-	37.2	19	-
Sewers, hand[1]	43	40	-3	VL	-6.6	VL	37.3	8	VL
Tailors, dressmakers, and custom sewers[1]	58	51	-7	VL	-11.4	VL	37.1	11	VL
Textile bleaching and dyeing machine operators and tenders[1]	37	41	4	VL	10.8	L	.0	3	VL
Textile cutting machine setters, operators, and tenders[1]	38	35	-2	VL	-6.5	VL	.0	7	VL
Textile knitting and weaving machine setters, operators, and tenders[1]	70	68	-2	VL	-2.4	VL	.0	14	VL
Textile winding, twisting, and drawing out machine setters, operators, and tenders[1]	90	86	-4	VL	-4.4	VL	.0	19	VL
Upholsterers[1]	58	53	-6	VL	-9.5	VL	25.9	9	VL
All other textile, apparel, and furnishings workers[1]	95	112	17	L	18.0	H	1.9	21	VL
Woodworkers	409	446	37	-	9.0	-	10.8	49	-
Cabinetmakers and bench carpenters	159	175	16	L	9.8	L	12.7	10	VL
Furniture finishers[1]	45	49	4	VL	8.4	L	17.8	5	VL
Model makers and patternmakers, wood[1]	10	12	2	VL	16.0	H	.0	1	VL
Sawing machine setters, operators, and tenders, wood	57	64	7	VL	11.7	L	7.9	10	VL
Woodworking machine setters, operators, and tenders, except sawing[1]	103	108	5	VL	5.3	VL	3.8	15	VL
All other woodworkers[1]	35	38	4	VL	10.6	L	21.0	5	VL
Other production occupations	3,293	3,563	269	-	8.2	-	2.7	567	-
Cementing and gluing machine operators and tenders[1]	36	38	2	VL	6.7	VL	.0	6	VL
Chemical processing machine setters, operators, and tenders	100	110	10	-	9.9	-	.0	16	-

[1] One or more Current Population Survey (CPS) proxy occupations are used to estimate CPS based data.
[2] Bachelor's degree or higher, plus work experience.
[3] Work experience in a related occupation.

NOTE: Rankings are based on employment in all detailed occupations in the National Employment Matrix. For details, see "Data presented" section of text. Codes for describing the ranked variables are: VH = Very high, H = High, L = Low, VL = Very low, and n. a. = data not available. A dash indicates data are not applicable.

Table 2. Occupational employment and job openings data, 2000-10, and worker characteristics, 2000 — Continued

(Numbers in thousands)

Annual average job openings due to growth and net replacement needs, 2000-10		Median annual earnings		Ranking of:		Most significant source of postsecondary education or training	2000 national employment matrix occupation
Number	Rank	Dollars	Rank	Unemployment rate	Percent part-time		
5	VL	27,570	H	H	VL	Moderate-term on-the-job	All other metal workers and plastic workers[1]
13	-	-	-	-	-	-	Plant and system operators
2	-	-	-	-	-	-	Power plant operators, distributors, and dispatchers
0	VL	57,220	VH	VL	VL	Long-term on-the-job	Nuclear power reactor operators[1]
0	VL	48,570	VH	VL	VL	Long-term on-the-job	Power distributors and dispatchers[1]
1	VL	46,090	VH	VL	VL	Long-term on-the-job	Power plant operators[1]
2	VL	40,420	VH	VL	VL	Long-term on-the-job	Stationary engineers and boiler operators[1]
4	VL	31,380	H	VL	VL	Long-term on-the-job	Water and liquid waste treatment plant and system operators[1]
6	-	-	-	-	-	-	Miscellaneous plant and system operators
2	VL	40,750	VH	L	VL	Long-term on-the-job	Chemical plant and system operators[1]
0	VL	44,730	VH	L	VL	Long-term on-the-job	Gas plant operators[1]
1	VL	45,180	VH	L	VL	Long-term on-the-job	Petroleum pump system operators, refinery operators, and gaugers[1]
2	VL	32,610	H	L	VL	Long-term on-the-job	All other plant and system operators[1]
16	-	-	-	-	-	-	Printing occupations
4	-	-	-	-	-	-	Bookbinders and bindery workers
4	VL	20,910	L	H	L	Moderate-term on-the-job	Bindery workers[1]
0	VL	23,760	L	H	L	Moderate-term on-the-job	Bookbinders[1]
2	VL	28,300	H	L	VL	Long-term on-the-job	Job printers
3	VL	30,310	H	L	H	Long-term on-the-job	Prepress technicians and workers[1]
7	VL	28,230	H	L	VL	Moderate-term on-the-job	Printing machine operators[1]
1	VL	22,470	L	VL	H	Moderate-term on-the-job	All other printing workers[1]
30	-	-	-	-	-	-	Textile, apparel, and furnishings occupations
1	VL	26,330	H	H	VL	Moderate-term on-the-job	Extruding and forming machine setters, operators, and tenders, synthetic and glass fibers[1]
0	VL	24,070	L	L	L	Long-term on-the-job	Fabric and apparel patternmakers[1]
9	L	15,790	VL	H	H	Moderate-term on-the-job	Laundry and dry-cleaning workers[1]
2	VL	16,170	VL	H	H	Short-term on-the-job	Pressers, textile, garment, and related materials[1]
4	VL	16,220	VL	VH	L	Moderate-term on-the-job	Sewing machine operators
1	VL	17,300	VL	VH	H	Long-term on-the-job	Shoe and leather workers and repairers[1]
0	VL	18,490	VL	H	VL	Moderate-term on-the-job	Shoe machine operators and tenders[1]
2	-	-	-	-	-	-	Tailors, dressmakers, and sewers
1	VL	16,820	VL	H	H	Short-term on-the-job	Sewers, hand[1]
1	VL	21,100	L	H	H	Related work experience[3]	Tailors, dressmakers, and custom sewers[1]
1	VL	19,580	L	H	VL	Moderate-term on-the-job	Textile bleaching and dyeing machine operators and tenders[1]
1	VL	19,200	L	H	VL	Moderate-term on-the-job	Textile cutting machine setters, operators, and tenders[1]
1	VL	21,460	L	H	VL	Long-term on-the-job	Textile knitting and weaving machine setters, operators, and tenders[1]
2	VL	20,570	L	H	VL	Moderate-term on-the-job	Textile winding, twisting, and drawing out machine setters, operators, and tenders[1]
2	VL	23,760	L	L	L	Long-term on-the-job	Upholsterers[1]
4	VL	19,240	L	H	VL	Moderate-term on-the-job	All other textile, apparel, and furnishings workers[1]
19	-	25,930	-	-	-	-	Woodworkers
7	VL	22,530	L	L	L	Long-term on-the-job	Cabinetmakers and bench carpenters
2	VL	21,500	L	H	L	Long-term on-the-job	Furniture finishers
1	VL	26,343	H	VL	VL	Long-term on-the-job	Model makers and patternmakers, wood[1]
3	VL	21,270	L	VH	VL	Moderate-term on-the-job	Sawing machine setters, operators, and tenders, wood
5	VL	20,790	L	H	VL	Moderate-term on-the-job	Woodworking machine setters, operators, and tenders, except sawing[1]
2	VL	19,720	L	VH	VL	Moderate-term on-the-job	All other woodworkers[1]
102	-	-	-	-	-	-	Other production occupations
1	VL	21,810	L	VH	VL	Moderate-term on-the-job	Cementing and gluing machine operators and tenders[1]
3	-	-	-	-	-	-	Chemical processing machine setters, operators, and tenders

[1] One or more Current Population Survey (CPS) proxy occupations are used to estimate CPS based data.
[2] Bachelor's degree or higher, plus work experience.
[3] Work experience in a related occupation.

NOTE: Rankings are based on employment in all detailed occupations in the National Employment Matrix. For details, see "Data presented" section of text. Codes for describing the ranked variables are: VH = Very high, H = High, L = Low, VL = Very low, and n. a. = data not available. A dash indicates data are not applicable.

Table 2. Occupational employment and job openings data, 2000-10, and worker characteristics, 2000 — Continued

(Numbers in thousands)

2000 national employment matrix occupation	Employment		Employment change, 2000-10				Per-cent self-emp-loyed, 2000	Annual average job openings due to growth and total replacement needs, 2000-10	
			Numeric		Percent				
	2000	2010	Number	Rank	Number	Rank		Number	Rank
Chemical equipment operators and tenders[1]	61	70	9	VL	14.9	H	.0	10	VL
Separating, filtering, clarifying, precipitating, and still machine setters, operators, and tenders[1]	39	40	1	VL	2.2	VL	.0	6	VL
Cleaning, washing, and metal pickling equipment operators and tenders[1]	20	17	-3	VL	-14.2	VL	.0	3	VL
Cooling and freezing equipment operators and tenders	7	7	0	VL	-1.3	VL	.0	1	VL
Crushing, grinding, polishing, mixing, and blending workers	202	222	21	-	10.3	-	.0	22	-
Crushing, grinding, and polishing machine setters, operators, and tenders[1]	44	49	4	VL	9.8	L	.0	5	VL
Grinding and polishing workers, hand[1]	49	55	7	VL	13.7	L	.0	5	VL
Mixing and blending machine setters, operators, and tenders[1]	109	118	10	VL	9.0	L	.0	12	VL
Cutting workers	115	117	2	-	1.8	-	.0	22	-
Cutters and trimmers, hand[1]	32	33	1	VL	2.2	VL	.0	6	VL
Cutting and slicing machine setters, operators, and tenders[1]	83	84	1	VL	1.7	VL	.0	16	VL
Etchers and engravers[1]	15	16	2	VL	11.1	L	25.3	2	VL
Extruding, forming, pressing, and compacting machine setters, operators, and tenders[1]	73	80	7	VL	9.0	L	.0	12	VL
Furnace, kiln, oven, drier, and kettle operators and tenders[1]	33	34	1	VL	3.2	VL	.0	5	VL
Helpers-Production workers[1]	525	587	62	L	11.9	L	.0	149	H
Inspectors, testers, sorters, samplers, and weighers[1]	602	591	-11	VL	-1.9	VL	1.2	91	L
Jewelers and precious stone and metal workers[1]	43	44	1	VL	1.3	VL	30.4	3	VL
Medical, dental, and ophthalmic laboratory workers	88	95	7	-	7.9	-	4.7	7	-
Dental laboratory technicians	43	46	3	VL	6.3	VL	7.3	3	VL
Medical appliance technicians	13	15	2	VL	19.0	H	7.7	1	VL
Ophthalmic laboratory technicians	32	34	2	VL	5.7	VL	.0	3	VL
Molders, shapers, and casters, except metal and plastic[1]	42	45	3	VL	7.4	VL	9.1	7	VL
Packaging and filling machine operators and tenders	379	433	54	L	14.4	H	.0	62	L
Painting workers	195	223	28	-	14.5	-	7.3	35	-
Coating, painting, and spraying machine setters, operators, and tenders[1]	108	121	13	VL	11.9	L	7.4	19	VL
Painters, transportation equipment[1]	49	57	9	VL	17.5	H	7.4	9	VL
Painting, coating, and decorating workers[1]	38	45	7	VL	17.9	H	7.2	7	VL
Paper goods machine setters, operators, and tenders[1]	123	116	-7	VL	-5.4	VL	.0	18	VL
Photographic process workers and processing machine operators	76	77	2	-	2.2	-	2.5	10	-
Photographic process workers	26	24	-2	VL	-8.2	VL	2.4	3	VL
Photographic processing machine operators	50	53	4	VL	7.6	VL	2.5	7	VL
Semiconductor processors	52	69	17	L	32.4	VH	.0	9	VL
Tire builders	18	20	2	VL	8.6	L	.0	3	VL
All other production workers[1]	549	619	70	H	12.7	L	7.2	108	H
Transportation and material moving occupations	10,088	11,618	1,530	-	15.2	-	4.1	1,940	-
Supervisors, transportation and material moving workers	357	427	70	-	19.7	-	3.6	39	-
Aircraft cargo handling supervisors[1]	10	13	3	VL	27.7	VH	.0	1	VL
First-line supervisors/managers of helpers, laborers, and material movers, hand[1]	153	182	29	L	18.9	H	3.6	16	VL
First-line supervisors/managers of transportation and material-moving machine and vehicle operators[1]	194	233	39	L	19.9	VH	3.8	21	VL
Air transportation occupations	166	186	20	-	12.2	-	1.1	10	-
Aircraft pilots and flight engineers	117	129	11	-	9.8	-	1.6	7	-
Airline pilots, copilots, and flight engineers[1]	98	104	6	VL	6.4	VL	.0	5	VL
Commercial pilots[1]	19	24	5	VL	26.9	VH	9.5	1	VL
Air traffic controllers and airfield operations specialists	31	35	3	-	10.2	-	.0	2	-
Air traffic controllers[1]	27	29	2	VL	7.2	VL	.0	2	VL
Airfield operations specialists[1]	5	6	1	VL	27.1	VH	.0	0	VL

[1] One or more Current Population Survey (CPS) proxy occupations are used to estimate CPS based data.
[2] Bachelor's degree or higher, plus work experience.
[3] Work experience in a related occupation.

NOTE: Rankings are based on employment in all detailed occupations in the National Employment Matrix. For details, see "Data presented" section of text. Codes for describing the ranked variables are: VH = Very high, H = High, L = Low, VL = Very low, and n. a. = data not available. A dash indicates data are not applicable.

(Numbers in thousands)

Annual average job openings due to growth and net replacement needs, 2000-10		Median annual earnings		Ranking of:		Most significant source of postsecondary education or training	2000 national employment matrix occupation
Number	Rank	Dollars	Rank	Unemployment rate	Percent part-time		
2	VL	35,800	H	L	VL	Moderate-term on-the-job	Chemical equipment operators and tenders[1]
1	VL	27,230	H	L	VL	Moderate-term on-the-job	Separating, filtering, clarifying, precipitating, and still machine setters, operators, and tenders[1]
0	VL	21,140	L	VH	L	Moderate-term on-the-job	Cleaning, washing, and metal pickling equipment operators and tenders[1]
0	VL	20,180	L	L	VL	Moderate-term on-the-job	Cooling and freezing equipment operators and tenders
6	-	-	-	-	-	-	**Crushing, grinding, polishing, mixing, and blending workers**
1	VL	24,950	L	H	VL	Moderate-term on-the-job	Crushing, grinding, and polishing machine setters, operators, and tenders[1]
2	VL	21,800	L	H	VL	Moderate-term on-the-job	Grinding and polishing workers, hand[1]
3	VL	26,170	H	H	VL	Moderate-term on-the-job	Mixing and blending machine setters, operators, and tenders[1]
2	-	-	-	-	-	-	Cutting workers
1	VL	20,330	L	H	VL	Short-term on-the-job	Cutters and trimmers, hand[1]
2	VL	23,870	L	H	VL	Moderate-term on-the-job	Cutting and slicing machine setters, operators, and tenders[1]
1	VL	21,050	L	VH	H	Long-term on-the-job	**Etchers and engravers[1]**
2	VL	24,840	L	H	VL	Moderate-term on-the-job	Extruding, forming, pressing, and compacting machine setters, operators, and tenders[1]
1	VL	27,320	H	L	VL	Moderate-term on-the-job	Furnace, kiln, oven, drier, and kettle operators and tenders[1]
19	L	18,000	VL	VH	L	Short-term on-the-job	Helpers-Production workers[1]
13	L	25,420	L	H	VL	Moderate-term on-the-job	Inspectors, testers, sorters, samplers, and weighers[1]
1	VL	26,330	H	L	L	Postsecondary vocational award	Jewelers and precious stone and metal workers[1]
3	-	-	-	-	-	-	Medical, dental, and ophthalmic laboratory workers
1	VL	26,920	H	VL	L	Long-term on-the-job	Dental laboratory technicians
1	VL	24,900	L	VL	L	Long-term on-the-job	Medical appliance technicians
1	VL	20,550	L	VL	L	Moderate-term on-the-job	Ophthalmic laboratory technicians
1	VL	23,380	L	H	L	Moderate-term on-the-job	Molders, shapers, and casters, except metal and plastic[1]
14	L	19,660	L	VH	L	Short-term on-the-job	Packaging and filling machine operators and tenders
7	-	-	-	-	-	-	**Painting workers**
4	VL	23,660	L	VH	VL	Moderate-term on-the-job	Coating, painting, and spraying machine setters, operators, and tenders[1]
2	VL	30,440	H	VH	VL	Moderate-term on-the-job	Painters, transportation equipment[1]
2	VL	19,850	L	VH	VL	Short-term on-the-job	Painting, coating, and decorating workers[1]
2	VL	26,530	H	H	VL	Moderate-term on-the-job	Paper goods machine setters, operators, and tenders[1]
2	-	-	-	-	-	-	Photographic process workers and processing machine operators
1	VL	19,630	L	H	H	Moderate-term on-the-job	Photographic process workers
2	VL	17,450	VL	H	H	Short-term on-the-job	Photographic processing machine operators
3	VL	25,430	L	L	VL	Associate degree	Semiconductor processors
0	VL	36,510	H	L	VL	Moderate-term on-the-job	Tire builders
17	L	20,170	L	H	VL	Moderate-term on-the-job	All other production workers[1]
395	-	-	-	-	-	-	**Transportation and material moving occupations**
15	-	-	-	-	-	-	Supervisors, transportation and material moving workers
0	VL	37,830	H	VL	L	Related work experience[3]	Aircraft cargo handling supervisors[1]
6	VL	34,800	H	VL	L	Related work experience[3]	First-line supervisors/managers of helpers, laborers, and material movers, hand[1]
8	L	40,300	VH	VL	L	Related work experience[3]	First-line supervisors/managers of transportation and material-moving machine and vehicle operators[1]
7	-	-	-	-	-	-	**Air transportation occupations**
4	-	-	-	-	-	-	Aircraft pilots and flight engineers
3	VL	110,940	VH	VL	H	Bachelor's degree	Airline pilots, copilots, and flight engineers[1]
1	VL	43,300	VH	VL	H	Postsecondary vocational award	Commercial pilots[1]
2	-	-	-	-	-	-	Air traffic controllers and airfield operations specialists
1	VL	82,520	VH	VL	VL	Long-term on-the-job	Air traffic controllers[1]
0	VL	32,080	H	VL	VL	Short-term on-the-job	Airfield operations specialists[1]

[1] One or more Current Population Survey (CPS) proxy occupations are used to estimate CPS based data.
[2] Bachelor's degree or higher, plus work experience.
[3] Work experience in a related occupation.

NOTE: Rankings are based on employment in all detailed occupations in the National Employment Matrix. For details, see "Data presented" section of text. Codes for describing the ranked variables are: VH = Very high, H = High, L = Low, VL = Very low, and n. a. = data not available. A dash indicates data are not applicable.

Table 2. Occupational employment and job openings data, 2000-10, and worker characteristics, 2000 — Continued

(Numbers in thousands)

2000 national employment matrix occupation	Employment		Employment change, 2000-10				Per-cent self-emp-loyed, 2000	Annual average job openings due to growth and total replacement needs, 2000-10	
			Numeric		Percent				
	2000	2010	Number	Rank	Number	Rank		Number	Rank
All other air transportation workers[1]	17	22	5	VL	32.2	VH	.0	2	VL
Motor vehicle operators	4,237	4,982	745	-	17.6	-	7.8	674	-
Ambulance drivers and attendants, except emergency medical technicians	15	20	5	VL	33.7	VH	.0	4	VL
Bus drivers	666	754	88	-	13.2	-	.9	96	-
Bus drivers, school	481	537	56	L	11.6	L	.9	68	L
Bus drivers, transit and intercity	185	217	32	L	17.4	H	.8	27	VL
Driver/sales workers and truck drivers	3,268	3,857	589	-	18.0	-	8.5	507	-
Driver/sales workers	402	430	29	L	7.1	VL	8.8	58	L
Truck drivers, heavy and tractor-trailer	1,749	2,095	346	VH	19.8	H	8.2	275	VH
Truck drivers, light or delivery services	1,117	1,331	215	VH	19.2	H	8.9	175	H
Taxi drivers and chauffeurs	176	219	43	L	24.4	VH	27.0	41	L
All other motor vehicle operators[1]	112	132	20	L	18.2	H	.0	18	VL
Rail transportation occupations	115	94	-21	-	-18.5	-	.0	11	-
Locomotive engineers and firers[1]	37	38	1	VL	2.3	VL	.0	4	VL
Railroad brake, signal, and switch operators[1] ..	22	9	-13	VL	-60.8	VL	.0	2	VL
Railroad conductors and yardmasters[1]	45	36	-8	VL	-18.9	VL	.0	4	VL
Rail yard engineers, dinkey operators, and hostlers ..	4	4	0	VL	-4.5	VL	.0	0	VL
All other rail transportation workers	7	7	0	VL	-4.1	VL	.0	1	VL
Water transportation occupations	70	74	3	-	4.4	-	.0	6	-
Sailors and marine oilers	32	33	2	VL	4.9	VL	.0	3	VL
Ship and boat captains and operators	25	26	1	VL	3.4	VL	.0	2	VL
Ship engineers	9	9	0	VL	5.8	VL	.0	1	VL
All other water transportation workers[1]	5	5	0	VL	4.2	VL	.0	0	VL
Related transportation occupations	309	341	32	-	10.4	-	1.6	85	-
Bridge and lock tenders[1]	4	4	-1	VL	-19.1	VL	.0	0	VL
Parking lot attendants	117	140	23	L	19.8	H	.0	19	VL
Service station attendants	112	110	-2	VL	-1.7	VL	2.4	45	L
Traffic technicians[1]	4	5	1	VL	14.1	L	.0	1	VL
Transportation inspectors	25	28	3	VL	11.3	L	9.0	3	VL
All other related transportation workers[1]	46	54	8	VL	17.9	H	.0	10	VL
Material moving occupations	4,833	5,514	681	-	14.1	-	1.2	1,134	-
Cleaners of vehicles and equipment	322	382	60	L	18.8	H	6.0	91	L
Conveyor operators and tenders	63	71	8	VL	13.3	L	.0	9	VL
Crane and tower operators[1]	55	59	5	VL	8.6	L	.0	5	VL
Excavating and loading machine and dragline operators[1]	76	88	11	VL	14.8	H	8.3	6	VL
Hoist and winch operators[1]	9	10	1	VL	8.3	L	.0	1	VL
Industrial truck and tractor operators	635	707	72	H	11.3	L	.3	99	H
Laborers and freight, stock, and material movers, hand[1]	2,084	2,373	289	VH	13.9	L	1.1	548	VH
Machine feeders and offbearers	182	159	-22	VL	-12.3	VL	.0	41	L
Packers and packagers, hand[1]	1,091	1,300	210	VH	19.3	H	.4	263	H
Pumping station operators	32	32	0	-	.0	-	.0	3	-
Gas compressor and gas pumping station operators	7	7	0	VL	4.8	VL	.0	1	VL
Pump operators, except wellhead pumpers	14	15	1	VL	4.8	VL	.0	1	VL
Wellhead pumpers	12	11	-1	VL	-8.5	VL	.0	1	VL
Refuse and recyclable material collectors[1]	124	145	21	L	16.6	H	1.7	36	L
Tank car, truck, and ship loaders	19	21	3	VL	13.5	L	.0	3	VL
All other material moving workers[1]	142	165	23	L	16.4	H	1.0	16	VL

[1] One or more Current Population Survey (CPS) proxy occupations are used to estimate CPS based data.
[2] Bachelor's degree or higher, plus work experience.
[3] Work experience in a related occupation.

NOTE: Rankings are based on employment in all detailed occupations in the National Employment Matrix. For details, see "Data presented" section of text. Codes for describing the ranked variables are: VH = Very high, H = High, L = Low, VL = Very low, and n. a. = data not available. A dash indicates data are not applicable.

Annual average job openings due to growth and net replacement needs, 2000-10		Median annual earnings		Ranking of:		Most significant source of postsecondary education or training	2000 national employment matrix occupation
Number	Rank	Dollars	Rank	Unemployment rate	Percent part-time		
1	VL	21,410	L	VL	VL	Moderate-term on-the-job	All other air transportation workers[1]
140	-	-	-	-	-	-	**Motor vehicle operators**
1	VL	17,820	VL	H	H	Moderate-term on-the-job	Ambulance drivers and attendants, except emergency medical technicians
26	-	-	-	-	-	-	Bus drivers
18	L	20,910	L	H	VH	Short-term on-the-job	Bus drivers, school
8	L	25,710	L	H	VH	Moderate-term on-the-job	Bus drivers, transit and intercity
104	-	-	-	-	-	-	Driver/sales workers and truck drivers
8	L	20,360	L	H	L	Short-term on-the-job	Driver/sales workers
59	VH	31,710	H	H	L	Moderate-term on-the-job	Truck drivers, heavy and tractor-trailer
37	H	22,350	L	H	L	Short-term on-the-job	Truck drivers, light or delivery services
6	VL	17,040	VL	H	H	Short-term on-the-job	Taxi drivers and chauffeurs
4	VL	19,360	L	VH	VL	Short-term on-the-job	All other motor vehicle operators[1]
5	-	44,450	-	-	-	-	**Rail transportation occupations**
2	VL	44,308	VH	VL	VL	Related work experience[3]	Locomotive engineers and firers[1]
1	VL	39,150	H	VL	VL	Related work experience[3]	Railroad brake, signal, and switch operators[1]
2	VL	39,220	H	VL	VL	Related work experience[3]	Railroad conductors and yardmasters[1]
0	VL	36,800	H	VL	VL	Related work experience[3]	Rail yard engineers, dinkey operators, and hostlers
0	VL	39,950	VH	VL	VL	Moderate-term on-the-job	All other rail transportation workers
3	-	44,990	-	-	-	-	**Water transportation occupations**
1	VL	28,120	H	VH	L	Short-term on-the-job	Sailors and marine oilers
1	VL	44,965	VH	H	VL	Related work experience[3]	Ship and boat captains and operators
0	VL	47,530	VH	VL	VL	Postsecondary vocational award	Ship engineers
0	VL	24,340	L	VH	L	Short-term on-the-job	All other water transportation workers[1]
14	-	-	-	-	-	-	**Related transportation occupations**
0	VL	32,420	H	VL	L	Short-term on-the-job	Bridge and lock tenders[1]
4	VL	14,880	VL	H	VH	Short-term on-the-job	Parking lot attendants
6	VL	15,280	VL	VH	H	Short-term on-the-job	Service station attendants
0	VL	30,830	H	VH	H	Short-term on-the-job	Traffic technicians[1]
1	VL	45,090	VH	L	VL	Related work experience[3]	Transportation inspectors
3	VL	26,610	H	VH	H	Short-term on-the-job	All other related transportation workers[1]
212	-	23,890	-	-	-	-	**Material moving occupations**
18	L	15,710	VL	VH	H	Short-term on-the-job	Cleaners of vehicles and equipment
3	VL	22,260	L	VH	VL	Short-term on-the-job	Conveyor operators and tenders
2	VL	33,050	H	H	VL	Moderate-term on-the-job	Crane and tower operators[1]
3	VL	31,070	H	H	VL	Moderate-term on-the-job	Excavating and loading machine and dragline operators[1]
0	VL	29,960	H	VH	VL	Moderate-term on-the-job	Hoist and winch operators[1]
16	L	24,410	L	H	VL	Short-term on-the-job	Industrial truck and tractor operators
99	VH	18,810	L	VH	H	Short-term on-the-job	Laborers and freight, stock, and material movers, hand[1]
6	VL	20,140	L	VH	L	Short-term on-the-job	**Machine feeders and offbearers**
49	H	15,660	VL	VH	H	Short-term on-the-job	Packers and packagers, hand[1]
1	-	-	-	-	-	-	Pumping station operators
0	VL	42,260	VH	L	VL	Moderate-term on-the-job	Gas compressor and gas pumping station operators
0	VL	35,700	H	VH	VL	Moderate-term on-the-job	Pump operators, except wellhead pumpers
0	VL	34,010	H	L	VL	Moderate-term on-the-job	Wellhead pumpers
7	VL	24,610	L	L	L	Short-term on-the-job	Refuse and recyclable material collectors[1]
1	VL	28,660	H	VH	VL	Moderate-term on-the-job	Tank car, truck, and ship loaders
6	VL	23,652	L	VH	VL	Short-term on-the-job	All other material moving workers[1]

[1] One or more Current Population Survey (CPS) proxy occupations are used to estimate CPS based data.
[2] Bachelor's degree or higher, plus work experience.
[3] Work experience in a related occupation.

NOTE: Rankings are based on employment in all detailed occupations in the National Employment Matrix. For details, see "Data presented" section of text. Codes for describing the ranked variables are: VH = Very high, H = High, L = Low, VL = Very low, and n. a. = data not available. A dash indicates data are not applicable.

Table 3. Employment for selected occupations not presented in the national employment matrix, 2000

(Numbers in thousands)

National employment matrix occupation	Occupation type	2000 employment
Medical scientists	Rollup	37
Epidemiologists	Current	3
Medical scientists, except epidemiologists	Current	34
Astronomers and physicists	Rollup	10
Astronomers	Current	1
Physicists	Current	9
Social scientists, other	Rollup	15
Anthropologists and archeologists	Current	5
Geographers	Current	1
Historians	Current	2
Political scientists	Current	6
Sociologists	Current	1
Postsecondary teachers	Rollup	1,344
Agricultural sciences teachers, postsecondary	Current	9
Anthropology and archeology teachers, postsecondary	Current	4
Architecture teachers, postsecondary	Current	5
Area, ethnic, and cultural studies teachers, postsecondary	Current	4
Art, drama, and music teachers, postsecondary	Current	60
Atmospheric, earth, marine, and space sciences teachers, postsecondary	Current	9
Biological science teachers, postsecondary	Current	36
Business teachers, postsecondary	Current	67
Chemistry teachers, postsecondary	Current	17
Communications teachers, postsecondary	Current	17
Computer science teachers, postsecondary	Current	30
Criminal justice and law enforcement teachers, postsecondary	Current	11
Economics teachers, postsecondary	Current	12
Education teachers, postsecondary	Current	41
Engineering teachers, postsecondary	Current	26
English language and literature teachers, postsecondary	Current	55
Environmental science teachers, postsecondary	Current	4
Foreign language and literature teachers, postsecondary	Current	19
Forestry and conservation science teachers, postsecondary	Current	1
Geography teachers, postsecondary	Current	4
Graduate teaching assistants	Current	164
Health specialties teachers, postsecondary	Current	93
History teachers, postsecondary	Current	17
Home economics teachers, postsecondary	Current	4
Law teachers, postsecondary	Current	11
Library science teachers, postsecondary	Current	4
Mathematical science teachers, postsecondary	Current	41
Nursing instructors and teachers, postsecondary	Current	38
Philosophy and religion teachers, postsecondary	Current	15
Physics teachers, postsecondary	Current	13
Political science teachers, postsecondary	Current	12
Psychology teachers, postsecondary	Current	26
Recreation and fitness studies teachers, postsecondary	Current	14
Social work teachers, postsecondary	Current	7
Sociology teachers, postsecondary	Current	15
Vocational education teachers, postsecondary	Current	125
All other postsecondary teachers	Current	313
Fire inspectors	Rollup	13
Fire inspectors and investigators	Current	12
Forest fire inspectors and prevention specialists	Current	1
Tour and travel guides	Rollup	44
Tour guides and escorts	Current	38
Travel guides	Current	6
All other installation, maintenance, and repair workers	Rollup	228
Commercial divers	Current	3
Fabric menders, except garment	Current	3
Refractory materials repairers, except brickmasons	Current	6
Signal and track switch repairers	Current	6
Installation, maintenance, and repair workers, all other	Current	210
Model makers and patternmakers, wood	Rollup	10
Model makers, wood	Current	5
Patternmakers, wood	Current	5
Ship and boat captains and operators	Rollup	25
Captains, mates, and pilots of water vessels	Current	22
Motorboat operators	Current	3

The data in table 2 have many potential uses. At times, users may want to know how a particular occupation—cashiers, except gaming, for example—compares with others. The "VH" (very high) rankings in table 2 for the increase in the number of jobs and for both categories of job openings point out that many jobs are available, certainly a favorable rating. The "VL" (very low) ranking for earnings and the "VH" (very high) ranking for unemployment, however, are unfavorable in comparison with other occupations, and these characteristics detract from the desirability of employment in the occupation. Table 2 also shows that cashiers, except gaming, require only short-term on-the-job training.

Some readers might wish to identify occupations with favorable characteristics that jobseekers can pursue through a specific type of training. For example, a student might be interested in a technical occupation, but does not care to obtain a 4-year college degree. In another instance, a planner might wish to ensure that training programs provided by junior colleges in the area are consistent with the needs of the national labor market. To obtain appropriate information, both the student and the planner could examine information on occupations for which the associate degree is the most significant source of education or training.

Although table 2 contains a great deal of information that is useful for career guidance, information about occupational comparisons should be used as an aid, not a sole source of information for making career choices. After using the table to identify occupations with favorable prospects, the reader should obtain additional information from other sources such as the *Occupational Outlook Handbook*, the *Occupational Outlook Quarterly*, and local sources, if available. Consideration should be given to individual aptitudes and preferences, and alternative sources of training available in the local area should be investigated. The appendix identifies sources of State and local area information.

An electronic version of table 2 is available on the Internet at:
ftp://ftp.bls.gov/pub/special.requests/ep/optddata/

Chapter III. Factors Affecting Occupational Employment, 2000-10

Occupational employment may change over time for several reasons. An occupation's employment could increase because of growing demand for goods and services produced by industries in which the employment is concentrated, for example. In addition, increases in an occupation's utilization in those industries could boost its overall employment. This chapter presents information about both categories of factors—those affecting industry employment, and those affecting occupational utilization within industries—that drive changes in occupational employment.

Industry employment

Many assumptions underlie the Bureau of Labor Statistics (BLS) projections of the aggregate economy and of industry output, productivity, and employment. Often, these assumptions bear specifically on macroeconomic factors, such as the aggregate unemployment rate, the expected time path of labor productivity, and expectations regarding the Federal budget surplus or deficit. Other assumptions deal with factors that affect industry-specific measures of economic activity.

Detailed industry employment projections are based largely on time series models, which, by their very nature, project future economic behavior based on a continuation of economic relationships that held in the past. For the most part, the determinants of industry employment are expressed in the structure of the model equations, and as adjustments imposed on the specific equations to ensure that the models are indeed making a smooth transition from actual historical data to projected future results. However, one of the most important steps associated with the preparation of the BLS projections is a detailed review of the results by analysts who studied recent economic trends in specific industries. In some cases, the results of the aggregate and industry models are modified because of the analysts' judgment that historical relationships need to be redefined in some manner. Table 4 presents historical and projected information about employment and output for detailed industries. Specific factors that underlie the determination of projected industry employment are presented in table 5 to allow the user of the projections to better understand the rationale for projected changes in industry employment and output.

Occupation utilization

BLS projections of wage and salary employment are developed within the framework of an industry-occupation matrix, which shows the occupational distribution in an industry. Historical data show that the occupational distribution of industries changes over time as the utilization of some occupations changes relative to that of other occupations.

Several factors may affect the changes in the utilization of workers in an occupation in particular industries, including changes in technology, business practices, the mix of goods and services produced, and the size of business establishments. BLS staff analyze each occupation in the matrix to identify the factors likely to cause an increase or decrease in its utilization within a particular industry in the future. The analyses incorporate judgments about new trends that may have not been influential in the past, such as the use of the Internet or e-commerce. Table 6 contains brief descriptions of the factors underlying projected changes in occupation utilization within industries between 2000 and 2010. Occupations appear in alphabetical order. Although all detailed occupations were analyzed, utilization for many occupations was projected not to change. These occupations are not included in table 6. Additionally, factors are discussed for only the most significant industries—those that have the highest share of an occupation's employment.

In developing the projections, BLS staff made hundreds of analytical decisions of this nature. To maintain consistency among analysts, guidelines for changing distributions were established as follows: small change = ± 10 percent; moderate change = ± 20 percent; large change = ± 35 percent; and very large change = ± 50 percent.

Table 4. Employment and output by industry, 1990, 2000, and projected 2010

Industry title and Standard Industrial Classification code	Employment							Output[1]				
	Thousands of jobs			Change		Average annual rate of growth (percent)		Billions of chained 1996 dollars			Average annual rate of growth (percent)	
	1990	2000	2010	1990-2000	2000-10	1990-2000	2000-10	1990	2000	2010	1990-2000	2000-10
Nonfarm wage and salary [2]	108,760	130,639	152,447	21,879	21,808	1.8	1.6	10672	15,128	20,761	3.6	3.2
Mining (10-14)	709	543	487	167	55	2.6	1.1	205	212	230	.3	.8
Metal mining (10)	58	41	35	17	6	3.5	1.5	11	13	16	1.2	2.6
Coal mining (12)	147	77	54	69	23	6.2	3.5	25	26	33	.4	2.4
Crude petroleum, natural gas, and gas liquids (131, 132)	196	129	100	67	29	4.1	2.5	133	122	130	.8	.6
Oil and gas field services (138)	198	182	188	17	7	.9	.4	22	31	28	3.3	1.0
Nonmetallic minerals, except fuels (14)	110	114	110	3	4	.3	.3	15	19	24	2.1	2.3
Construction (15, 16, 17)	5,120	6,698	7,522	1,578	825	2.7	1.2	730	910	1,182	2.2	2.6
Manufacturing (20-39)	19,077	18,469	19,047	607	577	.3	.3	3,022	4,601	6,279	4.3	3.2
Durable manufacturing (24, 25, 32-39)	11,109	11,138	11,780	29	642	.0	.6	1,481	2,785	4,136	6.5	4.0
Lumber and wood products (24)	733	832	905	99	73	1.3	.8	106	115	146	.8	2.4
Logging (241)	85	80	80	5	1	.6	.1	23	15	18	3.9	1.7
Sawmills and planing mills (242)	198	185	185	13	0	.7	.0	27	34	44	2.2	2.6
Millwork, plywood, and structural members (243)	262	335	361	74	25	2.5	.7	31	36	44	1.6	2.1
Wood containers and miscellaneous wood product (244, 249)	130	142	152	12	10	.9	.7	17	19	23	1.6	1.9
Wood buildings and mobile homes (245)	59	91	127	31	36	4.3	3.4	8	10	16	2.0	5.1
Furniture and fixtures (25)	506	558	630	52	72	1.0	1.2	50	84	111	5.3	2.9
Household furniture (251)	289	293	283	4	11	.1	.4	24	32	38	3.0	1.8
Partitions and fixtures (254)	78	91	116	12	25	1.5	2.5	7	14	16	6.8	1.2
Office and miscellaneous furniture and fixtures (252, 253, 259)	138	174	231	36	57	2.3	2.9	19	37	57	7.2	4.3
Glass and glass products (321-323)	160	148	140	12	8	.8	.6	19	25	34	2.9	2.9
Hydraulic cement (324)	18	18	16	0	2	.2	1.0	6	7	11	2.8	3.7
Stone, clay, and miscellaneous mineral products (325, 326, 328)	172	165	152	7	13	.4	.8	20	29	32	3.7	1.0
Concrete, gypsum, and plaster products (327)	206	248	263	42	14	1.9	.6	29	42	53	3.7	2.4
Primary metal industries (33)	756	698	650	58	47	.8	.7	152	200	239	2.8	1.8
Blast furnaces and basic steel products (331)	276	225	176	52	49	2.1	2.4	65	79	73	1.8	.7
Iron and steel foundries (332)	132	123	125	10	2	.7	.2	13	18	26	2.7	4.0
Primary nonferrous smelting and refining (333)	46	36	34	10	2	2.5	.4	14	18	21	2.5	1.3
All other primary metals (334, 339)	46	45	43	2	1	.3	.3	10	11	17	1.6	4.4
Nonferrous rolling and drawing (335)	172	176	173	4	3	.2	.2	42	60	81	3.7	3.1
Nonferrous foundries (336)	84	94	99	11	5	1.2	.5	7	14	19	6.6	2.9
Fabricated metal products (34)	1,419	1,537	1,661	118	124	.8	.8	176	273	387	4.5	3.6
Metal cans and shipping containers (341)	50	36	26	14	10	3.3	3.3	14	13	18	.5	3.7
Cutlery, handtools, and hardware (342)	131	121	110	11	11	.9	.9	16	21	30	2.5	3.6
Plumbing and nonelectric heating equipment (343)	60	60	55	0	5	.0	.8	7	11	12	4.6	.9
Fabricated structural metal products (344)	427	498	540	72	42	1.6	.8	49	76	102	4.5	2.9
Screw machine products, bolts, rivets, etc. (345)	96	107	123	11	1	1.1	1.4	9	26	42	10.6	5.0
Metal forgings and stampings (346)	225	255	254	30	1	1.3	.0	31	53	70	5.5	2.9
Metal coating, engraving, and allied services (347)	120	146	191	27	45	2.0	2.7	10	17	32	4.9	6.8
Ordinance and ammunition (348)	75	38	35	37	3	6.5	.9	8	6	7	3.3	2.1
Miscellaneous fabricated metal products (349)	237	277	327	40	51	1.6	1.7	32	51	74	4.9	3.7
Industrial machinery and equipment (35)	2,095	2,120	2,222	26	102	.1	.5	214	618	1,117	11.2	6.1
Engines and turbines (351)	89	85	83	4	2	.5	.2	19	30	42	4.6	3.6
Farm and garden machinery (352)	106	96	105	9	9	.9	.9	18	24	40	3.0	5.3
Construction and related machinery (353)	229	240	284	11	44	.5	1.7	33	53	78	4.9	3.9
Metal working machinery and equipment (354)	330	330	330	0	0	.0	.0	29	38	51	2.8	3.0
Special industry machinery (355)	159	172	158	13	14	.8	.8	23	44	40	6.5	.9
General industrial machinery and equipment (356)	247	251	260	4	9	.2	.3	34	41	55	2.0	2.9
Computer and office equipment (357)	438	361	350	76	11	1.9	.3	28	386	1,531	30.1	14.8
Refrigeration and service industry machinery (358)	177	212	242	35	30	1.8	1.3	29	47	65	5.1	3.2
Industrial machinery, nec (359)	320	373	410	53	37	1.5	1.0	26	36	72	3.5	7.0

See footnotes at end of table.

Industry title and Standard Industrial Classification code	Employment							Output[1]				
	Thousands of jobs			Change		Average annual rate of growth (percent)		Billions of chained 1996 dollars			Average annual rate of growth (percent)	
	1990	2000	2010	1990-2000	2000-10	1990-2000	2000-10	1990	2000	2010	1990-2000	2000-10
Electronic and other electronic equipment (36)	1,674	1,719	1,820	45	102	.3	.6	154	587	984	14.3	5.3
Electric distribution equipment (361)	97	85	77	12	8	1.3	1.0	11	15	19	3.3	2.0
Electrical industrial apparatus (362)	169	150	127	19	23	1.2	1.7	20	31	51	4.2	5.2
Household appliances (363)	124	116	97	8	19	.7	1.8	17	24	26	3.9	.5
Electric lighting and wiring equipment (364)	189	183	194	5	11	.3	.6	21	32	42	4.4	2.6
Household audio and video equipment (365)	85	80	77	5	3	.6	.3	9	12	18	2.5	4.0
Communication equipment (366)	264	276	290	13	14	.5	.5	41	107	175	10.2	5.0
Electronic components and accessories (367)	582	682	800	100	118	1.6	1.6	29	386	760	29.3	7.0
Miscellaneous electrical equipment (369)	165	146	158	19	13	1.2	.8	22	32	47	4.0	3.8
Transportation equipment (37)	1,989	1,849	2,063	140	214	.7	1.1	411	613	881	4.1	3.7
Motor vehicles and equipment (371)	812	1,013	1,100	201	87	2.2	.8	236	433	665	6.3	4.4
Aerospace (372, 376)	897	551	655	346	104	4.8	1.7	142	136	162	.4	1.7
Ship and boat building and repairing (373)	188	166	170	22	4	1.2	.2	20	18	17	1.0	.4
Railroad equipment (374)	33	36	38	3	2	.8	.7	5	10	16	5.9	5.0
Miscellaneous transportation equipment (375, 379)	59	83	99	24	16	3.5	1.8	8	16	22	7.7	3.1
Instruments and related products (38)	1,006	853	869	153	17	1.6	.2	130	177	238	3.2	3.0
Search and navigation equipment (381)	284	154	140	130	14	5.9	1.0	40	37	56	.6	4.2
Measuring and controlling devices (382)	323	302	300	21	2	.7	.1	33	46	74	3.2	4.9
Medical equipment, instruments, and supplies (384)	246	288	338	42	50	1.6	1.6	33	63	87	6.5	3.4
Ophthalmic goods (385)	43	33	34	10	1	2.5	.2	2	4	5	7.3	2.1
Photographic equipment and supplies (386)	100	70	55	29	15	3.4	2.4	20	27	15	3.2	5.6
Watches, clocks, and parts (387)	11	5	2	6	3	7.0	7.2	2	1	0	8.1	14.7
Miscellaneous manufacturing industries (39)	375	394	390	19	4	.5	.1	41	52	79	2.5	4.3
Jewelry, silverware, and plated ware (391)	52	49	47	3	2	.6	.4	6	8	9	2.6	1.3
Toys and sporting goods (394)	104	104	109	0	5	.0	.5	11	16	36	3.6	8.4
Manufactured products, nec (393, 395, 396, 3999)	220	242	234	22	8	1.0	.3	23	28	34	1.9	2.1
Nondurable manufacturing (20-23, 26-31)	7,968	7,331	7,267	637	64	.8	.1	1,553	1,835	2,220	1.7	1.9
Food and kindred products (20)	1,661	1,684	1,634	23	50	.1	.3	411	499	542	2.0	.8
Meat products (201)	422	504	542	82	38	1.8	.7	87	113	140	2.7	2.1
Dairy products (202)	155	146	121	10	24	.6	1.8	53	59	67	1.1	1.2
Preserved fruits and vegetables (203)	247	220	195	27	25	1.2	1.2	49	57	45	1.6	2.3
Grain mill products, fats and oils (204, 207)	159	152	150	7	2	.5	.1	70	87	96	2.2	1.0
Bakery products (205)	213	204	191	9	13	.4	.7	29	32	35	1.0	1.0
Sugar and confectionery products (206)	99	92	85	7	7	.7	.8	24	28	32	1.7	1.3
Beverages (208)	184	187	165	3	22	.2	1.3	66	85	89	2.6	.4
Miscellaneous foods and kindred products (209)	182	180	185	2	5	.1	.3	35	39	42	1.0	.7
Tobacco products (21)	49	34	29	15	5	3.6	1.6	36	36	39	.2	.8
Textile mill products (22)	692	529	500	163	29	2.7	.6	69	78	86	1.3	1.0
Weaving, finishing, yarn, and thread mills (221-224, 226, 228)	374	284	250	90	34	2.7	1.3	34	39	41	1.4	.4
Knitting mills (225)	205	126	120	80	6	4.8	.5	15	15	18	.0	1.7
Carpets and rugs (227)	61	66	73	5	7	.7	1.1	11	14	15	1.6	1.2
Miscellaneous textile goods (229)	51	54	57	2	3	.5	.6	8	10	12	2.4	2.0
Apparel and other textile products (23)	1,036	633	530	403	103	4.8	1.8	65	68	87	.3	2.6
Apparel (231-238)	832	418	315	414	103	6.7	2.8	47	44	51	.6	1.3
Miscellaneous fabricated textile products (239)	204	215	215	11	0	.5	.0	18	23	36	2.6	4.7
Paper and allied products (26)	697	657	626	40	31	.6	.5	149	168	195	1.2	1.5
Pulp, paper, and paperboard mills (261-263)	246	199	176	48	23	2.1	1.2	64	59	65	.8	.9
Paperboard containers and boxes (265)	209	218	210	9	8	.4	.4	36	45	50	2.2	1.2
Converted paper products except containers (267)	241	240	240	1	0	.1	.0	49	64	79	2.7	2.2
Printing and publishing (27)	1,570	1,547	1,545	22	3	.1	.0	195	214	240	1.0	1.1
Newspapers (271)	474	442	432	33	10	.7	.2	48	44	43	1.0	.2
Periodicals (272)	129	149	165	20	16	1.5	1.0	25	38	44	4.0	1.5
Books (273)	121	126	136	5	10	.4	.7	24	23	31	.5	2.9
Miscellaneous publishing (274)	82	95	105	13	10	1.5	1.0	11	18	27	4.5	4.3

See footnotes at end of table.

60

Industry title and Standard Industrial Classification code	Employment							Output[1]				
	Thousands of jobs			Change		Average annual rate of growth (percent)		Billions of chained 1996 dollars			Average annual rate of growth (percent)	
	1990	2000	2010	1990-2000	2000-10	1990-2000	2000-10	1990	2000	2010	1990-2000	2000-10
Commercial printing and business forms (275, 276)	602	603	585	1	18	.0	.3	71	76	79	.6	.4
Greeting cards (277)	25	25	27	0	1	.0	.6	4	4	4	.1	.3
Blankbooks and bookbinding (278)	72	60	55	13	4	1.9	.8	6	6	7	1.5	.3
Service industries for the printing trade (279)	64	47	40	16	7	2.9	1.6	5	5	5	.1	.9
Chemicals and allied products (28)	1,086	1,038	1,081	48	43	.5	.4	337	403	560	1.8	3.3
Industrial chemicals (281, 286)	293	218	190	75	28	2.9	1.4	116	100	94	1.4	.7
Plastics materials and synthetics (282)	180	154	130	26	24	1.5	1.7	52	69	101	2.8	4.0
Drugs (283)	237	315	390	78	75	2.9	2.2	63	99	171	4.7	5.6
Soap, cleaners, and toilet goods (284)	159	155	164	4	9	.3	.6	47	63	89	2.9	3.6
Paints and allied products (285)	61	52	56	9	4	1.7	.7	16	20	28	1.8	3.8
Agricultural chemicals (287)	56	51	56	5	5	.9	.9	22	25	36	1.2	3.7
Miscellaneous chemical products (289)	100	93	95	7	2	.7	.2	23	27	38	1.7	3.5
Petroleum and coal products (29)	157	128	113	30	15	2.1	1.2	171	189	208	1.0	.9
Petroleum refining (291)	118	85	65	33	20	3.3	2.6	157	169	181	.7	.7
Miscellaneous petroleum and coal products (295, 299)	40	43	48	3	5	.8	1.0	14	21	27	3.6	2.5
Rubber and miscellaneous plastics products (30)	888	1,011	1,166	123	156	1.3	1.4	110	170	253	4.5	4.0
Tires and inner tubes (301)	84	79	82	5	2	.6	.3	12	15	23	2.5	4.4
Rubber products, plastics hose and footwear (302, 5, 6)	177	187	184	10	2	.6	.1	18	26	34	3.4	2.8
Miscellaneous plastics products, nec (308)	626	744	900	118	156	1.7	1.9	79	129	196	5.0	4.2
Leather and leather products (31)	133	72	44	62	27	6.0	4.7	10	10	5	.2	6.3
Footwear, except rubber and plastics (313, 4)	80	30	14	50	16	9.3	7.2	5	3	2	6.3	1.5
Luggage, handbags, and leather products, nec (311, 315-317, 3)	53	41	30	12	11	2.5	3.2	6	8	4	3.2	6.4
Transportation, communications, and utilities (40-42, 44-49)	5,776	7,019	8,274	1,243	1,255	2.0	1.7	931	1,278	1,962	3.2	4.4
Transportation (40-42, 44-47)	3,510	4,529	5,466	1,019	937	2.6	1.9	387	531	798	3.2	4.2
Railroad transportation (40)	279	236	175	43	60	1.7	2.9	35	37	48	.5	2.7
Local and interurban passenger transit (41)	338	476	624	138	148	3.5	2.7	21	24	31	1.4	2.5
Trucking and warehousing (42)	1,395	1,856	2,262	460	407	2.9	2.0	163	255	394	4.6	4.4
Trucking and courier services, except air (421-423)	1,278	1,649	1,962	371	313	2.6	1.8	154	237	359	4.4	4.2
Warehousing and storage (422)	117	206	300	89	94	5.8	3.8	10	17	35	6.2	7.2
Water transportation (44)	177	196	208	19	13	1.0	.6	37	40	50	.9	2.3
Air transportation (45)	968	1,281	1,600	314	319	2.8	2.2	96	125	192	2.6	4.4
Pipelines, except natural gas (46)	19	14	11	5	2	3.0	1.7	8	7	9	2.2	3.3
Transportation services (47)	336	471	585	135	114	3.4	2.2	26	43	73	5.1	5.5
Passenger transportation arrangement (472)	188	219	235	30	17	1.5	.7	10	19	34	6.7	6.0
Miscellaneous transportation services (473-474, 478)	148	253	350	105	97	5.5	3.3	16	24	40	4.0	5.2
Communications (48)	1,309	1,639	1,916	330	277	2.3	1.6	245	419	750	5.5	6.0
Telephone, telegraph, and other communications (481-482, 489)	950	1,168	1,310	218	143	2.1	1.2	185	341	638	6.3	6.5
Cable and pay television services (484)	126	216	325	90	109	5.5	4.2	26	35	60	2.8	5.7
Radio and televsion broadcasting (483)	234	255	280	22	25	.9	.9	35	45	59	2.6	2.7
Utilities (49)	957	851	893	106	42	1.2	.5	299	326	417	.9	2.5
Electric utilities (491)	454	357	324	98	33	2.4	1.0	176	212	275	1.9	2.6
Gas utilities (492)	165	128	120	37	8	2.5	.6	66	49	63	3.0	2.6
Combined utilities (493)	193	152	138	41	14	2.4	1.0	32	38	46	1.5	2.1
Water and sanitation (494-497)	145	214	310	69	96	4.0	3.8	24	29	34	1.8	1.8
Wholesale trade (50, 51)	6,173	7,024	7,800	851	776	1.3	1.1	608	920	1,410	4.2	4.4
Retail trade (52-59)	19,601	23,307	26,400	3,706	3,093	1.7	1.3	897	1,222	1,628	3.1	2.9
Retail trade, excluding eating and drinking places (52-57, 59)	13,092	15,194	16,800	2,102	1,606	1.5	1.0	652	926	1,237	3.6	2.9
Eating and drinking places (58)	6,509	8,114	9,600	1,605	1,486	2.2	1.7	245	298	393	2.0	2.8

See footnotes at end of table.

Industry title and Standard Industrial Classification code	Employment							Output[1]				
	Thousands of jobs			Change		Average annual rate of growth (percent)		Billions of chained 1996 dollars			Average annual rate of growth (percent)	
	1990	2000	2010	1990-2000	2000-10	1990-2000	2000-10	1990	2000	2010	1990-2000	2000-10
Finance, insurance and real estate (60-67)	6,709	7,560	8,247	851	687	1.2	.9	1,198	1,806	2,429	4.2	3.0
Depository institutions (60)	2,251	2,029	1,999	221	31	1.0	.2	266	446	596	5.3	2.9
Nondepository institutions, holding and investment offices (61, 67)	593	932	1,075	339	143	4.6	1.4	70	122	152	5.8	2.2
Security and commodity brokers (62)	424	748	900	324	152	5.8	1.9	57	292	540	17.7	6.4
Insurance carriers (63)	1,462	1,589	1,632	127	43	.8	.3	211	228	259	.8	1.3
Insurance agents, brokers, and service (64)	663	757	865	93	109	1.3	1.3	68	81	103	1.8	2.4
Real estate (65)	1,315	1,504	1,776	189	272	1.4	1.7	535	653	822	2.0	2.3
Royalties	-	-	-	-	-	-	-	55	96	191	5.8	7.1
Owner-occupied dwellings	-	-	-	-	-	-	-	493	631	943	2.5	4.1
Services (70-87, 89)[2]	27,291	39,340	52,233	12,049	12,893	3.7	2.9	2,057	3,032	4,378	4.0	3.7
Hotels (701)	1,578	1,845	2,100	267	255	1.6	1.3	85	108	136	2.5	2.3
Other lodging places (702-704)	53	67	67	14	0	2.3	.0	5	7	10	2.8	4.7
Personal services (72)	1,104	1,251	1,354	147	103	1.3	.8	76	101	147	2.9	3.8
Laundry, cleaning, and shoe repair (721, 725)	433	451	470	18	19	.4	.4	22	25	28	1.6	.8
Personal services, nec (722, 729)	200	266	287	66	21	2.9	.8	26	40	64	4.6	4.9
Beauty and barber shops (723-724)	389	433	490	44	57	1.1	1.2	20	26	40	2.6	4.5
Funeral service and crematories (726)	83	101	107	18	6	2.0	.6	9	10	14	1.0	4.1
Business services (73)	5,139	9,858	14,923	4,719	5,064	6.7	4.2	342	713	1,278	7.6	6.0
Advertising (731)	235	302	400	68	98	2.6	2.9	27	47	67	5.8	3.5
Service to buildings (734)	807	994	1,120	188	126	2.1	1.2	31	50	71	5.0	3.6
Miscellaneous equipment rental and leasing (735)	208	279	397	71	118	3.0	3.6	28	39	60	3.2	4.4
Personnel supply services (736)	1,535	3,887	5,800	2,353	1,913	9.7	4.1	38	101	167	10.2	5.1
Computer and data processing services (737)	772	2,095	3,900	1,323	1,805	10.5	6.4	99	278	601	10.8	8.0
Miscellaneous business services (732-733, 738)	1,584	2,301	3,305	717	1,004	3.8	3.7	119	198	313	5.2	4.7
Auto repair, services, and garages (75)	914	1,248	1,527	335	278	3.2	2.0	104	166	286	4.8	5.6
Automotive rentals, without drivers (751)	173	225	265	52	41	2.7	1.7	17	63	151	14.0	9.1
Automobile parking, repair, and services (752-754)	741	1,024	1,262	283	238	3.3	2.1	87	103	136	1.7	2.8
Miscellaneous repair shops (76)	374	366	405	9	39	.2	1.0	44	51	62	1.5	2.1
Electrical repair shops (762)	112	104	103	8	1	.7	.1	15	15	14	.3	.2
Watch, jewelry, and furniture repair (763, 764)	30	29	27	0	2	.1	.8	2	3	5	3.5	3.2
Miscellaneous repair shops and related services (769)	233	233	275	1	42	.0	1.7	26	33	43	2.3	2.8
Motion pictures (78)	408	594	672	186	78	3.8	1.2	45	77	86	5.7	1.1
Motion pictures and video tape distribution (781-783)	274	426	499	152	73	4.5	1.6	40	69	77	5.6	1.1
Video tape rental (784)	134	168	173	34	5	2.3	.3	5	9	9	5.8	.6
Amusement and recreation services (79)	1,076	1,728	2,325	652	597	4.9	3.0	75	137	212	6.2	4.4
Producers, orchestras, and entertainers (792)	136	181	225	45	44	2.9	2.2	18	28	35	4.6	2.3
Bowling centers (793)	91	81	70	10	11	1.2	1.5	4	3	3	2.4	2.0
Commercial sports (794)	101	153	180	52	28	4.2	1.7	13	15	19	1.4	1.9
Amusement and recreation services, nec (791, 9)	748	1,314	1,850	566	536	5.8	3.5	40	91	156	8.4	5.6
Health services (80)	7,814	10,095	12,934	2,281	2,839	2.6	2.5	595	762	882	2.5	1.5
Offices of health practitioners (801-804)	2,166	3,099	4,344	933	1,245	3.6	3.4	254	317	374	2.3	1.7
Nursing and personal care facilities (805)	1,415	1,796	2,190	381	394	2.4	2.0	55	69	85	2.4	2.1
Hospitals (806)	3,549	3,990	4,500	442	510	1.2	1.2	236	292	315	2.1	.8
Health services, nec (807-809)	685	1,210	1,900	525	690	5.9	4.6	52	84	108	5.0	2.5
Legal services (81)	908	1,010	1,350	102	340	1.1	2.9	134	143	195	.7	3.2
Educational services (82)	1,661	2,325	2,852	664	527	3.4	2.1	91	113	142	2.1	2.3
Social services (83)	1,734	2,903	4,128	1,169	1,225	5.3	3.6	76	103	171	3.1	5.2
Individual and miscellaneous social services (832, 839)	634	1,005	1,300	372	295	4.7	2.6	31	47	77	4.1	5.1
Job training and related services (833)	248	380	500	131	120	4.3	2.8	9	9	14	.2	4.8
Child day care services (835)	391	712	1,010	321	298	6.2	3.6	20	24	40	2.0	5.2
Residential care (836)	461	806	1,318	345	512	5.7	5.0	16	24	41	4.2	5.5
Museums, botanical and zoological gardens (84)	66	106	135	40	29	4.9	2.4	3	6	9	5.0	4.6
Membership organizations (86)	1,945	2,475	2,734	529	259	2.4	1.0	79	96	122	2.0	2.4

See footnotes at end of table.

Industry title and Standard Industrial Classification code	Employment							Output[1]				
	Thousands of jobs			Change		Average annual rate of growth (percent)		Billions of chained 1996 dollars			Average annual rate of growth (percent)	
	1990	2000	2010	1990-2000	2000-10	1990-2000	2000-10	1990	2000	2010	1990-2000	2000-10
Engineering, management, and other services (87, 89)	2,516	3,469	4,729	953	1,260	3.3	3.1	290	434	640	4.1	3.9
Engineering and architectural services (871)	786	1,017	1,330	231	313	2.6	2.7	103	133	211	2.6	4.7
Research and testing services (873)	549	642	886	94	244	1.6	3.3	39	67	108	5.6	4.9
Management and public relations (874)	610	1,090	1,550	479	460	6.0	3.6	79	147	195	6.5	2.8
Accounting, auditing, and other services (872, 89)	571	720	963	149	243	2.3	3.0	70	87	127	2.3	3.8
Government	18,304	20,680	22,436	2,376	1,757	1.2	.8	1,043	1,162	1,287	1.1	1.0
Federal Government	3,085	2,777	2,622	308	154	1.0	.6	389	353	360	1.0	.2
Federal enterprises	1,026	975	952	51	23	.5	.2	69	85	94	2.1	.9
U.S. Postal Service	819	860	850	41	10	.5	.1	55	65	74	1.7	1.4
Federal electric utilities	31	27	22	4	5	1.3	2.2	6	11	10	5.8	1.4
Federal Government enterprises, nec	177	88	80	89	8	6.7	.9	9	10	10	.9	.5
Federal general government	2,059	1,802	1,671	257	131	1.3	.8	256	200	190	2.4	.5
Federal Government capital services	-	-	-	-	-	-	-	65	68	78	.5	1.3
State and local government	15,219	17,903	19,814	2,684	1,911	1.6	1.0	655	808	928	2.1	1.4
State and local enterprises	913	869	918	44	49	.5	.5	103	139	189	3.1	3.2
Local government passenger transit	207	223	225	16	2	.7	.1	6	7	8	1.9	.6
State and local electric utilities	82	89	95	7	6	.8	.7	19	24	28	2.4	1.3
State and local government enterprises, nec	624	557	598	67	41	1.1	.7	77	107	154	3.3	3.7
State and local general government	14,306	17,034	18,896	2,728	1,862	1.8	1.0	552	670	738	2.0	1.0
State and local government hospitals	1,072	970	948	102	22	1.0	.2	42	45	51	.8	1.2
State and local government education	7,771	9,472	10,548	1,700	1,076	2.0	1.1	265	303	302	1.3	.0
State and local general government, nec	5,462	6,592	7,400	1,130	808	1.9	1.2	199	227	255	1.3	1.2
State and local government capital services	-	-	-	-	-	-	-	46	96	135	7.5	3.5
Agriculture (01, 02, 07, 08, 09)[3]	3,340	3,526	3,849	186	323	.5	.9	257	334	405	2.6	1.9
Agricultural production (01, 02)	2,174	1,979	1,824	196	155	.9	.8	210	260	315	2.2	1.9
Agricultural services (7)	1,166	1,548	2,025	382	477	2.9	2.7	36	58	70	4.8	1.9
Veterinary services (74)	143	240	336	97	96	5.3	3.4	8	16	20	6.7	2.5
Landscape and horticultural services (78)	576	808	1,093	233	285	3.5	3.1	18	27	36	4.4	2.7
Agricultural services, nec (071, 072, 075, 076)	339	403	501	63	99	1.7	2.2	10	15	14	3.9	.6
Forestry, fishing, hunting, and trapping (08, 09)	108	97	95	11	2	1.1	.2	12	15	19	2.5	2.3
Private household wage and salary (88)	1,014	890	664	124	226	1.3	2.9	13	15	13	1.5	1.0
Nonagricultural self-employed and unpaid family [4,5]	8,921	8,731	9,062	190	331	.2	.4	-	-	-	-	-
Secondary wage and salary jobs in agriculture (except agricultural services); forestry, fishing, hunting, and trapping; private households	205	155	150	50	5	2.8	.3	-	-	-	-	-
Secondary job as a self-employed or unpaid family worker[6]	2,084	1,652	1,582	432	70	2.3	.0	-	-	-	-	-
Total[7,8]	124,324	145,594	167,754	21,269	22,160	1.6	1.4	11472	16,180	22,286	3.5	3.3

[1] Excludes SIC 074,5,8 (agricultural services) and 99 (nonclassifiable establishments). The data therefore are not exactly comparable with data published in Employment and Earnings.

[2] Excludes government wage and salary workers, and includes private sector for SIC 08,09 (forestry, fishing, hunting, and trapping; and private households).

[3] Excludes SIC 08,09 (forestry, fishing, hunting, and trapping).

[4] Comparable estimate of output growth is not available.

[5] Workers who hold a secondary wage and salary job in agriculture (except agricultural services); forestry, fishing, hunting, and trapping; and private households.

[6] Wage and salary workers who hold a secondary wage and salary job as a self-employed or unpaid family worker.

[7] Wage and Salary data are from the Current Employment Statistics (payroll) survey, which counts jobs, whereas self-employed, unpaid family workers, agricultural, forestry, fishing, hunting, and trapping, and private household data are from the Current Population Survey (household survey), which counts workers.

[8] Subcategories do not necessarily add to higher categories as a byproduct of chain-weighting.

NOTE: Dash indicates data not available. n.e.c. = not elsewhere classified.

Source: Historical output data are from the Bureau of Economic Analysis, U.S. Department of Commerce.

Table 5. Factors affecting industry output and employment, 2000-10

SIC code	Industry title	Factors affecting output and employment
01, 02	Agricultural production	Output will increase due to a growing population with rising disposable income consuming more agricultural products. The industry is being affected by increasing concentration of producers in some agricultural sectors, and downward pressure on prices because of increased competition in global markets. Productivity, spurred by improved farm equipment, will continue to increase. Employment, especially of self-employed farmers, will continue to decline.
074	Veterinary services	Output is increasing as a result of demand for preventative medical services for pets, and an increase in the number of households owning pets. Employment growth will continue.
078	Landscape and horticultural services	Output will increase due to projected construction growth and increasing reliance of homeowners on these services. As interest rates decline, home sales should increase which would propel demand. Declining productivity growth is expected to result in employment growth.
071, 072 075, 076	Agricultural services, n.e.c.	Initiatives such as the Freedom to Farm Act and a rising concentration in agricultural sectors will continue to lead to lower farm income, depressing output for these agricultural services. Falling productivity will lead to increasing employment.
08, 09	Forestry, fishing, hunting, and trapping	Output in this industry will increase because of demand for its products as inputs to the logging and food processing industries. Productivity will increase causing total employment to continue to decrease. Self-employed workers will decline while wage and salary employment will increase slightly.
10	Metal mining	Output will increase as demand for ore as an input to the primary nonferrous metals, steel, industrial chemicals, and nonresidential construction industries continues to grow. Employment in this industry will decline due to advances in productivity through improved mine technology and automation.
12	Coal mining	Coal is currently used to generate about half of the country's electricity and as an input to producing primary steel products. Output will increase primarily on the strength of expected increases in demand for electricity. As a result of continuing strong regulation of sulfur emissions, more low-sulfur Western coal is expected to be mined. Western coal is far easier to extract as it is generally located closer to the surface, resulting in lower demand for labor input. Additional employment declines are expected due to advances in productivity through improved mine technology and automation.
131, 132	Crude petroleum, natural gas, and gas liquids	Output is entirely consumed as an input to the petroleum refining and gas utilities industries. Output will increase as a result of growth in these industries. Productivity will increase as a result of continued technological advances in drilling and exploration techniques. Employment will decline as productivity increases and American companies shift to foreign exploration and production. The oil and gas industry is experiencing mergers that eliminate redundant positions and decrease employment. Outsourcing to specialized firms for key operations such as exploration results in employees moving from this sector to oil and gas field services.
138	Oil and gas field services	This industry is affected by the global market price for oil and gas. Output is primarily measured as the value of new oil and gas well exploration and drilling and is mostly consumed as an investment purchase. Output is expected to decline slightly. A productivity decline, however, will offset any employment decline associated with the decline in output resulting in a slight employment increase.
14	Nonmetallic minerals, except fuels	This sector is sensitive to economic cycles. Output will increase primarily because of intermediate demand as an input to the concrete products, residential construction, and agricultural chemicals industries. Employment is expected to decline due to increased productivity and mergers that lead to layoffs. Imports will decrease employment in chemicals and fertilizers.

Table 5. Factors affecting industry output and employment, 2000-10—Continued

SIC code	Industry title	Factors affecting output and employment
15, 16, 17	Construction	The industry is primarily engaged in construction of residential and nonresidential buildings and infrastructure such as highways, bridges, sewers, and railroads. All are expected to be growth areas so output will increase. Technology trends will favor productivity increases, but employment is expected to increase as well.
241	Logging	Output growth results from projected growth for timber as an input to pulp and paper processing, and to the veneer and plywood sector that supplies materials used in providing an expanding population's new housing needs. Productivity gains due to increased mechanization should result in low employment growth.
242	Sawmills and planing mills	Output is purchased for new single-unit housing construction, other wood processing industries, and the maintenance and repair sector. A growing population and increasing numbers of new housing starts will result in output growth. Increasing imports of foreign timber, however, will limit output growth. Productivity will increase, and as a result employment is expected to remain unchanged.
243	Millwork, plywood, and structural members	Output is primarily consumed as an input to the residential construction and wood processing industries. These will grow due to demand from an expanding population and increasing new housing starts. Rising productivity and imports will result in slow employment growth.
324	Hydraulic cement	Output will increase because construction buys virtually all of the intermediate output, and construction will increase. There have been substantial increases in productivity as a result of the industry automating production and the concentration of new capital investment in energy efficient plants that use the dry process of cement manufacture. Imports will continue to increase as well. Employment has declined dramatically during the past 20 years and is expected to do so in the future.
325, 326 328, 329	Stone, clay, and miscellaneous mineral products	Output continues to increase as a result of demand by many manufacturing industries and as an input to the construction industry. Productivity and imports likewise continue to increase, contributing to a decline in employment.
327	Concrete, gypsum, and plaster products	The products are used by virtually every sector of the growing construction industry causing output to increase. Productivity will continue to increase, but at a slower rate; employment will continue to grow as it has since the early 1990s.
331	Blast furnaces and basic steel products	Output is overwhelmingly purchased as an intermediate input to other industries such as automotive stampings and industrial machinery. Demand is expected to grow for this industry's product. However, increasing imports and gains in productivity through expansion of minimills will result in a continuing decrease in employment.
332	Iron and steel foundries	Output will grow from continued intermediate demand in the rail, motor vehicles, and heavy construction industries, as well as from overall growth in the economy, but will be limited as motor vehicle manufacturers use other materials, such as light weight alloys and plastics, in production. Productivity continues to make gains due to improved technology, and as a result employment will increase only slightly.
333	Primary nonferrous smelting and refining	Output growth is expected as a result of intermediate demand in the jewelry, silverware, and lighter weight copper and aluminum industrial products industries. Productivity will increase, though at a slower rate than previously, and employment is expected to decline as a result.
334, 339	All other primary metals	Output is primarily sold as an intermediate commodity to metalworking machinery, motor vehicle parts, and other manufacturing industries. Output will increase as a result of increased demand from the motor vehicles industries. Employment is expected to decline due to increased productivity.
341	Metal cans and shipping containers	Output is consumed as an intermediate input to the beverage, food, soap, paint, and petroleum product industries, and will increase as these industries grow; although a trend towards plastic bottles will cut production of metal cans. Shipping containers will be in

Table 5. Factors affecting industry output and employment, 2000-10—Continued

SIC code	Industry title	Factors affecting output and employment
		demand for shipping an increasing number of goods. Employment will drop due to productivity increases.
342	Cutlery, handtools, and hardware	Products are purchased by individuals, and as inputs to a variety of industries (principally the motor vehicle industry), which will cause output to increase. Strong imports, and increasing automation in metal cutting and molding machine industries that increases productivity, will reduce employment.
343	Plumbing and nonelectric heating equipment	Output growth will result from demand for nonelectric heating equipment, which is primarily an input to the construction industry. The increase in demand for electric heating has dampened output growth. Productivity will increase and employment will decline as a result.
344	Fabricated structural metal products	Output is consumed mainly as an input to construction and as an investment purchase by electric utilities, and will grow as these industries expand. Productivity increases will continue and somewhat dampen the growth in employment.
348	Ordnance and ammunition	Output will increase as the result of purchases by government for military and law enforcement use, and by private individuals. Productivity has increased markedly as new manufacturing facilities have been built and is expected to continue to increase. Employment will decline as a result of increasing productivity and mergers.
349	Miscellaneous fabricated metal products	Output is purchased mainly by the construction, utilities, and oil and gas extraction industries. Demand for many of these fabricated products will increase as these industries expand. Productivity growth and vigorous imports will limit the rate of employment increase.
351	Engines and turbines	Output will rise as a result of increasing exports, and as investment by the defense and electric power plant industries grows. Increased productivity will lead to a decrease in employment.
352	Farm and garden machinery and equipment	Output is primarily consumed as investment from the agricultural and real estate industries, and will increase as a result of growth in most of these industries. Productivity will increase as the industry moves toward smart agriculture that relies on very sophisticated and technologically-advanced equipment. Employment will continue to increase slowly.
353	Construction and related machinery	Output is primarily purchased as investment by the construction, petroleum, coal mining, and various manufacturing industries and will increase as the majority of these industries grow. This is a cyclical industry that is affected by housing starts and consumer confidence. Increasing intermediate demand, such as that arising from expenditures in search of new energy supplies, will increase employment.
354	Metalworking machinery and equipment	Output is consumed as investment by the motor vehicle industry and as an intermediate input for replacement parts, and will increase as the industries grow. Rising productivity will occur through new investment in computer-controlled equipment, and industrial consolidation. Employment will be unchanged as imports and productivity offset output growth.
355	Special industry machinery	Output will fall as a result of demand for investment in special industry machinery such as food processing machinery being met largely by imports. Employment will fall due to the continuing consolidation of many of the small and medium-sized shops that comprise this industry.
356	General industrial machinery and equipment	Output gains will result from increasing investment and intermediate input purchases of automated and flexible general industrial machinery by many industries. Output growth will be accompanied by productivity increases caused by growing automation, and mergers among the small shops that comprise this industry. Employment will increase slowly due to a high level of imports.

Table 5. Factors affecting industry output and employment, 2000-10—Continued

SIC code	Industry title	Factors affecting output and employment
357	Computer and office equipment	Output will grow faster than in most other industries, driven by ever more consumers and businesses conducting commerce using computers and the Internet. Productivity, driven by newer and more powerful microchips, will rise even faster. There will be a slight decline in employment, however, since imports are large and growing even faster than output and productivity.
358	Refrigeration and service industry machinery	Output will increase as capital purchases by retail and eating and drinking establishments increase with industry growth. Productivity increases that lag those in output growth will result in employment growth.
359	Industrial machinery, n.e.c.	Output is expected to increase due to growth in demand by the aircraft, motor vehicle, and other manufacturing industries. Rising productivity will result as investment in affordable, flexible computer-controlled technology increases. Employment growth will continue but will be moderated by productivity increases.
361	Electric distribution equipment	Increasing intermediate demand for communications and telephone apparatus, computers, and semiconductors will increase output. Productivity will increase, though at lower levels than previously. Employment will increase slowly because of productivity improvements.
362	Electrical industrial apparatus	Industry output will continue to increase with the demand for electricity. However, employment will decline due to gains in productivity.
363	Household appliances	The significance of U.S.-based firms will diminish even as demand for major home appliances rises. Relatively slow growth in output is expected. Employment will decline because of the large penetration of imports from Japan and other Asian countries.
364	Electric lighting and wiring equipment	Demand is expected to cause output to increase. However, increased productivity is expected to cause employment declines.
365	Household audio and video equipment	Output will increase as consumers continue to demand the latest technologies for their entertainment. Productivity also will increase as more efficient technology is applied to the production process. Employment will decrease as a result.
366	Communication equipment	Broadband will be a significant factor in the next few years as growing numbers of Internet users demand higher speeds and greater connectivity to take advantage of various Internet applications. Output will increase as firms continue to make major investments in technology through the purchasing of communications equipment. Popular applications (e-mail, Internet, messaging) will be increasingly capable of being run on wireless handheld devices. Employment growth will result.
367	Electronic components and accessories	Output will grow as the market for these products remains strong. Electronic components and accessories are needed in cars, computers, cell phones, and cable modems, all of whose markets are expected to expand in the next decade. Demand for these parts is being met largely by U.S. firms that are extremely competitive when very sophisticated and intricate production processes are needed. Employment will increase despite productivity increases.
369	Miscellaneous electrical equipment	Output will increase due to increased intermediate demand and capital purchases for parts and accessories from the computer, communications, and various electronics industries. More efficient manufacturing techniques will increase productivity. Limited employment growth will result as output growth exceeds that of productivity.
371	Motor vehicles and equipment	The automobile industry is becoming more decentralized due to outsourcing. Increased personal consumption of vehicles coupled with intermediate demand from businesses such as wholesale and retail trade will drive up industry output. Productivity will increase almost as fast as output, and imports will continue to rise, so employment will increase only slightly.

SIC code	Industry title	Factors affecting output and employment
372, 376	Aerospace	Output is expected to increase to satisfy growth in domestic air transportation, defense purchases, and exports. Employment and output growth will be similar.
373	Ship and boat building and repairing	Output is consumed by the military services and individuals, and as capital investment by the water transport and energy industries. Rebounding prices for oil and natural gas will spur demand for oil drilling platforms. In addition, the deadline imposed by the Oil Pollution Act of 1990, under which all tankers and tank barges must be converted to double-hulls by 2015, means that vessels will need to be refitted. Output will decline, however, due to increasing imports. Increasing employment results from falling productivity.
374	Railroad equipment	Output is consumed as an investment or as an intermediate input by the rail transportation industry. As the industry improves their tracks and equipment to accommodate the increased demand for freight and passenger rail transportation, output will increase. Productivity will increase due to technological advances, but at a rate slower than output growth; employment will increase slightly.
375, 379	Miscellaneous transportation equipment	Output is purchased by individuals, the military services (tanks), and exported. Output will increase as demand for recreational equipment such as bicycles, motorcycles, RVs, and snowmobiles, continues to grow. Automation will continue to prompt productivity growth, but at a much lower rate than output. As a result, employment will increase.
381	Search and navigation equipment	Output is used by the defense, aerospace, ship, and transportation industries. More satellites and greater accessibility of global positioning system (GPS) signals will spur growth in ground-based navigation systems and thus increase output. The Federal Radio Navigation Plan's goal is to have GPS technology replace older, ground-based systems by 2010. Technology-driven productivity increases will decrease employment.
384	Medical equipment, instruments, and supplies	Some output is consumed by individuals with the balance used as an investment or intermediate input by hospitals and other medical services. Output will continue to grow as an aging population requires additional medical care and seeks treatments using the latest technology. Productivity increases continue, but at a slower pace than previously. Employment will increase as output increases surpass productivity increases.
385	Ophthalmic goods	Output is expected to grow due to increased demand for eyeglasses and contact lenses by an aging population. Lasik surgery will dampen demand from some of the population, since it is an alternative to corrective lenses for normal eyesight. Productivity will increase due to improved technology from more efficient equipment. A modest increase in employment is expected, however, because output will increase faster than productivity.
386	Photographic equipment and supplies	A sharp increase in imports, which has been going on for decades and is expected to continue, will cause output and employment to decline. A further decrease in output will result from the overlapping of products in the imaging and information technology industries—some of the traditional photographic industry output now is part of the computer and office equipment industry. Industry restructuring that includes alliances among manufacturers in the two industries is expected to depress employment. Productivity also will decline.
391	Jewelry, silverware, and plated ware	Output is purchased primarily by individuals and will increase due to increasing demand from consumers with higher disposable income. Employment will fall slightly as productivity grows, and imports increase fairly rapidly.
201	Meat products	Output is consumed by individuals and as an intermediate input to eating and drinking places, and will increase due to a growing population with rising disposable income. Productivity will increase due to technological advances including safety-enhancing packaging to extend meat shelf life, and automated packaging to reduce human error and contamination. Employment will continue to increase.
202	Dairy products	Output is consumed by individuals and as an intermediate input to eating and drinking places. Output will increase due to a growing population with rising disposable income.

Table 5. Factors affecting industry output and employment, 2000-10—Continued

SIC code	Industry title	Factors affecting output and employment
		New plants and equipment, combined with improved methods for processing milk products will raise productivity, resulting in declining employment.
203	Preserved fruits and vegetables	Output is consumed by individuals and as an intermediate input to eating and drinking places, and will decline slightly as a result of increased imports. Productivity and employment will fall at about half the rate of decline in output.
204, 207	Grain mill products, fats, and oils	Output is consumed as an input by the livestock and food processing industries, eating and drinking places, individuals, and is exported. Output will increase due to a growing population with rising disposable income. Productivity will continue to rise and employment will decline slightly as a result.
205	Bakery products	Output is consumed by individuals and as an intermediate input by eating and drinking places, and will increase due to a growing population with rising disposable income. Increased numbers of in-store bakeries and new bakery products also will increase output. Employment is expected to decline as a result of productivity gains.
206	Sugar and confectionery products	Output is consumed by individuals and is an intermediate input to the food processing industries, and will increase due to the growing population with rising disposable income. Rapidly increasing productivity caused by new plants and equipment will cause employment to decline.
208	Beverages	Output will increase as individuals, eating and drinking places, and the food processing industries consume more beverages, including bottled water. Productivity will continue to increase due to automation of filling and packaging tasks; employment in this capital-intensive industry is expected to decline as a result.
209	Miscellaneous foods and kindred products	Output will increase as individuals, eating and drinking places, and the food processing industries demand more miscellaneous food products such as frozen fish and seafood. Productivity will fall slightly because of the labor-intensive nature of some of the production in this industry, leading to slightly higher employment.
21	Tobacco products	Output is consumed primarily by individuals and is exported. Output will increase, despite rising prices and an anti-smoking public relations campaign against domestic consumption, as exports increase sharply. Productivity will rise due to advancing technology; employment will continue to fall as a result.
221-224 226, 228	Weaving, finishing, yarn, and thread mills	Output is purchased as an intermediate input by apparel and textile industries, and is expected to grow. Productivity will rise due to faster looms, automated inspection machines, and continued consolidation among textile producers. Employment is expected to decline primarily as a result of increased productivity.
225	Knitting mills	Output is purchased by individuals and used as an intermediate input by the apparel industry, and will increase as a result of industry growth. Productivity will continue to increase, encouraged by faster knitting machines, though at a slower rate than previously. Employment will continue to decline.
227	Carpets and rugs	Output is consumed by individuals, is an investment purchase by the real estate industry, or is an intermediate purchase by the construction industry. Output will grow due to increasing demand from residential and commercial construction. Productivity will continue to increase, though at a slower rate than previously and, in conjunction with rapidly growing imports, will cause employment to decline.
229	Miscellaneous textile goods	Output is used primarily as an intermediate input by a variety of industries. Output will increase as a result of GDP growth despite brisk growth in imports. Productivity gains will continue but at half the rate of output growth and employment will increase as a result.
231-238	Apparel	Output is primarily consumed by individuals and will increase in response to demand from a growing population with rising disposable income. Productivity will continue to

Table 5. Factors affecting industry output and employment, 2000-10—Continued

SIC code	Industry title	Factors affecting output and employment
		increase due in part to new work structures like cellular manufacturing. Employment will continue to decline as a result of rapid growth in imports and productivity.
239	Miscellaneous fabricated textile products	Output is consumed mainly by individuals and is an intermediate input to the motor vehicle and apparel industries. Productivity increases will continue, enhanced by the invention of new fiber technologies. Rising imports and productivity will offset the increase in output, resulting in no change in employment.
271	Newspapers	Almost all output is sold to individuals and will decline due to competition from nonprint media sources. People will continue to shift from reading print newspapers to accessing news through sources like the Internet. Productivity will increase due to automation, so employment will decline.
272	Periodicals	Most output is purchased by consumers with about a third consumed by intermediate demand. Output will grow due to increased consumption by individuals and increased advertising revenues. U.S. publishers have expanded their titles to foreign markets and have created spin-off titles to attract more advertising and readers. Exports exceed imports, with both growing briskly. Productivity will increase slowly, resulting in employment growth.
273	Books	Output is purchased by consumers, government, and as an intermediate input to service industries, especially educational services. Output will increase due to demand from a growing and aging population with rising disposable income and leisure time. Productivity will increase due to efficiency gains, but at a slower rate than output, and employment will increase as a result.
274	Miscellaneous publishing	Output will increase due to growing personal consumption and intermediate purchases by industries. Technological change is expected to have an impact with productivity increasing due to the efficiencies of expanding business markets and computer technology, but at a slower rate than output growth. The resulting impact on employment will be continued growth.
275, 276	Commercial printing and business forms	Output is purchased primarily by government and as an intermediate input by a wide variety of industries. Output will increase slightly as government and industry require printing services and forms. Productivity will increase due to technical innovations such as digital processors that can produce color-corrected film or digital text and images directly to printing plates. Employment will continue to decline as a result.
277	Greeting cards	Virtually all output is purchased as personal consumption, and will decline slightly due to strong growth in imports. Productivity will decrease slightly, and as a result employment will increase slightly.
278	Blankbooks and bookbinding	Output is used primarily as an intermediate input to the banking and book publishing industries, and will increase as these industries grow. Import growth is rapid. Productivity will increase due to technology such as new graphics software and automated binding capabilities. Employment will decrease due to rising productivity and more product lines being manufactured overseas.
279	Service industries for the printing trade	Output is mainly directed to the commercial printing, publishing, and advertising industries and will decline due to reduced demand as services industries are replaced with in-house operations. Productivity will continue to increase due to technological advances. Employment will decline due to technology in the form of digital imaging.
281, 286	Industrial chemicals	Output is mainly an intermediate input to the chemical, plastics, and petroleum refining industries and will decline as imports continue to cause downward pressure. Productivity will increase slightly over the projection period. Employment will decline as the inorganic chemicals industry loses jobs to firms in Latin America and Asia.
282	Plastics materials and synthetics	Output is consumed as an intermediate input to the construction, motor vehicles, goods packaging, and textiles industries and will increase as these industries grow. Rising imports and productivity will result in declining employment.

Table 5. Factors affecting industry output and employment, 2000-10—Continued

SIC code	Industry title	Factors affecting output and employment
283	Drugs	Output is consumed by individuals and the medical services industries and will grow rapidly due to a growing and aging population. Productivity will also grow rapidly. Sustained demand for lifestyle drugs and other promising new drugs should further stimulate employment.
284	Soap, cleaners, and toilet goods	Output is primarily consumed by individuals, with a variety of industries using these products as intermediate input. Output will increase due to the growing and the aging population coupled with the rising standard of living. Productivity will increase, but at a slower rate than output, resulting in employment growth.
285	Paints and allied products	Output is consumed as an intermediate input by the construction, motor vehicle, and other manufacturing industries and will increase due to industry growth. Productivity will increase, but at a slower rate than output, so employment will increase. In addition, increased environmental awareness and new legislation will encourage firms to create more environmentally friendly paint and other protective chemicals, further increasing employment.
287	Agricultural chemicals	Output is consumed by the agricultural industries and is exported, and will increase as these industries grow. The industry produces fertilizers and pesticides, among other products, for which export markets are opening in Latin America and Asia as developing nations advance in their agricultural methods. Productivity will increase at a slower rate than output, which along with export growth, will generate an employment increase.
289	Miscellaneous chemical products	Output is primarily consumed as an intermediate input to various manufacturing and construction industries and will increase due to industry growth. Productivity will increase as environmental concerns increase efforts to produce more environmentally friendly substances to replace current adhesives, sealants, and printing inks. Employment will grow as a function of overall growth in GDP.
291	Petroleum refining	Output is consumed by individuals and as an input to the electric utilities and transportation industries, and will increase due to continued demand from motor vehicle users, as well as demand for kerosene and fuel oils. Advancing technology will continue to increase productivity, and employment will decline. Foreign competition and an imbalance of imports over exports will further depress employment.
295, 299	Miscellaneous petroleum and coal products	Output is consumed as an input to various industries and will increase with GDP growth. Productivity also will grow, but not as fast as output. Employment will continue to increase as a result.
308	Miscellaneous plastics products, n.e.c.	Output is used as an intermediate input by a wide variety of industries and will increase due to growing demand for plastic products and continuing substitution of plastic for other materials in production. Productivity will increase with adaptation of labor-saving, computer-controlled automation in the industry, but at a slower rate than output, so employment will increase.
40	Railroad transportation	Output is consumed as a transportation and export margin on virtually all manufactured products and will expand with GDP growth. Productivity gains—stemming from centralized rail yards equipped with efficient material handling equipment, declining crew sizes, and automated dispatching systems—will cause employment to decline.
41	Local and interurban passenger transit	Output and employment will rise due to population growth. Productivity will be unchanged. Public funding levels and pollution control measures may benefit the subway and bus service sectors.
421, 423	Trucking and courier services, except air	Output is consumed by individuals and as a transportation margin on shipping goods to market, and will grow as GDP and the population increase. Productivity will increase as the trucking industry increasingly provides logistical management services developed with the warehousing industry. Employment will continue to increase.
422	Warehousing and storage	Output is consumed by individuals and as a transportation margin on shipping goods to market, and will grow as GDP and population continue to increase. Logistical

Table 5. Factors affecting industry output and employment, 2000-10—Continued

SIC code	Industry title	Factors affecting output and employment
		management services permitting manufacturers to outsource their delivery process also will increase output. Productivity will grow, but at less than half the level of output's increase. Employment will increase.
44	Water transportation	Output is consumed by individuals and as a transportation margin on shipping goods to market. Output will grow as GDP and the population increase. Productivity will rise more slowly than output, and employment will increase as a result.
45	Air transportation	Output is consumed by individuals, business travelers, and as a transportation margin on shipping goods to market. Output will grow as GDP and the population increase. Productivity will rise, but at a slower rate than output, resulting in employment growth.
46	Pipelines, except natural gas	Output is consumed as a transportation margin on shipping petroleum, and will grow as GDP and the population increase. Productivity will increase even faster than output due to advances in pipeline/pumping station technology, resulting in a continued decline in employment.
472	Passenger transportation arrangement	Output is mainly purchased by the airline industry and individuals. Rapid growth in output is expected, reflecting increasing business and leisure travel. However, rising productivity will result from increased use of technology, especially the Internet. Employment will increase as travel becomes more affordable and leisure time increases, but new technologies that allow consumers to research and plan their own trips will dampen employment growth.
473, 474 478	Miscellaneous transportation services	Output is purchased by transportation industries and is closely related to the trucking and warehousing industries. Output will increase rapidly as packaging, freight, cargo arrangement, and other transportation-related services remain instrumental to logistics management. Productivity will grow, but at a slower rate than output, resulting in rapid employment growth.
481, 482 489	Telephone communications and services	Output is purchased by individuals and as an intermediate input to businesses and other organizations and will increase strongly. New telecommunications services, such as Internet access and wireless communications, will lead to rapid output growth. Fast growth in productivity will dampen employment growth.
483	Radio and television broadcasting	Output is mainly purchased by individuals and will increase with population and GDP growth. Increasing commute times will account for a strong radio advertising market. Digital broadcasting and recording technology will continue to improve productivity at a faster rate than output growth, causing employment to decrease.
484	Cable and pay television services	Output is mainly purchased by individuals. Rapid output growth will result from population and GDP growth. Productivity will increase at a much slower rate than output as companies upgrade cable and other pay television infrastructure, allowing providers to deliver telephone and Internet services as well as television programming. Employment will increase.
491	Electric utilities	Output is consumed by individuals and as an input in many industries and is expected to increase as the demand for electricity increases with population and GDP growth. Increased productivity will cause employment to decline.
492	Gas utilities	Output is consumed by individuals and as an input to many industries and will rise as the demand for gas increases with population and GDP growth. Productivity gains will outpace output growth and, along with industry deregulation and restructuring, will lead to declining employment.
493	Combined utilities	Output is consumed by individuals and as an input to many industries and is expected to increase with population and GDP. Increased productivity will cause employment to decline.
494-497	Water and sanitation	Output is consumed by individuals and as an input by many industries and is expected to increase as population growth in rural areas increases the demand for water and sanitation

SIC code	Industry title	Factors affecting output and employment
		services, including municipal solid waste and recycling programs. Productivity will continue to decline, generating many additional employment opportunities.
50, 51	Wholesale trade	Output is consumed as a trade margin on goods being sold at various stages of production and will continue to increase. Labor will be used more efficiently, although productivity growth will be outpaced by output growth, resulting in increasing employment.
52-57, 59	Retail trade, except eating and drinking places	Output is consumed as a trade margin on goods sold to individuals and will increase with population and GDP growth. Productivity will increase due to gains in technology and mergers, but at a slower pace than output. As a result, employment is expected to increase.
58	Eating and drinking places	Output is consumed primarily by individuals and will increase as disposable income and the population increase. Productivity will increase, but at a slower rate than output, and as a result, employment will increase.
60	Depository institutions	Output is consumed by individuals and organizations and will increase as banks offer a variety of financial products to compete with other financial service companies. Productivity will increase faster than output, as automation will cause continued streamlining of back office functions and reduce the need for tellers. Employment will decline due to mergers and the resulting layoffs of redundant workers.
61, 67	Nondepository institutions; holding and investment offices	Output is consumed by individuals and organizations and will increase as low interest rates help sustain demand for loans from these nonbank lenders. Productivity gains, due to credit scoring, will dampen employment growth in the loan and credit business. Banks are opening their own finance and mortgage banking companies, causing an employment shift to this industry from the banking industry.
62	Security and commodity brokers	Output is consumed by individuals, and financial and insurance firms. Rapid output growth is expected as the baby boomers enter their peak savings years, and the population, in general, becomes more sophisticated about investing. Productivity will increase as the securities and mutual fund markets are automated to grow and attract investors seeking higher returns on their investments. The increase in self-directed pension plans will continue to drive demand in this industry and increase the demand for investment advisors to help people invest this pool of money, so employment will increase.
63	Insurance carriers	Output is purchased primarily by individuals and a variety of intermediate sectors and will increase as a growing and increasingly affluent population demands more insurance coverage, particularly health insurance. Increased motor vehicle and home sales will result in higher demand for property and casualty insurance. Also, an increasing number of businesses will require property and liability insurance. Productivity will increase with more direct sales by insurance carriers through the Internet and the telephone. Employment will increase, especially for computer specialists, customer service representatives, and telemarketers.
64	Insurance agents, brokers, and service	Output will grow as a result of increased demand for insurance coverage by a growing and increasingly affluent population. Productivity will increase at a slower rate than output, and downsizing of agent staff in the insurance carrier segment will raise employment growth in this sector, as some employees opt to work for independent agencies or start their own business.
65	Real estate	Rising output will be purchased by individuals and organizations as rent, real estate commissions, or fees. The industry is more sensitive to the business cycle than most. New technology and consolidation will increase productivity; employment growth will continue.
701	Hotels	Output in this cyclical industry is consumed by individuals and organizations and will grow as an increasingly affluent, growing population travels more for business or leisure. Productivity will increase, but at a slower rate than output, and employment will rise.

Table 5. Factors affecting industry output and employment, 2000-10—Continued

SIC code	Industry title	Factors affecting output and employment
702-704	Other lodging places	Output is consumed by individuals and will continue to increase, but rising productivity will cause employment to remain unchanged.
721, 725	Laundry, cleaning, and shoe repair	Output is mainly used by individuals and businesses and will increase, driven by a growing, increasingly affluent population. The industry has been dominated by family owned and operated stores historically, but will be less so over the projection period. Use of central dry-cleaning facilities that process work for multiple stores will increase productivity. Total employment will decline slowly, despite an increase in wage and salary workers, as self-employed and unpaid family workers leave the industry.
722, 729	Personal services, n.e.c.	All output is purchased by individuals and will continue to grow as demand for personal services—such as portrait photography and tanning salons—increases due to population growth and rising disposable income. Productivity will increase, but at a much slower rate than output, resulting in modest employment growth.
723, 724	Beauty and barber shops	Output is consumed by individuals and will increase due to population growth and rising incomes. Productivity growth will lag behind output growth. The labor-intensive nature of the industry will generate employment growth.
726	Funeral service and crematories	The aging of the population will be partially offset by better healthcare, resulting in increasing output. Productivity will increase in areas like embalming, but at a slower rate than output, so employment will increase.
731	Advertising	Output is purchased by many industries, the largest being retail trade sector, and will increase because of demand for advertising by increasing numbers of producers and vendors. Productivity will increase in part due to use of the Internet, but at a much slower rate than output, so employment will increase.
734	Services to buildings	Output is purchased by individuals, government, and as an input by a variety of industries, and will increase as this industry benefits from outsourcing, as reflected by increasing intermediate demand. Productivity will increase at a slower rate than output, resulting in modest employment growth.
735	Miscellaneous equipment rental and leasing	Output is purchased by individuals and as an intermediate input by a variety of industries. Output growth will result from firms' preference for leasing business-related assets, due to smaller capital outlays and protection against shorter product cycles. Productivity will increase, but at a much slower rate than output. Employment will increase rapidly as the industry benefits from outsourcing.
736	Personnel supply services	Rapid growth in output and employment will be encouraged by expansion of the industry to include many professional occupations, such as accountants, lawyers, managers, and engineers. In addition, firms will increasingly use personnel supply services to reduce costs, improve flexibility, and screen candidates for permanent positions. Productivity will increase slowly.
737	Computer and data processing services	This industry includes computer software development; networking and data communications; Internet and online services; data processing, maintenance and repair; and other specialized consulting. Output will increase rapidly as businesses contract out computer-related functions to establishments in this industry. Computer networking and data communications has become one of the fastest growing and technologically dynamic segments. Factors increasing demand for networks and network products and services include the Internet, the expansion of intranets and extranets, remote access needs, an increase in the number of PCs connected to LANs, and the growing importance of security. Employment will show strong growth for the projection period.
732, 733 738	Miscellaneous business services	As firms seek lower-cost alternatives to hiring and outsource support and clerical functions, output will grow. Firms operating businesses in this sector range from armored car services to photocopy centers. Productivity will increase, though at a much slower rate than output, resulting in rapid employment growth.

Table 5. Factors affecting industry output and employment, 2000-10—Continued

SIC code	Industry title	Factors affecting output and employment
751	Automotive rentals, without drivers	Output is mainly consumed as an intermediate input by a variety of industries and, continuing historical trends, should show strong future growth due to firms' preference for leasing and renting motor vehicles. Strong productivity growth will continue and as a result, employment will increase modestly.
752-754	Automobile parking, repair, and services	Output is primarily consumed by individuals and will increase as the growing population of increasingly affluent individuals demands services such as car washes and quick oil changes. Productivity will increase, but at a much slower rate than output, and employment will increase as a result.
762	Electrical repair shops	Output is purchased by individuals and will decline as mass-produced electrical equipment becomes cheaper to replace than repair. Productivity will increase and employment will decline as a result.
763, 764	Watch, jewelry, and furniture repair	Virtually all output is purchased by individuals, and will rise as population growth and increasing affluence increase sales of expensive items including watches and jewelry. In turn, this should drive demand in the repair industry. Productivity will increase and as a result employment will decline.
781-783	Motion pictures	Most output is consumed as an input to motion picture theaters and television. Output will increase as a growing population continues to enjoy movies as entertainment. Blockbuster films will dominate the industry, especially with continued expansion of multiplex theaters and increased exports from film distribution rights. Productivity will decline; employment is expected to increase.
784	Video tape rental	Output is consumed by individuals and will increase slightly as a result of increasing leisure time and interest in movies as entertainment. Productivity is increasing, but employment will continue to grow at a slow pace.
792	Producers, orchestras, and entertainers	A growing population with increased leisure time fuels the demand for musicians and other entertainers. Output and employment will grow roughly together; productivity will not change.
793	Bowling centers	All output is consumed by individuals and will continue to fall due to competition from other forms of entertainment. Productivity will increase as technology allows larger alleys to use fewer workers, and employment will continue to decline.
794	Commercial sports	Output is consumed by individuals and will grow as a larger population with more leisure time becomes increasingly interested in sports. Productivity will increase slowly for all jobs and remain unchanged for wage and salary workers. Employment will continue to increase as a result.
791, 799	Amusement and recreation services, n.e.c.	Output is purchased by individuals and will grow rapidly due to increasing disposable income, leisure time, and awareness of the benefits of exercise. Productivity will increase, but at a slower rate than output. Employment will increase as a result.
801-804	Offices of health practitioners	Output is consumed by individuals and will increase, though at a slower rate than previously, driven by a growing and aging population that will continue to demand a high level of quality healthcare services. Productivity will continue to decline and as a result employment will increase rapidly.
805	Nursing and personal care facilities	Output is consumed by individuals and will increase at a slower pace than previously, driven by a growing and aging population. Industry growth will be somewhat restricted by attempts to control costs by providing services in alternate settings, such as adult daycare centers, residential care facilities, and patients' homes.
806	Hospitals	Output is consumed by individuals and will increase at a slower pace than previously, driven by a growing and aging population. Productivity will decline and employment growth will be slower-than-average. Continued emphasis on controlling costs will result in faster employment growth in more cost-effective outpatient and ambulatory care departments.

SIC code	Industry title	Factors affecting output and employment
807-809	Health services, n.e.c.	Most output is consumed by individuals and will increase due to strong demand from a growing and aging population for home health and other outpatient care services. Productivity will decline and employment will increase rapidly as a result.
81	Legal services	Output is purchased by individuals and as an intermediate input by a wide variety of industries. Output growth will be stimulated by increased litigation due to a rise in the amount and complexity of business activities. Productivity will increase, but at a much slower rate than output; employment will increase rapidly as a result.
82	Educational services	Output is consumed by government and individuals and will continue to grow in response to the needs of a larger school age population. Productivity will increase slowly, but faster than previously, and employment will increase.
832, 839	Individual and miscellaneous social services	Output is purchased entirely by individuals and will increase due to sustained demand for individual and family counseling, adult daycare, senior citizens' associations, and other services. Productivity will increase at a much slower rate than output, resulting in continued strong employment growth.
833	Job training and related services	Output is consumed primarily by individuals and is expected to increase as unemployed and underemployed workers require retraining for welfare-to-work programs. Productivity will increase at a slower rate than output and will spur employment growth.
835	Child daycare services	Output is consumed entirely by individuals. Continued rapid output growth will result from growth in the child population and increased parental labor force participation rates. Productivity will increase, but at a slower rate than output. Growth in government funding for preschool education and before- and after-school programs will drive strong employment growth.
836	Residential care	Output consists entirely of individual consumption. Rapid growth will occur due to increasing levels of government spending, growth in the eligible, noninstitutionalized population, increasing levels of disposable income, and an aging population that will require more services. Institutionalization of disabled and nonviolent criminals and substance abusers is on the decline. Productivity will increase, but at a much slower rate than output, and as a result employment will increase rapidly.
84	Museums, botanical, and zoological gardens	Most output is consumed by individuals and will grow as public interest in science, art, and history increases due to growth in the amount of leisure time available. Productivity will increase at the same rate as employment.
871	Engineering and architectural services	Most output is purchased by the construction and engineering industries and will increase as firms contract out for engineering and architectural services. Productivity will increase at a slower rate than output, so employment will continue to grow.
873	Research and testing services	Output is consumed by government and a variety of manufacturing and professional services. Growth in R&D expenditures for advancing commercial, physical, and biological research will stimulate demand for output. Productivity will increase at a slower rate than output, so strong employment growth will continue.
874	Management and public relations	Output is primarily consumed as an intermediate input by a wide variety of industries and will continue to increase as firms contain expenses by outsourcing or using consultants. Productivity will decline, assuring continued strong employment growth.
872, 89	Accounting, auditing, and other services	Output is primarily consumed as an intermediate input by a wide variety of industries and will continue to increase as firms contain expenses by outsourcing or using consultants. The industry will be less dependent on traditional accounting and auditing services for revenue than on the demand for consulting, management, financial, and assurance services. Productivity will increase, but not enough to offset rapid employment growth arising from the expansion of services offered.
88	Private households	Output is purchased by individuals and will decrease because childcare and house-cleaning services will increasingly be provided by specialized, efficient firms in other

SIC code	Industry title	Factors affecting output and employment
		industry sectors. Government regulation of the workplace makes the use of private household workers expensive relative to the use of specialized firms. Productivity will increase and employment will decline as a result.
...	U.S. Postal Service	Output will increase slightly as the Postal Service delivers increasing numbers of packages shipped by manufacturers and delivery services on the final leg of their local delivery as First class mail. Productivity will increase with automation and employment will decline as a result.
...	Federal electric utilities	Output will decline while productivity increases. Employment will decline as a result.
...	Federal Government enterprises, n.e.c.	Output will increase as a result of demand for Federally-delivered services. Productivity will increase and employment will decrease significantly as a result. The trend toward outsourcing of sales, technical, and blue-collar jobs will continue.
...	Federal general Government	Output will decline as the trend toward a smaller role for the Federal Government continues. Productivity will increase, and employment will decline as a result.
...	Local government passenger transit	Output will increase as more people use public transportation. The relative size of Government and the influence of mass transit programs and initiatives will shape the industry. Productivity will only increase slightly and employment will increase even more slowly.
...	State and local electric utilities	Output will increase as a result of industry deregulation on the national level, which will increase State and local participation in some areas of the country. Productivity will increase, but at a slower rate than output; employment will increase as a result.
...	State and local government enterprises, n.e.c.	Output will increase as a result of demand from consumers for such services as State liquor stores. Productivity will increase almost as fast as output and employment will increase only slightly as a result.
...	State and local government hospitals	Output will increase as public hospitals provide intensive services to trauma victims, the poor, and uninsured. Productivity will increase even more rapidly, however, and employment will decrease as a result. In addition, more communities will stop providing safety-net services directly and more State and local government hospitals will either close or be converted into community general hospitals, usually private, not-for-profit institutions.
...	State and local general government, n.e.c.	Output, which is measured as the compensation of government employees not elsewhere classified, will increase. There will be no change in productivity, so employment will increase at the same rate as output.

Table 6. Factors changing occupational utilization, 2000-10

Matrix occupation	Factors changing occupational utilization
Accountants and auditors	A small decrease in accounting, auditing, and bookkeeping firms and a moderate decrease in Federal Government are expected as powerful accounting software and information technology make accountants more productive. Accounting firms also will continue to diversify their services, hiring more nonaccountant personnel. A moderate increase is expected in management and public relations as consulting firms seek to provide a varied package of services to business, including accounting.
Administrative law judges, adjudicators, and hearing officers	A small decrease is expected across all industries due to budgetary constraints. These workers will be expected to take on greater caseloads.
Administrative services managers	A moderate increase in management and public relations is anticipated as firms contract out administrative functions, such as facility management.
Advertising and promotions managers	A small increase is expected in most industries as the Internet increases the complexity and diversity of work, along with the number of sales agents to manage.
Advertising sales agents	A small increase is expected in most industries due to increasing Internet usage and the need for more specialists to sell multimedia advertising space.
Agricultural inspectors	A small increase is expected in Federal Government because of growing concern over the quality of agricultural products.
Air traffic controllers	A small increase in Federal Government is expected due to increases in air traffic, primarily commercial aviation.
Airline pilots, copilots, and flight engineers	A small decrease is expected in all industries as larger and better aircraft and technological and managerial advances allow faster turnaround of aircraft on the ground and make pilots more productive.
Amusement and recreation attendants	A moderate increase is expected in hotels and motels as they offer more amusement services, such as arcades and water rides.
Announcers	Moderate declines in all industries due to the effects of consolidation, use of digital technology, and growth of alternative media sources.
Art directors	A small increase is expected in advertising as use of the Internet and other electronic media expands the vehicles for advertising. A small increase also is expected in mailing, reproduction, and stenographic services as art directors increasingly plan and lay out reports, documents, and other printed matter.
Athletic trainers	Small decreases are expected in education and miscellaneous amusement and recreation services because, as athletic departments are streamlined due to budget constraints, coaches and assistant coaches will perform duties traditionally performed by athletic trainers.
Audiologists	There will be moderate increases in offices of other health practitioners and hospitals due to growing demand for services for children and the elderly. Also, a moderate increase is anticipated in education, as children with disabilities move into mainstream schools.
Automotive service technicians and mechanics	A large decrease in department stores is anticipated because discount stores will continue to shift their focus away from standard repair services and towards accessories. A moderate decrease is expected in gasoline service stations, as it is remains more profitable to offer carwashes and convenience store amenities rather than repair services. There will be a moderate increase in automotive services, except repair, as the industry increasingly offers services, such as oil changes, previously performed by workers in other industries or by vehicle owners.
Avionics technicians	All industries will experience a small decrease due to technological and design advancements, such as modular equipment, making repair and replacement of components more efficient.
Bakers	A moderate increase in grocery stores is anticipated as more of these establishments have their own bakeries.

Table 6. Factors changing occupational utilization, 2000-10—Continued

Matrix occupation	Factors changing occupational utilization
Barbers	A moderate decline is expected in beauty shops because more men will receive hair-cutting services from hairdressers, hairstylists, and cosmetologists.
Bill and account collectors	A small increase is expected in credit reporting and collection as more firms outsource bill collection. A small increase also is expected in hospitals as the need to collect payments in a timely fashion grows.
Billing and posting clerks and machine operators	Most industries will experience small declines due to increased use of electronic bill payment.
Bindery workers	A small increase is expected in commercial printing and business forms as new businesses continue to contract out specialized bindery work to establishments in this industry. Small decreases in most other industries are anticipated due to the implementation of more-sophisticated technology.
Biological scientists	A small increase is expected in research and testing services as the availability of more research and grant money and an expedited Food and Drug Administration approval process will lead to increases in the number of tests conducted.
Biological technicians	A small increase in research and testing services is expected as drug and biotechnology companies contract out clinical trials. Small declines are expected at all levels of government due to downsizing and contracting out.
Biomedical engineers	A small increase is expected in all industries due to the aging of the population and increased emphasis on health issues expanding the need for sophisticated biomedical equipment.
Boilermakers	A small decrease is expected across all industries due to the use of small boilers, which generally require less onsite assembly. Advances in production technology also will be a factor.
Bookbinders	The commercial printing and business forms industry will experience a small increase as new businesses continue to contract out the specialized binding of materials to establishments in this industry.
Bookkeeping, accounting, and auditing clerks	A small decline across most industries is expected because increasing automation will make these workers more productive.
Broadcast technicians	A small decrease in radio and television broadcasting is anticipated due to laborsaving technology, consolidation, and growth in alternative media sources.
Brokerage clerks	A small increase is expected in commercial banks, savings institutions, and credit unions as banks start to sell securities. A moderate decrease is expected in security and commodity brokers and dealers due to the growth of online trading.
Budget analysts	A moderate increase is expected in Federal Government as the industry downsizes in efforts to be more efficient and to shift some duties to the States. Budget analysts, necessary for the operation of agencies regardless of size, should increase their share of employment.
Bus and truck mechanics and diesel engine specialists	Small decreases are expected in local and long-distance trucking and terminals, education, and local government due to contracting out of repair services to specialty shops. A small increase in automotive repair shops is anticipated because these firms will be the beneficiaries of the contracting out. A small to moderate increase is expected in motor vehicles, parts, and supplies because an increasing proportion of diesel-trained mechanics and specialists will be needed to repair and tune the increasing number of diesel-powered engines.
Busdrivers, school	A small decrease is expected in education as local school districts contract out these services.
Butchers and meatcutters	Groceries and related products and grocery stores will experience moderate decreases as more meat processing is done in manufacturing plants.

Table 6. Factors changing occupational utilization, 2000-10—Continued

Matrix occupation	Factors changing occupational utilization
Cabinetmakers and bench carpenters	A small decrease is expected in household furniture as more home furnishings are sold unassembled or are cut by machines from composition wood products, requiring minimal assembly and finishing.
Camera and photographic equipment repairers	Small to moderate decreases are expected due to increased use of inexpensive cameras that often are not worth repairing, and the growing popularity of digital cameras, which should be more reliable because they have fewer moving parts.
Camera operators, television, video, and motion picture	A small increase is expected in cable and other pay television services because of expanding outlets and markets, and the growing need to provide videotape and onair images. A moderate increase is expected in motion picture production and distribution because technological changes will expand the variety of cameras available, leading to a need for more operators.
Cardiovascular technologists and technicians	A moderate increase is expected in hospitals to allow them to better meet the surgical needs of an aging population that is more susceptible to heart disease.
Cargo and freight agents	Small decreases are expected in most industries as firms consolidate and as computerization increases automated tracking capabilities, reducing the need for agents.
Carpet installers	A small decrease is expected across all industries for wage and salary carpet installers, as more become self-employed, working contractually with firms.
Cashiers, except gaming	A small increase is expected in grocery and hardware stores as the number of cashiers grows relative to that of retail sales workers.
Cement masons and concrete finishers	A small decrease is expected across all industries. Improved tools and equipment and prefabricated masonry systems will make these workers more productive.
Cementing and gluing machine operators and tenders	Faster and more highly automated gluing machines will result in a small decrease in paperboard containers and boxes.
Chefs and head cooks	A large decrease in hotels and motels is anticipated due to the growing proportion of extended-stay facilities with no food service.
Chemical technicians	Small declines are expected in plastics materials and synthetics and in industrial organic chemicals as more work is contracted out to research and testing services firms. This, in turn, will cause a small increase in research and testing services.
Chemists	Small declines are expected in industrial inorganic and organic chemicals as these firms contract out research and development to research and testing services firms. A small increase is expected in the drug manufacturing industry as a wealthier, more diverse, and older population demands new and improved drugs. An expedited Food and Drug Administration drug approval process and advances in research and development will further stimulate drug research.
Childcare workers	Growth of funding for before- and after-school programs should increase the need for childcare workers in public and private education.
Child, family, and school social workers	A small increase is expected in educational services due to the growing need to help students with their academic and social problems and to integrate physically challenged children into mainstream education. A small increase also is expected in local government due to expansion of social services provided by local governments.
Choreographers	A moderate increase is expected in miscellaneous amusement and recreation services because of increasing demand for choreography at theme parks and other entertainment venues, and in fitness centers, aerobic studios, or other athletic facilities.
Civil engineering technicians	State and local government will experience moderate decreases as these agencies contract out more services.

Table 6. Factors changing occupational utilization, 2000-10—Continued

Matrix occupation	Factors changing occupational utilization
Claims adjusters, examiners, and investigators	An aging population and increasing access to medical insurance will result in a small increase in medical service and health insurance. A small increase in fire, marine, and casualty insurance should occur as the number of policies grows, resulting in more claims.
Cleaners of vehicles and equipment	Small decreases in motor vehicle dealers and in automotive services, except repair, are expected as hand carwashing and detailing is replaced by automated equipment. A small to moderate increase is expected in gasoline service stations because some stations will forego repair services for carwashing services. Small increases in automotive repair shops and automotive rentals, no drivers, are anticipated due to an increasing focus on improving customer service.
Cleaning, washing, and metal pickling equipment operators and tenders	Moderate decreases will result in all industries as advances in technology improve worker productivity.
Coin, vending, and amusement machine servicers and repairers	A moderate decrease is expected in nonstore retailers as newer, electronic machinery makes repair and servicing less labor intensive. A moderate decrease also is anticipated in eating and drinking places as demand for cigarette machines is affected by changing attitudes towards smoking. Growing demand for arcades and coin-operated gambling machines will cause a small increase in miscellaneous amusement and recreation services.
Combined food preparation and serving workers, including fast food	A moderate increase is expected in eating and drinking places as more preparers and servers are needed to handle the expected increase in takeout meals.
Commercial and industrial designers	A large increase is expected in motor vehicles and equipment, reflecting the growing use of industrial design in the manufacture of auto safety devices and visual displays. A small increase is expected in engineering and architectural services as designers increasingly work in smaller firms, rather than large corporations.
Computer and information systems managers	Moderate increases are expected in most industries as firms continue to embrace new technologies and employ more computer specialists. As a component of management, computer and information systems managers should increase relative to other managers.
Computer hardware engineers	The computer and data processing services industry will experience a small decrease due to increasing emphasis on developing software applications.
Computer operators	Large decreases are expected in all industries as systems are automated and as other computer-related workers take on functions previously performed by computer operators.
Computer programmers	Moderate decreases are expected in most industries. Although establishments still need programmers to write programs and maintain old code, emphasis on design, development, and analysis will continue to boost demand for other computer specialists relative to demand for programmers.
Computer software engineers, applications	Large increases are expected in almost all industries due to increasing demand for computer applications software and specialized utility programs designed and developed to meet users' needs. Emphasis on design and analysis will continue to boost demand for software applications engineers relative to demand for programmers who only write code.
Computer software engineers, systems software	Large increases are projected for all industries due to the continuous need to design and develop operating systems-level software, compilers, and network distribution software, as well as to implement, safeguard, and update systems and resolve problems.
Computer support specialists	As computers and software become more complex, more support specialists will be needed to provide technical assistance to users, resulting in a large increase in computer and data processing services and very large increases in most other industries.

Table 6. Factors changing occupational utilization, 2000-10—Continued

Matrix occupation	Factors changing occupational utilization
Computer systems analysts	A small increase is expected in computer and data processing services and a moderate increase is anticipated in most other industries due to new applications of technology, specifically the demand for networking and systems integration. Computer systems analysts continue to play an instrumental role in businesses by using technology to make operations more efficient and productive.
Computer-controlled machine tool operators, metal and plastic	Small increases will result across all industries due to improvements in computer-controlled machine tools.
Conservation scientists	A small increase is expected in State government due to expanded funding for conservation initiatives. A small increase also is expected in research and testing services as environmental consulting firms require the expertise of these scientists to ensure compliance with government environmental regulations.
Construction and building inspectors	Small decreases in State and local governments and a moderate decrease in Federal Government are expected as governments contract out to private firms rather than employ inspectors in-house. This, in turn, will cause a moderate increase in engineering and architectural services.
Cooks, fast food	A moderate decline in all industries is expected because, although more people are eating out, fast-food operations are no longer the main providers of quick-service foods. Increased health awareness also will reduce the proportion of sales in the fast-food segment of eating and drinking places.
Cooks, institution and cafeteria	Small decreases in nursing and personal care facilities, hospitals, and residential care, and a moderate decrease in education will result as services are contracted out. Religious organizations will experience a moderate increase as more churches add feeding ministries to their services.
Cooks, restaurant	A small increase in eating and drinking places is anticipated due to growth of full-service food establishments.
Cooks, short order	Eating and drinking places will experience a moderate decrease as chefs replace short-order cooks.
Correctional officers and jailers	A moderate increase in State government is expected because State penal facilities tend to house long-sentence criminals incarcerated for serious crimes, for whom there is little hope of parole. A moderate increase is expected in Federal Government because prisoner populations will increase due to mandatory sentences with less likelihood of parole for Federal crimes. As governments contract out an increasing proportion of correctional services, a moderate increase in management and public relations will result.
Correspondence clerks	Small decreases are expected in many industries as notification regarding delinquent accounts and bills due is increasingly automated.
Counter attendants, cafeteria, food concession, and coffee shop	A moderate increase in grocery stores will result from increasing demand for prepared meals.
Couriers and messengers	Moderate decreases are expected in all industries because of widespread use of electronic information-handling technology.
Credit analysts	Advances in technology that make the development of credit ratings faster and easier will result in small to moderate decreases in Federal and business credit and personal credit institutions.
Credit authorizers, checkers, and clerks	A moderate decrease is expected in commercial banks, savings institutions, and credit unions and small decreases are expected in most other industries as new, productivity-enhancing software makes checking credit ratings faster and easier.

Table 6. Factors changing occupational utilization, 2000-10—Continued

Matrix occupation	Factors changing occupational utilization
Customer service representatives	The increase in business transacted over the Internet and the use of 24-hour call centers to respond to customer inquiries and resolve complaints will result in large increases in finance, insurance, and real estate. Customer service representatives continue to take on responsibilities previously performed by other workers in these industries.
Cutting, punching, and press machine setters, operators, and tenders, metal and plastic	Productivity improvements, resulting from increased mechanization, will cause moderate decreases in all industries.
Dancers	A small increase is expected in dance studios, schools, and halls to meet an increased demand for dance education. A moderate decline is expected in eating and drinking places as the trend away from live entertainment continues.
Data entry keyers	A moderate to large decrease is expected for all industries due to the effects of new technologies, such as scanners, that automate the data entry process.
Database administrators	Small to moderate increases are expected in most industries and very large increases are anticipated in finance, insurance, and real estate. Data integrity, backup, and security have become increasingly important to all types of organizations as the Internet and electronic business continuously create tremendous volumes of data.
Demonstrators and product promoters	A moderate increase is expected in department stores as retail outlets compete more intensely with the Internet and catalogs and make greater use of in-store promotions to attract buyers. A moderate decrease is expected in personnel supply services, reflecting the decline in demand for product promotion services in this industry.
Dental assistants	A small increase is expected in offices and clinics of dentists as dentists delegate more tasks to dental assistants.
Dental hygienists	A small increase is expected in offices and clinics of dentists as hygienists perform more services traditionally performed by dentists.
Dental laboratory technicians	A moderate decline is expected in offices and clinics of dentists as these establishments contract out laboratory work. Another moderate decline is expected in medical and dental laboratories as technological advancements improve productivity.
Dentists	A small decline is expected in offices and clinics of dentists as dental support staff perform more services.
Derrick operators, oil and gas	A small increase is expected in oil and gas field services because derrick operators are less likely to be eliminated due to technology change than are other workers in the industry.
Desktop publishers	Very large increases are expected in most industries as advances in computer software simplify the publication process and these workers replace traditional compositors, typesetters, and pasteup workers.
Detectives and criminal investigators	Increased awareness and proliferation of various crimes, especially electronic crimes, will cause a large increase in Federal Government.
Diagnostic medical sonographers	Because health service providers will increasingly contract out many services, including sonography, a large increase in medical and dental laboratories is expected.
Dietetic technicians	Small increases are expected in hospitals and nursing and personal care facilities as cost saving efforts cause dietetic technicians to assume more responsibilities relative to dietitians and nutritionists.
Dietitians and nutritionists	Small decreases in hospitals and State government and a moderate decrease in nursing and personal care facilities are expected due to budget constraints and contracting out.
Dining room and cafeteria attendants and bartender helpers	Moderate decreases in all industries are anticipated as automation increases and as more cafeterias become self-service.

Table 6. Factors changing occupational utilization, 2000-10—Continued

Matrix occupation	*Factors changing occupational utilization*
Dishwashers	The automation of dishwashing will cause moderate declines across all industries.
Drilling and boring machine tool setters, operators, and tenders, metal and plastic	Small decreases are expected in all industries due to replacement of these workers by computer numeric control machine tools and robots.
Driver/sales workers	A moderate to large increase in motor vehicles, parts, and supplies is expected due to an increase in parts and tools sold off the truck by local suppliers who work with the local dealerships. A small to moderate decrease in wholesale trade, other, is anticipated because efficiencies gained in management of inventories and the sequencing of deliveries will reduce reliance on labor-intensive positions. A small decrease is expected in groceries and related products as most grocery stores purchase their inventory from large wholesale distributors rather than from driver/sales workers.
Editors	A large increase in periodicals and moderate increases in newspapers and in books are expected as more editors are needed to review the growing volume of written submissions.
Educational, vocational, and school counselors	There will be a small increase in public and private education as school boards continue efforts to reduce student-to-counselor ratios. A small increase also is anticipated in job training and related services due to the growing number of career changers and welfare-to-work programs.
Electrical and electronic engineering technicians	A small decrease is expected in Federal Government due to increased contracting out. A moderate increase is expected in personnel supply services as more technicians are employed on a temporary basis.
Electrical and electronic equipment assemblers	Moderate decreases are expected for all industries as improved designs and engineering simplify the assembly process.
Electrical and electronics drafters	A small increase is expected in personnel supply services as more drafters are employed on a temporary basis. A moderate increase is projected for engineering and architectural services as some drafters assume engineering responsibilities that entail use of computer-aided drafting (CAD) systems.
Electrical and electronics repairers, commercial and industrial equipment	A moderate decrease in Federal Government is anticipated as these services are contracted out.
Electrical engineers	A small increase is expected in engineering and architectural services as firms contract out to establishments in this industry.
Electrical power-line installers and repairers	As deregulated utilities contain costs through contracting out, a large increase in heavy construction will result.
Electricians	A small increase is expected in all industries as new technologies, such as digital communications, programmable controllers, and automated systems and equipment stimulate the demand for electricians.
Electromechanical technicians	Personnel supply services will experience a moderate increase due to increasing use of technicians on a temporary basis.
Electronic home entertainment equipment installers and repairers	Appliance, radio, television, and music stores and electrical repair shops will experience very large decreases due to lower maintenance requirements of equipment with microelectronic circuitry. Also, as the equipment becomes more affordable, breakdowns are more likely to result in replacement rather than repair.
Electronics engineers, except computer	A small increase is projected in search and navigation equipment due to increased defense expenditures and continued development of Global Positioning System (GPS) applications. A moderate increase is expected for engineering and architectural services as the trend toward contracting out continues. A small decline is expected in Federal Government because of the outsourcing of research and engineering support jobs to contractors.

Table 6. Factors changing occupational utilization, 2000-10—Continued

Matrix occupation	Factors changing occupational utilization
Eligibility interviewers, government programs	Moderate decreases are projected in all industries as government programs are reformed.
Embalmers	A small decrease is expected in funeral service and crematories due to a continuing trend towards cremation and the ability of funeral home chains to meet their needs with fewer embalmers. Most funeral directors are trained, licensed, practicing embalmers.
Emergency medical technicians and paramedics	A moderate increase is expected in local government because these workers will increasingly enter the job market as paid professionals working for fire and rescue companies, rather than joining volunteer organizations.
Engineering managers	Small increases are expected in engineering and architectural services and in management and public relations as firms expand management to keep up with growing computer workforces and demand for technical consulting services.
Environmental engineers	A small increase is expected in many industries due to growing emphasis and spending on the environment.
Environmental science and protection technicians, including health	As contracting out of environmental testing increases, a small increase is expected in research and testing services.
Environmental scientists and specialists, including health	A small increase is expected in engineering and architectural services, as more companies need consultants to advise on an increasing number of new environmental regulations, issues of remediation, and other environmental concerns.
Excavating and loading machine and dragline operators	There will be moderate increases in highway and street construction and heavy construction, except highway and street, due to increased clearing of land for suburban development.
Executive secretaries and administrative assistants	Small decreases are expected in many industries as office automation redistributes traditional secretarial responsibilities and makes these workers more productive.
Extruding and forming machine setters, operators, and tenders, synthetic and glass fibers	A moderate increase is expected in both weaving, finishing, yarn, and thread mills and in miscellaneous textile goods as the demand for synthetic and glass fibers grows.
Fallers	A small decrease in logging is expected as workers become more productive through advances in technology.
Farm and home management advisors	Loss of farms and a shrinking agricultural population will result in a small decrease in educational services.
Farm, ranch, and other agricultural managers	A small increase is expected in most industries as more farmland becomes the property of nonfamily entities.
Fashion designers	A very large increase is expected in the apparel industry as the role of fashion designers increases relative to those of other apparel workers. A small increase is expected in wholesale trade, other, reflecting the growing number of wholesale distributors who design and sell clothing under their own labels.
File clerks	Small to moderate decreases are expected in most industries due to automation and consolidation of recordkeeping functions.
Financial analysts	As a result of deregulation that allows commercial banks to expand into financial services traditionally offered by security and investment banking firms, a moderate increase is projected in commercial banks, savings institutions, and credit unions.

Table 6. Factors changing occupational utilization, 2000-10—Continued

Matrix occupation	Factors changing occupational utilization
Financial managers	Moderate increases are expected in wholesale trade, other and accounting, auditing, and bookkeeping and a small increase is expected in security and commodity brokers and dealers due to increasing regulation, resulting in a rising need for these workers to oversee daily operations and growth in international business ventures. A small decrease is expected in commercial banks, savings institutions, and credit unions due to automation and industry consolidation.
First-line supervisors/managers of correctional officers	A moderate increase is expected in Federal Government because of growing prisoner populations. There will be a moderate increase in State government because State penal facilities tend to harbor long-sentence criminals incarcerated for serious crimes for which there is little likelihood of parole.
First-line supervisors/managers of helpers, laborers, and material movers, hand	A small increase is expected in groceries and related products because technological advances in this industry require more supervisors and managers with computer expertise to monitor and evaluate inventories. There will be a small to moderate increase in wholesale trade, other, because new inventory and logistical services increase the relative need for these workers.
First-line supervisors/managers of housekeeping and janitorial workers	Contracting out will cause moderate decreases in miscellaneous amusement and recreation services and hospitals and large decreases in nursing and personal care facilities and residential care.
First-line supervisors/managers of nonretail sales workers	A small decrease is expected in many industries because Internet sales, electronic commerce, and automated order and purchasing systems are expected to reduce the need for supervisors. This is partly because there will be fewer sales personnel to supervise and partly because technological developments are expected to reduce the need for the managerial functions these workers perform.
First-line supervisors/managers of police and detectives	Growth in the number of law enforcement officers and a downsizing of nonprofessional personnel will result in a small increase in State government.
First-line supervisors/managers of production and operating workers	Because the proportion of production workers in the workforce is expected to decrease, the proportion accounted for by their supervisors also is expected to decrease in all industries.
First-line supervisors/managers of transportation and material-moving machine and vehicle operators	A small increase in air carriers is anticipated because more of these workers will be needed to facilitate the movement of goods from airplanes to other modes of transportation. A small to moderate increase is expected in wholesale trade, other, because more managers and supervisors with computer and logistics expertise will be needed.
Fitness trainers and aerobics instructors	A small increase in all industries is expected due to the aging of the population and greater concern for health and fitness.
Food and tobacco roasting, baking, and drying machine operators and tenders	Automation advances in cooking and roasting equipment will result in small decreases in all industries.
Food preparation workers	Grocery stores will experience a moderate increase as these establishments increasingly offer hot meals.
Food servers, nonrestaurant	Nursing and personal care facilities and hospitals will experience small decreases due to contracting out.
Food service managers	A small increase is anticipated in eating and drinking places due to the requirement that there be a manager at every shift in an increasing number of restaurants.
Forest and conservation technicians	A small increase is expected in State government because of budgetary increases for water and soil conservation at the State level.
Forging machine setters, operators, and tenders, metal and plastic	All industries except miscellaneous plastics products and personnel supply services will experience small decreases due to improved automation and other technological advances.

Table 6. Factors changing occupational utilization, 2000-10—Continued

Matrix occupation	Factors changing occupational utilization
Foundry mold and coremakers	Small decreases will result in all industries as advances in making molds and cores continue to improve the productivity of moldmakers.
Funeral attendants	A small increase is expected in funeral service and crematories due to an increased need for individuals to assist funeral directors in the many tasks involved with funeral services.
Geoscientists, except hydrologists and geographers	A small increase in crude petroleum, natural gas, and gas liquids is anticipated as exploration for oil and gas deposits expands. A small increase also is expected in engineering and architectural services, as geoscientists perform more environmental audits and site and risk assessments resulting from environmental regulations. There should be a small increase in management and public relations due to increased demand for physical scientists in consulting firms.
Glaziers	A small decrease in paint, glass, and wallpaper stores is expected as these businesses contract out to glass wholesalers.
Graphic designers	A moderate increase is expected in advertising, as the importance of graphic designers grows along with the volume of Internet advertising. Small increases are expected in commercial printing and business forms and in mailing, reproduction, and stenographic services due to increased use of graphic designers in the highly computerized printing process.
Hairdressers, hairstylists, and cosmetologists	A small decline is expected in department stores as fewer establishments offer beauty shops and salons.
Hazardous materials removal workers	A small increase is expected in miscellaneous special trade contractors as governments and private industry become more conscious of environmental and biological hazards.
Health and safety engineers, except mining safety engineers and inspectors	A small increase is expected in management and public relations, reflecting growing concern for safety in the workplace.
Heating, air-conditioning, and refrigeration mechanics and installers	A small increase is expected in most industries due to renewed concerns regarding increasing energy efficiency, the need for continual maintenance and repair, and population shifts to warmer climates.
Helpers—Installation, maintenance, and repair workers	There will be small increases in motor vehicle dealers and automotive repair shops due to increased use of helpers to boost productivity and the volume of repairs.
Helpers—Production workers	A small decrease in personnel supply services is expected because increasing automation and more-efficient machinery will dampen manufacturers' demand for the temporary services of these lesser-skilled workers, compared with demand for other workers.
Highway maintenance workers	Small decreases in State and local governments will result from increased contracting out to private firms. This, in turn, will cause a moderate increase in highway and street construction and in other heavy construction.
Home appliance repairers	A moderate increase is expected in fuel dealers because they will increasingly sell large appliances and service contracts, requiring more repairers.
Home health aides	A moderate increase is expected in hospitals as they provide more home health care services to a growing and aging population. A small decrease is expected in residential care as facilities continue to utilize other workers, such as personal and home care aides, to meet the increasing demand for social services.
Hotel, motel, and resort desk clerks	A moderate increase is expected in hotels and motels due to the shift away from luxury hotels toward more-practical, extended-stay hotels. In the latter type of establishment, the desk clerk often is responsible for all front office operations.
Human resources assistants, except payroll and timekeeping	A small decrease is projected in Federal Government due to continuing emphasis on making government smaller and more efficient.

Table 6. Factors changing occupational utilization, 2000-10—Continued

Matrix occupation	Factors changing occupational utilization
Hydrologists	A moderate increase is expected in management and public relations as more management services are contracted out to this industry. A small increase is expected in engineering and architectural services as hydrologists continue to perform environmental audits and site and risk assessments resulting from environmental regulations.
Industrial truck and tractor operators	A small decrease is expected in public warehousing and storage because logistical services and inventory management will increase the productivity of these workers. A small increase is expected in groceries and related products as more of these workers are needed to move, sort, and redistribute merchandise to chain grocery stores.
Inspectors, testers, sorters, samplers, and weighers	A moderate increase is expected in personnel supply services as firms hire temporary inspectors with more-technical skills, rather than train their own workers. Small to moderate decreases are expected in most other industries as automated inspection machines replace inspectors, or as the job shifts to temporary workers or other production workers.
Instructional coordinators	A small increase is expected in educational services as mandatory testing becomes more prevalent in schools.
Insulation workers	A small decrease is expected in masonry, stonework, and plastering firms as insulation workers move into special trade contracting, hiring their services out to general contractors rather than working directly for them. This will result in a moderate increase in miscellaneous special contracting firms.
Insurance appraisers, auto damage	A small increase in fire, marine, and casualty insurance is expected due to increases in sales of auto policies and in the processing of associated claims.
Insurance claims and policy processing clerks	A large decrease is expected as these workers become more efficient due to technology change. Additionally, some of these workers will be replaced by customer service representatives, who, with the aid of more-advanced tools, will be able to take on more complex duties.
Insurance sales agents	A small increase in commercial banks, savings institutions, and credit unions is expected due to new legislation allowing financial institutions to compete in the delivery of a wide range of financial services. A moderate decrease is expected in life insurance; medical service and health insurance; and fire, marine, and casualty insurance as these industries reduce the number of agents and rely more heavily on direct marketing via telephone and the Internet to cut costs. A small increase in insurance agents, brokers, and services is anticipated as displaced agents from other sectors join independent agencies or open their own businesses.
Insurance underwriters	A small increase in life insurance is expected due to the need for individual attention to each life insurance policy, allowing less automation. As the insurance industry declines, underwriters will be less affected than other workers. A large decrease is expected in insurance agents, brokers, and services as underwriters move back into insurance carriers, where they are more productive due to the implementation of underwriting software and information technology.
Interior designers	A small increase is expected in wholesale trade, other, as demand for interior design services grows. A moderate decline is expected in furniture and homefurnishing stores as these establishments contract out design work for their customers.
Interviewers, except eligibility and loan	A small increase is expected in hospitals as the duties of these workers expand to include customer service and other related duties. For example, they will increasingly handle financial questions and serve as patient advocates.
Janitors and cleaners, except maids and housekeeping cleaners	Educational services will experience a small decrease as services are contracted out.
Jewelers and precious stone and metal workers	A moderate increase is expected in jewelry, silverware, and plated ware, reflecting the labor-intensive work of jewelers that is not as easily automated as the work of others in the industry. A moderate decrease is expected in miscellaneous shopping goods stores as competition from television and Internet sales increases.

Table 6. Factors changing occupational utilization, 2000-10—Continued

Matrix occupation	Factors changing occupational utilization
Judges, magistrate judges, and magistrates	A small decrease is anticipated as budgetary pressures reduce their relative proportion in all industries.
Laborers and freight, stock, and material movers, hand	Small decreases across all industries are anticipated due to automation and advances in moving machinery and equipment.
Landscape architects	A small increase is expected in engineering and architectural services due to increasing demand for these workers by design firms.
Lathe and turning machine toolsetters, operators, and tenders, metal and plastic	Moderate decreases are expected across all industries as specialized workers with limited skills are replaced by workers with broader skills. Also, advances in computer numeric control latheing will improve productivity among lathe operators.
Laundry and drycleaning workers	A small decrease in hospitals is anticipated as laundry services, like many other non-medical services, are contracted out to contain costs.
Law clerks	A small decrease is expected because firms will replace law clerks with paralegals and legal assistants in an effort to contain the costs of delivering legal services.
Lawyers	A moderate increase in Federal Government and a small increase in State government are expected as caseloads at both levels continue to increase.
Layout workers, metal and plastic	As automated machining increases and many tasks become unnecessary, moderate decreases will result in all industries.
Legal secretaries	A small decrease is expected in legal services as paralegals expand their role and take on many of the tasks previously assigned to legal secretaries.
Librarians	Increasing quality of Internet access to medical literature and information networks will contribute to a moderate decrease in hospitals. A small decrease is expected in educational services as libraries employ more library technicians and automate procedures.
Library assistants, clerical	A small increase is expected in local government as more relatively low-paid library assistants assume greater responsibilities.
Library technicians	A small increase is expected in public and private education as libraries continue to automate operations with sophisticated equipment and computers. Additionally, technicians will be hired as an alternative to higher paid librarians.
Licensed practical and licensed vocational nurses	A moderate decrease is expected in hospitals as they substitute a combination of registered nurses and lower cost nursing aides to provide nursing care.
Loan interviewers and clerks	A large decrease is expected in most industries as the loan process becomes increasingly standardized and a simpler credit scoring system further reduces the need for followup interviews to resolve problems.
Locomotive engineers and firers	A large increase is expected in railroad transportation due to consolidation of job functions, which will result in engineers taking on more responsibilities.
Machine feeders and offbearers	There will be moderate decreases across all industries due to increased use of robots and other automation.
Maids and housekeeping cleaners	Small decreases in hospitals and residential care are anticipated as services are contracted out. Services to buildings will experience a small increase due to contracting out.
Mail clerks and mail machine operators, except postal service	Small to moderate decreases are expected in most industries as more communications are sent electronically.
Maintenance and repair workers, general	Small decreases in all industries will result from technical advances.

Table 6. Factors changing occupational utilization, 2000-10—Continued

Matrix occupation	*Factors changing occupational utilization*
Management analysts	A small increase in expected in computer and data processing services and in accounting, auditing, and bookkeeping as firms capitalize on high demand for electronic business by increasing consulting in the areas of electronic commerce and corporate reorganization and restructuring. A moderate increase is expected in Federal Government because the expertise of these workers in streamlining business practices and reducing costs will be valued as the Government continues to downsize.
Manicurists and pedicurists	Moderate increases are expected in beauty shops due to rising demand for manicure and pedicure services.
Market research analysts	A moderate decrease is expected in computer and data processing services because growth in the demand for other industry services, such as computer programming and maintenance and repair, will outpace growth in demand for market research services.
Marketing managers	Small to moderate increases are expected in most industries because of the increasing complexity of Internet services and the rising demand for these workers to conduct marketing promotions previously performed in-house by a general manager or information technology worker.
Materials scientists	Small declines are expected in industrial organic chemicals as firms contract out research and development to research and testing services. This, in turn, will result in a small increase in research and testing services.
Mechanical drafters	A small increase in engineering and architectural services is expected as drafters take over some engineering responsibilities using computer-aided drafting (CAD) systems.
Mechanical engineering technicians	A small decline is expected in Federal Government due to contracting out.
Medical and clinical laboratory technicians	A small decrease is expected in hospitals and a small increase is expected in medical and dental laboratories as hospitals continue to control costs by contracting out to commercial laboratories.
Medical and clinical laboratory technologists	A small decrease is expected in hospitals and a moderate increase is expected in medical and dental laboratories as hospitals continue to control costs by contracting out to commercial laboratories.
Medical and health services managers	The increasing complexity of hospitals and large health networks, and reliance on managers for effective office operations, will result in a small increase in hospitals and a moderate increase in offices of physicians. A moderate decrease is expected in home health care services as a result of higher worker/manager ratios and increasing emphasis on clinical care.
Medical and public health social workers	There will be a small increase in nursing and personal care facilities as the elderly population grows rapidly and as more social workers are needed to coordinate the care of patients in nursing homes. A small increase is expected in hospitals, where workers will be needed to counsel patients after their discharge, while a moderate increase is expected in home health care services because of the need to assist patients recovering outside of hospitals.
Medical assistants	A small increase is expected in offices of physicians as group practices employ a higher proportion of medical assistants who can handle both clinical and clerical duties. A moderate increase is expected in offices of other heath practitioners as practitioners delegate more low-level duties. A large increase is expected in hospitals as ambulatory and outpatient departments continue to grow rapidly.
Medical records and health information technicians	A large increase in offices of physicians and small increases in nursing and personal care facilities and in hospitals are expected due to the increasing complexity of health information and insurance company requirements.
Medical scientists	Small increases are expected in drug manufacturing and Federal Government as funding for research increases, and as an expedited Food and Drug Administration drug approval process and advances in biotechnology increase the number of clinical trials performed.

Table 6. Factors changing occupational utilization, 2000-10—Continued

Matrix occupation	Factors changing occupational utilization
Medical secretaries	Most industries will experience small decreases as automation allows each secretary to support a larger number of workers.
Mental health and substance abuse social workers	A moderate increase is expected in individual and miscellaneous social services due to increased demand for social services aimed at the mentally ill and at substance abuse prevention and treatment. A small increase is expected in residential care and in State and local government due to growing demand for services for substance abusers and the mentally ill as they become better integrated into society.
Merchandise displayers and window trimmers	A moderate decrease is expected in department stores due to an increase in the number of discount department stores that do not emphasize store displays. A small decrease is expected in clothing and accessories stores as more stores become integrated into homogenous shopping malls.
Meter readers, utilities	Large decreases are expected in all industries because of increased use of remote, automated meter-reading systems.
Milling and planing machine setters, operators, and tenders, metal and plastic	Improvements in computer numeric control machining and robotics will increase productivity, resulting in small decreases in all industries. Advances in factory technology and new production techniques requiring more highly skilled workers also are factors in the decreases.
Millwrights	Moderate increases in miscellaneous special trade contractors will result as independent contractors are hired by firms to do installation. Moderate decreases are expected in blast furnaces and basic steel products and in motor vehicles and equipment due to contracting out.
Mobile heavy equipment mechanics, except engines	A small increase is anticipated in machinery, equipment, and supplies because other sectors within this industry are not expected to grow as fast as the construction and mining machinery sectors, in which mobile heavy equipment mechanics are concentrated. A small increase is expected in miscellaneous equipment rental and leasing because more construction companies will lease and rent their equipment rather than make large capital investments themselves.
Model makers, metal and plastic	Small decreases across all industries will stem from improved productivity in computer-aided manufacturing and large-scale, multiaxis computer numeric control machining.
Models	A large increase is expected in clothing and accessories stores as the increased volume of catalog and Internet sales requires more models to advertise merchandise.
Motion picture projectionists	A large decrease is expected in motion picture theaters because better film technology allows projectionists to oversee more than one screen at a time.
Multimedia artists and animators	A large increase is expected in motion picture production and distribution as the use of special effects, animation, and computer graphics in movies increases. A moderate increase is expected in advertising as Internet advertising with sound, special effects, and animation becomes more prevalent.
Musicians and singers	A small increase is expected in the producers, orchestras, and entertainers industry because of increased interest in live music performances. A small increase also is expected in religious organizations because of increases in the number of performers and in the size of performing groups, such as professional choirs. A small decline is expected in eating and drinking places as the trend away from live entertainment in those establishments continues.
Network and computer systems administrators	Large increases are expected in all industries as organizations develop and expand network, Internet, and intranet systems and conduct more business electronically. More network and computer systems administrators will be needed to provide day-to-day onsite administrative support for software users in a variety of work environments, as well as to plan, coordinate, and implement security measures.
Network systems and data communications analysts	A moderate increase is expected in computer and data processing services and a large increase is anticipated for most other industries due to the growing need for workers to design, develop, and maintain Web sites, intranets, and other data communications systems.

91

Table 6. Factors changing occupational utilization, 2000-10—Continued

Matrix occupation	Factors changing occupational utilization
Occupational therapist aides	There will be small increases across all industries due to the growth and aging of the population and to improvements in technology that will allow more medical conditions to be treated.
Occupational therapist assistants	Small increases are expected in all industries due to the growth and aging of the population and to improvements in technology that will allow more medical conditions to be treated.
Occupational therapists	A small increase is anticipated in offices of other health practitioners, nursing and personal care facilities, and hospitals due to the continuing high level of demand for therapy services from a growing and aging population.
Office clerks, general	Moderate declines are expected in commercial banks, savings institutions, and credit unions; hospitals; and educational services. Increased automation and a trend towards hiring employees with more-specialized, technical skills will contribute to this decline. A small decline in personnel supply services also is expected because of increased office automation and a resulting decrease in demand for general office workers.
Office machine operators, except computer	Large decreases are projected in all industries as automation eliminates the need for these workers and other office workers take over tasks previously performed by office machine operators.
Operating engineers and other construction equipment operators	A small decrease is expected in all industries as technological improvements to equipment increase productivity, moderating demand for operators.
Opticians, dispensing	A moderate increase is expected in department stores because more people will choose the convenience of full-service department stores for eye care. A moderate decrease in offices of other health practitioners and a small decrease in used merchandise and retail stores will result as growth in demand for optical services is outpaced by growth in demand for other services provided by these industries.
Optometrists	A small decline is expected in offices of other health practitioners because demand for optometric care is not expected to increase as fast as demand for other types of healthcare provided by this industry.
Order clerks	Moderate to large decreases are expected in all industries as the spread of electronic data interchange, electronic commerce, and automatic billing systems increases productivity.
Parking lot attendants	There will be a small increase in miscellaneous personal services due to increased contracting out of valet parking.
Parts salespersons	A moderate decrease is expected in most industries due to automation resulting from the use of electronic data interchange, electronic commerce, and the Internet.
Patternmakers, metal and plastic	Improved productivity in computer-aided manufacturing and large-scale, multiaxis computer numeric control machining will result in small decreases throughout all industries.
Payroll and timekeeping clerks	Small declines are expected in most industries due to increased use of automated timekeeping systems. A moderate decline is expected in personnel supply services as the proportion of clerical workers declines in relation to those of other types of temporary workers.
Personal and home care aides	A small increase is expected in hospitals as they continue to expand their services into the home care sector. A large increase in nursing and personal care facilities and a small increase in residential care will result as cost containment pressures and greater demand for social services increase reliance on aides. A moderate increase is anticipated in individual and miscellaneous social services due to growing demand for adult daycare and homemaker services.
Personal financial advisors	Moderate increases are expected for most industries due to a growing need for financial planning for retirement and to deregulation of the financial services industries, which allows insurance agents, stockbrokers, and bankers to take on broader roles of financial advisors.

Table 6. Factors changing occupational utilization, 2000-10—Continued

Matrix occupation	Factors changing occupational utilization
Pesticide handlers, sprayers, and applicators, vegetation	Standard maintenance of existing grounds or creation of new grounds, as opposed to use of costlier chemical treatments, will lead to a small decrease in landscape and horticultural services.
Pharmacists	Large increases are expected in department and grocery stores as more add pharmacy departments.
Pharmacy aides	A small increase in drugstores and proprietary stores is anticipated as they employ a greater share of front-line workers to ring up transactions.
Pharmacy technicians	Large increases are expected in department and grocery stores as these establishments continue to add pharmacy departments. A large increase is expected for drugstores and proprietary stores as more lower paid and efficient technicians take over routine tasks previously handled by pharmacists.
Photographic process workers	Very large declines are expected in mailing, reproduction, and stenographic services and in miscellaneous business services due to wider use of digital photography and Web-based marketing, which increases the use of desktop publishing and in-house processing. A large decline also is expected in photographic studios, portrait, due to increased use of digital photography.
Photographic processing machine operators	A large decline is expected in miscellaneous business services because film processing is less labor-intensive due to improved photo processing technology. A small decline is expected in mailing, reproduction, and stenographic services because digital photography and desktop publishing allow much of this work to be done in-house.
Physical therapist aides	There will be small increases across all industries due to the growth and aging of the population and to improvements in technology that will allow more medical conditions to be treated.
Physical therapist assistants	Small increases are expected in all industries due to the growth and aging of the population and to improvements in technology that will allow more medical conditions to be treated.
Physical therapists	There will be small increases in offices of other health practitioners, nursing and personal care facilities, and hospitals due to the continuing high level of demand for therapy services from a growing and aging population.
Physician assistants	A large increase in hospitals and a small increase in offices of physicians, including osteopaths, will result as these cost-efficient workers continue to provide a growing proportion of services previously provided by physicians.
Physicians and surgeons	There will be a small increase in hospitals and a small decrease in offices of physicians, including osteopaths, due to the continued movement from "solo" practices to large group practices or managed care organizations. A small increase is expected in Federal Government due to an aging Veterans Administration hospital population who will require more care.
Plumbers, pipefitters, and steamfitters	A moderate decrease is expected in Federal Government, reflecting continuing efforts to reduce expenses by contracting out.
Podiatrists	Offices of other health practitioners will experience a small decrease because demand for podiatric care is not expected to grow as fast as demand for other types of medical services.
Police and sheriff's patrol officers	A large increase is expected in Federal Government due to increased hiring of Federal agents. A small increase is anticipated in local government, reflecting increased police department budgets.
Postal service mail sorters, processors, and processing machine operators	There will be a small decrease in the Postal Service due to increasing automation of mail sorting.
Postsecondary teachers	A small increase is anticipated in educational services because of an expected increase in college enrollments. A growing percentage of high school graduates are going to college and more adults are returning to school in order to update their skills.

Table 6. Factors changing occupational utilization, 2000-10—Continued

Matrix occupation	Factors changing occupational utilization
Power distributors and dispatchers	Small decreases are expected in electric services and local government because of increased automation, as well as job consolidation resulting from industry deregulation.
Private detectives and investigators	As liability for employing detectives and investigators becomes higher in retail establishments and as other businesses seek lower-cost contracts for investigative and detective services, there should be small decreases across most industries, with a moderate increase in miscellaneous business services.
Probation officers and correctional treatment specialists	Small increases are expected in most industries due to an increase in the number of offenders in prison and on parole and probation.
Procurement clerks	As direct communication between businesses and their suppliers increases as a result of electronic commerce, moderate declines are expected in all industries as fewer clerks are needed to process purchase orders.
Producers and directors	A moderate increase is expected in radio and television broadcasting due to greater programming needs by stations. A small increase is expected in motion picture production and distribution because of the growing number of films produced each year. A small increase also is expected in the producers, orchestras, and entertainers industry because of the growing complexity of operating an entertainment business.
Proofreaders and copy markers	Small to moderate decreases are projected in all industries as automated proofreading programs allow authors and writers to quickly proof their own work for spelling, grammar, and graphics errors.
Property, real estate, and community association managers	A small decrease is expected for real estate operators and lessors and a small increase is expected for real estate agents and managers as the real estate industry moves from owner-operators toward more-professional third-party management.
Psychiatric aides	A small decrease is expected in hospitals as cost pressures limit inpatient psychiatric treatment.
Psychiatric technicians	A small decrease will occur in hospitals as cost pressures limit inpatient psychiatric treatment.
Psychologists	A small decrease is anticipated in hospitals because of patient and insurer preference for psychiatrists over psychologists, who are unable to prescribe medications.
Public relations managers	Small increases are expected in most industries as firms take a more active approach to possible product failures, company scandals, and other events.
Public relations specialists	Small increases are expected for most industries as firms take a more active approach to possible product failures, company scandals, and other events.
Purchasing agents, except wholesale, retail, and farm products	A small increase is expected in State government as purchasing agents oversee and administer a growing number of contractors handling outsourced programs.
Purchasing managers	A small to moderate decrease is expected in all industries due to the impact of electronic commerce on the ordering and reordering goods and services.
Radio mechanics	Very large declines will result in all industries except telephone communications due to the improved reliability and lower cost of equipment.
Radio operators	Small decreases are anticipated across all industries due to technological advancements and automation.
Railcar repairers	A small decrease in railroad transportation is expected due to consolidation of worker responsibilities.
Rail yard engineers, dinkey operators, and hostlers	As the responsibilities of these workers are assumed by locomotive engineers, a moderate decrease in railroad transportation will result.

Table 6. Factors changing occupational utilization, 2000-10—Continued

Matrix occupation	Factors changing occupational utilization
Railroad brake, signal, and switch operators	Technological improvements and consolidation of job responsibilities will cause a very large decrease in railroad transportation.
Rail-track laying and maintenance equipment operators	A moderate decrease is expected in railroad transportation as track laying is automated and requires less labor.
Real estate brokers	A small decrease is expected in the real estate agents and managers industry as the Internet makes searching for and buying a home more efficient and easier to transact, and the trend towards commission-only compensation continues.
Real estate sales agents	A small to moderate increase is projected in the real estate operators and lessors industry as real estate owners employ agents directly and contract them out to work on the developer's site. A small decrease is expected in the real estate agents and managers and the subdividers and developers industries as the need for agents is reduced by the increase in Internet resources and the contracting out of sales services.
Receptionists and information clerks	A moderate increase is expected in beauty shops as the number of independent operators increases. A small decrease is projected in the offices of physicians, including osteopaths, because of the move toward larger group practices, in which many practitioners share the services of one receptionist.
Recreation workers	Nursing and personal care facilities will experience a small decrease as cost-cutting measures are implemented. Individual and miscellaneous social services also will experience a small decrease as recreation services are contracted out. Similarly, a small decrease is projected in residential care as recreation services are contracted out due to health and safety requirements. A small increase is expected in civic and social associations as participation in sports activities increases.
Recreational therapists	A small decrease is expected in hospitals and a moderate decrease is projected for nursing and personal care facilities as pressure to cut costs mounts.
Refuse and recyclable material collectors	There will be a small decrease in local government and a small to moderate decrease in water supply and sanitary services due to increased contracting out.
Registered nurses	A small increase is expected in nursing and personal care facilities as patients are transferred out of hospitals more quickly and require more-extensive and highly skilled care. A small increase also is expected in Federal Government, reflecting more spending on healthcare for the aging veteran population and on medical research.
Reservation and transportation ticket agents and travel clerks	A small decrease is expected for air carriers because of the emergence of electronic ticketing, the Internet, and other technological advances affecting the ways in which travel is arranged and tickets are purchased.
Residential advisors	The residential care industry will experience a moderate decrease due to the shift of job duties to other workers.
Respiratory therapists	A moderate increase is expected in hospitals because of increased incidence of heart attacks and pulmonary disease attributable to an aging population.
Respiratory therapy technicians	A moderate increase is expected in hospitals because of increased incidence of heart attacks and pulmonary disease attributable to an aging population.
Retail salespersons	A small increase is expected in lumber and other building materials and in used merchandise and retail stores as more emphasis is placed on improving customer service. Small decreases are projected for hardware and grocery stores as the proportion of salespersons declines relative to those of other employees, such as cashiers.
Rotary drill operators, oil and gas	A small to moderate decrease is expected in oil and gas field services as improved drilling techniques and automation make these workers more productive.

Table 6. Factors changing occupational utilization, 2000-10—Continued

Matrix occupation	Factors changing occupational utilization
Roustabouts, oil and gas	A moderate decrease is expected in crude petroleum, natural gas, and gas liquids as technology increases productivity and workers shift into oil and gas field services to work for contract firms.
Sailors and marine oilers	A small decrease is expected in ocean, Great Lakes, and other transportation of freight by water as newer ships and technological improvements increase efficiency.
Sales engineers	A small to moderate increase is expected in wholesale trade, other, because of the increasing proportion of high-technology products and services that will be sold.
Sales managers	Small to moderate increases are expected in most industries as the duties of sales managers become more specialized and complex and as more organizations add divisions to implement and oversee Internet sales.
Secondary school teachers, except special and vocational education	A small increase is anticipated in public and private education because of expected higher growth rates in the number of high school students compared with those of elementary and middle school students.
Secretaries, except legal, medical, and executive	Most industries will experience small to moderate decreases as office automation redistributes traditional secretarial responsibilities and makes these workers more productive.
Securities, commodities, and financial services sales agents	Moderate increases are expected in banking and closely related functions, not elsewhere classified, and in commercial banks, savings institutions, and credit unions due to deregulation of financial services that will continue to allow commercial banks to expand into investment banking. A small increase also is expected in security and commodity exchanges and services because of an increased need for financial advice.
Security guards	All industries, except miscellaneous business services, will experience small decreases as businesses and government attempt to reduce costs by contracting out guard services.
Semiconductor processors	A small to moderate increase is expected in electronic components and accessories as lower-skilled production and processing jobs continue to be performed abroad.
Service station attendants	A very large decrease is expected in petroleum and petroleum products as petroleum companies divest themselves of gasoline stations, reducing the need for these workers. There will be a large decrease in gasoline service stations due to increased automation and the elimination of full-service amenities requiring a service attendant.
Sewers, hand	Small increases are expected as automation continues to dampen demand for other occupations relative to hand sewers.
Sewing machine operators	A moderate decrease in knitting mills is expected as technology simplifies processes and makes operators more efficient. Additionally, movement of work overseas will reduce the relative number of sewing machine operators.
Sheet metal workers	A moderate increase is expected in plumbing, heating, and air-conditioning. Growth in the air-conditioning component of the industry is expected to outpace growth in the others, creating more opportunities for sheet metal workers. A small to moderate decrease is expected in aircraft and parts as designers and builders turn to composite materials rather than sheet metal for construction. A moderate decrease is expected in Federal Government due to efforts to reduce expenses by contracting out.
Shoe machine operators and tenders	A moderate decrease is expected in all industries as jobs in this low-skilled occupation are moved overseas and as imports from international companies increase.
Slaughterers and meatpackers	Small decreases are expected in the meat products industry due to automation of processing plants.

Table 6. Factors changing occupational utilization, 2000-10—Continued

Matrix occupation	Factors changing occupational utilization
Social and human service assistants	There will be small increases in nursing and personal care facilities, health and allied services, and State government; moderate increases in hospitals, job training and related services, and local government; and a large increase in individual and miscellaneous social services as these assistants are increasingly hired in place of higher paid social workers in an effort to reduce costs as the elderly population increases. A moderate increase is expected in residential care as more substance abusers are treated instead of imprisoned.
Special education teachers, middle school	Because of an increase in the number of children classified as learning disabled, a small increase is expected across all industries.
Special education teachers, preschool, kindergarten, and elementary school	A moderate increase is expected across all industries because of growth in the number of children classified as learning disabled, which demonstrates its largest increase at this age level.
Special education teachers, secondary school	A small increase is expected because of an increase in the number of children classified as learning disabled.
Speech-language pathologists	There will be a moderate increase in offices of other health practitioners and hospitals due to growing demand for services for children and the elderly. A moderate increase is anticipated in education as children with disabilities move into mainstream schools.
Stationary engineers and boiler operators	Most industries will experience small decreases as automation continues to increase worker productivity.
Stock clerks and order fillers	Moderate decreases are expected in grocery stores, drugstores, and Federal Government because of continued use of bar coding, hand-held scanners, computerized inventory control systems, and automated warehouse vehicles.
Stonemasons	A small increase is expected across all industries due to increasing use of stone in construction.
Surgical technologists	A very large increase is expected in offices of physicians, including osteopaths, because of an increase in the number of surgeries performed in outpatient settings. A small increase is expected in hospitals because of their preference for using more cost-effective surgical technologists rather than surgical registered nurses.
Surveyors	Engineering and architectural services will experience a moderate decrease due to increasing use of new mapping technologies, such as Global Positioning Systems (GPS).
Switchboard operators, including answering service	All industries will experience a significant decrease due to improvements in voice-mail technology, voice recognition software, and personal board exchange technology.
Tailors, dressmakers, and custom sewers	A small decrease is expected in nearly all industries as consumers choose lower cost, ready-to-wear garments requiring little or no fitting or altering. The apparel industry will see a small decrease as automation makes the labor-intensive, highly skilled work easier for lesser skilled workers. This also will allow producers to move jobs overseas to reduce costs.
Tax preparers	A small decrease is expected in miscellaneous personal services because an increasing number of people will use tax preparation software instead of the services of tax preparers.
Taxi drivers and chauffeurs	A small to moderate increase is expected in hotels and motels as more offer complimentary shuttle service. A small increase is expected in individual and miscellaneous social services because, as the elderly population increases, so will the demand for transportation services.
Teacher assistants	Small increases are expected in educational services and child daycare services due to the growing role of teacher assistants in bilingual and special education.
Telecommunications equipment installers and repairers, except line installers	Moderate decreases will result in all industries due to improvements in equipment capabilities and reliability.

Table 6. Factors changing occupational utilization, 2000-10—Continued

Matrix occupation	Factors changing occupational utilization
Telephone operators	Very large decreases are projected across all industries due to increasing automation, improved voice-recognition technology, foreign competition, and the use of Internet-based phone directories.
Tellers	Small to moderate declines are expected in all industries as increased use of automatic teller machines, online banking, and other new technology decreases the need for tellers.
Terrazzo workers and finishers	A small decrease is expected. Improved tools, equipment, and materials will make these workers more productive, reducing the demand for labor.
Textile bleaching and dyeing machine operators and tenders	A small increase in carpet and rug manufacturing is expected as trade incentives continue to encourage the dyeing of these products domestically.
Textile knitting and weaving machine setters, operators, and tenders	A moderate increase is expected in carpet and rug manufacturing, because weaving is very labor-intensive and therefore less susceptible to automation, unlike many other occupations in the industry.
Tire repairers and changers	There will be a moderate to large decrease in department stores as resources are diverted from automobile service areas back to the core business of the department store.
Title examiners, abstractors, and searchers	A small decrease is anticipated in all industries as advanced technology and computer software boost productivity. Additionally, many title examiners will be replaced by legal assistants.
Tool grinders, filers, and sharpeners	All industries will experience small decreases due to the trend toward replacing tools rather than sharpening them.
Transit and railroad police	There will be a small decrease in railroad transportation due to declining demand for rail travel.
Transportation, storage, and distribution managers	A small increase in railroad transportation and moderate increases in local and long-distance trucking and terminals, as well as in public warehousing and storage, are anticipated because highly educated and technologically proficient managers will be in greater demand to manage inventories and provide advanced logistical support.
Travel agents	Small decreases are projected in all industries due to the abundance of online travel information sites, such as those for airlines and hotels, which reduce the need for travel agents.
Tree trimmers and pruners	A small decrease is expected in landscape and horticultural services due to the relatively expensive nature of the services these workers provide.
Truckdrivers, heavy and tractor-trailer	A moderate to large increase is expected in air carriers because of expansion of services provided by logistics-oriented companies. A small to moderate increase is expected in groceries and related products because many franchise groceries will gain returns to scale by dealing in larger lots of merchandise and by using warehouse distribution rather than providing personalized local service.
Truckdrivers, light or delivery services	A small decrease in local and long-distance trucking and terminals is anticipated because of an emphasis on the use of large trucks, which yields larger returns to scale. A small to moderate increase is expected in air carriers because of expansion of services provided by logistics-oriented companies. There will be a small decrease in groceries and related products and a small to moderate decrease in eating and drinking places because many franchises will gain returns to scale by dealing in larger lots of merchandise and by using warehouse distribution rather than providing personalized local service.
Upholsterers	Small to moderate decreases are expected in all industries, attributable to the use of more-durable fabrics that reduce the need for repairs in automobiles and on some furniture. Also, more products will be designed to reduce the need to reupholster, and the availability of lower priced furniture will cause consumers to buy new furniture instead of repairing.
Waiters and waitresses	A small increase in eating and drinking places will result from an increase in full-service restaurants. Growth in the proportion of extended-stay hotels and motels, which often do not offer dining facilities, will cause a large decline in the hotel and motel industry.

Table 6. Factors changing occupational utilization, 2000-10—Continued

Matrix occupation	Factors changing occupational utilization
Water and liquid waste treatment plant and system operators	A small increase is expected in water supply and sanitary services as new Federal guidelines on operator certification encourage some communities to contract out plant operations to firms in this sector.
Welders, cutters, solderers, and brazers	Moderate increases are expected in fabricated structural metal products as newer techniques and technologies and lighter alloys continue to increase the popularity of welding as a joining technique.
Wholesale and retail buyers, except farm products	A moderate decrease is projected in almost all industries as efficiency gains from electronic commerce allow customers to circumvent buyers and connect directly with business Web sites and more-centralized purchasing operations.
Woodworking machine setters, operators, and tenders, except sawing	Small to moderate decreases will result in wood containers and miscellaneous wood products, household furniture, and office and miscellaneous furniture and fixtures due to laborsaving automation such as computer-controlled woodworking machinery.
Word processors and typists	All industries will experience large decreases because of the proliferation of personal computers.
Writers and authors	A moderate increase in periodicals is expected due to the rapidly expanding market for periodicals and trade journals—many in electronic format—requiring a larger staff of writers to provide copy for these publications. A moderate increase also is anticipated in business and professional organizations because of increasing services to members on their Internet sites and through newsletters. A small increase is expected in newspapers because writers form the core of industry employment and are not as easily eliminated as others through technological gains.

Chapter IV. Estimating Occupational Replacement Needs

Information about projected job openings by occupation—openings resulting from employment growth or the need to replace workers who leave an occupation—has many important applications. For example, students and vocational counselors use this information to make career choice decisions; planners of training programs use it to develop education policies; and personnel specialists use it to plan their recruiting efforts. The Bureau of Labor Statistics (BLS) has provided information on employment growth biennially through its occupational outlook program for more than 50 years and, in 1992, resumed estimating job openings resulting from replacement needs.

After completing a comprehensive research effort, BLS researchers concluded that two definitions and two estimates of separations were needed to provide appropriate replacement needs information for different users. The first type of estimate, *total separations*, measures all individuals who leave their occupation. The second, *net separations*, measures the net movements of new and experienced workers into and out of occupations. As discussed below, both measures of separations use data from the Current Population Survey (CPS). After developing historical total and net separation rates, BLS calculates projected total and net replacement rates. The projected total and net replacement rates are used to estimate future total and net replacement needs for each occupation in the employment matrix.

Concepts and definitions

During the past several decades, a variety of concepts have been used to calculate estimates of occupational replacement needs and job openings. These different concepts result in significantly different estimates of separations for the same occupation that often have confused users of the information. This section briefly summarizes the concepts currently used by BLS to calculate replacement needs data. Figure 1 illustrates the differences between total and net separations.

Total separations. Total separations identify the flow of individuals leaving an occupation, for any reason whatsoever, without regard to persons entering the occupation. Total separations are the larger measure of separations. During a given period, individuals may leave an occupation for a variety of reasons, and must be replaced. Some become employed in a different occupation as a result of a promotion, a desire to change careers, the loss of an existing job, the need for a different job while attending school or training or caring for family, or some other reason. Oth-

ers who leave an occupation stop working altogether because they retire, desire more time for leisure or for an extended vacation, assume family responsibilities, return to school, move out of the geographic area, or become ill, or for some other reason. If employment in an occupation is to increase or remain the same, those individuals who left the occupation must be replaced. In most cases, total occupational separations are thus replacement needs and a source of job openings. If employment is declining, however, occupational separations exceed replacement needs by the amount of decline in employment because some persons who leave the occupation are not replaced. (Individuals who change employers but remain employed in the same occupation—events often referred to as "turnover"—are not included in counts of replacement needs because job changes by these individuals have no impact on the number of openings for persons wishing to enter an occupation.)

Net separations. Net separations summarize movements of workers into and out of an occupation over a specific period. If employment is not declining, net separations approximate the number of persons who permanently leave an occupation: they quantify the need for new entrants and, if training is required, identify minimum training requirements.

Employment data, by age, for two points in time are used to estimate net separations. For example, occupational employment, by age, is prepared for a base year and for a second year 5 years later. Employment figures for each age group in the base year are then compared with employment figures for the group that is 5 years older. For example, in a given occupation, employment in the base year for the 55- to 59-year-old group is compared with employment in the second year for the 60- to 64-year-old group. If employment has increased from the base-year group to the older, second-year group, then the increase measures net entrants into the occupation for the second-year group, and net separations from the occupation for that group are zero. If, instead, employment has declined across the two groups, the decline is recorded as net separations from that occupation for the second age group. The total net separations from the occupation in question are then the sum of the net separations from that occupation for all age groups.

It is important to note that, within any age group, individuals may have done any of the following to stop being included in employment data for the area: Left the occupation and started working in another occupation, stopped

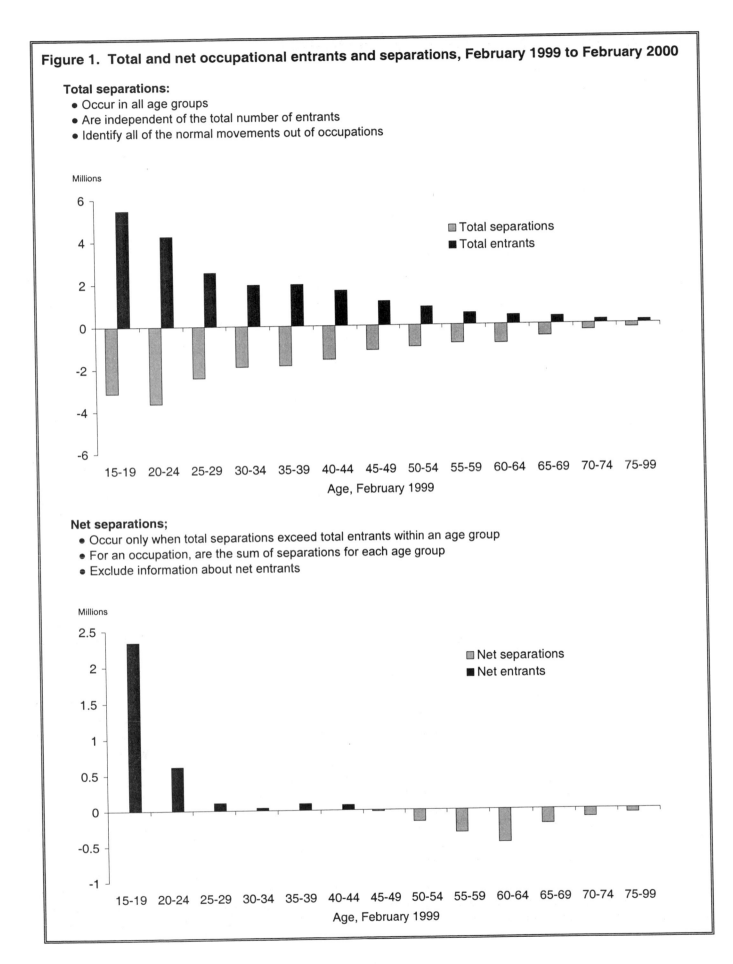

Figure 1. Total and net occupational entrants and separations, February 1999 to February 2000

Total separations:
- Occur in all age groups
- Are independent of the total number of entrants
- Identify all of the normal movements out of occupations

Net separations;
- Occur only when total separations exceed total entrants within an age group
- For an occupation, are the sum of separations for each age group
- Exclude information about net entrants

working altogether, or left the region. Similarly, individuals entering the occupation in an area may have been working in another occupation, may not have been working at all, or may have come from another region. The change measured over the period in question thus reveals only whether there were more or fewer entrants than separations, and tells nothing about the numbers of total entrants, total separations, or any of their components. That is, the change indicates whether the size of the original age group increased or decreased, but it indicates nothing about the specific actions of individuals making up the group.

Replacement needs. In developing estimates of replacement needs, the distinction between total and net separations and replacement needs pertaining to an occupation must not be overlooked. When employment in an occupation remains the same or increases over a given period, replacement needs equal separations. Conversely, when employment declines, replacement needs are less than separations because some individuals leaving an occupation are not replaced.

During a period when employment in an occupation declines, total separations will be greater than they would be if employment were increasing because more individuals lose their jobs. Net separations would be greater not only because more individuals leave, but also because fewer enter the occupation. A decline in employment represents individuals who left an occupation and were not replaced; therefore, replacement needs during a time of declining employment are determined by reducing observed separations by the decline in employment.

Although it is conceptually possible that employment could decline to zero, the possibility is remote, especially with national data. In such an unlikely scenario, separations would equal the previous number of employees because all lost their jobs, and replacement needs would be zero (replacement needs = separations - employment decline = 0). During periods of employment decline, displaced workers are available to reenter the occupation later, and thus may reduce the need to train additional workers.

Developing measures of total separations

All individuals who leave an occupation—those who transfer to another occupation or who stop working for any reason—must be included in a measure of total separations. Producing such a measure requires longitudinal data that include information about individuals at two points in time. During the late 1970s, BLS researchers developed a procedure for using CPS data to estimate the total number of job openings arising from workers who leave their occupation between two points in time that are 1 year apart. Annual data are preferable to data with other periodicities because most data on training program completions are compiled on an annual basis. Annual total separation data thus facilitate analyses of occupational supply and demand.

The method of measuring total separations entailed using computer records to track the same individuals in the CPS over a 1-year period. Matched data, from August 1998 to August 1999 through July 1999 to July 2000, were created for each of the 12 months and were combined. Use of data from the matched sample permitted changes in an individual's employment status and occupation to be tabulated. Next, the matched data dealing with changes in labor force status were merged with data on February 1999-2000 occupational transfers that were collected in the February 2000 CPS supplement.

An excessively large estimate of occupational transfers in matched CPS data occurs because, over time individuals may respond differently to the same CPS question about their occupation, responses may be recorded differently by interviewers collecting the data, or recorded information may be interpreted and coded differently by persons preparing files for computer processing. All these actions result in a different occupation being recorded in the second year when, in fact, no change of occupation occurred.

Combining 1999-2000 matched CPS data and occupational transfer data from the February 2000 CPS yields *merged data* that provide a composite description of movements into, out of, and between occupations over two points that are 1 year apart. The resulting merged data identify the numbers and types of separations and the characteristics of workers who change occupations, become unemployed, or leave the labor force.

Total separations data for occupations with fewer than 50,000 employees in 2000 were judged unreliable because of the limited number of observations in the sample. Data for the remaining occupations were examined individually and, if data identifying specific reasons for leaving the occupation appeared suspect, another detailed occupational group was selected to serve as a proxy and provide substitute data.

The CPS is conducted primarily to obtain current data on the labor force status of individuals, rather than data that measure changes over time. As a result, there are significant limitations to the data that describe change. The CPS is a household survey that collects data from persons living at specific addresses. One limitation to the matched sample is that information can be developed only from the responses of individuals who do not change their residence. Movers tend to change their labor force status more than do nonmovers; hence, the separation rates are biased downward because movers are not included. Separation rates also are biased downward because the CPS excludes individuals who die between surveys.

By contrast, response and coding errors bias the separation rates upward. For example, if employed persons were incorrectly classified as not being in the labor force during the second survey, the matched data would indicate movement where none occurred. Although the net effect of the various biases on the movements is not known, their various impacts are offsetting and not concentrated by occupation.

It must be emphasized that total separation rates developed from merged CPS data are not measured rates based on longitudinal data about individuals, but rather are a composite estimate of movements from occupations based on CPS data from two distinct sources. However, the rates are occupation-specific and are extremely valuable for describing the labor market.

Developing measures of net separations

Changes in age groups over a 5-year period provide a comprehensive measure of occupation-specific net separations. When the size of a group increases, a measure of net entrants is recorded; when it declines, net separations are identified. Net changes in an age group capture the net effect of transfers into and out of occupations, immigration, and emigration, as well as labor force entries and separations, including deaths. A 5-year period was chosen so as to reduce the impact of cyclical variations that might affect comparisons made over a shorter period. Estimates for other periods can be developed, however. Estimates also can be developed for industry, educational level, sex, and a variety of other demographic variables. This new "cohort" technique thus becomes a powerful tool for analyzing labor market changes.

Employment estimates for appropriate age groups, by occupation, were developed for 1992-97, 1993-98, 1994-99, and 1995-2000. Initially, several hundred thousand records containing information on occupation, age, and many other characteristics for all employed persons in 1992 were combined, and occupational employment by age group was tabulated. The process was repeated to obtain estimates for desired age groups in 1997. To increase the sample size and reduce cyclical fluctuations, estimates for the age groups for which 1992 employment was tabulated also were developed for 1993, 1994, and 1995, and estimates for the age groups used in 1997 were developed for 1998, 1999, and 2000. Data on employment by occupation, by age group, were then averaged and used to prepare the es-

Table 7. Net separations for registered nurses and for waiters and waitresses, by age group, 1995-2000

(Numbers in thousands)

1995 employment[1]		2000 employment[2]		Net Change, 1995-2000	Net separations, 1995-2000	Separation rate, 1995-2000 (percent)
Age	Number	Age	Number			
Registered nurses						
16-99...................	1,902	—	2,088	186	140	7.4
		16-20	1	1		
16-19..................	1	21-24	59	58	0	0
20-24..................	67	25-29	207	140	0	0
25-29..................	204	30-34	266	62	0	0
30-34..................	296	35-39	327	31	0	0
35-39..................	377	40-44	411	34	0	0
40-44..................	343	45-49	341	-3	3	0.8
45-49..................	249	50-54	225	-24	24	9.5
50-54..................	173	55-59	142	-32	32	18.2
55-59..................	108	60-64	73	-35	35	32.2
60-64..................	59	65-69	24	-35	35	59.1
65-69..................	18	70-74	9	-8	8	48.3
70-74..................	5	75-79	2	-3	3	58.3
75-99..................	2	80-99	1	-1	1	34.6
Waiters and waitresses						
16-99..................	1,414	—	1,411	-3	451	31.9
		16-20	393	393		
16-19..................	237	21-24	292	55	0	0
20-24..................	412	25-29	205	-208	208	50.3
25-29..................	213	30-34	136	-78	78	36.4
30-34..................	181	35-39	130	-51	51	28.3
35-39..................	138	40-44	93	-45	45	32.4
40-44..................	78	45-49	59	-19	19	24.5
45-49..................	55	50-54	43	-12	12	21.6
50-54..................	42	55-59	24	-17	17	41.6
55-59..................	25	60-64	20	-5	5	19.6
60-64..................	21	65-69	10	-11	11	53.0
65-69..................	9	70-74	5	-4	4	46.4
70-74..................	2	75-79	1	0	0	25.0
75-99..................	2	80-99	1	-1	1	47.3

[1] 1995 data are averages of 1992, 1993, 1994, and 1995.
[2] 2000 data are averages of 1997, 1998, 1999, and 2000.

timates presented in this chapter. To simplify the presentation, all references to 1995 data represent averages for 1992, 1993, 1994, and 1995, and references to 2000 data represent averages for 1997, 1998, 1999, and 2000.

In most occupations, net leavers occur only in the older age groups, usually above age 45. This pattern typically describes individuals leaving in large numbers to retire. A different pattern displayed in some occupations is the vast majority of all net separations taking place in the youngest age groups. In this case, large numbers of workers probably obtained employment in the occupation when they first entered the workforce. When they were ready to begin full-time jobs, or when they qualified for higher paying jobs, they transferred to another occupation. In both patterns, the net separations quantify the number of persons who permanently left the occupation. Table 7 shows these

Table 8. Net separations in selected teaching occupations, by age group, 1995-2000

(Numbers in thousands)

Current Population Survey occupation	Number employed, 1995[1]	Age group												
		16 to 19	20 to 24	25 to 29	30 to 34	35 to 39	40 to 44	45 to 49	50 to 54	55 to 59	60 to 64	65 to 69	70 to 74	75 to 79
Teachers, except college and university.........	4,211	0	0	0	0	0	0	39	85	98	66	22	6	7
Teachers, prekindergarten and kindergarten..	478	0	0	0	0	0	7	5	0	5	5	2	1	1
Teachers, elementary school.....................	1,636	0	0	0	0	0	0	19	44	43	29	7	1	2
Teachers, secondary school....................	1,178	0	0	0	0	0	3	26	46	39	21	5	1	1
Teachers, special education....................	274	0	0	0	0	0	0	0	2	4	3	1	0	0
Teachers, n.e.c.[2]....................................	646	0	0	0	0	0	0	0	0	7	9	8	3	2

[1] 1995 data are averages of 1992, 1993, 1994, and 1995.
[2] n.e.c. = not elsewhere classified.

different patterns, and also illustrates how net separations for registered nurses and for waiters and waitresses were calculated.

In table 7, employment data by age group for registered nurses and for waiters and waitresses in 1995 are compared with corresponding data for a 5-year-older group in 2000. For example, the number of registered nurses aged 20 to 24 in 1995 is compared with the number of registered nurses aged 25 to 29 in 2000, and the difference is calculated. If the difference is positive, more individuals aged 20 to 24 in 1995 entered than left the occupation. Nothing is known about the numbers of persons transferring into the occupation, entering the labor force, immigrating from another country, transferring out of the occupation, leaving the labor force, or leaving the United States. The difference between the two groups simply identifies the amount by which total entrants exceed total leavers. If, by contrast, the difference is negative, more individuals left than entered the occupation. Only a negative difference results in a measure of net separations. Positive differences are recorded as zero net separations for the age group. The separation rate for an age group is calculated by dividing net separations by 1995 employment in the age group. Net separations for all age groups were totaled and divided by total employment in 1995 to obtain the 5-year net separation rate for the occupation.

Table 7 also presents information on the percentage of leavers in each age group for registered nurses and for waiters and waitresses. This measure is calculated by dividing net leavers in the age group by 1995 employment for that age group. Information about the percentage of leavers in each age group is valuable because it permits estimates of net leavers in the future, which will be discussed later.

Because registered nurses and waiters and waitresses are large occupations, the CPS sample provides quite reliable employment data for each age group within them. However, for small occupations, such as actuaries, the sample is too small and the net separation data are unreliable. For example, actuaries have an irregular distribution of net separations among the age groups, and the net separation rate of about 19 percent is inconsistent with rates for other professional and related occupations.

To obtain a separation rate for each detailed CPS occu-

pation, one of two procedures was used when data for an occupation were judged to be unreliable. When a larger detailed occupation had characteristics similar to those of the occupation in question, the larger occupation was chosen as a proxy, and the separation and employment data for the proxy occupation were substituted for the unreliable data and were used to calculate separation rates. When there was no larger detailed occupation with characteristics similar to those of the occupation in question, separation and employment data for a summary occupation group were substituted for the unreliable data.

The procedure for determining separation rates for summary occupations, however, was not as straightforward as that for detailed occupations. Note that, in table 8, no net separations are measured for the summary occupation group, teachers, except college and university, until age 45. Yet, two of the detailed occupations that make up the group, prekindergarten and kindergarten and secondary schoolteachers, exhibit net separations prior to that age. The summary occupation does not register those separations because total net entrants in the other detailed occupations—elementary, special education, and not elsewhere covered teachers—exceeded the total of net separations among prekindergarten and kindergarten and secondary schoolteachers. To exclude the measure of net separations from the summary occupation, however, would result in an understatement of separations from detailed occupations. To overcome this limitation, net separations in each age group for summary occupations were calculated by totaling the net separations for each detailed occupation in that age group. Thus, the net separation data for each age group for the summary occupation group, teachers, except college and university, in table 9 is the sum of the data measured for prekindergarten and kindergarten, elementary, secondary, special education, and not elsewhere covered teachers. (Because unrounded data are used, the totals shown may not be the sum of the data for detailed occupations.)

Projected replacement rates

Thus far, all information presented about separations has been descriptive and retrospective; that is, it has described what occurred in the past. The BLS employment projections program, however, focuses on future opportunities, a pur-

Table 9. Net separations in selected teaching occupations, adjusted summary occupation, by age group, 1995-2000

(Numbers in thousands)

Current Population Survey Occupation	Number employed, 1995[1]	Age group												
		16 to 19	20 to 24	25 to 29	30 to 34	35 to 39	40 to 44	45 to 49	50 to 54	55 to 59	60 to 64	65 to 69	70 to 74	75 to 79
Teachers, except college and university.........	4,211	0	0	0	0	0	10	51	92	98	66	22	6	7
Teachers, prekindergarten and kindergarten..	478	0	0	0	0	0	7	5	0	5	5	2	1	1
Teachers, elementary school.....................	1,636	0	0	0	0	0	0	19	44	43	29	7	1	2
Teachers, secondary school.....................	1,178	0	0	0	0	0	3	26	46	39	21	5	1	1
Teachers, special education.....................	274	0	0	0	0	0	0	0	2	4	3	1	0	0
Teachers, n.e.c.[2].................................	646	0	0	0	0	0	0	0	0	7	9	8	3	2

[1] 1995 data are averages of 1992, 1993, 1994, and 1995.

[2] n.e.c. = not elsewhere classified.

pose that requires projections of employment change and, in addition, projections of replacement needs due to total and net separations.

Total replacement rates. Total separation rates for all detailed occupations were developed from merged CPS data for the period 1999-2000. As described earlier, total separation rates from proxy occupations were substituted for those for small occupations when the latter data appeared unreliable. If employment in the occupation in question remained the same or increased from 1999 to 2000, the 1999-2000 total separation rate also was the replacement rate and should be used to estimate replacement needs during a projection period. However, if employment declined, the replacement rate was calculated by subtracting the employment decline from the separations. Total replacement rates were used without adjustment for the 2000-10 projection period. Employment for 2005, the midpoint of the projection period, was multiplied by the annual average replacement rates for the 1999-2000 period to project annual average replacement needs over the period 2000-10. Although labor market conditions affect the replacement rates, attempts to adjust the rates would be fraught with difficulties because not enough is known about how cyclical factors and other labor market conditions affect the rates.

Net replacement rates. To develop a net separation rate for an occupation, employment figures for that occupation in a given age group in 1995 were compared with employment in the occupation in 2000 for a group that was 5 years older. (As noted earlier, data for 1995 actually consist of the average of data for 1992, 1993, 1994, and 1995, and data for 2000 consist of the average for 1997, 1998, 1999, and 2000.) If employment for the group increased, no net separations occurred, and separations were recorded as zero. If employment declined, the number was recorded as net separations for that age group. The 5-year net separation rate for the age group was calculated by dividing the number of net separations by employment in 1995. (See table 7.) The 5-year net separation rates for 1995-2000 for each age group could then be applied to employment in future years to obtain a projection of net separations. Excluded from these projections are the replacement needs attributable to those entering the occupation within the projection period.

Between 1995 and 2000, employment in most occupations increased or remained the same. It should also be noted that the 1995-2000 net separation rates, by age, were used without adjustment to estimate replacement needs during the projection period. If employment declined, however, one of several adjustments to the age-specific separation rates was used to obtain a replacement rate that reduced the occupational separation rate by the rate of decline in employment. When the employment decline was less than the number of net separations among persons aged 16 to 49 in 1995, the number of net separations for that age group was reduced by the employment decline. The decline was distributed in proportion to the number of net separations in each age subgroup of the group aged 16 to 49. This technique was the one most frequently used; it confines the adjustments to the ages most affected by adverse economic conditions. Older workers are more likely to remain employed until they retire. In most of the remaining cases, the net separations were reduced in a like fashion for persons aged 16 to 54 or persons aged 16 to 65, depending on the distribution of net separations in the occupation and the amount by which employment declined. Then, the adjusted age-specific rates were used to calculate future net replacement needs for persons employed in 2000.

Showing data for the persons employed as registered nurses in 2000, table 10 illustrates the method for calculating net leavers over the period 2000-10. First, net leavers were calculated for 2000-2005 by multiplying 2000 employment obtained from the CPS for each age group by the replacement rate in 1995-2000 for the same age group. Before net leavers in 2005-10 were calculated, employment in 2005 for each age group was estimated by identifying employment in 2000 for a 5-year-younger age group and subtracting any projected net leavers for the period 2000-2005. For example, table 10 shows the 2005 employment figure for registered nurses aged 55 to 59 to be 184,000. This estimate was arrived at by identifying the 2000 employment figure for nurses aged 50 to 54 (225,000) and subtracting the 41,000 net leavers in 2000-2005 from that age group (discrepancies due to rounding). When employment for each age group for 2005 was developed, the resulting figure was multiplied by the replacement rate for that age group to estimate net leavers for 2005-10. Summing the number of net leavers for each of the 5-year groups provided an estimate of net leavers for the 10-year period 2000-10. Net leavers over the 10-year projection period 2000-10 were determined by combining estimates for the 5-year periods 2000-2005 and 2005-10. Dividing the net separations for 2000-10 by 10 yielded annual average net separations, which were then divided by 2000 employment to yield an annual average net separation rate.

New entrants—individuals who were younger than age 16 in 2000 but who can be expected to join the group of employed persons after 2000—are not included in the estimate of separations for 2000-10. If they were included, estimates of separations with net transfers in the younger age groups—such as those for waiters and waitresses—would be larger.

Replacement rates based on the Occupational Employment Statistics survey

The preceding sections described procedures for estimating annual average replacement rates of total and net separations for detailed CPS occupations. To estimate current and projected occupational employment, the BLS projections program uses an employment matrix that is based primarily on data from the Occupational Employment Statistics (OES) survey. The current and projected occupational employment estimates are used to calculate the employment change component of projected job openings. To obtain the replacement needs components of projected total and net job openings, estimates of total and net separations based on the OES survey had to be developed. The procedure required use of total and net separation rates for all detailed occupations based on the OES survey. These rates

Table 10. Net replacement data for registered nurses, by age group, 2000-10

(Numbers in thousands)

| Age | 2000 employment[1] | | Net replacement needs, 2000-2005 | 2005 employment | Net replacement needs, 2005-10 |
	Number	Replacement rate, 1995-2000 (percent)		Number	
16-99......	2,088	7.4	183	—	235
16-19....	1	0	0	0	0
20-24....	59	0	0	1	0
25-29....	207	0	0	59	0
30-34....	266	0	0	207	0
35-39....	327	0	0	266	0
40-44....	411	0.8	3	327	3
45-49....	341	9.5	32	398	38
50-54....	225	18.2	41	308	56
55-59....	142	32.2	46	184	59
60-64....	73	59.1	43	96	57
65-69....	24	48.3	12	30	14
70-74....	9	58.3	5	12	7
75-99....	3	34.6	1	4	1

[1] 2000 data are averages of 1997, 1998, 1999, and 2000.

were developed by (1) identifying the CPS occupation or occupations that are equivalent to the detailed OES survey-based occupation, and (2) either using the CPS rate directly or calculating a weighted rate, using OES or CPS employment figures as weights, if the occupation consisted of more than one OES or CPS occupation. Table 11 presents 2000-10 total and net replacement rates for 2000 OES-based matrix occupations and shows 2000-10 annual average total and net replacement needs. Information identifying OES occupations for which CPS equivalent occupational data were replaced with that of a proxy CPS occupation is available from the Division of Occupational Outlook at (202) 691-5703.

Frequently asked questions about replacement data

Q. *Why does BLS compute estimates of both total and net replacement needs data?*
A. A single estimate is not appropriate for all purposes. Vocational guidance counseling, for example, requires information about growth and replacement needs that quantifies all opportunities in the labor market. However, training program planning is better served with information about opportunities for new entrants. Thus, two different estimates are provided.

Q. *Why is the estimate of growth and net replacement needs described as providing a minimum measure of training needs?*
A. In the younger age groups, more individuals are entering than leaving the occupation, and the measure of net separations for that age group is zero. A trained person who dies may require a replacement, but would not be included in net replacement needs estimates. More significantly, not all persons completing training enter the occupation for which they qualify. As a result, more workers must be trained to ensure that the minimum number enter the occupation.

Q. *Do the 2000-10 projected net replacement rates assume that future labor market behavior will not change from past patterns?*
A. Yes, 1995-2000 occupation- and age-specific rates are used in calculating the projected rates. The 1995-2000 rates are applied to projected occupational age-distribution data. The result is an occupation-specific replacement rate that captures the impact of demographic, but not behavioral, changes.

Q. *Are total and net separation rates the same as total and net replacement needs?*
A. In most occupations, yes. If employment declines during the period being examined, however, separations will exceed replacement needs by the employment decline. When employment is declining, not all persons separating from the occupation are replaced.

Q. *Should a projected decline in employment be subtracted from replacement needs to estimate job opportunities?*
A. No! If employment declines, the number of opportunities resulting from growth is zero, with replacement needs constituting the only source. When employment declines, separations increase both because individuals are losing their jobs and, in the case of net separations, because fewer are entering the occupation. Replacement needs—calculated by reducing separations by any decline in employment—should not be further reduced by projected employment declines.

Q. *If employment is declining rapidly, is it possible for replacement needs to be zero?*
A. In the extreme case, yes. For example, assume that, in a limited geographic area, a single firm is the sole employer of tool and die makers. If the firm ceases operations, all tool and die makers in the area will leave the occupation; separations will equal the decline in employment and there are no replacement needs. An analogous situation, though possible, is unlikely to occur at the national level because not all areas of the country share the same market conditions.

Table 11. Total and net replacement rates and annual average replacement needs, 2000-10

(Numbers in thousands)

2000 Matrix occupation	Total employment, 2000	Replacement rate (Percent) Total, 1999-2000	Net, 2000-10 Annual average	Net, 2000-10 10-year	Annual average replacement needs, 2000-10 Total	Annual average replacement needs, 2000-10 Net
Total, all occupations	145,594	14.3	2.4	23.7	20,858	3,453
Management, business, and financial occupations	15,519	9.9	1.7	17.0	1,544	265
Management occupations	10,564	9.8	1.6	16.3	1,032	172
Administrative services managers	362	8.5	1.6	16.3	31	6
Advertising, marketing, promotions, public relations, and sales managers	707	6.4	1.4	14.4	45	10
Advertising and promotions managers	100	6.5	1.4	14.3	7	1
Marketing and sales managers	533	6.1	1.4	14.4	32	8
Marketing managers	190	6.1	1.4	14.4	12	3
Sales managers	343	6.1	1.4	14.3	21	5
Public relations managers	74	9.0	1.5	15.3	7	1
Agricultural managers	1,462	10.9	0.6	6.4	159	9
Farm, ranch, and other agricultural managers[1]	169	8.5	1.1	11.5	14	2
Farmers and ranchers[1]	1,294	11.3	0.6	5.7	146	7
Chief executives	547	8.7	3.1	31.4	48	17
Computer and information systems managers	313	9.0	1.7	16.9	28	5
Construction managers	308	8.5	1.6	16.3	26	5
Education administrators	453	7.7	2.6	25.9	35	12
Engineering managers	282	8.5	1.6	16.3	24	5
Financial managers	658	8.1	1.5	15.3	53	10
Food service managers	465	11.8	1.2	11.8	55	6
Funeral directors	32	9.2	1.7	17.2	3	1
Gaming managers	4	9.9	1.9	18.5	(2)	(2)
General and operations managers	2,398	9.8	1.7	16.8	235	40
Human resources managers	219	6.5	1.7	17.3	14	4
Industrial production managers	255	8.5	1.6	16.3	22	4
Legislators	54	9.8	3.1	31.4	5	2
Lodging managers	68	11.8	1.2	11.8	8	1
Medical and health services managers	250	10.7	1.7	17.2	27	4
Natural sciences managers	42	9.3	1.8	17.6	4	1
Postmasters and mail superintendents	25	9.2	1.7	17.2	2	(2)
Property, real estate, and community association managers	270	8.9	1.6	16.3	24	4
Purchasing managers	132	12.9	3.1	31.3	17	4
Social and community service managers	128	9.9	1.9	18.8	13	2
Transportation, storage, and distribution managers	149	8.5	1.6	16.3	13	2
All other managers	981	9.8	1.8	17.7	96	17
Business and financial operations occupations	4,956	10.5	1.9	18.6	522	92
Business operations specialists	2,841	10.4	2.0	19.8	295	56
Agents and business managers of artists, performers, and athletes	17	10.9	2.0	20.2	2	(2)
Buyers and purchasing agents	404	10.8	2.4	23.6	44	10
Purchasing agents and buyers, farm products	20	9.8	2.0	19.8	2	(2)
Purchasing agents, except wholesale, retail, and farm products	237	9.8	2.0	19.8	23	5
Wholesale and retail buyers, except farm products	148	12.0	3.0	30.3	18	4
Claims adjusters, appraisers, examiners, and investigators	207	12.1	1.1	11.1	25	2
Claims adjusters, examiners, and investigators	194	12.1	1.1	11.1	24	2
Insurance appraisers, auto damage	13	12.1	1.1	11.1	2	(2)
Compliance officers, except agriculture, construction, health and safety, and transportation[1]	140	6.8	2.5	25.5	9	4
Cost estimators	211	13.1	2.2	22.0	28	5
Emergency management specialists	10	13.5	2.9	28.5	1	(2)
Human resources, training, and labor relations specialists	490	9.7	1.9	19.3	48	9
Compensation, benefits, and job analysis specialists	87	9.7	1.9	19.3	8	2
Employment, recruitment, and placement specialists	199	9.7	1.9	19.3	19	4
Training and development specialists	204	9.7	1.9	19.3	20	4
Management analysts	501	9.9	0.9	8.8	50	4
Meeting and convention planners	34	9.9	1.8	18.5	3	1
All other business operations specialists	827	10.4	2.5	25.4	86	21
Financial specialists	2,115	10.9	1.7	17.0	230	36
Accountants and auditors	976	10.3	1.5	14.8	100	14
Appraisers and assessors of real estate	57	9.8	2.8	28.4	6	2

See footnotes at end of table.

(Numbers in thousands)

2000 Matrix occupation	Total employ-ment, 2000	Replacement rate (Percent)			Annual average replacement needs, 2000-10	
		Total, 1999-2000	Net, 2000-10		Total	Net
			Annual average	10-year		
Budget analysts	70	11.7	2.0	20.0	8	1
Credit analysts	60	11.7	2.0	20.0	7	1
Financial analysts	145	13.5	1.4	13.6	20	2
Financial examiners	25	10.0	1.9	19.2	2	(2)
Insurance underwriters	107	9.9	1.5	15.2	11	2
Loan counselors and officers	265	11.7	2.0	20.0	31	5
Loan counselors	29	11.7	2.0	20.0	3	1
Loan officers	236	11.7	2.0	20.0	28	5
Personal financial advisors	94	14.2	1.2	11.6	13	1
Tax examiners, collectors, and revenue agents	79	7.9	2.7	26.6	6	2
Tax preparers	69	11.7	2.0	20.0	8	1
All other financial specialists	169	11.7	2.0	20.0	20	3
Professional and related occupations	26,758	9.4	1.9	19.4	2,505	520
Computer and mathematical occupations	2,993	7.4	1.0	9.7	221	29
Computer specialists	2,903	7.3	0.9	9.2	212	27
Computer programmers	585	6.1	2.1	21.0	36	12
Computer scientists and systems analysts	459	7.9	0.9	8.8	36	4
Computer and information scientists, research	28	7.9	0.9	8.8	2	(2)
Computer systems analysts	431	7.9	0.9	8.8	34	4
Computer software engineers	697	7.4	0.7	6.7	51	5
Computer software engineers, applications	380	7.4	0.7	6.7	28	3
Computer software engineers, systems software	317	7.4	0.7	6.7	23	2
Computer support specialists	506	7.9	0.4	4.2	40	2
Database administrators	106	7.9	0.4	4.2	8	(2)
Network and computer systems administrators	229	7.9	0.4	4.2	18	1
Network systems and data communications analysts	119	7.9	0.4	4.2	9	1
All other computer specialists	203	7.9	0.9	8.8	16	2
Mathematical science occupations	89	8.6	2.3	23.0	8	2
Mathematical scientists and technicians	85	8.6	2.4	23.6	7	2
Actuaries	14	8.1	1.3	12.8	1	(2)
Mathematicians	4	8.1	1.3	12.8	(2)	(2)
Operations research analysts	47	8.8	3.2	32.2	4	2
Statisticians	19	8.1	1.3	12.8	2	(2)
Miscellaneous mathematical science occupations	5	8.1	1.3	12.8	(2)	(2)
Architecture and engineering occupations	2,605	6.3	2.1	20.8	165	54
Architects, surveyors, and cartographers	196	4.8	1.4	14.0	9	3
Architects, except naval	124	3.8	0.6	5.7	5	1
Architects, except landscape and naval	102	3.8	0.6	5.7	4	1
Landscape architects	22	3.8	0.6	5.7	1	(2)
Surveyors, cartographers, and photogrammetrists	65	12.2	3.0	30.4	8	2
Cartographers and photogrammetrists	7	12.2	3.0	30.4	1	(2)
Surveyors	58	12.2	3.0	30.4	7	2
All other architects, surveyors, and cartographers	6	12.2	0.6	5.7	1	(2)
Engineers	1,465	4.5	2.0	20.0	65	29
Aerospace engineers	50	4.7	3.0	29.5	2	1
Agricultural engineers	2	4.7	2.2	21.8	(2)	(2)
Biomedical engineers	7	6.1	2.0	19.9	(2)	(2)
Chemical engineers	33	4.7	1.8	17.5	2	1
Civil engineers	232	1.8	1.6	15.6	4	4
Computer hardware engineers	60	5.7	1.4	14.3	3	1
Electrical and electronics engineers	288	4.9	1.8	18.3	14	5
Electrical engineers	157	4.9	1.8	18.3	8	3
Electronics engineers, except computer	130	4.9	1.8	18.3	6	2
Environmental engineers	52	6.1	2.0	19.9	3	1
Industrial engineers, including health and safety	198	6.3	1.7	16.7	13	3
Health and safety engineers, except mining safety engineers and inspectors	44	6.3	1.7	16.7	3	1
Industrial engineers	154	6.3	1.7	16.7	10	3
Marine engineers and naval architects	5	4.7	2.2	21.8	(2)	(2)
Materials engineers	33	4.7	2.2	21.8	2	1
Mechanical engineers	221	3.2	2.9	29.3	7	6

See footnotes at end of table.

Table 11. Total and net replacement rates and annual average replacement needs, 2000-10 — Continued

(Numbers in thousands)

2000 Matrix occupation	Total employment, 2000	Replacement rate (Percent)			Annual average replacement needs, 2000-10	
		Total, 1999-2000	Net, 2000-10		Total	Net
			Annual average	10-year		
Mining and geological engineers, including mining safety engineers	6	4.7	2.2	21.8	(^{2})	(^{2})
Nuclear engineers	14	4.7	2.2	21.8	1	(^{2})
Petroleum engineers	9	4.7	2.2	21.8	(^{2})	(^{2})
All other engineers	253	6.1	2.0	19.9	15	5
Drafters, engineering, and mapping technicians	944	10.1	2.3	23.4	96	22
Drafters	213	11.9	3.0	30.3	25	6
Architectural and civil drafters	102	11.9	3.0	30.3	12	3
Electrical and electronics drafters	41	11.9	3.0	30.3	5	1
Mechanical drafters	70	11.9	3.0	30.3	8	2
Engineering technicians, except drafters	519	9.3	2.0	20.2	48	10
Aerospace engineering and operations technicians[1]	21	9.3	2.0	20.2	2	(^{2})
Civil engineering technicians[1]	94	9.3	2.0	20.2	9	2
Electrical and electronic engineering technicians[1]	233	9.3	2.0	20.2	22	5
Electro-mechanical technicians[1]	43	9.3	2.0	20.2	4	1
Environmental engineering technicians[1]	18	9.3	2.0	20.2	2	(^{2})
Industrial engineering technicians[1]	52	9.3	2.0	20.2	5	1
Mechanical engineering technicians[1]	58	9.3	2.0	20.2	5	1
Surveying and mapping technicians[1]	55	13.4	3.2	32.3	7	2
All other drafters, engineering, and mapping technicians[1]	156	10.2	2.2	21.6	16	3
Life, physical, and social science occupations	1,164	10.1	2.9	28.9	118	34
Life scientists	184	6.3	3.2	32.4	12	6
Agricultural and food scientists	17	6.9	3.3	32.5	1	1
Biological scientists	73	7.5	3.6	35.9	5	3
Conservation scientists and foresters	29	6.9	3.3	32.5	2	1
Conservation scientists	16	6.9	3.3	32.5	1	1
Foresters	12	6.9	3.3	32.5	1	(^{2})
Medical scientists	37	4.1	2.3	22.7	2	1
All other life scientists	28	4.1	3.6	35.9	1	1
Physical scientists	239	7.1	3.3	33.5	17	8
Astronomers and physicists	10	6.9	3.3	32.5	1	(^{2})
Atmospheric and space scientists	7	6.9	3.3	32.5	(^{2})	(^{2})
Chemists and materials scientists	92	7.3	3.1	31.4	7	3
Chemists	84	7.3	3.1	31.4	6	3
Materials scientists	8	7.3	3.1	31.4	1	(^{2})
Environmental scientists and geoscientists	97	6.9	3.3	32.5	7	3
Environmental scientists and specialists, including health	64	6.9	3.3	32.5	4	2
Geoscientists, except hydrologists and geographers	25	6.9	3.3	32.5	2	1
Hydrologists	8	6.9	3.3	32.5	1	(^{2})
All other physical scientists[1]	33	7.7	4.2	42.4	3	1
Social scientists and related occupations	410	11.6	2.3	23.2	48	10
Economists	22	14.9	2.2	22.1	3	(^{2})
Market and survey researchers	113	14.9	2.2	22.1	17	2
Market research analysts	90	14.9	2.2	22.1	13	2
Survey researchers	23	14.9	2.2	22.1	3	(^{2})
Psychologists	182	9.7	2.3	23.3	18	4
Social scientists, other[1]	15	10.3	2.5	25.0	2	(^{2})
Urban and regional planners[1]	30	10.3	2.5	25.0	3	1
All other social scientists and related workers[1]	49	9.9	2.4	24.2	5	1
Life, physical, and social science technicians	330	15.4	3.1	30.6	51	10
Agricultural and food science technicians	18	17.6	2.3	23.2	3	(^{2})
Biological technicians	41	17.6	2.3	23.2	7	1
Chemical technicians[1]	73	17.6	2.3	23.2	13	2
Geological and petroleum technicians[1]	10	17.6	2.3	23.2	2	(^{2})
Nuclear technicians	3	6.7	3.0	30.0	(^{2})	(^{2})
Other life, physical, and social science technicians	184	11.0	3.6	36.4	20	7
Environmental science and protection technicians, including health[1]	27	11.0	3.6	36.4	3	1
Forensic science technicians[1]	6	11.0	3.6	36.4	1	(^{2})
Forest and conservation technicians[1]	18	11.0	3.6	36.4	2	1
All other life, physical, and social science technicians[1]	133	11.0	3.6	36.4	15	5
Community and social services occupations	1,869	11.8	1.7	17.0	221	32

See footnotes at end of table.

110

Table 11. Total and net replacement rates and annual average replacement needs, 2000-10 — Continued

(Numbers in thousands)

2000 Matrix occupation	Total employ-ment, 2000	Replacement rate (Percent)			Annual average replacement needs, 2000-10	
		Total, 1999-2000	Net, 2000-10		Total	Net
			Annual average	10-year		
Counselors	465	10.9	2.0	20.5	51	10
Educational, vocational, and school counselors	205	10.9	2.0	20.5	22	4
Marriage and family therapists	21	10.9	2.0	20.5	2	(2)
Mental health counselors	67	10.9	2.0	20.5	7	1
Rehabilitation counselors	110	10.9	2.0	20.5	12	2
Substance abuse and behavioral disorder counselors	61	10.9	2.0	20.5	7	1
Miscellaneous community and social service specialists	398	16.5	1.5	14.8	66	6
Health educators[1]	43	16.5	1.5	14.8	7	1
Probation officers and correctional treatment specialists[1]	84	16.5	1.5	14.9	14	1
Social and human service assistants[1]	271	16.5	1.5	14.8	45	4
Religious workers	293	8.6	2.3	23.0	25	7
Clergy	171	6.9	2.7	27.3	12	5
Directors, religious activities and education	121	18.9	1.7	17.0	23	2
Social workers	468	12.6	1.1	11.2	59	5
Child, family, and school social workers	281	12.6	1.1	11.2	35	3
Medical and public health social workers	104	12.6	1.1	11.2	13	1
Mental health and substance abuse social workers	83	12.6	1.1	11.2	10	1
All other counselors, social, and religious workers[1]	244	13.6	1.7	17.5	33	4
Legal occupations	1,119	7.2	0.8	7.9	80	9
Judges, magistrates, and other judicial workers	43	9.8	2.8	28.4	4	1
Administrative law judges, adjudicators, and hearing officers[1]	14	9.8	2.8	28.4	1	(2)
Arbitrators, mediators, and conciliators[1]	4	9.8	2.8	28.4	(2)	(2)
Judges, magistrate judges, and magistrates[1]	24	9.8	2.8	28.3	2	1
Lawyers	681	5.1	0.7	6.7	35	5
Paralegals and legal assistants	188	12.2	0.6	6.1	23	1
Miscellaneous legal support workers	98	10.2	0.9	9.2	10	1
Court reporters	18	10.2	0.9	9.2	2	(2)
Law clerks	31	10.2	0.9	9.2	3	(2)
Title examiners, abstractors, and searchers	48	10.2	0.9	9.2	5	(2)
All other legal and related workers	109	10.2	0.9	9.2	11	1
Education, training, and library occupations	8,260	11.4	2.2	21.6	943	179
Postsecondary teachers[1]	1,344	13.7	2.7	27.3	184	37
Primary, secondary, and special education teachers	4,284	8.7	2.2	22.2	372	95
Preschool and kindergarten teachers	597	13.1	1.2	12.4	78	7
Preschool teachers, except special education	423	13.1	1.2	12.4	55	5
Kindergarten teachers, except special education	175	13.1	1.2	12.4	23	2
Elementary and middle school teachers	2,122	9.4	2.3	22.7	199	48
Elementary school teachers, except special education	1,532	9.4	2.3	22.7	144	35
Middle school teachers, except special and vocational education	570	9.4	2.3	22.7	54	13
Vocational education teachers, middle school	20	9.4	2.3	22.7	2	(2)
Secondary school teachers	1,113	6.0	3.0	30.5	67	34
Secondary school teachers, except special and vocational education	1,004	6.0	3.0	30.4	60	31
Vocational education teachers, secondary school	109	6.0	3.0	30.5	7	3
Special education teachers	453	6.4	1.3	12.7	29	6
Special education teachers, preschool, kindergarten, and elementary school	234	6.4	1.3	12.7	15	3
Special education teachers, middle school	96	6.4	1.3	12.7	6	1
Special education teachers, secondary school	123	6.4	1.3	12.7	8	2
Other teachers and instructors	901	18.4	1.0	10.0	166	9
Adult literacy, remedial education, and GED teachers and instructors	67	18.4	1.0	10.0	12	1
Self-enrichment education teachers	186	18.4	1.0	10.0	34	2
All other teachers, primary, secondary, and adult	648	18.4	1.0	10.0	119	7
Library, museum, training, and other education occupations	1,731	16.6	2.2	21.7	287	38
Archivists, curators, and museum technicians[1]	21	4.2	2.1	20.5	1	(2)
Librarians	149	4.1	2.1	20.8	6	3
Library technicians	109	26.6	4.4	44.5	29	5
Teacher assistants	1,262	20.3	2.1	20.9	256	26
Other education, training, library, and museum workers	190	19.0	1.5	14.5	36	3
Audio-visual collections specialists	11	19.0	1.5	14.5	2	(2)
Farm and home management advisors	11	19.0	1.5	14.5	2	(2)
Instructional coordinators	81	19.0	1.5	14.5	15	1
All other library, museum, training, and other education workers	87	19.0	1.5	14.5	17	1

See footnotes at end of table.

(Numbers in thousands)

2000 Matrix occupation	Total employment, 2000	Replacement rate (Percent)			Annual average replacement needs, 2000-10	
		Total, 1999-2000	Net, 2000-10		Total	Net
			Annual average	10-year		
Arts, design, entertainment, sports, and media occupations	2,371	14.0	1.9	19.0	333	45
Art and design occupations	750	14.2	1.3	13.1	106	10
Artists and related workers	147	12.2	2.1	20.6	18	3
Art directors[1]	47	12.2	2.1	20.6	6	1
Fine artists, including painters, sculptors, and illustrators[1]	31	12.2	2.1	20.6	4	1
Multi-media artists and animators[1]	69	12.2	2.1	20.6	8	1
Designers	492	14.8	1.0	10.0	73	5
Commercial and industrial designers	50	14.8	1.0	10.0	7	1
Fashion designers	16	14.8	1.0	10.0	2	(2)
Floral designers	102	14.8	1.0	10.0	15	1
Graphic designers	190	14.8	1.0	10.0	28	2
Interior designers	46	14.8	1.0	10.0	7	(2)
Merchandise displayers and window trimmers	76	14.8	1.0	10.0	11	1
Set and exhibit designers	12	14.8	1.0	10.0	2	(2)
All other art and design workers[1]	112	13.7	1.6	16.4	15	2
Entertainers and performers, sports and related occupations	626	18.2	1.9	19.2	114	12
Actors, producers, and directors	158	19.5	1.9	19.2	31	3
Actors	99	20.2	1.9	19.2	20	2
Producers and directors[1]	58	19.2	1.9	19.2	11	1
Athletes, coaches, umpires, and related workers	129	19.2	2.0	19.8	25	3
Athletes and sports competitors	18	19.2	2.0	19.8	3	(2)
Coaches and scouts	99	19.2	2.0	19.8	19	2
Umpires, referees, and other sports officials	11	19.2	2.0	19.8	2	(2)
Dancers and choreographers	26	14.7	1.9	19.3	4	1
Dancers[1]	15	14.7	1.9	19.2	2	(2)
Choreographers[1]	11	14.7	1.9	19.3	2	(2)
Musicians, singers, and related workers	240	17.2	1.9	18.9	41	5
Music directors and composers	50	17.2	1.9	18.9	9	1
Musicians and singers	191	17.2	1.9	18.9	33	4
All other entertainers and performers, sports and related workers[1]	74	14.7	1.9	19.3	11	1
Media and communication occupations	703	12.3	2.3	22.5	87	16
Announcers	71	5.9	1.5	15.0	4	1
News analysts, reporters and correspondents	78	12.1	3.2	32.4	9	3
Public relations specialists	137	13.9	1.7	17.0	19	2
Writers and editors	305	12.3	2.5	25.4	37	8
Editors	122	11.9	3.2	32.4	14	4
Technical writers	57	8.7	3.0	30.1	5	2
Writers and authors	126	14.3	1.6	16.4	18	2
Miscellaneous media and communications workers	112	14.7	1.9	19.3	17	2
Interpreters and translators[1]	22	14.7	1.9	19.3	3	(2)
All other media and communication workers[1]	90	14.7	1.9	19.3	13	2
Media and communication equipment occupations	291	9.3	2.5	25.2	27	7
Broadcast and sound engineering technicians and radio operators	87	8.2	3.0	29.7	7	3
Audio and video equipment technicians[1]	37	8.2	3.0	29.7	3	1
Broadcast technicians[1]	36	8.2	3.0	29.7	3	1
Radio operators[1]	3	8.2	3.0	29.7	(2)	(2)
Sound engineering technicians[1]	11	8.2	3.0	29.7	1	(2)
Photographers	131	9.9	2.0	19.9	13	3
Television, video, and motion picture camera operators and editors	43	9.9	2.0	20.0	4	1
Camera operators, television, video, and motion picture	27	9.9	2.0	20.0	3	1
Film and video editors	16	9.9	2.0	20.0	2	(2)
All other media and communication equipment workers[1]	31	6.1	4.2	42.4	2	1
Healthcare practitioners and technical occupations	6,379	6.9	2.2	21.9	443	140
Health diagnosing and treating practitioners	3,921	6.0	2.1	20.6	233	81
Chiropractors	50	4.0	1.8	18.2	2	1
Dentists	152	4.0	2.3	22.6	6	3
Dietitians and nutritionists	49	10.8	2.7	26.9	5	1
Optometrists	31	4.0	1.8	18.2	1	1
Pharmacists	217	9.4	3.0	29.9	20	6
Physicians and surgeons	598	4.5	1.5	14.8	27	9
Physician assistants	58	9.4	2.2	21.7	5	1

See footnotes at end of table.

(Numbers in thousands)

2000 Matrix occupation	Total employ-ment, 2000	Replacement rate (Percent)			Annual average replacement needs, 2000-10	
		Total, 1999-2000	Net, 2000-10		Total	Net
			Annual average	10-year		
Podiatrists	18	4.0	1.8	18.2	1	(2)
Registered nurses	2,194	6.4	2.0	20.2	140	44
Therapists	439	4.5	2.5	24.9	20	11
Audiologists[1]	13	4.5	2.5	25.1	1	(2)
Occupational therapists	78	4.5	2.5	25.1	4	2
Physical therapists[1]	132	4.5	2.5	25.1	6	3
Radiation therapists	16	6.1	2.0	20.5	1	(2)
Recreational therapists[1]	29	4.5	2.5	25.1	1	1
Respiratory therapists	83	4.5	2.5	25.1	4	2
Speech-language pathologists[1]	88	4.5	2.5	25.1	4	2
Veterinarians	59	4.0	1.8	18.2	2	1
All other health diagnosing and treating practitioners	57	4.5	2.2	21.6	3	1
Other health professionals and technicians	2,457	9.4	2.4	24.0	230	59
Clinical laboratory technologists and technicians	295	13.1	2.3	23.5	39	7
Medical and clinical laboratory technologists	148	13.1	2.3	23.5	19	3
Medical and clinical laboratory technicians	147	13.1	2.3	23.5	19	3
Dental hygienists	147	3.4	1.4	14.5	5	2
Diagnostic related technologists and technicians	257	7.7	2.2	22.0	20	6
Cardiovascular technologists and technicians	39	7.7	2.2	22.0	3	1
Diagnostic medical sonographers	33	7.7	2.2	22.0	3	1
Nuclear medicine technologists	18	7.7	2.2	22.0	1	(2)
Radiologic technologists and technicians	167	7.7	2.2	22.0	13	4
Emergency medical technicians and paramedics	172	11.2	2.5	25.3	19	4
Health diagnosing and treating practitioner support technicians	417	11.5	2.6	25.9	48	11
Dietetic technicians	26	11.5	2.6	25.9	3	1
Pharmacy technicians	190	11.5	2.6	25.9	22	5
Psychiatric technicians	54	11.5	2.6	25.9	6	1
Respiratory therapy technicians	27	11.5	2.6	25.9	3	1
Surgical technologists	71	11.5	2.6	25.9	8	2
Veterinary technologists and technicians	49	11.5	2.6	25.9	6	1
Licensed practical and licensed vocational nurses	700	8.3	2.6	25.7	58	18
Medical records and health information technicians[1]	136	10.4	2.2	22.3	14	3
Opticians, dispensing	68	2.1	1.8	18.5	1	1
Other health practitioners and technical workers	266	8.2	2.6	25.8	22	7
Athletic trainers	15	11.5	2.6	25.8	2	(2)
Occupational health and safety specialists and technicians	35	11.5	2.6	25.8	4	1
Orthotists and prosthetists	5	11.5	2.6	25.9	1	(2)
All other health practitioners and technical workers[1]	212	8.0	2.6	25.8	17	5
Service occupations	26,075	21.5	3.2	31.9	5,594	832
Healthcare support occupations	3,196	17.5	1.7	17.1	558	55
Dental assistants	247	6.3	1.8	17.9	16	4
Massage therapists	34	20.8	2.3	22.8	7	1
Nursing, psychiatric, and home health aides	2,053	19.5	1.3	12.8	400	26
Home health aides	615	19.5	1.3	12.7	120	8
Nursing aides, orderlies, and attendants	1,373	19.5	1.3	12.8	268	18
Psychiatric aides	65	19.5	1.3	12.8	13	1
Occupational therapist assistants and aides	25	20.2	2.9	29.4	5	1
Occupational therapist assistants	17	20.2	2.9	29.4	3	(2)
Occupational therapist aides	9	20.2	2.9	29.4	2	(2)
Physical therapist assistants and aides	80	20.2	2.9	29.4	16	2
Physical therapist assistants	44	20.2	2.9	29.4	9	1
Physical therapist aides	36	20.2	2.9	29.4	7	1
Medical assistants and other healthcare support occupations	757	15.0	2.7	26.5	113	20
Medical assistants	329	15.0	2.7	26.5	49	9
Medical equipment preparers	33	15.0	2.7	26.5	5	1
Medical transcriptionists	102	15.0	2.7	26.5	15	3
Pharmacy aides	57	15.0	2.7	26.5	9	2
Veterinary assistants and laboratory animal caretakers	55	15.0	2.7	26.5	8	1
All other healthcare support workers	181	15.0	2.7	26.5	27	5

See footnotes at end of table.

(Numbers in thousands)

2000 Matrix occupation	Total employ-ment, 2000	Replacement rate (Percent)			Annual average replacement needs, 2000-10	
		Total, 1999-2000	Net, 2000-10		Total	Net
			Annual average	10-year		
Protective service occupations	3,087	12.6	2.8	28.1	389	87
First-line supervisors/managers, protective service workers	273	8.2	2.8	27.8	22	8
First-line supervisors/managers of correctional officers	30	9.2	1.7	17.2	3	1
First-line supervisors/managers of fire fighting and prevention workers[1]	62	8.6	3.2	31.9	5	2
First-line supervisors/managers of police and detectives	121	7.8	2.7	27.0	9	3
First-line supervisors/managers of protective service workers, except police, fire and corrections[1]	61	8.6	3.1	30.6	5	2
Fire fighters	258	4.6	2.6	25.9	12	7
Fire inspectors[1]	13	4.5	2.7	26.5	1	(2)
Law enforcement workers	1,150	4.9	2.2	22.3	57	26
Bailiffs, correctional officers, and jailers	427	7.2	2.4	24.3	31	10
Bailiffs[1]	14	7.2	2.4	24.3	1	(2)
Correctional officers and jailers[1]	414	7.2	2.4	24.3	30	10
Detectives and criminal investigators	93	4.2	2.2	22.4	4	2
Fish and game wardens[1]	8	3.4	1.2	12.1	(2)	(2)
Parking enforcement workers[1]	9	3.4	1.2	12.1	(2)	(2)
Police and sheriff's patrol officers[1]	607	3.4	2.1	21.1	21	13
Transit and railroad police	6	3.4	2.2	22.4	(2)	(2)
Other protective service workers	1,394	24.9	3.3	33.5	347	47
Animal control workers	9	45.9	7.6	76.5	4	1
Crossing guards[1]	74	24.6	3.4	34.0	18	3
Private detectives and investigators	39	22.7	2.8	27.6	9	1
Security guards and gaming surveillance officers	1,117	21.9	2.7	27.3	245	30
Gaming surveillance officers and gaming investigators[1]	11	21.9	2.7	27.3	2	(2)
Security guards[1]	1,106	21.9	2.7	27.3	242	30
All other protective service workers	156	45.9	7.6	76.5	72	12
Food preparation and serving related occupations	10,140	28.5	4.5	45.3	2,886	460
Supervisors, food preparation and serving workers	788	21.9	2.6	26.2	173	21
Chefs and head cooks	139	25.0	3.1	30.8	35	4
First-line supervisors/managers of food preparation and serving workers	649	21.0	2.5	25.2	136	16
Cooks and food preparation workers	2,709	24.4	3.2	31.6	661	86
Cooks	1,864	23.7	2.8	28.4	442	53
Cooks, fast food[1]	522	23.7	2.8	28.4	124	15
Cooks, institution and cafeteria[1]	465	23.7	2.8	28.4	110	13
Cooks, private household[1]	5	23.7	2.8	28.4	1	(2)
Cooks, restaurant[1]	668	23.7	2.8	28.4	158	19
Cooks, short order[1]	205	23.7	2.8	28.4	49	6
Food preparation workers	844	27.4	3.9	38.6	231	33
Food and beverage serving workers	5,201	31.9	5.8	58.4	1,659	304
Bartenders	387	21.8	3.9	39.5	84	15
Combined food preparation and serving workers, including fast food	2,206	33.4	6.1	61.2	737	135
Counter attendants, cafeteria, food concession, and coffee shop	421	51.3	7.7	77.5	216	33
Food servers, nonrestaurant	205	41.4	4.4	44.4	85	9
Waiters and waitresses	1,983	30.0	5.6	56.3	596	112
Other food preparation and serving related workers	1,442	33.1	3.5	34.5	477	50
Dining room and cafeteria attendants and bartender helpers	431	37.4	3.4	33.6	161	14
Dishwashers	525	29.8	3.8	37.5	156	20
Hosts and hostesses, restaurant, lounge, and coffee shop	343	24.6	3.0	29.8	84	10
All other food preparation and serving related workers	143	29.8	3.8	37.5	43	5
Building and grounds cleaning and maintenance occupations	5,549	20.4	2.0	20.4	1,131	113
Supervisors, building and grounds cleaning and maintenance workers	378	7.3	1.8	18.0	28	7
First-line supervisors/managers of housekeeping and janitorial workers	219	8.1	2.7	27.2	18	6
First-line supervisors/managers of landscaping, lawn service, and groundskeeping workers	159	6.5	0.5	5.5	10	1
Building cleaning workers	3,981	21.4	2.0	19.6	852	78
Janitors and cleaners, except maids and housekeeping cleaners	2,348	21.6	1.8	18.1	507	42
Maids and housekeeping cleaners[1]	1,633	21.2	2.2	21.7	346	35
Grounds maintenance workers	973	21.5	2.5	25.1	210	24
Landscaping and groundskeeping workers	894	21.5	2.5	25.1	193	22

See footnotes at end of table.

(Numbers in thousands)

2000 Matrix occupation	Total employment, 2000	Replacement rate (Percent)			Annual average replacement needs, 2000-10	
		Total, 1999-2000	Net, 2000-10		Total	Net
			Annual average	10-year		
Pesticide handlers, sprayers, and applicators, vegetation	27	21.5	2.5	25.1	6	1
Tree trimmers and pruners	52	21.5	2.5	25.1	11	1
Pest control workers[1]	58	11.5	2.0	20.2	7	1
All other building and grounds cleaning and maintenance workers	159	21.6	2.0	19.8	34	3
Personal care and service occupations	4,103	19.5	2.9	28.8	801	118
First-line supervisors/managers of personal service workers	125	6.8	2.8	27.6	8	3
Animal care and service workers	145	15.4	2.1	21.0	22	3
Animal trainers[1]	15	14.7	1.9	19.3	2	([2])
Nonfarm animal caretakers	131	15.5	2.1	21.1	20	3
Child care workers	1,193	31.0	3.4	33.9	370	40
Entertainment attendants and related workers	344	29.5	4.8	48.5	101	17
Motion picture projectionists[1]	11	15.1	2.4	23.5	2	([2])
Ushers, lobby attendants, and ticket takers[1]	112	22.8	8.0	80.2	26	9
Miscellaneous entertainment attendants and related workers	221	31.6	3.4	33.6	70	7
Amusement and recreation attendants	197	31.6	3.4	33.6	62	7
Costume, locker room, and other attendants	24	31.6	3.4	33.6	8	1
Funeral service workers	33	20.8	2.3	22.8	7	1
Embalmers	7	20.8	2.3	22.8	1	([2])
Funeral attendants	26	20.8	2.3	22.8	5	1
Gaming occupations	167	28.5	3.2	32.5	48	5
First-line supervisors/managers, gaming workers	46	6.8	2.8	27.6	3	1
Gaming supervisors	31	6.8	2.8	27.6	2	1
Slot key persons	14	6.8	2.8	27.6	1	([2])
Gaming services workers	100	32.4	3.4	34.4	32	3
Gaming and sports book writers and runners	12	32.4	3.4	34.4	4	([2])
Gaming dealers	88	32.4	3.4	34.4	28	3
All other gaming service workers	21	32.4	3.4	33.9	7	1
Personal appearance workers	790	11.3	2.5	24.8	89	20
Barbers	73	4.1	2.8	28.5	3	2
Hairdressers, hairstylists, and cosmetologists	636	12.3	2.4	24.4	78	16
Miscellaneous personal appearance workers	81	12.3	2.4	24.4	10	2
Manicurists and pedicurists	40	12.3	2.4	24.4	5	1
Shampooers	20	12.3	2.4	24.4	2	([2])
Skin care specialists	21	12.3	2.4	24.4	3	1
Personal and home care aides[1]	414	20.3	1.5	15.2	84	6
Recreation and fitness workers	427	11.9	2.1	20.7	51	9
Fitness trainers and aerobics instructors	158	11.9	2.1	20.7	19	3
Recreation workers	269	11.9	2.1	20.7	32	6
Residential advisors	44	20.8	2.3	22.8	9	1
Transportation, tourism, and lodging attendants	259	12.7	3.4	33.9	33	9
Baggage porters, bellhops, and concierges	68	22.8	3.4	34.4	16	2
Baggage porters and bellhops[1]	51	22.8	3.4	34.4	12	2
Concierges[1]	18	22.8	3.4	34.4	4	1
Tour and travel guides[1]	44	22.8	3.1	31.1	10	1
Transportation attendants	147	6.4	3.4	34.4	9	5
Flight attendants[1]	124	6.4	3.4	34.4	8	4
Transportation attendants, except flight attendants and baggage porters[1]	23	6.4	3.4	34.4	1	1
All other personal care and service workers	163	16.7	2.3	22.8	27	4
Sales and related occupations	15,513	18.0	3.1	31.2	2,792	484
Advertising sales agents	155	15.9	2.0	20.3	25	3
Cashiers	3,363	33.8	4.5	45.4	1,138	153
Cashiers, except gaming	3,325	33.8	4.5	45.4	1,125	151
Gaming change persons and booth cashiers	38	33.8	4.5	45.4	13	2
Counter and rental clerks	423	35.5	4.5	45.3	150	19
Door-to-door sales workers, news and street vendors, and related workers	166	25.3	2.6	25.6	42	4
Insurance sales agents	378	11.4	2.5	25.5	43	10
Models, demonstrators, and product promoters	121	29.2	3.3	32.6	35	4
Demonstrators and product promoters	118	29.2	3.3	32.6	34	4
Models	4	29.2	3.3	32.6	1	([2])
Parts salespersons	260	8.2	3.0	29.8	21	8

See footnotes at end of table.

Table 11. Total and net replacement rates and annual average replacement needs, 2000-10 — Continued

(Numbers in thousands)

2000 Matrix occupation	Total employment, 2000	Replacement rate (Percent)			Annual average replacement needs, 2000-10	
		Total, 1999-2000	Net, 2000-10		Total	Net
			Annual average	10-year		
Real estate brokers and sales agents	432	8.3	1.7	17.3	36	7
Real estate brokers	93	8.3	1.7	17.3	8	2
Real estate sales agents	339	8.3	1.7	17.3	28	6
Retail salespersons	4,109	27.4	3.8	38.0	1,124	156
Sales engineers[1]	85	4.7	2.6	25.8	4	2
Sales representatives, wholesale and manufacturing	1,821	6.0	2.7	27.1	110	49
Sales representatives, wholesale and manufacturing, technical and scientific products[1]	396	6.0	2.7	27.2	24	11
Sales representatives, wholesale and manufacturing, except technical and scientific products[1]	1,425	6.0	2.7	27.1	86	39
Securities, commodities, and financial services sales agents	367	15.1	0.8	8.1	55	3
Supervisors, sales workers	2,504	9.9	1.4	14.5	247	36
First-line supervisors/managers of retail sales workers	2,072	9.9	1.4	14.4	206	30
First-line supervisors/managers of non-retail sales workers	432	9.5	1.5	14.7	41	6
Telemarketers	572	25.4	2.1	20.6	145	12
Travel agents	135	16.8	2.4	24.2	23	3
All other sales and related workers[1]	621	15.9	2.2	22.0	99	14
Office and administrative support occupations	23,882	17.4	2.1	21.0	4,146	502
First-line supervisors/managers of office and administrative support workers[1]	1,392	10.5	1.9	19.3	146	27
Communications equipment operators	339	18.5	3.0	29.8	63	10
Switchboard operators, including answering service[1]	259	18.5	3.0	29.5	48	8
Telephone operators	54	18.5	2.9	29.5	10	2
All other communications equipment operators[1]	26	19.0	3.3	33.1	5	1
Financial, information, and record clerks	9,006	19.5	2.1	20.8	1,760	187
Financial clerks	3,696	15.6	2.5	25.1	577	93
Bill and account collectors	400	17.7	2.5	24.9	71	10
Billing and posting clerks and machine operators[1]	506	13.6	2.4	24.5	69	12
Bookkeeping, accounting, and auditing clerks	1,991	15.0	1.9	19.0	298	38
Gaming cage workers	22	33.8	4.5	45.4	7	1
Payroll and timekeeping clerks	201	12.7	2.9	29.0	26	6
Procurement clerks	76	16.6	2.3	22.8	13	2
Tellers	499	19.7	4.8	48.1	98	24
Information and record clerks	5,099	22.2	1.8	18.0	1,131	92
Brokerage clerks	70	10.7	1.3	13.1	7	1
Correspondence clerks[1]	38	14.1	2.9	29.3	5	1
Court, municipal, and license clerks	105	13.4	1.6	15.9	14	2
Credit authorizers, checkers, and clerks	86	19.9	0.9	9.1	17	1
Customer service representatives	1,946	18.4	0.8	8.5	359	17
Eligibility interviewers, government programs[1]	117	11.2	2.9	29.3	13	3
File clerks	288	27.3	3.2	31.9	79	9
Hotel, motel, and resort desk clerks	177	41.5	4.4	43.6	73	8
Human resources assistants, except payroll and timekeeping[1]	177	14.1	2.3	22.7	25	4
Interviewers, except eligibility and loan	154	34.2	2.1	21.2	53	3
Library assistants, clerical	98	26.6	4.4	44.5	26	4
Loan interviewers and clerks	139	18.3	0.7	6.8	25	1
New accounts clerks	87	34.2	2.1	21.2	30	2
Order clerks[1]	348	14.1	2.1	21.2	49	7
Receptionists and information clerks	1,078	24.9	2.2	22.0	269	24
Reservation and transportation ticket agents and travel clerks	191	20.4	2.7	27.0	39	5
All other financial, information, and record clerks	211	10.7	1.3	13.1	23	3
Material recording, scheduling, dispatching, and distributing occupations	4,238	17.2	2.7	27.3	729	116
Cargo and freight agents	60	14.9	2.0	20.1	9	1
Couriers and messengers	141	26.0	2.7	27.2	37	4
Dispatchers	254	4.7	1.6	16.5	12	4
Dispatchers, except police, fire, and ambulance[1]	168	4.7	1.6	16.5	8	3
Police, fire, and ambulance dispatchers[1]	86	4.7	1.6	16.5	4	1
Meter readers, utilities[1]	49	15.5	2.4	24.4	8	1
Postal service workers	688	4.1	2.6	25.8	28	18

See footnotes at end of table.

116

(Numbers in thousands)

2000 Matrix occupation	Total employment, 2000	Replacement rate (Percent)			Annual average replacement needs, 2000-10	
		Total, 1999-2000	Net, 2000-10		Total	Net
			Annual average	10-year		
Postal service clerks	74	4.1	2.2	21.9	3	2
Postal service mail carriers[1]	324	4.1	3.0	30.3	13	10
Postal service mail sorters, processors, and processing machine operators	289	4.1	2.2	21.9	12	6
Production, planning, and expediting clerks[1]	332	11.0	1.7	16.7	36	6
Shipping, receiving, and traffic clerks	890	14.9	2.0	20.1	133	18
Stock clerks and order fillers[1]	1,679	27.8	3.6	35.6	467	60
Weighers, measurers, checkers, and samplers, recordkeeping[1]	83	15.5	2.4	24.4	13	2
All other material recording, scheduling, dispatching, and distributing workers[1]	63	27.8	3.6	35.6	17	2
Secretaries, administrative assistants, and other office support occupations	8,908	15.8	1.8	18.2	1,405	162
Computer operators[1]	194	16.0	1.8	17.9	31	3
Data entry and information processing workers	806	16.8	1.7	17.4	136	14
Data entry keyers	509	17.7	1.6	15.8	90	8
Word processors and typists	297	15.7	2.0	20.2	47	6
Desktop publishers	38	12.7	1.8	17.9	5	1
Insurance claims and policy processing clerks[1]	289	12.2	1.7	17.3	35	5
Mail clerks and mail machine operators, except postal service[1]	188	11.9	2.9	29.2	22	5
Office clerks, general	2,705	25.0	1.9	19.2	676	52
Office machine operators, except computer[1]	84	21.6	3.5	35.2	18	3
Proofreaders and copy markers[1]	35	18.7	3.6	36.2	7	1
Secretaries and administrative assistants	3,902	12.8	1.7	17.0	500	66
Executive secretaries and administrative assistants	1,445	12.8	1.7	17.0	185	25
Legal secretaries	279	12.8	1.7	17.0	36	5
Medical secretaries	314	12.8	1.7	17.0	40	5
Secretaries, except legal, medical, and executive	1,864	12.8	1.7	17.0	239	32
Statistical assistants	21	9.7	0.9	8.8	2	(2)
All other secretaries, administrative assistants, and other office support workers[1]	645	13.8	1.6	16.1	89	10
Farming, fishing, and forestry occupations	1,429	18.7	3.0	29.7	267	42
First-line supervisors/managers/contractors of farming, fishing, and forestry workers[1]	100	8.4	0.8	7.6	8	1
Agricultural workers	987	20.5	3.3	32.6	202	32
Agricultural inspectors[1]	15	9.4	2.5	24.6	1	(2)
Farmworkers[1]	909	21.2	3.3	33.4	192	30
Graders and sorters, agricultural products[1]	63	19.3	2.3	23.2	12	1
Fishers and fishing vessel operators[1]	53	10.2	3.2	31.6	5	2
Forest, conservation, and logging workers	90	16.4	2.0	20.2	15	2
Forest and conservation workers[1]	21	16.8	2.4	24.4	4	1
Logging workers	69	15.8	1.9	18.8	11	1
Fallers	13	15.8	1.9	18.8	2	(2)
Logging equipment operators	47	15.8	1.9	18.8	7	1
Log graders and scalers	8	15.8	1.9	18.8	1	(2)
All other farming, fishing, and forestry workers[1]	199	19.7	3.0	30.5	39	6
Construction and extraction occupations	7,451	13.6	2.0	19.7	1,011	147
First-line supervisors/managers of construction trades and extraction workers[1]	792	5.4	2.3	22.8	43	18
Construction trades and related workers	6,466	14.9	1.9	18.9	963	122
Boilermakers[1]	27	7.7	2.6	25.9	2	1
Brickmasons, blockmasons, and stonemasons	158	12.6	1.9	18.6	20	3
Brickmasons and blockmasons[1]	144	12.6	1.9	18.6	18	3
Stonemasons[1]	14	12.6	1.9	18.6	2	(2)
Carpenters[1]	1,204	13.4	1.7	16.9	161	20
Carpet, floor, and tile installers and finishers	167	8.6	1.7	16.8	14	3
Carpet installers	76	8.6	1.7	16.8	7	1
Floor layers, except carpet, wood, and hard tiles	23	8.6	1.7	16.8	2	(2)
Floor sanders and finishers	14	8.6	1.7	16.8	1	(2)
Tile and marble setters	54	8.6	1.7	16.8	5	1
Cement masons, concrete finishers, and terrazzo workers	166	2.4	0.9	8.6	4	1
Cement masons and concrete finishers	162	2.4	0.9	8.6	4	1
Terrazzo workers and finishers	3	2.4	0.9	8.6	(2)	(2)
Construction laborers	791	29.8	0.9	9.1	236	7

See footnotes at end of table.

(Numbers in thousands)

2000 Matrix occupation	Total employment, 2000	Replacement rate (Percent)			Annual average replacement needs, 2000-10	
		Total, 1999-2000	Net, 2000-10		Total	Net
			Annual average	10-year		
Construction equipment operators	416	7.5	2.1	21.4	31	9
Operating engineers and other construction equipment operators[1]	357	7.1	2.2	21.8	25	8
Paving, surfacing, and tamping equipment operators[1]	55	11.3	1.9	19.3	6	1
Pile-driver operators	4	16.8	1.7	17.1	1	([2])
Drywall installers, ceiling tile installers, and tapers	188	13.1	1.0	9.6	25	2
Drywall and ceiling tile installers	143	13.1	1.0	9.6	19	1
Tapers	44	13.1	1.0	9.6	6	([2])
Electricians[1]	698	9.4	1.9	18.7	66	13
Glaziers[1]	49	12.6	1.9	18.6	6	1
Insulation workers	53	23.5	3.0	30.3	12	2
Painters, construction and maintenance	491	13.6	1.8	17.6	67	9
Paperhangers[1]	27	12.6	1.9	18.6	3	([2])
Pipelayers, plumbers, pipefitters, and steamfitters	568	9.7	1.6	16.5	55	9
Pipelayers[1]	65	9.7	1.6	16.5	6	1
Plumbers, pipefitters, and steamfitters[1]	503	9.7	1.6	16.5	49	8
Plasterers and stucco masons[1]	54	12.6	1.9	18.6	7	1
Reinforcing iron and rebar workers	27	12.9	1.1	10.7	4	([2])
Roofers	158	24.0	2.3	22.8	38	4
Sheet metal workers[1]	224	6.0	2.1	20.7	13	5
Structural iron and steel workers	84	13.9	1.1	10.7	12	1
Helpers, construction trades	450	23.7	5.0	49.6	107	22
Helpers-brickmasons, blockmasons, stonemasons, and tile and marble setters	58	23.7	5.0	49.6	14	3
Helpers-carpenters	101	23.7	5.0	49.6	24	5
Helpers-electricians	114	23.7	5.0	49.6	27	6
Helpers-painters, paperhangers, plasterers, and stucco masons	27	23.7	5.0	49.6	6	1
Helpers-pipelayers, plumbers, pipefitters, and steamfitters	86	23.7	5.0	49.6	20	4
Helpers-roofers	23	23.7	5.0	49.6	6	1
All other helpers, construction trades	41	23.7	5.0	49.6	10	2
Other construction and related workers	465	16.0	1.9	19.4	75	9
Construction and building inspectors	75	3.1	2.3	22.6	2	2
Elevator installers and repairers[1]	23	10.8	3.2	32.4	2	1
Fence erectors	29	16.8	1.7	17.1	5	([2])
Hazardous materials removal workers	37	23.5	3.0	30.3	9	1
Highway maintenance workers	151	20.8	1.5	15.0	31	2
Rail-track laying and maintenance equipment operators	12	24.1	2.2	21.5	3	([2])
Septic tank servicers and sewer pipe cleaners	15	26.3	2.2	22.4	4	([2])
All other construction and related workers	123	16.8	1.7	17.0	21	2
Extraction workers	193	8.0	3.5	35.1	15	7
Derrick, rotary drill, and service unit operators, oil, gas, and mining	45	6.2	3.5	35.0	3	2
Derrick operators, oil and gas[1]	16	6.2	3.5	35.0	1	1
Rotary drill operators, oil and gas[1]	18	6.2	3.5	35.0	1	1
Service unit operators, oil, gas, and mining[1]	11	6.2	3.5	35.0	1	([2])
Earth drillers, except oil and gas[1]	24	12.2	2.0	20.0	3	([2])
Explosives workers, ordnance handling experts, and blasters[1]	5	6.2	3.5	35.0	([2])	([2])
Helpers-Extraction workers[1]	37	16.1	4.5	45.1	6	2
Mining machine operators	22	6.2	3.5	35.0	1	1
Continuous mining machine operators[1]	10	6.2	3.5	35.0	1	([2])
Miscellaneous mining machine operators[1]	12	6.2	3.5	35.0	1	([2])
Roustabouts, oil and gas[1]	41	6.2	3.5	35.0	3	1
All other extraction workers[1]	19	7.4	3.5	35.0	1	1
Installation, maintenance, and repair occupations	5,820	9.2	2.2	21.8	535	127
First-line supervisors/managers of mechanics, installers, and repairers[1]	442	8.7	2.6	26.0	38	11
Electrical and electronic equipment mechanics, installers, and repairers	683	9.8	1.8	17.6	67	12
Avionics technicians	16	10.5	2.0	20.4	2	([2])
Computer, automated teller, and office machine repairers	172	13.9	1.1	10.8	24	2
Electric motor, power tool, and related repairers	37	9.4	2.3	23.0	3	1
Electrical and electronics installers and repairers, transportation equipment	14	9.7	1.9	19.1	1	([2])
Electrical and electronics repairers, industrial and utility	108	11.1	2.0	20.1	12	2
Electrical and electronics repairers, commercial and industrial equipment	90	11.1	2.0	20.1	10	2

See footnotes at end of table.

(Numbers in thousands)

2000 Matrix occupation	Total employment, 2000	Replacement rate (Percent)			Annual average replacement needs, 2000-10	
		Total, 1999-2000	Net, 2000-10		Total	Net
			Annual average	10-year		
Electrical and electronics repairers, powerhouse, substation, and relay	18	11.1	2.0	20.1	2	(²)
Electronic equipment installers and repairers, motor vehicles	13	9.4	2.3	23.0	1	(²)
Electronic home entertainment equipment installers and repairers	37	11.2	1.9	18.5	4	1
Radio and telecommunications equipment installers and repairers	196	4.9	1.9	18.8	10	4
Radio mechanics[1]	7	4.9	1.9	18.8	(²)	(²)
Telecommunications equipment installers and repairers, except line installers[1]	189	4.9	1.9	18.8	9	4
Security and fire alarm systems installers ...	44	9.5	1.9	18.6	4	1
All other electrical and electronic equipment mechanics, installers, and repairers[1]	48	4.9	2.3	23.0	2	1
Vehicle and mobile equipment mechanics, installers, and repairers	1,931	10.7	2.5	25.4	206	49
Aircraft mechanics and service technicians[1] ...	158	6.9	2.1	21.2	11	3
Automotive body and related repairers	199	9.1	2.5	24.7	18	5
Automotive glass installers and repairers	22	8.5	2.5	25.0	2	1
Automotive service technicians and mechanics[1] ...	840	12.4	2.4	23.6	104	20
Bus and truck mechanics and diesel engine specialists ...	285	6.9	2.6	25.7	20	7
Heavy vehicle and mobile equipment service technicians and mechanics	185	8.5	2.6	25.9	16	5
Farm equipment mechanics[1] ...	41	8.5	2.6	25.9	3	1
Mobile heavy equipment mechanics, except engines[1] ...	130	8.5	2.6	25.9	11	3
Rail car repairers[1] ...	14	8.5	2.6	25.9	1	(²)
Small engine mechanics ...	73	20.2	2.5	25.1	15	2
Motorboat mechanics ...	25	20.2	2.5	25.1	5	1
Motorcycle mechanics ...	14	20.2	2.5	25.1	3	(²)
Outdoor power equipment and other small engine mechanics	33	20.2	2.5	25.1	7	1
Miscellaneous vehicle and mobile equipment mechanics, installers, and repairers	170	29.8	3.8	38.3	51	6
Bicycle repairers ...	9	29.8	3.8	38.3	3	(²)
Recreational vehicle service technicians ...	12	29.8	3.8	38.3	4	(²)
Tire repairers and changers ...	89	29.8	3.8	38.3	27	3
All other vehicle and mobile equipment mechanics, installers, and repairers	60	29.8	3.8	38.3	18	2
Other installation, maintenance, and repair occupations	2,764	7.7	2.0	19.5	212	54
Coin, vending, and amusement machine servicers and repairers	37	12.0	2.2	22.1	4	1
Control and valve installers and repairers	46	10.8	3.2	32.4	5	1
Control and valve installers and repairers, except mechanical door[1] ...	34	10.8	3.2	32.4	4	1
Mechanical door repairers[1] ...	11	10.8	3.2	32.4	1	(²)
Heating, air conditioning, and refrigeration mechanics and installers	243	8.6	1.0	10.4	21	3
Helpers-Installation, maintenance, and repair workers[1] ...	145	23.7	5.1	51.0	35	7
Home appliance repairers[1] ...	43	12.2	2.1	20.5	5	1
Industrial machinery mechanics	198	3.5	2.7	27.0	7	5
Line installers and repairers	263	4.9	2.4	24.1	13	6
Electrical power-line installers and repairers ...	99	4.6	3.3	32.5	5	3
Telecommunications line installers and repairers[1] ...	164	5.3	1.9	19.0	9	3
Locksmiths and safe repairers[1] ...	23	10.8	3.2	32.4	3	1
Maintenance and repair workers, general	1,251	8.3	1.3	13.0	103	16
Maintenance workers, machinery[1] ...	114	3.4	2.7	27.0	4	3
Manufactured building and mobile home installers ...	17	10.3	2.0	20.4	2	(²)
Millwrights	72	10.2	3.0	30.1	7	2
Precision instrument and equipment repairers ...	63	10.5	2.5	25.0	7	2
Camera and photographic equipment repairers[1] ...	7	10.5	2.5	25.0	1	(²)
Medical equipment repairers[1] ...	28	10.5	2.5	25.0	3	1
Musical instrument repairers and tuners[1] ...	7	10.5	2.5	25.0	1	(²)
Watch repairers[1] ...	5	10.5	2.5	25.0	1	(²)
All other precision instrument and equipment repairers[1] ...	15	10.5	2.5	25.0	2	(²)
Riggers	20	10.3	2.0	20.4	2	(²)
All other installation, maintenance, and repair workers	228	7.1	2.0	20.4	16	5
Production occupations	13,060	14.6	2.3	22.8	1,906	297
First-line supervisors/managers of production and operating workers	819	8.7	2.6	26.3	71	22
Assemblers and fabricators	2,653	18.8	1.9	19.1	500	51
Aircraft structure, surfaces, rigging, and systems assemblers[1] ...	20	7.7	2.6	25.9	2	1
Electrical, electronics, and electromechanical assemblers ...	508	17.5	2.6	25.6	89	13
Coil winders, tapers, and finishers ...	56	17.5	2.6	25.6	10	1
Electrical and electronic equipment assemblers ...	379	17.5	2.6	25.6	66	10

See footnotes at end of table.

Table 11. Total and net replacement rates and annual average replacement needs, 2000-10 — Continued

(Numbers in thousands)

2000 Matrix occupation	Total employ-ment, 2000	Total, 1999-2000	Net, 2000-10 Annual average	Net, 2000-10 10-year	Annual average replacement needs, 2000-10 Total	Annual average replacement needs, 2000-10 Net
Electromechanical equipment assemblers	73	17.5	2.6	25.6	13	2
Engine and other machine assemblers[1]	67	15.9	2.0	19.9	11	1
Structural metal fabricators and fitters	101	19.8	1.5	15.4	20	2
Miscellaneous assemblers and fabricators	1,957	19.4	1.7	17.5	380	34
Fiberglass laminators and fabricators[1]	48	19.4	1.7	17.5	9	1
Team assemblers[1]	1,458	19.4	1.8	17.5	283	26
Timing device assemblers, adjusters, and calibrators[1]	12	19.4	1.8	17.5	2	(2)
All other assemblers and fabricators[1]	439	19.4	1.7	17.5	85	8
Food processing occupations	760	12.9	2.2	22.2	98	17
Bakers	160	15.9	1.6	15.8	25	3
Butchers and other meat, poultry, and fish processing workers	411	11.1	2.4	24.3	45	10
Butchers and meat cutters[1]	141	11.1	2.4	24.3	16	3
Meat, poultry, and fish cutters and trimmers[1]	148	11.1	2.4	24.3	16	4
Slaughterers and meat packers[1]	122	11.1	2.4	24.3	13	3
Food and tobacco roasting, baking, and drying machine operators and tenders[1]	18	15.1	2.4	23.5	3	(2)
Food batchmakers[1]	66	13.0	2.4	24.4	9	2
Food cooking machine operators and tenders	37	18.9	1.7	17.5	7	1
All other food processing workers[1]	69	13.0	2.4	24.3	9	2
Metal workers and plastic workers	2,907	11.2	2.5	24.5	327	71
Computer control programmers and operators	186	9.5	3.6	35.5	18	7
Computer-controlled machine tool operators, metal and plastic[1]	162	9.5	3.6	35.5	15	6
Numerical tool and process control programmers[1]	24	9.5	3.6	35.5	2	1
Cutting, punching, and press machine setters, operators, and tenders, metal and plastic[1]	372	9.5	2.0	19.5	35	7
Drilling and boring machine tool setters, operators, and tenders, metal and plastic[1]	71	11.2	3.3	32.7	8	2
Extruding and drawing machine setters, operators, and tenders, metal and plastic[1]	126	17.9	2.2	22.0	23	3
Forging machine setters, operators, and tenders, metal and plastic[1]	54	11.2	3.3	32.7	6	2
Grinding, lapping, polishing, and buffing machine tool setters, operators, and tenders, metal and plastic[1]	145	17.6	2.4	24.4	26	4
Heat treating equipment setters, operators, and tenders, metal and plastic[1]	43	21.8	2.0	20.3	9	1
Lathe and turning machine tool setters, operators, and tenders, metal and plastic[1]	84	14.4	3.9	39.2	12	3
Lay-out workers, metal and plastic[1]	18	7.7	2.6	25.9	1	(2)
Machinists[1]	430	6.6	2.1	20.5	28	9
Metal furnace and kiln operators and tenders	40	13.9	2.7	27.5	6	1
Metal-refining furnace operators and tenders[1]	24	13.9	2.7	27.5	3	1
Pourers and casters, metal[1]	16	13.9	2.7	27.5	2	(2)
Milling and planing machine setters, operators, and tenders, metal and plastic[1]	34	11.2	3.3	32.7	4	1
Model makers and patternmakers, metal and plastic	19	11.0	2.7	27.3	2	1
Model makers, metal and plastic[1]	11	11.0	2.7	27.3	1	(2)
Patternmakers, metal and plastic[1]	9	11.0	2.7	27.3	1	(2)
Molders and molding machine setters, operators, and tenders, metal and plastic	235	21.7	2.0	20.3	51	5
Foundry mold and coremakers[1]	59	21.7	2.0	20.3	13	1
Molding, coremaking, and casting machine setters, operators, and tenders, metal and plastic[1]	176	21.7	2.0	20.3	38	4
Multiple machine tool setters, operators, and tenders, metal and plastic	105	19.8	1.5	15.4	21	2
Plating and coating machine setters, operators, and tenders, metal and plastic[1]	65	21.8	2.0	20.3	14	1
Rolling machine setters, operators, and tenders, metal and plastic[1]	49	11.2	3.3	32.7	6	2
Tool and die makers[1]	130	4.7	2.5	25.1	6	3
Tool grinders, filers, and sharpeners[1]	29	7.7	2.6	25.9	2	1
Welding, soldering, and brazing workers	521	11.5	2.8	28.1	60	15
Welders, cutters, solderers, and brazers[1]	446	11.5	2.8	28.1	51	13
Welding, soldering, and brazing machine setters, operators, and tenders[1]	74	11.5	2.8	28.1	9	2
All other metal workers and plastic workers[1]	150	13.7	1.9	19.4	20	3
Plant and system operators	368	7.2	3.0	30.2	27	11
Power plant operators, distributors, and dispatchers	55	7.0	3.0	29.9	4	2
Nuclear power reactor operators[1]	4	7.0	3.0	29.9	(2)	(2)
Power distributors and dispatchers[1]	15	7.0	3.0	29.9	1	(2)
Power plant operators[1]	36	7.0	3.0	29.9	3	1
Stationary engineers and boiler operators[1]	57	7.6	2.8	27.8	4	2
Water and liquid waste treatment plant and system operators[1]	88	7.0	3.1	31.5	6	3
Miscellaneous plant and system operators	167	7.0	3.0	30.4	12	5

See footnotes at end of table.

(Numbers in thousands)

2000 Matrix occupation	Total employment, 2000	Replacement rate (Percent)			Annual average replacement needs, 2000-10	
		Total, 1999-2000	Net, 2000-10		Total	Net
			Annual average	10-year		
Chemical plant and system operators[1]	71	7.0	3.0	30.3	5	2
Gas plant operators[1]	12	7.0	3.0	30.4	1	(²)
Petroleum pump system operators, refinery operators, and gaugers[1]	35	7.0	3.0	30.3	2	1
All other plant and system operators[1]	49	7.0	3.0	30.3	3	1
Printing occupations	534	11.1	2.5	25.3	59	14
Bookbinders and bindery workers	115	12.1	2.6	26.4	14	3
Bindery workers[1]	105	12.1	2.6	26.4	13	3
Bookbinders[1]	10	12.1	2.6	26.4	1	(²)
Job printers	56	10.8	2.5	25.2	6	1
Prepress technicians and workers[1]	107	11.3	2.5	24.6	12	3
Printing machine operators[1]	222	10.9	2.5	25.2	24	6
All other printing workers[1]	34	10.9	2.5	25.2	4	1
Textile, apparel, and furnishings occupations	1,317	20.4	1.9	18.9	269	25
Extruding and forming machine setters, operators, and tenders, synthetic and glass fibers[1]	41	14.2	2.5	25.1	6	1
Fabric and apparel patternmakers[1]	15	13.4	3.2	31.5	2	(²)
Laundry and dry-cleaning workers[1]	236	26.1	2.6	26.4	62	6
Pressers, textile, garment, and related materials[1]	110	17.5	1.4	13.7	19	2
Sewing machine operators	399	20.4	1.1	10.6	81	4
Shoe and leather workers and repairers[1]	19	15.0	4.0	39.7	3	1
Shoe machine operators and tenders[1]	9	20.4	0.9	9.5	2	(²)
Tailors, dressmakers, and sewers	101	18.9	2.2	22.1	19	2
Sewers, hand[1]	43	18.9	2.2	22.1	8	1
Tailors, dressmakers, and custom sewers[1]	58	18.9	2.2	22.1	11	1
Textile bleaching and dyeing machine operators and tenders[1]	37	6.8	2.0	19.7	2	1
Textile cutting machine setters, operators, and tenders[1]	38	19.2	1.7	17.1	7	1
Textile knitting and weaving machine setters, operators, and tenders[1]	70	20.4	1.6	16.1	14	1
Textile winding, twisting, and drawing out machine setters, operators, and tenders[1]	90	21.4	2.2	21.6	19	2
Upholsterers[1]	58	15.0	3.3	32.9	9	2
All other textile, apparel, and furnishings workers[1]	95	20.5	2.0	20.4	19	2
Woodworkers	409	11.0	3.7	36.8	45	15
Cabinetmakers and bench carpenters	159	5.0	3.2	31.8	8	5
Furniture finishers[1]	45	9.1	4.0	39.7	4	2
Model makers and patternmakers, wood[1]	10	9.1	4.0	39.7	1	(²)
Sawing machine setters, operators, and tenders, wood	57	16.1	3.9	39.2	9	2
Woodworking machine setters, operators, and tenders, except sawing[1]	103	14.4	4.0	40.3	15	4
All other woodworkers[1]	35	12.3	4.0	40.3	4	1
Other production occupations	3,293	16.3	2.2	22.0	538	72
Cementing and gluing machine operators and tenders[1]	36	15.1	2.4	23.5	5	1
Chemical processing machine setters, operators, and tenders	100	15.1	2.4	23.5	15	2
Chemical equipment operators and tenders[1]	61	15.1	2.4	23.5	9	1
Separating, filtering, clarifying, precipitating, and still machine setters, operators, and tenders[1]	39	15.1	2.4	23.5	6	1
Cleaning, washing, and metal pickling equipment operators and tenders[1]	20	15.1	2.4	23.5	3	(²)
Cooling and freezing equipment operators and tenders	7	13.9	1.7	17.5	1	(²)
Crushing, grinding, polishing, mixing, and blending workers	202	9.9	2.2	21.8	20	4
Crushing, grinding, and polishing machine setters, operators, and tenders[1]	44	9.9	2.2	21.8	4	1
Grinding and polishing workers, hand[1]	49	9.9	2.2	21.8	5	1
Mixing and blending machine setters, operators, and tenders[1]	109	9.9	2.2	21.8	11	2
Cutting workers	115	18.7	1.8	17.8	22	2
Cutters and trimmers, hand[1]	32	18.7	1.8	17.8	6	1
Cutting and slicing machine setters, operators, and tenders[1]	83	18.7	1.8	17.8	16	1
Etchers and engravers[1]	15	13.2	2.5	25.0	2	(²)
Extruding, forming, pressing, and compacting machine setters, operators, and tenders[1]	73	16.1	2.3	23.0	12	2
Furnace, kiln, oven, drier, and kettle operators and tenders[1]	33	13.9	2.7	27.5	5	1
Helpers-Production workers[1]	525	27.2	2.5	25.1	143	13
Inspectors, testers, sorters, samplers, and weighers[1]	602	15.1	2.2	22.1	91	13
Jewelers and precious stone and metal workers[1]	43	7.7	2.6	25.9	3	1

See footnotes at end of table.

2000 Matrix occupation	Total employ-ment, 2000	Replacement rate (Percent)			Annual average replacement needs, 2000-10	
		Total, 1999-2000	Net, 2000-10		Total	Net
			Annual average	10-year		
Medical, dental, and ophthalmic laboratory workers	88	7.3	2.7	27.1	6	2
Dental laboratory technicians	43	7.3	2.7	27.1	3	1
Medical appliance technicians	13	7.3	2.7	27.1	1	(2)
Ophthalmic laboratory technicians	32	7.3	2.7	27.1	2	1
Molders, shapers, and casters, except metal and plastic[1]	42	15.1	2.6	26.1	6	1
Packaging and filling machine operators and tenders	379	14.9	2.2	22.0	56	8
Painting workers	195	16.3	2.2	22.4	32	4
Coating, painting, and spraying machine setters, operators, and tenders[1]	108	16.3	2.2	22.4	18	2
Painters, transportation equipment[1]	49	16.3	2.2	22.4	8	1
Painting, coating, and decorating workers[1]	38	16.3	2.2	22.4	6	1
Paper goods machine setters, operators, and tenders[1]	123	14.2	2.0	19.5	18	2
Photographic process workers and processing machine operators	76	13.0	2.6	26.0	10	2
Photographic process workers	26	13.0	2.6	26.0	3	1
Photographic processing machine operators	50	13.0	2.6	26.0	6	1
Semiconductor processors	52	13.9	1.7	17.5	7	1
Tire builders	18	13.9	1.7	17.5	3	(2)
All other production workers[1]	549	18.4	1.8	17.9	101	10
Transportation and material moving occupations	**10,088**	**17.7**	**2.3**	**23.5**	**1,782**	**237**
Supervisors, transportation and material moving workers	357	8.8	2.1	21.5	32	8
Aircraft cargo handling supervisors[1]	10	8.8	2.1	21.5	1	(2)
First-line supervisors/managers of helpers, laborers, and material movers, hand[1]	153	8.8	2.1	21.5	14	3
First-line supervisors/managers of transportation and material-moving machine and vehicle operators[1]	194	8.8	2.1	21.5	17	4
Air transportation occupations	166	4.9	2.9	28.6	8	5
Aircraft pilots and flight engineers	117	4.7	2.3	22.9	6	3
Airline pilots, copilots, and flight engineers[1]	98	4.7	2.3	22.9	5	2
Commercial pilots[1]	19	4.7	2.3	22.9	1	(2)
Air traffic controllers and airfield operations specialists	31	6.1	4.2	42.4	2	1
Air traffic controllers[1]	27	6.1	4.2	42.4	2	1
Airfield operations specialists[1]	5	6.1	4.2	42.4	(2)	(2)
All other air transportation workers[1]	17	6.1	4.2	42.4	1	1
Motor vehicle operators	4,237	14.1	1.5	15.4	599	65
Ambulance drivers and attendants, except emergency medical technicians	15	19.7	0.8	8.1	3	(2)
Bus drivers	666	13.0	2.5	25.4	87	17
Bus drivers, school	481	13.0	2.5	25.4	63	12
Bus drivers, transit and intercity	185	13.0	2.5	25.4	24	5
Driver/sales workers and truck drivers	3,268	13.7	1.4	13.7	448	45
Driver/sales workers	402	13.7	1.4	13.7	55	6
Truck drivers, heavy and tractor-trailer	1,749	13.7	1.4	13.7	240	24
Truck drivers, light or delivery services	1,117	13.7	1.4	13.7	153	15
Taxi drivers and chauffeurs	176	20.9	0.8	8.1	37	1
All other motor vehicle operators[1]	112	14.2	1.7	16.9	16	2
Rail transportation occupations	115	9.4	4.5	44.6	11	5
Locomotive engineers and firers[1]	37	9.4	4.5	44.6	3	2
Railroad brake, signal, and switch operators[1]	22	9.4	4.5	44.6	2	1
Railroad conductors and yardmasters[1]	45	9.4	4.5	44.6	4	2
Rail yard engineers, dinkey operators, and hostlers	4	9.4	4.5	44.6	(2)	(2)
All other rail transportation workers	7	9.4	4.5	44.6	1	(2)
Water transportation occupations	70	7.7	3.4	34.1	5	2
Sailors and marine oilers	32	7.7	3.4	34.1	2	1
Ship and boat captains and operators	25	7.8	3.4	34.0	2	1
Ship engineers	9	7.7	3.4	34.1	1	(2)
All other water transportation workers[1]	5	7.8	3.4	34.1	(2)	(2)
Related transportation occupations	309	26.3	3.4	33.7	81	10
Bridge and lock tenders[1]	4	7.7	3.4	34.1	(2)	(2)
Parking lot attendants	117	14.2	1.7	16.9	17	2
Service station attendants	112	40.2	5.1	51.0	45	6
Traffic technicians[1]	4	20.1	3.8	38.2	1	(2)

See footnotes at end of table.

Table 11. Total and net replacement rates and annual average replacement needs, 2000-10 — Continued

(Numbers in thousands)

2000 Matrix occupation	Total employ-ment, 2000	Replacement rate (Percent)			Annual average replacement needs, 2000-10	
		Total, 1999-2000	Net, 2000-10		Total	Net
			Annual average	10-year		
Transportation inspectors	25	10.6	2.5	24.7	3	1
All other related transportation workers[1]	46	20.1	3.8	38.2	9	2
Material moving occupations	4,833	22.0	2.9	29.3	1,063	141
Cleaners of vehicles and equipment	322	26.5	3.8	38.2	85	12
Conveyor operators and tenders	63	12.6	2.9	28.5	8	2
Crane and tower operators[1]	55	8.5	3.0	29.9	5	2
Excavating and loading machine and dragline operators[1]	76	6.2	3.0	29.7	5	2
Hoist and winch operators[1]	9	7.5	2.1	20.6	1	(2)
Industrial truck and tractor operators	635	14.4	1.4	13.9	91	9
Laborers and freight, stock, and material movers, hand[1]	2,084	24.9	3.3	33.4	519	70
Machine feeders and offbearers	182	22.3	3.5	34.7	41	6
Packers and packagers, hand[1]	1,091	22.1	2.5	25.5	242	28
Pumping station operators	32	9.6	2.8	28.1	3	1
Gas compressor and gas pumping station operators	7	9.6	2.8	28.1	1	(2)
Pump operators, except wellhead pumpers	14	9.6	2.8	28.1	1	(2)
Wellhead pumpers	12	9.6	2.8	28.1	1	(2)
Refuse and recyclable material collectors[1]	124	27.6	4.3	43.4	34	5
Tank car, truck, and ship loaders	19	12.6	2.9	28.5	2	1
All other material moving workers[1]	142	9.9	2.8	27.5	14	4

[1] One or more Current Population Survey (CPS) proxy occupations may be used to estimate CPS based data. See Chapter 2.
[2] Less than 500

123

Chapter V. Education and Training Statistics

Nearly 3 million postsecondary degrees were earned during the 1999-2000 academic year: about 564,000 associate degrees, 1.2 million bachelor's degrees, 464,000 master's degrees, 44,000 doctoral degrees, and 79,000 first professional degrees.

Table 12 presents data on the number of awards and degrees earned during 1999-2000 by type of educational program and detailed field of study. Data covering the period from July 1, 1999, to June 30, 2000, were provided by the National Center for Education Statistics (NCES), U. S. Department of Education, from the Integrated Postsecondary Education Data System (IPEDS). These data, collected in fall 2000, were the first to be collected through the IPEDS Web-based data collection system. The NCES surveyed institutions of higher education that offer awards at the bachelor's degree level and higher, institutions with 2-year programs, and public and private institutions with programs of less than 2 years. The 1990 version of the *Classification of Instructional Programs* was used to categorize the data.[1]

Nondegree formal awards for the completion of 1- to 4-year curriculums totaled 286,000 during the 1999-2000 academic year, while awards earned for the completion of programs of less than 1 year numbered 273,000. The majority of both types of awards were earned in personal and miscellaneous services, computer and information sciences, mechanic and repairer occupations, health professions and related sciences, and business management and administrative services.

Associate degrees earned totaled 564,000, up nearly 20 percent from 10 years earlier. Almost two-thirds were earned in three disciplines: Liberal arts and sciences, general studies, and humanities; business management and administrative services; and health professions and related sciences. NCES projects the number of earned associate degrees to rise to 625,000 by 2010-11, an increase of 12 percent from 1997-98.

A total of 1,244,000 bachelor's degrees were earned during 1999-2000, an increase of nearly 17 percent from the 1989-90 academic year. About 40 percent were earned in three disciplines: Business management and administrative services; education; and social sciences and history. Over the 1989-90 to 1999-2000 period, the number of degrees earned increased substantially in nearly all

disciplines, including biological and life sciences (up 25,300), psychology (up 19,900), health professions and related sciences (up 19,400), and visual and performing arts (up 19,400). Decreases were seen in bachelor's degrees earned in disciplines such as engineering (down 7,300) and engineering-related technology (down 4,200). NCES projects the number of earned bachelor's degrees to rise to 1,392,000 by the 2010-11 academic year, an increase of 18 percent from 1997-98.

Some 464,000 master's degrees were granted in 1999-2000, about 41 percent more than in 1989-90. More than 60 percent were earned in education, business management and administrative services, and health professions and related sciences. Nearly all disciplines experienced increases in degrees earned over the period 1989-90 to 1999-2000. Some of the largest increases were in education (up 43,200), business administration and management (up 29,300), and health sciences and related professions (up 22,300). NCES projects the number of earned master's degrees to increase to 477,000 by the 2010-11 academic year, an increase of 11 percent from 1997-98.

Doctoral degrees totaled about 44,000 during 1999-2000, up about 12 percent from 10 years earlier. Nearly 40 percent were earned in education, engineering, and biological and life sciences. Almost all disciplines experienced increases in degrees earned over the period 1989-90 to 1999-2000. NCES projects the number of earned doctoral degrees to grow to 49,100 by the 2010-11 academic year, an increase of 7 percent from 1997-98.

About 79,000 first professional degrees were earned during 1999-2000, about 9 percent more than in the 1989-90 academic year. Virtually all were earned in law and legal studies, health professions and related sciences, and theological studies and religious vocations. NCES projects the number of earned first professional degrees to increase to 88,300 by the 2010-11 academic year, an increase of 12 percent from 1997-98.

Information on obtaining postsecondary education data from NCES is available on the Internet. Access the NCES site (**http://nces.ed.gov**) for the *Digest of Education Statistics*, IPEDS data back to 1989-90, and data from other statistical series.

---

[1] *Classification of Instructional Programs*, 1990 ed. (National Center for Education Statistics, August 1991).

Table 12. Earned awards and degrees, by field of study, 1999-2000

Classification of Instructional Programs (CIP) codes and titles	Awards, curriculums of under 1 year	1- to 4-year awards	Associate degrees	Bachelor's degrees	Master's degrees	Doctoral degrees	First profes-sional degrees
Total, all programs	272,758	285,566	563,639	1,244,359	463,572	44,275	78,975
01. Agricultural business and production	2,147	2,045	4,349	5,816	528	183	0
01.01 Agricultural business and management	468	348	988	3,828	394	150	0
01.0101 Agricultural business and management, general	147	38	543	885	33	0	0
01.0102 Agricultural business/agribusiness operations	2	50	227	1,500	10	0	0
01.0103 Agricultural economics	0	0	7	934	337	150	0
01.0104 Farm and ranch management	305	260	128	112	12	0	0
01.0199 Agricultural business and management, other	14	0	83	397	2	0	0
01.02 Agricultural mechanization	191	367	300	266	0	0	0
01.0201 Agricultural mechanization, general	1	108	155	239	0	0	0
01.0204 Agricultural power machinery operator	190	194	138	0	0	0	0
01.0299 Agricultural mechanization, other	0	65	7	27	0	0	0
01.03 Agricultural production workers and managers	67	182	693	285	49	8	0
01.0301 Agricultural production workers and managers, general	14	106	349	69	6	0	0
01.0302 Agricultural animal husbandry and production management	48	69	237	143	0	0	0
01.0303 Aquaculture operations and production management	5	6	24	73	30	4	0
01.0304 Crop production operations and management	0	0	83	0	11	4	0
01.0399 Agricultural production workers and managers, other	0	1	0	0	2	0	0
01.04 Agricultural and food products processing	0	25	26	189	7	6	0
01.05 Agricultural supplies and related services	286	56	348	214	0	0	0
01.0501 Agricultural supplies retailing and wholesaling	45	11	140	82	0	0	0
01.0505 Animal trainer	1	0	43	0	0	0	0
01.0507 Equestrian/equine studies, horse management and training	148	43	153	132	0	0	0
01.0599 Agricultural supplies and related services, other	92	2	12	0	0	0	0
01.06 Horticulture services operations and management	948	1,032	1,935	746	31	17	0
01.0601 Horticulture services operations and management, general	495	434	700	205	18	11	0
01.0603 Ornamental horticulture operations and management	174	153	379	264	13	2	0
01.0604 Greenhouse operations and management	14	17	35	0	0	0	0
01.0605 Landscaping operations and management	168	284	342	133	0	0	0
01.0606 Nursery operations and management	62	86	79	0	0	0	0
01.0607 Turf management	33	52	342	131	0	0	0
01.0699 Horticulture services operations and management, other	2	6	58	13	0	4	0
01.07 International agriculture	0	0	0	11	11	0	0
01.99 Agricultural business and production, other	187	35	59	277	36	2	0
01.9999 Agricultural business and production, other	187	35	59	277	36	2	0
02. Agricultural sciences	19	179	943	8,656	1,566	652	0
02.01 Agriculture/agricultural sciences	0	10	457	1,450	176	6	0
02.0101 Agriculture/agricultural sciences, general	0	10	457	1,405	155	6	0
02.0102 Agricultural extension	0	0	0	45	21	0	0
02.02 Animal sciences	10	140	331	3,976	431	167	0
02.0201 Animal sciences, general	10	79	137	3,506	328	132	0
02.0202 Agricultural animal breeding and genetics	0	0	0	27	10	3	0
02.0203 Agricultural animal health	0	20	33	2	5	0	0
02.0204 Agricultural animal nutrition	0	0	0	0	5	13	0
02.0205 Agricultural animal physiology	0	0	0	0	4	1	0
02.0206 Dairy science	0	32	7	112	19	2	0
02.0209 Poultry	0	9	38	110	28	2	0
02.0299 Animal sciences, other	0	0	116	219	32	14	0
02.03 Food sciences and technology	0	3	26	672	270	148	0
02.04 Plant sciences	3	26	83	2,177	520	256	0
02.0401 Plant sciences, general	0	0	7	421	70	36	0
02.0402 Agronomy and crop science	0	14	11	677	199	115	0
02.0403 Horticulture science	3	7	58	801	127	51	0
02.0405 Plant breeding and genetics	0	0	0	0	10	10	0
02.0406 Agricultural plant pathology	0	0	1	9	5	8	0
02.0407 Agricultural plant physiology	0	0	0	0	6	4	0
02.0408 Plant protection (pest management)	0	5	5	35	16	5	0
02.0409 Range science and management	0	0	1	113	54	15	0
02.0499 Plant sciences, other	0	0	0	121	33	12	0
02.05 Soil sciences	0	0	0	106	111	60	0
02.99 Agriculture/agricultural sciences, other	6	0	46	275	58	15	0
03. Conservation and renewable natural resources	156	211	1,374	9,696	2,266	346	0
03.01 Natural resources conservation	13	69	273	5,494	1,313	118	0

125

Classification of Instructional Programs (CIP) codes and titles		Awards, curriculums of under 1 year	1- to 4-year awards	Associate degrees	Bachelor's degrees	Master's degrees	Doctoral degrees	First profes- sional degrees
03.0101	Natural resources conservation, general	1	65	185	1,343	380	49	0
03.0102	Environmental science/studies	12	4	88	4,151	933	69	0
03.02	Natural resources management and protective services	30	32	307	643	176	3	0
03.0201	Natural resources management and policy	17	9	107	548	169	2	0
03.0203	Natural resources law enforcement and protective services	7	0	68	18	0	0	0
03.0299	Natural resources management and protective services, other	6	23	132	77	7	1	0
03.03	Fishing and fisheries sciences and management	87	0	88	170	89	21	0
03.04	Forest production and processing	18	64	392	242	16	14	0
03.0401	Forest harvesting and production technology/technician	2	25	294	173	16	14	0
03.0404	Forest products technology/technician	16	38	52	15	0	0	0
03.0499	Forestry production and processing, other	0	1	46	54	0	0	0
03.05	Forestry and related sciences	5	42	178	1,550	449	129	0
03.0501	Forestry, general	2	38	115	735	303	82	0
03.0502	Forestry sciences	0	0	7	205	64	26	0
03.0506	Forest management	3	0	31	229	26	7	0
03.0509	Wood science and pulp/paper technology	0	4	25	205	23	7	0
03.0599	Forestry and related sciences, other	0	0	0	176	33	7	0
03.06	Wildlife and wildlands management	3	4	114	1,091	173	37	0
03.99	Conservation and renewable natural resources, other	0	0	22	506	50	24	0
04.	Architecture and related programs	28	83	392	8,415	4,246	125	0
04.02	Architecture	0	2	56	4,974	2,278	45	0
04.03	City/urban, community, and regional planning	0	0	0	451	1,290	62	0
04.04	Architectural environmental design	0	0	0	692	29	2	0
04.05	Interior architecture	4	81	291	704	36	0	0
04.06	Landscape architecture	2	0	18	944	338	1	0
04.07	Architectural urban design and planning	0	0	0	0	75	1	0
04.99	Architecture and related programs, other	22	0	27	650	200	14	0
05.	Area, ethnic, and cultural studies	227	87	259	6,416	1,625	217	0
05.01	Area studies	107	20	9	3,708	1,096	167	0
05.0101	African studies	1	0	0	30	34	5	0
05.0102	American studies/civilization	0	2	7	1,492	221	91	0
05.0103	Asian studies	36	0	2	493	92	0	0
05.0104	East Asian studies	0	7	0	374	123	18	0
05.0105	Eastern European area studies	0	0	0	7	14	0	0
05.0106	European studies	0	0	0	89	18	0	0
05.0107	Latin American studies	34	11	0	477	232	11	0
05.0108	Middle Eastern studies	8	0	0	98	95	29	0
05.0109	Pacific area studies	0	0	0	4	8	0	0
05.0110	Russian and Slavic area studies	11	0	0	94	83	0	0
05.0111	Scandinavian area studies	0	0	0	23	2	1	0
05.0112	South Asian studies	0	0	0	15	15	1	0
05.0113	Southeast Asian studies	0	0	0	8	11	2	0
05.0114	Western European studies	17	0	0	27	40	3	0
05.0115	Canadian studies	0	0	0	2	0	0	0
05.0199	Area studies, other	0	0	0	475	108	6	0
05.02	Ethnic and cultural studies	104	67	244	2,340	378	35	0
05.0201	Afro-American (black) studies	13	11	0	610	63	7	0
05.0202	American Indian/Native American studies	0	15	30	77	22	0	0
05.0203	Hispanic-American studies	0	0	0	256	13	0	0
05.0204	Islamic studies	0	0	0	3	6	1	0
05.0205	Jewish/Judaic studies	3	0	146	167	42	11	0
05.0206	Asian-American studies	0	0	0	98	9	0	0
05.0207	Women's studies	87	34	9	818	99	5	0
05.0299	Ethnic and cultural studies, other	1	7	59	311	124	11	0
05.99	Area, ethnic, and cultural studies, other	16	0	6	368	151	15	0
08.	Marketing operations/marketing and distribution	5,644	1,468	5,546	4,178	593	3	0
08.01	Apparel and accessories marketing operations	19	96	1,624	936	3	1	0
08.0101	Apparel and accessories marketing operations, general	1	6	26	82	2	0	0
08.0102	Fashion merchandising	18	90	1,574	761	1	1	0
08.0199	Apparel and accessories marketing operations, other	0	0	24	93	0	0	0
08.02	Business and personal services marketing operations	27	35	109	10	0	0	0
08.0204	Business services marketing operations	13	33	14	0	0	0	0
08.0205	Personal services marketing operations	0	0	47	0	0	0	0
08.0299	Business and personal services marketing operations, other	14	2	48	10	0	0	0

Classification of Instructional Programs (CIP) codes and titles	Awards, curriculums of under 1 year	1- to 4-year awards	Associate degrees	Bachelor's degrees	Master's degrees	Doctoral degrees	First profes- sional degrees
08.03 Entrepreneurship	43	34	51	198	133	0	0
08.04 Financial services marketing operations	0	2	19	12	0	0	0
08.05 Floristry marketing operations	179	50	5	0	0	0	0
08.06 Food products retailing and wholesaling operations	144	53	11	83	6	0	0
08.07 General retailing and wholesaling operations and skills	2,793	420	2,085	2,340	359	2	0
08.0701 Auctioneering	11	0	0	0	0	0	0
08.0704 General buying operations	46	0	41	36	0	0	0
08.0705 General retailing operations	193	94	605	114	0	0	0
08.0706 General selling skills and sales operations	1,199	147	470	493	0	0	0
08.0708 General marketing operations	185	142	551	1,489	359	2	0
08.0709 General distribution operations	6	6	52	0	0	0	0
08.0799 General retailing and wholesaling operations and skills, other	1,153	31	366	208	0	0	0
08.08 Home and office products marketing operations	2	2	2	33	0	0	0
08.0809 Home products marketing operations	2	2	2	33	0	0	0
08.0810 Office products marketing operations	0	0	0	0	0	0	0
08.0899 Home and office products marketing operations, other	0	0	0	0	0	0	0
08.09 Hospitality and recreation marketing operations	42	142	156	84	0	0	0
08.0901 Hospitality and recreation marketing operations, general	12	18	111	7	0	0	0
08.0902 Hotel/motel services marketing operations	9	15	30	0	0	0	0
08.0903 Recreational products/services marketing operations	1	0	15	54	0	0	0
08.0906 Food sales operations	0	109	0	23	0	0	0
08.0999 Hospitality and recreation marketing operations, other	20	0	0	0	0	0	0
08.10 Insurance marketing operations	109	0	17	0	0	0	0
08.11 Tourism and travel services marketing operations	2,266	385	1,032	146	7	0	0
08.1104 Tourism promotion operations	64	69	234	122	2	0	0
08.1105 Travel services marketing operations	744	154	410	6	5	0	0
08.1199 Tourism and travel services marketing operations, other	1,458	162	388	18	0	0	0
08.12 Vehicle and petroleum products marketing operations	13	71	72	72	0	0	0
08.1203 Vehicle parts and accessories marketing operations	13	71	34	4	0	0	0
08.1208 Vehicle marketing operations	0	0	38	68	0	0	0
08.13 Health products and services marketing operations	0	0	0	0	0	0	0
08.99 Marketing operations/marketing and distribution, other	7	178	363	264	85	0	0
09. Communications	635	1,018	2,754	55,783	5,179	347	0
09.01 Communications, general	45	162	838	27,705	2,019	229	0
09.02 Advertising	6	186	456	3,146	256	3	0
09.04 Journalism and mass communications	98	33	416	13,838	1,581	71	0
09.0401 Journalism	64	8	259	9,360	1,292	24	0
09.0402 Broadcast journalism	0	9	114	632	21	0	0
09.0403 Mass communications	34	15	42	3,325	223	44	0
09.0499 Journalism and mass communications, other	0	1	1	521	45	3	0
09.05 Public relations and organizational communications	1	2	43	3,024	165	0	0
09.07 Radio and television broadcasting	245	541	511	5,461	339	13	0
09.99 Communications, other	240	94	490	2,609	819	31	0
10. Communications technologies	1,452	702	1,709	1,152	446	10	0
10.01 Communications technologies	1,452	702	1,709	1,152	446	10	0
10.0101 Educational/instructional media technology/technician	86	36	284	2	80	0	0
10.0103 Photographic technology/technician	15	29	138	11	0	0	0
10.0104 Radio and television broadcasting technology/technician	725	408	820	614	266	10	0
10.0199 Communications technologies/technicians, other	626	229	467	525	100	0	0
11. Computer and information sciences	23,197	17,433	20,437	36,349	14,256	770	0
11.01 Computer and information sciences, general	5,139	3,035	5,556	21,808	9,102	570	0
11.02 Computer programming	2,805	4,218	4,173	374	117	1	0
11.03 Data processing technology/technician	6,225	2,454	2,133	205	5	0	0
11.04 Information science and systems	528	785	2,213	7,346	2,369	49	0
11.05 Computer systems analysis	592	1,225	514	171	88	0	0
11.07 Computer science	129	371	751	5,327	1,310	105	0
11.99 Computer and information sciences, other	7,779	5,345	5,097	1,118	1,265	45	0
12. Personal and miscellaneous services	23,910	44,650	9,580	369	2	0	0
12.02 Gaming and sports officiating services	494	145	0	0	0	0	0

Classification of Instructional Programs (CIP) codes and titles	Awards, curriculums of under 1 year	1- to 4-year awards	Associate degrees	Bachelor's degrees	Master's degrees	Doctoral degrees	First profes-sional degrees
12.0203 Card dealer	469	145	0	0	0	0	0
12.0299 Gaming and sports officiating services, other	25	0	0	0	0	0	0
12.03 Funeral services and mortuary science	32	249	1,370	174	0	0	0
12.04 Cosmetic services	19,547	40,390	564	1	0	0	0
12.0401 Cosmetic services, general	2,310	79	6	0	0	0	0
12.0402 Barber/hairstylist	262	2,283	0	0	0	0	0
12.0403 Cosmetologist	3,850	35,363	191	0	0	0	0
12.0404 Electrolysis technician	46	0	0	0	0	0	0
12.0405 Massage	4,312	1,486	367	1	0	0	0
12.0406 Makeup artist	3,016	336	0	0	0	0	0
12.0499 Cosmetic services, other	5,751	843	0	0	0	0	0
12.05 Culinary arts and related services	2,759	3,863	7,598	194	2	0	0
12.0501 Baker/pastry chef	386	147	380	12	0	0	0
12.0502 Bartender/mixologist	668	0	0	0	0	0	0
12.0503 Culinary arts/chef training	1,125	3,270	5,505	159	0	0	0
12.0504 Food and beverage/restaurant operations manager	143	62	501	9	0	0	0
12.0505 Kitchen personnel/cook and assistant training	163	92	10	0	0	0	0
12.0506 Meatcutter	65	25	6	0	0	0	0
12.0507 Waiter/waitress and dining room manager	0	2	0	0	0	0	0
12.0599 Culinary arts and related services, other	209	265	1,196	14	2	0	0
12.99 Personal and miscellaneous services, other	1,078	3	48	0	0	0	0
13. Education	2,277	1,043	8,207	115,660	129,589	6,830	0
13.01 Education, general	39	6	3,041	2,980	16,743	1,206	0
13.02 Bilingual/bicultural education	58	0	16	660	710	32	0
13.03 Curriculum and instruction	0	0	0	295	11,741	824	0
13.04 Education administration and supervision	250	3	12	680	18,182	2,265	0
13.0401 Education administration and supervision, general	0	3	0	489	12,280	1,633	0
13.0402 Administration of special education	0	0	0	0	29	6	0
13.0403 Adult and continuing education administration	0	0	0	9	177	77	0
13.0404 Educational supervision	0	0	0	31	1,178	46	0
13.0405 Elementary, middle school, and secondary education administration	0	0	7	112	2,982	41	0
13.0406 Higher education administration	0	0	0	28	405	266	0
13.0407 Community and junior college education administration	0	0	0	0	8	0	0
13.0499 Education administration and supervision, other	250	0	5	11	1,123	196	0
13.05 Educational/instructional media design	0	1	18	105	2,024	53	0
13.06 Educational evaluation, research, and statistics	0	0	0	1	137	85	0
13.0601 Educational evaluation and research	0	0	0	0	22	26	0
13.0603 Educational statistics and research methods	0	0	0	1	38	28	0
13.0604 Educational assessment, testing, and measurement	0	0	0	0	58	11	0
13.0699 Educational evaluation, research, and statistics, other	0	0	0	0	19	20	0
13.07 International and comparative education	0	0	9	0	95	1	0
13.08 Educational psychology	0	0	0	134	1,387	421	0
13.09 Social and philosophical foundations of education	0	0	0	106	455	130	0
13.10 Special education, total	2	124	275	10,012	12,047	210	0
13.1001 Special education, general	0	7	96	7,574	9,261	166	0
13.1003 Education of the deaf and hearing impaired	0	15	41	228	203	3	0
13.1004 Education of the gifted and talented	0	0	0	10	173	3	0
13.1005 Education of the emotionally handicapped	0	0	0	253	286	9	0
13.1006 Education of the mentally handicapped	0	0	1	318	118	0	0
13.1007 Education of the multiple handicapped	0	0	0	123	248	2	0
13.1008 Education of the physically handicapped	0	0	1	33	34	0	0
13.1009 Education of the blind and visually handicapped	0	0	0	22	28	0	0
13.1011 Education of specific learning disabled	0	0	0	486	726	16	0
13.1012 Education of the speech impaired	0	0	2	586	295	0	0
13.1099 Special education, other	2	102	134	379	675	11	0
13.11 Student counseling and personnel services	0	0	0	326	12,392	296	0
13.1101 Counselor education counseling and guidance services	0	0	0	303	11,831	283	0
13.1102 College/postsecondary student counseling and personnel services	0	0	0	23	561	13	0
13.12 General teacher education	63	228	3,067	64,646	28,180	338	0
13.1201 Adult and continuing teacher education	0	77	88	176	923	112	0
13.1202 Elementary teacher education	0	44	1,389	49,707	14,463	67	0
13.1203 Junior high/intermediate/middle school teacher education	0	0	4	1,627	804	3	0
13.1204 Preelementary/early childhood/kindergarten teacher education	42	82	1,065	6,559	2,320	18	0
13.1205 Secondary teacher education	0	16	303	4,913	5,424	49	0
13.1299 Teacher education, multiple levels	10	0	119	680	3,048	81	0

Classification of Instructional Programs (CIP) codes and titles	Awards, curriculums of under 1 year	1- to 4-year awards	Associate degrees	Bachelor's degrees	Master's degrees	Doctoral degrees	First professional degrees
13.13 Teacher education, specific academic and vocational programs	278	216	519	34,006	17,787	654	0
13.1301 Agricultural teacher education (vocational)	0	0	22	585	293	32	0
13.1302 Art teacher education	0	1	5	1,806	635	28	0
13.1303 Business teacher education (vocational)	0	0	9	828	351	8	0
13.1304 Driver and safety teacher education	24	0	0	0	16	0	0
13.1305 English teacher education	0	0	20	2,517	804	16	0
13.1306 Foreign languages teacher education	0	2	10	237	346	13	0
13.1307 Health teacher education	93	0	29	1,905	630	70	0
13.1308 Home economics teacher education (vocational)	0	0	19	267	62	4	0
13.1309 Technology teacher education/industrial arts teacher education	0	3	17	1,090	483	8	0
13.1310 Marketing operations teacher education/marketing and distributive teacher education (vocational)	0	0	0	57	3	0	0
13.1311 Mathematics teacher education	0	1	13	1,455	760	40	0
13.1312 Music teacher education	0	3	17	3,279	774	72	0
13.1314 Physical education teaching and coaching	0	4	284	12,447	3,036	142	0
13.1315 Reading teacher education	0	0	2	176	4,680	71	0
13.1316 Science teacher education, general	0	0	6	1,057	735	38	0
13.1317 Social science teacher education	0	0	5	828	129	1	0
13.1318 Social studies teacher education	0	0	2	1,928	594	3	0
13.1319 Technical teacher education (vocational)	125	4	37	182	221	37	0
13.1320 Trade and industrial education (vocational)	6	4	6	1,088	379	26	0
13.1321 Computer teacher education	8	0	0	16	1,186	0	0
13.1322 Biology teacher education	0	0	0	379	154	0	0
13.1323 Chemistry teacher education	0	0	2	48	25	0	0
13.1324 Drama and dance teacher education	0	4	0	79	31	0	0
13.1325 French language teacher education	0	0	0	49	20	0	0
13.1326 German language teacher education	0	0	0	16	1	0	0
13.1327 Health occupations teacher education (vocational)	0	11	0	65	34	1	0
13.1328 History teacher education	0	0	4	532	51	0	0
13.1329 Physics teacher education	0	0	0	23	8	0	0
13.1330 Spanish language teacher education	0	0	0	275	37	0	0
13.1331 Speech teacher education	0	0	4	77	3	0	0
13.1399 Teacher education, specific academic and vocational programs, other	22	179	6	715	1,306	44	0
13.14 Teaching English as a second language/foreign language	1,088	12	10	183	1,635	15	0
13.15 Teacher assistant/aide	198	452	913	0	0	0	0
13.99 Education, other	301	1	327	1,526	6,074	300	0
14. Engineering	129	206	1,752	57,477	25,449	5,302	0
14.01 Engineering, general	1	24	1,147	1,847	1,239	202	0
14.02 Aerospace, aeronautical, and astronautical engineering	0	0	1	1,150	562	198	0
14.03 Agricultural engineering	0	0	0	750	176	68	0
14.04 Architectural engineering	0	0	4	570	64	0	0
14.05 Bioengineering and biomedical engineering	0	0	0	1,256	515	204	0
14.06 Ceramic sciences and engineering	0	0	0	102	35	21	0
14.07 Chemical engineering	0	0	13	5,746	1,073	581	0
14.08 Civil engineering	2	0	20	8,069	3,394	534	0
14.0801 Civil engineering, general	2	0	20	7,900	3,262	510	0
14.0802 Geotechnical engineering	0	0	0	0	0	0	0
14.0803 Structural engineering	0	0	0	11	10	0	0
14.0804 Transportation and highway engineering	0	0	0	1	45	2	0
14.0805 Water resources engineering	0	0	0	9	45	17	0
14.0899 Civil engineering, other	0	0	0	148	32	5	0
14.09 Computer engineering	32	0	24	4,488	1,403	123	0
14.10 Electrical, electronics, and communications engineering	1	150	256	12,743	6,882	1,363	0
14.11 Engineering mechanics	57	0	0	65	95	41	0
14.12 Engineering physics	0	0	0	248	23	13	0
14.13 Engineering science	0	0	77	241	288	56	0
14.14 Environmental/environmental health engineering	21	0	31	636	650	85	0
14.15 Geological engineering	0	0	2	156	42	8	0
14.16 Geophysical engineering	0	0	0	25	7	1	0
14.17 Industrial/manufacturing engineering	0	1	37	3,415	1,955	188	0
14.18 Materials engineering	0	0	0	501	543	320	0
14.19 Mechanical engineering	0	0	56	12,577	3,263	772	0
14.20 Metallurgical engineering	0	0	0	210	72	51	0
14.21 Mining and mineral engineering	0	0	0	152	39	8	0
14.22 Naval architecture and marine engineering	0	17	0	212	29	3	0
14.23 Nuclear engineering	0	0	4	125	126	93	0
14.24 Ocean engineering	0	0	0	81	75	17	0

Classification of Instructional Programs (CIP) codes and titles	Awards, curriculums of under 1 year	1- to 4-year awards	Associate degrees	Bachelor's degrees	Master's degrees	Doctoral degrees	First profes- sional degrees
14.25 Petroleum engineering	0	0	0	260	163	44	0
14.27 Systems engineering	0	0	4	362	571	45	0
14.28 Textile sciences and engineering	0	0	0	189	53	14	0
14.29 Engineering design	0	14	15	0	0	0	0
14.30 Engineering/industrial management	8	0	30	274	950	25	0
14.31 Materials science	0	0	11	96	78	54	0
14.32 Polymer/plastics engineering	0	0	0	37	99	31	0
14.99 Engineering, other	7	0	20	894	985	139	0
15. Engineering-related technology	12,896	12,128	35,249	13,742	873	6	0
15.01 Architectural engineering technology	99	87	1,202	569	0	0	0
15.02 Civil engineering/civil technology	15	146	1,065	394	0	0	0
15.03 Electrical and electronic engineering-related technology	5,312	3,920	19,684	3,851	12	0	0
15.0301 Computer engineering technology/technician	4,072	696	3,220	342	5	0	0
15.0303 Electrical/electronic and communications engineering technology/technician	880	2,610	8,458	2,443	7	0	0
15.0304 Laser and optical technology/technician	0	17	166	3	0	0	0
15.0399 Electrical and electronic engineering-related technologies/technicians, other	360	597	7,840	1,063	0	0	0
15.04 Electromechanical instrumentation and maintenance technology	4,796	3,657	4,223	512	0	1	0
15.0401 Biomedical engineering-related technology/technician	1	5	262	49	0	1	0
15.0402 Computer maintenance technology/technician	4,482	2,816	2,659	2	0	0	0
15.0403 Electromechanical technology/technician	123	426	530	103	0	0	0
15.0404 Instrumentation technology/technician	71	212	430	4	0	0	0
15.0405 Robotics technology/technician	37	148	275	344	0	0	0
15.0499 Electromechanical instrumentation and maintenance technologies/technicians, other	82	50	67	10	0	0	0
15.05 Environmental control technologies	1,122	2,235	1,276	153	156	0	0
15.0501 Heating, air-conditioning, and refrigeration technology/technician	813	2,015	617	8	0	0	0
15.0503 Energy management and system technology/technician	0	1	17	33	20	0	0
15.0506 Water quality and wastewater treatment technology/technician	182	58	152	24	0	0	0
15.0507 Environmental and pollution control technology/technician	120	68	264	67	25	0	0
15.0599 Environmental control technologies/technicians, other	7	93	226	21	111	0	0
15.06 Industrial production technologies	402	601	1,726	3,500	304	2	0
15.0603 Industrial/manufacturing technology/technician	271	390	1,133	2,852	281	2	0
15.0607 Plastics technology/technician	55	45	163	150	0	0	0
15.0611 Metallurgical technology/technician	0	8	35	0	0	0	0
15.0699 Industrial production technologies/technicians, other	76	158	395	498	23	0	0
15.07 Quality control and safety technologies	308	282	427	476	203	0	0
15.0701 Occupational safety and health technology/technician	117	96	160	471	130	0	0
15.0702 Quality control technology/technician	179	173	246	4	72	0	0
15.0799 Quality control and safety technologies/technicians, other	12	13	21	1	1	0	0
15.08 Mechanical engineering-related technologies	296	576	3,253	1,423	0	0	0
15.0801 Aeronautical and aerospace engineering technology/technician	40	142	506	165	0	0	0
15.0803 Automotive engineering technology/technician	76	109	762	126	0	0	0
15.0805 Mechanical engineering/mechanical technology/technician	178	142	1,493	786	0	0	0
15.0899 Mechanical engineering-related technologies/technicians, other	2	183	492	346	0	0	0
15.09 Mining and petroleum technologies	108	24	86	7	0	0	0
15.0901 Mining technology/technician	108	2	20	2	0	0	0
15.0903 Petroleum technology/technician	0	22	65	3	0	0	0
15.0999 Mining and petroleum technologies/technicians, other	0	0	1	2	0	0	0
15.10 Construction/building technology	52	256	713	1,105	55	0	0
15.11 Miscellaneous engineering-related technologies	54	169	530	463	113	3	0
15.1101 Engineering-related technology/technician, general	21	37	272	321	93	0	0
15.1102 Surveying	32	68	219	142	20	3	0
15.1103 Hydraulic technology/technician	1	64	39	0	0	0	0
15.99 Engineering-related technologies/technicians, other	332	175	1,064	1,289	30	0	0
16. Foreign languages and literatures	1,007	18	501	14,962	2,891	884	0

Classification of Instructional Programs (CIP) codes and titles	Awards, curriculums of under 1 year	1- to 4-year awards	Associate degrees	Bachelor's degrees	Master's degrees	Doctoral degrees	First professional degrees
16.01 Foreign languages and literatures	10	5	196	1,792	872	238	0
16.0101 Foreign languages and literatures, general	0	0	196	1,044	224	45	0
16.0102 Linguistics	6	0	0	719	557	193	0
16.0103 Foreign language interpretation and translation	4	5	0	29	91	0	0
16.03 East and Southeast Asian languages and literatures	16	0	15	588	103	34	0
16.0301 Chinese language and literature	6	0	7	183	17	9	0
16.0302 Japanese language and literature	10	0	8	321	36	7	0
16.0399 East and Southeast Asian languages and literatures, other	0	0	0	84	50	18	0
16.04 East European languages and literatures	0	0	10	370	87	38	0
16.0402 Russian language and literature	0	0	10	339	33	8	0
16.0403 Slavic languages and literature (other than Russian)	0	0	0	27	48	27	0
16.0499 East European languages and literatures, other	0	0	0	4	6	3	0
16.05 Germanic languages and literatures	15	2	20	1,165	221	78	0
16.0501 German language and literature	15	2	20	1,125	201	70	0
16.0502 Scandinavian languages and literature	0	0	0	27	4	1	0
16.0599 Germanic languages and literatures, other	0	0	0	13	16	7	0
16.07 South Asian languages and literatures	0	0	0	8	2	5	0
16.09 Romance languages and literatures	966	11	254	9,913	1,260	370	0
16.0901 French language and literature	16	4	41	2,499	355	124	0
16.0902 Italian language and literature	0	0	3	237	51	13	0
16.0904 Portuguese language and literature	0	0	0	33	8	2	0
16.0905 Spanish language and literature	950	7	210	7,018	729	175	0
16.0999 Romance languages and literatures, other	0	0	0	126	117	56	0
16.11 Middle Eastern languages and literatures	0	0	0	55	70	23	0
16.1101 Arabic language and literature	0	0	0	6	4	5	0
16.1102 Hebrew language and literature	0	0	0	21	35	9	0
16.1199 Middle Eastern languages and literatures, other	0	0	0	28	31	9	0
16.12 Classical and Ancient Near Eastern languages and literatures	0	0	0	846	181	57	0
16.1201 Classics and classical languages and literatures	0	0	0	732	145	54	0
16.1202 Greek language and literature (Ancient and Medieval)	0	0	0	26	8	0	0
16.1203 Latin language and literature (Ancient and Medieval)	0	0	0	79	10	1	0
16.1299 Classical and Ancient Near Eastern languages and literatures, other	0	0	0	9	18	2	0
16.99 Foreign languages and literatures, other	0	0	6	225	95	41	0
19. Home economics	1,157	266	960	17,489	2,762	357	0
19.01 Home economics, general	39	12	106	2,751	367	55	0
19.02 Home economics business services	0	0	0	45	3	0	0
19.0201 Business home economics	0	0	0	31	0	0	0
19.0202 Home economics communications	0	0	0	14	3	0	0
19.03 Family and community studies	0	1	46	454	96	0	0
19.04 Family/consumer resource management	30	0	0	1,590	77	14	0
19.0401 Family resource management studies	30	0	0	729	32	9	0
19.0402 Consumer economics and science	0	0	0	558	35	0	0
19.0499 Family/consumer resource management, other	0	0	0	303	10	5	0
19.05 Foods and nutrition studies	344	5	109	4,086	642	44	0
19.0501 Foods and nutrition studies, general	41	1	7	2,297	396	30	0
19.0502 Foods and nutrition science	288	0	0	126	43	10	0
19.0503 Dietetics/human nutritional services	15	4	102	1,585	187	1	0
19.0505 Food systems administration	0	0	0	27	2	0	0
19.0599 Foods and nutrition studies, other	0	0	0	51	14	3	0
19.06 Housing studies	0	0	0	370	16	3	0
19.0601 Housing studies, general	0	0	0	307	14	2	0
19.0603 Interior environments	0	0	0	24	2	1	0
19.0699 Housing studies, other	0	0	0	39	0	0	0
19.07 Individual and family development studies	735	248	632	6,454	1,473	210	0
19.0701 Individual and family development studies, general	70	4	122	4,751	460	80	0
19.0703 Family and marriage counseling	0	0	0	7	735	29	0
19.0704 Family life and relations studies	260	0	0	725	98	15	0
19.0705 Gerontological services	14	44	108	75	63	2	0
19.0706 Child growth, care, and development studies	211	200	353	713	97	84	0
19.0799 Individual and family development studies, other	180	0	49	183	20	0	0
19.09 Clothing/apparel and textile studies	1	0	63	1,531	74	19	0
19.99 Home economics, other	8	0	4	208	14	12	0
20. Vocational home economics	8,312	5,744	7,414	464	52	0	0
20.02 Childcare and guidance workers and managers	5,144	4,257	5,705	144	47	0	0
20.0201 Childcare and guidance workers and managers, general	1,851	2,310	3,663	114	46	0	0

Classification of Instructional Programs (CIP) codes and titles	Awards, curriculums of under 1 year	1- to 4-year awards	Associate degrees	Bachelor's degrees	Master's degrees	Doctoral degrees	First professional degrees
20.0202 Childcare provider/assistant	2,053	1,767	1,180	24	0	0	0
20.0203 Childcare services manager	1,128	129	777	6	1	0	0
20.0299 Childcare and guidance workers and managers, other	112	51	85	0	0	0	0
20.03 Clothing, apparel, and textiles workers and managers	199	285	248	16	3	0	0
20.0301 Clothing, apparel, and textiles workers and managers, general	12	28	50	16	3	0	0
20.0303 Commercial garment and apparel workers	147	186	76	0	0	0	0
20.0305 Custom tailor	7	32	17	0	0	0	0
20.0306 Fashion and fabric consultant	18	33	29	0	0	0	0
20.0309 Drycleaner and launderer (commercial)	0	0	0	0	0	0	0
20.0399 Clothing, apparel, and textile workers and managers, other	15	6	76	0	0	0	0
20.04 Institutional food workers and administrators	1,920	760	1,204	299	2	0	0
20.0401 Institutional food workers and administrators, general	1,037	515	671	39	2	0	0
20.0404 Dietitian assistant	215	81	248	0	0	0	0
20.0405 Food caterer	44	0	0	0	0	0	0
20.0409 Institutional food services administrator	624	144	232	260	0	0	0
20.0499 Institutional food workers and administrators, other	0	20	53	0	0	0	0
20.05 Home furnishings and equipment installers and consultants	244	134	200	0	0	0	0
20.0501 Home furnishings and equipment installers and consultants, general	231	86	188	0	0	0	0
20.0502 Window treatment maker and installer	0	21	0	0	0	0	0
20.0599 Home furnishings and equipment installers and consultants, other	13	27	12	0	0	0	0
20.06 Custodial, housekeeping, and home services workers and managers	684	142	20	0	0	0	0
20.0601 Custodial, housekeeping, and home services workers and managers, general	49	51	0	0	0	0	0
20.0602 Elder care provider/companion	21	13	16	0	0	0	0
20.0604 Custodian/caretaker	568	47	0	0	0	0	0
20.0605 Executive housekeeper	568	47	0	0	0	0	0
20.0606 Homemaker's aide	0	0	0	0	0	0	0
20.0699 Custodial, housekeeping, and home services workers and managers, other	1	31	0	0	0	0	0
20.99 Vocational home economics, other	121	166	37	5	0	0	0
22. Law and legal studies	1,256	1,686	7,288	2,643	3,814	74	37,311
22.01 Law and legal studies	1,256	1,686	7,288	2,643	3,814	74	37,311
22.0101 Law (LL.B., J.D.)	0	0	0	0	0	0	37,311
22.0102 Prelaw studies	0	0	99	150	0	0	0
22.0103 Paralegal/legal assistant	1,102	1,569	7,046	1,731	58	0	0
22.0104 Juridical science/legal specialization (LL.M., M.C.L., J.S.D./S.J.D.)	0	0	0	17	1,988	46	0
22.0199 Law and legal studies, other	154	117	143	745	1,768	28	0
23. English language and literature/letters	936	90	947	50,730	7,316	1,614	0
23.01 English language and literature, general	717	22	671	37,484	4,615	1,205	0
23.03 Comparative literature	30	0	0	808	221	153	0
23.04 English composition	0	0	5	317	12	5	0
23.05 English creative writing	5	0	7	1,112	1,358	19	0
23.07 American literature (United States)	0	0	15	33	4	13	0
23.08 English literature (British and Commonwealth)	0	0	2	1,161	194	41	0
23.10 Speech and rhetorical studies	28	1	200	8,339	597	120	0
23.11 English technical and business writing	14	6	5	282	228	3	0
23.99 English language and literature/letters, other	142	61	42	1,194	87	55	0
24. Liberal arts and sciences, general studies, and humanities	371	2,038	187,191	34,763	3,334	83	0
24.01 Liberal arts and sciences/liberal studies	371	2,038	187,191	34,763	3,334	83	0
24.0101 Liberal arts and sciences/liberal studies	115	600	149,011	22,015	1,933	17	0
24.0102 General studies	59	1,311	24,088	7,575	131	5	0
24.0103 Humanities/humanistic studies	0	0	5,823	2,595	779	58	0
24.0199 Liberal art and sciences, general studies, and humanities, other	197	127	8,269	2,578	491	3	0
25. Library science	124	47	98	157	4,606	68	0
25.01 Library science/librarianship	9	6	3	157	4,479	61	0
25.03 Library assistant	115	40	95	0	0	0	0
25.99 Library science, other	0	1	0	0	127	7	0
26. Biological sciences/life sciences	21	36	1,434	63,344	6,335	4,838	0

Classification of Instructional Programs (CIP) codes and titles	Awards, curriculums of under 1 year	1- to 4-year awards	Associate degrees	Bachelor's degrees	Master's degrees	Doctoral degrees	First professional degrees
26.01 Biology, general	3	6	1,279	44,740	2,630	709	0
26.02 Biochemistry and biophysics	0	0	0	3,639	307	644	0
26.0202 Biochemistry	0	0	0	3,606	279	549	0
26.0203 Biophysics	0	0	0	33	28	95	0
26.03 Botany	0	0	3	379	215	203	0
26.0301 Botany, general	0	0	3	332	127	103	0
26.0305 Plant pathology	0	0	0	4	71	74	0
26.0307 Plant physiology	0	0	0	0	4	12	0
26.0399 Botany, other	0	0	0	43	13	14	0
26.04 Cell and molecular biology	0	0	0	2,590	296	642	0
26.0401 Cell biology	0	0	0	268	53	169	0
26.0402 Molecular biology	0	0	0	723	129	250	0
26.0499 Cell and molecular biology, other	0	0	0	1,599	114	223	0
26.05 Microbiology/bacteriology	0	0	3	2,950	328	383	0
26.06 Miscellaneous biological specializations	0	6	41	3,910	1,464	1,231	0
26.0601 Anatomy	0	0	0	174	87	75	0
26.0603 Ecology	0	0	1	982	177	126	0
26.0607 Marine/aquatic biology	0	0	0	711	98	44	0
26.0608 Neuroscience	0	0	0	625	78	283	0
26.0609 Nutritional sciences	0	0	0	490	330	125	0
26.0610 Parasitology	0	0	0	0	0	4	0
26.0611 Radiation biology/radiobiology	0	0	13	0	23	10	0
26.0612 Toxicology	0	3	5	50	55	76	0
26.0613 Genetics, plant and animal	0	0	0	286	143	255	0
26.0614 Biometrics	0	0	0	19	63	22	0
26.0615 Biostatistics	0	0	0	2	58	30	0
26.0616 Biotechnology research	0	3	13	147	187	0	0
26.0617 Evolutionary biology	0	0	0	8	10	18	0
26.0618 Biological immunology	0	0	0	0	7	28	0
26.0619 Virology	0	0	0	0	3	21	0
26.0699 Miscellaneous biological specializations, other	0	0	9	416	145	114	0
26.07 Zoology	18	24	27	3,309	754	821	0
26.0701 Zoology, general	0	1	12	2,629	210	137	0
26.0702 Entomology	18	23	0	80	138	130	0
26.0704 Pathology, human and animal	0	0	0	6	53	110	0
26.0705 Pharmacology, human and animal	0	0	0	60	89	231	0
26.0706 Physiology, human and animal	0	0	15	532	264	213	0
26.0799 Zoology, other	0	0	0	2	0	0	0
26.99 Biological sciences/life sciences, other	0	0	81	1,827	341	205	0
27. Mathematics	7	96	675	11,955	3,460	1,093	0
27.01 Mathematics	0	7	668	10,026	2,028	720	0
27.03 Applied mathematics	7	0	2	1,346	542	126	0
27.0301 Applied mathematics, general	7	0	0	701	329	95	0
27.0302 Operations research	0	0	2	609	208	31	0
27.0303 Applied mathematics, other	0	0	0	36	5	0	0
27.05 Mathematical statistics	0	0	0	388	787	220	0
27.99 Mathematics, other	0	89	5	195	103	27	0
29. Military technologies	40	0	65	0	0	0	0
30. Multi/interdisciplinary studies	192	188	11,783	27,865	3,092	379	0
30.01 Biological and physical sciences	1	0	7,072	2,422	343	24	0
30.05 Peace and conflict studies	0	13	0	120	136	4	0
30.06 Systems science and theory	0	0	0	264	133	18	0
30.08 Mathematics and computer science	0	0	1	299	31	14	0
30.10 Biopsychology	0	0	0	60	0	0	0
30.11 Gerontology	63	18	29	243	200	6	0
30.12 Historic preservation, conservation, and architectural history	0	1	15	70	66	0	0
30.13 Medieval and renaissance studies	2	0	0	30	21	3	0
30.14 Museology/museum studies	3	0	0	54	146	0	0
30.15 Science, technology, and society	9	0	26	257	76	6	0
30.99 Multi/interdisciplinary studies, other	114	156	4,640	24,046	1,940	304	0
31. Parks, recreation, leisure, and fitness studies	124	149	855	19,112	2,478	134	0
31.01 Parks, recreation, and leisure studies	10	16	98	2,608	204	15	0
31.03 Parks, recreation, and leisure facilities management	1	59	243	2,915	215	18	0
31.05 Health and physical education/fitness	109	69	409	13,432	2,036	97	0
31.0501 Health and physical education, general	96	14	219	5,624	649	43	0
31.0502 Adapted physical education/therapeutic recreation	0	3	0	211	38	0	0
31.0503 Athletic training and sports medicine	0	33	36	1,329	118	0	0
31.0504 Sport and fitness administration/management	2	12	106	2,041	416	2	0

Classification of Instructional Programs (CIP) codes and titles	Awards, curriculums of under 1 year	1- to 4-year awards	Associate degrees	Bachelor's degrees	Master's degrees	Doctoral degrees	First professional degrees
31.0505 Exercise sciences/physiology and movement studies	1	3	28	3,788	697	46	0
31.0506 Sociopsychological sports studies	0	0	0	32	16	0	0
31.0599 Health and physical education/fitness, other	10	4	20	407	102	6	0
31.99 Parks, recreation, leisure, and fitness studies, other	4	5	105	157	23	4	0
38. Philosophy and religion	1	27	63	8,365	1,343	579	0
38.01 Philosophy	0	0	32	4,769	595	349	0
38.02 Religion/religious studies	1	27	31	3,226	548	217	0
38.99 Philosophy and religion	0	0	0	370	200	13	0
39. Theological studies and religious vocations	101	1,073	461	6,848	5,009	1,443	5,309
39.01 Biblical and other theological languages and literatures	0	0	0	27	42	13	0
39.02 Bible/biblical studies	33	785	327	1,999	408	13	0
39.03 Missions/missionary studies and misology	0	0	9	261	274	58	0
39.04 Religious education	17	41	44	920	488	54	0
39.05 Religious/sacred music	1	3	4	171	57	0	0
39.06 Theological and ministerial studies	31	205	68	2,701	2,879	960	5,309
39.0601 Theology/theological studies	0	89	43	1,155	2,266	669	0
39.0602 Divinity/ministry (B.D., M.Div.)	0	0	0	0	0	0	5,137
39.0603 Rabbinical and Talmudic studies (M.H.L./Rav)	0	0	0	0	0	0	142
39.0604 Pretheological/Preministerial studies	0	2	1	142	0	0	0
39.0605 Ordination, other	0	0	0	0	0	0	30
39.0606 Talmudic Studies	0	11	0	754	69	16	0
39.0699 Theological and ministerial studies, other	31	103	24	650	544	275	0
39.07 Pastoral counseling and specialized ministries	12	27	3	362	549	161	0
39.99 Theological studies and religious vocations, other	7	12	6	407	312	184	0
40. Physical sciences	244	14	1,350	17,963	4,923	3,963	0
40.01 Physical sciences, general	0	0	772	290	58	5	0
40.02 Astronomy	0	0	1	95	76	79	0
40.03 Astrophysics	0	0	0	61	23	19	0
40.04 Atmospheric sciences and meteorology	0	0	0	485	163	87	0
40.05 Chemistry	0	3	301	9,968	1,927	2,065	0
40.0501 Chemistry, general	0	3	301	9,645	1,787	1,875	0
40.0502 Analytical chemistry	0	0	0	0	31	16	0
40.0503 Inorganic chemistry	0	0	0	0	0	4	0
40.0504 Organic chemistry	0	0	0	8	15	8	0
40.0505 Medicinal/pharmaceutical chemistry	0	0	0	54	31	55	0
40.0506 Physical and theoretical chemistry	0	0	0	4	6	13	0
40.0507 Polymer chemistry	0	0	0	0	15	42	0
40.0599 Chemistry, other	0	0	0	257	42	52	0
40.06 Geological and related sciences	0	0	28	2,789	964	302	0
40.0601 Geology	0	0	28	2,502	820	234	0
40.0602 Geochemistry	0	0	0	5	7	3	0
40.0603 Geophysics and seismology	0	0	0	60	70	37	0
40.0604 Paleontology	0	0	0	0	2	0	0
40.0699 Geological and related sciences, other	0	0	0	222	65	28	0
40.07 Miscellaneous physical sciences	244	0	78	713	301	195	0
40.0701 Metallurgy	0	0	0	0	1	0	0
40.0702 Oceanography	244	0	54	109	85	99	0
40.0703 Earth and planetary science	0	0	0	544	159	83	0
40.0799 Miscellaneous physical sciences, other	0	0	24	60	56	13	0
40.08 Physics	0	11	105	3,283	1,266	1,184	0
40.0801 Physics, general	0	11	105	3,176	1,170	1,101	0
40.0802 Chemical and atomic/molecular physics	0	0	0	18	1	12	0
40.0806 Nuclear physics	0	0	0	0	2	3	0
40.0807 Optics	0	0	0	6	31	22	0
40.0810 Theoretical and mathematical physics	0	0	0	7	0	0	0
40.0899 Physics, other	0	0	0	76	62	46	0
40.99 Physical sciences, other	0	0	65	279	145	27	0
41. Science technologies	139	150	1,110	163	18	2	0
41.01 Biological technology	22	30	128	46	0	2	0
41.02 Nuclear and industrial radiologic technologies	7	22	54	2	5	0	0
41.0204 Industrial radiologic technology/technician	2	18	36	1	0	0	0
41.0205 Nuclear/nuclear power technology/technician	5	4	13	1	5	0	0
41.0299 Nuclear and industrial radiologic technologies/technicians, other	0	0	5	0	0	0	0
41.03 Physical science technologies	110	74	601	13	0	0	0
41.0301 Chemical technology/technician	110	74	597	11	0	0	0
41.0399 Physical science technologies/technicians, other	0	0	4	2	0	0	0
41.99 Science technologies, other	0	24	327	102	13	0	0

Classification of Instructional Programs (CIP) codes and titles	Awards, curriculums of under 1 year	1- to 4-year awards	Associate degrees	Bachelor's degrees	Master's degrees	Doctoral degrees	First professional degrees
42. Psychology	117	23	1,455	73,964	15,092	4,305	0
42.01 Psychology	103	8	1,303	68,600	4,532	1,609	0
42.02 Clinical psychology	0	0	0	113	1,502	1,801	0
42.03 Cognitive psychology and psycholinguistics	0	0	0	71	30	19	0
42.04 Community psychology	0	0	25	107	334	3	0
42.06 Counseling psychology	3	2	1	394	4,829	293	0
42.07 Developmental and child psychology	0	0	0	795	150	65	0
42.08 Experimental psychology	0	0	0	246	47	44	0
42.09 Industrial and organizational psychology	0	0	0	179	1,115	101	0
42.11 Physiological psychology/psychobiology	0	0	0	254	18	18	0
42.16 Social psychology	0	13	26	860	198	52	0
42.17 School psychology	0	0	1	27	1,282	167	0
42.99 Psychology, other	11	0	99	2,318	1,055	133	0
43. Protective services	12,550	3,654	16,286	24,883	2,618	52	0
43.01 Criminal justice and corrections	9,240	2,699	13,475	24,494	2,576	52	0
43.0102 Corrections/correctional administration	2,332	174	632	595	40	0	0
43.0103 Criminal justice/law enforcement administration	733	777	3,324	7,168	1,096	4	0
43.0104 Criminal justice studies	98	84	2,422	14,206	1,240	48	0
43.0106 Forensic technology/technician	12	0	38	71	123	0	0
43.0107 Law enforcement/police science	4,657	1,588	6,662	1,597	62	0	0
43.0109 Security and loss prevention services	1,009	36	91	56	1	0	0
43.0199 Criminal justice and corrections, other	399	40	306	801	14	0	0
43.02 Fire protection	3,254	843	2,364	369	35	0	0
43.0201 Fire protection and safety technology/technician	1,288	411	1,502	186	2	0	0
43.0202 Fire services administration	64	18	167	153	8	0	0
43.0203 Fire science/firefighting	1,879	408	678	24	0	0	0
43.0299 Fire protection, other	23	6	17	6	25	0	0
43.99 Protective services, other	56	112	447	20	7	0	0
44. Public administration and services	515	386	3,648	20,346	25,619	536	0
44.02 Community organization, resources, and services	61	130	1,263	2,064	415	8	0
44.04 Public administration	16	11	64	2,279	7,512	167	0
44.05 Public policy analysis	0	0	7	620	865	94	0
44.07 Social work	117	51	1,462	14,891	16,133	256	0
44.99 Public administration and services, other	321	194	852	492	694	11	0
45. Social sciences and history	149	58	5,136	126,356	14,411	4,052	0
45.01 Social sciences, general	0	1	3,833	7,477	610	50	0
45.02 Anthropology	0	2	47	6,898	964	452	0
45.03 Archeology	7	11	5	120	27	18	0
45.04 Criminology	0	0	33	3,183	190	16	0
45.05 Demography/population studies	0	0	1	2	34	7	0
45.06 Economics	0	5	203	18,154	2,254	832	0
45.0601 Economics, general	0	5	198	17,497	1,878	811	0
45.0602 Applied and resource economics	0	0	0	131	115	10	0
45.0603 Econometrics and quantitative economics	0	0	0	27	1	0	0
45.0604 Development economics and international development	0	0	0	1	112	3	0
45.0605 International economics	0	0	0	125	121	7	0
45.0699 Economics, other	0	0	5	373	27	1	0
45.07 Geography	51	0	55	4,038	786	200	0
45.0701 Geography	7	0	40	3,947	773	200	0
45.0702 Cartography	44	0	15	91	13	0	0
45.08 History	37	5	324	25,052	2,683	972	0
45.0801 History, general	0	5	321	24,722	2,588	927	0
45.0802 American (United States) history	37	0	0	33	12	10	0
45.0803 European history	0	0	0	5	2	2	0
45.0804 History and philosophy of science and technology	0	0	0	92	20	20	0
45.0805 Public/applied history and archival administration	0	0	0	24	43	0	0
45.0899 History, other	0	0	3	176	18	13	0
45.09 International relations and affairs	2	33	3	5,227	2,225	54	0
45.10 Political science and government	19	0	107	27,339	1,669	684	0
45.1001 Political science, general	19	0	106	26,949	1,579	677	0
45.1002 American government and politics	0	0	0	35	77	3	0
45.1099 Political science and government, other	0	0	1	355	13	4	0
45.11 Sociology	30	1	365	25,581	2,045	594	0
45.12 Urban affairs/studies	0	0	14	643	318	49	0
45.99 Social sciences and history, other	3	0	146	2,642	606	124	0
46. Construction trades	6,847	7,909	2,319	186	12	0	0
46.01 Masons and tilesetters	337	308	47	1	0	0	0
46.02 Carpenters	1,418	1,635	346	0	0	0	0

Classification of Instructional Programs (CIP) codes and titles	Awards, curriculums of under 1 year	1- to 4-year awards	Associate degrees	Bachelor's degrees	Master's degrees	Doctoral degrees	First professional degrees
46.03 Electrical and power transmission installation	1,560	4,172	1,161	1	0	0	0
46.0301 Electrical and power transmission installation, general	161	173	65	0	0	0	0
46.0302 Electrician	1,371	3,714	971	1	0	0	0
46.0303 Lineworker	28	252	102	0	0	0	0
46.0399 Electrical and power transmission installation, other	0	33	23	0	0	0	0
46.04 Construction and building finishers and managers	2,425	835	319	164	12	0	0
46.0401 Building/property maintenance and manager	1,906	392	62	75	0	0	0
46.0403 Construction/building inspector	87	62	74	1	0	0	0
46.0408 Painter and wall coverer	30	1	0	0	0	0	0
46.0499 Construction and building finishers and managers, other	402	380	183	88	12	0	0
46.05 Plumbers and pipefitters	575	574	111	0	0	0	0
46.99 Construction trades, other	532	385	335	20	0	0	0
47. Mechanics and repairers	13,423	35,007	11,580	70	0	0	0
47.01 Electrical and electronics equipment installers and repairers	3,802	6,521	3,003	0	0	0	0
47.0101 Electrical and electronics equipment installer and repairer, general	1,440	2,796	1,137	0	0	0	0
47.0102 Business machine repairer	0	100	14	0	0	0	0
47.0103 Communications systems installer and repairer	243	488	348	0	0	0	0
47.0104 Computer installer and repairer	1,441	1,035	563	0	0	0	0
47.0105 Industrial electronics installer and repairer	234	1,411	716	0	0	0	0
47.0106 Major appliance installer and repairer	90	193	64	0	0	0	0
47.0199 Electrical and electronics equipment installer and repairer, other	354	498	161	0	0	0	0
47.02 Heating, air-conditioning, and refrigeration mechanics and repairers	1,914	5,793	853	0	0	0	0
47.03 Industrial equipment maintenance and repairers	1,215	1,287	477	2	0	0	0
47.0302 Heavy equipment maintenance and repairer	117	207	104	0	0	0	0
47.0303 Industrial machinery maintenance and repairer	520	824	305	2	0	0	0
47.0399 Industrial equipment maintenance and repairers, other	578	256	68	0	0	0	0
47.04 Miscellaneous mechanics and repairers	159	273	135	0	0	0	0
47.0401 Instrument calibration and repairer	31	20	1	0	0	0	0
47.0402 Gunsmith	30	26	84	0	0	0	0
47.0403 Locksmith and safe repairer	1	33	0	0	0	0	0
47.0404 Musical instrument repairer	42	68	14	0	0	0	0
47.0408 Watch, clock, and jewelry repairer	46	88	36	0	0	0	0
47.0499 Miscellaneous mechanics and repairers, other	9	38	0	0	0	0	0
47.05 Stationary energy sources installers and operators	29	33	2	0	0	0	0
47.06 Vehicle and mobile equipment mechanics and repairers	6,156	20,305	6,843	68	0	0	0
47.0603 Auto/automotive body repairer	599	2,488	629	2	0	0	0
47.0604 Auto/automotive mechanic/technician	4,404	10,725	3,820	24	0	0	0
47.0605 Diesel engine mechanic and repairer	361	2,033	1,131	14	0	0	0
47.0606 Small-engine mechanic and repairer	192	291	17	0	0	0	0
47.0607 Aircraft mechanic/technician, airframe	204	1,701	288	11	0	0	0
47.0608 Aircraft mechanic/technician, powerplant	91	1,078	255	0	0	0	0
47.0609 Aviation systems and avionics maintenance technologist/technician	67	642	370	17	0	0	0
47.0611 Motorcycle mechanic and repairer	193	1,054	0	0	0	0	0
47.0699 Vehicle and mobile equipment mechanics and repairers, other	45	293	333	0	0	0	0
47.99 Mechanics and repairers, other	148	795	267	0	0	0	0
48. Precision production trades	6,867	15,395	11,786	393	5	0	0
48.01 Drafting	1,872	5,131	8,306	212	0	0	0
48.0101 Drafting, general	1,032	2,260	5,496	93	0	0	0
48.0102 Architectural drafting	70	670	999	1	0	0	0
48.0103 Civil/structural drafting	10	71	32	0	0	0	0
48.0104 Electrical/electronics drafting	321	40	76	1	0	0	0
48.0105 Mechanical drafting	182	717	1,059	117	0	0	0
48.0199 Drafting, other	257	1,373	644	0	0	0	0
48.02 Graphic and printing equipment operators	555	1,532	1,200	148	0	0	0
48.0201 Graphic and printing equipment operators, general	163	605	670	128	0	0	0
48.0205 Mechanical typesetter and composer	2	4	13	0	0	0	0
48.0206 Lithographer and platemaker	6	12	44	0	0	0	0
48.0208 Printing press operator	6	220	46	7	0	0	0
48.0211 Computer typography and composition equipment operator	118	111	124	0	0	0	0
48.0212 Desktop publishing equipment operator	247	514	97	0	0	0	0

Classification of Instructional Programs (CIP) codes and titles	Awards, curriculums of under 1 year	1- to 4-year awards	Associate degrees	Bachelor's degrees	Master's degrees	Doctoral degrees	First professional degrees
48.0299 Graphic and printing equipment operators, other ...	13	66	206	13	0	0	0
48.03 Leatherworkers and upholsterers	249	364	5	0	0	0	0
48.0303 Upholster	247	363	1	0	0	0	0
48.0304 Shoe, boot, and leather repairer	2	1	0	0	0	0	0
48.0399 Leatherworkers and upholsterers, other	0	0	4	0	0	0	0
48.05 Precision metal workers	3,868	7,634	2,024	15	0	0	0
48.0501 Machinist/machine technologist	803	1,594	578	0	0	0	0
48.0503 Machine shop assistant	499	1,584	521	0	0	0	0
48.0506 Sheet metal workers	223	132	48	0	0	0	0
48.0507 Tool-and-die maker/technologist	145	561	425	14	0	0	0
48.0508 Welder/welding technologist	2,119	3,725	434	1	0	0	0
48.0599 Precision metal workers, other	79	38	18	0	0	0	0
48.07 Woodworkers	167	478	71	18	5	0	0
48.0701 Woodworkers, general	1	28	7	0	0	0	0
48.0702 Furniture designer and maker	24	30	17	18	5	0	0
48.0703 Cabinet maker and millworker	142	304	40	0	0	0	0
48.0799 Woodworkers, other	0	116	7	0	0	0	0
48.99 Precision production trades, other	156	256	180	0	0	0	0
49. Transportation and materials moving workers	16,498	1,796	1,016	3,395	697	0	0
49.01 Air transportation workers	3,800	341	844	3,192	697	0	0
49.0101 Aviation and airway science	28	0	201	1,863	5	0	0
49.0102 Aircraft pilot and navigator (professional)	1,098	316	468	688	594	0	0
49.0104 Aviation management	0	0	99	596	58	0	0
49.0105 Air traffic control	89	10	60	28	0	0	0
49.0106 Flight attendant	1,680	12	10	0	0	0	0
49.0107 Aircraft pilot (private)	62	0	3	14	0	0	0
49.0199 Air transportation workers, other	843	3	3	3	40	0	0
49.02 Vehicle and equipment operators	12,279	467	11	0	0	0	0
49.0202 Construction equipment operator	33	205	1	0	0	0	0
49.0205 Truck, bus, and other commercial vehicle operators	11,245	232	1	0	0	0	0
49.0299 Vehicle and equipment operators, other	1,001	30	9	0	0	0	0
49.03 Water transportation workers	319	971	103	186	0	0	0
49.0303 Fishing technology/commercial fishing	13	0	0	0	0	0	0
49.0304 Diver (professional)	201	577	38	0	0	0	0
49.0306 Marine maintenance and ship repairer	34	321	65	0	0	0	0
49.0309 Marine science/merchant marine officer	51	26	0	178	0	0	0
49.0399 Water transportation workers, other	20	47	0	8	0	0	0
49.99 Transportation and material moving workers, other	100	17	58	17	0	0	0
50. Visual and performing arts	6,572	5,265	17,018	58,854	11,065	1,117	0
50.01 Visual and performing arts	3	41	540	1,675	116	10	0
50.02 Crafts, folk art, and artisanry	0	6	0	156	5	0	0
50.03 Dance	4	49	81	1,296	162	12	0
50.04 Design and applied arts	1,661	3,598	11,891	10,048	920	0	0
50.0401 Design and visual communications	178	311	1,567	1,317	109	0	0
50.0402 Graphic design, commercial art, and illustration	1,219	2,697	6,527	5,255	510	0	0
50.0404 Industrial design	0	4	237	898	87	0	0
50.0406 Commercial photography	25	192	381	0	0	0	0
50.0407 Fashion design and illustration	1	48	1,108	615	32	0	0
50.0408 Interior design	54	254	1,305	1,518	105	0	0
50.0499 Design and applied arts, other	184	92	766	445	77	0	0
50.05 Dramatic/theater arts and stagecraft	156	535	411	7,526	1,422	70	0
50.0501 Drama/theater arts, general	12	141	360	7,037	1,269	70	0
50.0502 Technical theater/theater design and stagecraft	0	11	51	178	40	0	0
50.0503 Acting and directing	144	65	0	195	84	0	0
50.0504 Playwriting and screenwriting	0	0	0	12	5	0	0
50.0505 Drama/theater literature, history, and criticism	0	3	0	11	0	0	0
50.0599 Dramatic/theater arts and stagecraft, other	0	315	0	93	24	0	0
50.06 Film/video and photographic arts	199	256	1,362	4,124	724	12	0
50.0601 Film/cinema studies	7	0	0	902	118	5	0
50.0602 Film-video making/cinematography and production	9	11	778	1,596	427	3	0
50.0605 Photography	183	194	371	987	143	4	0
50.0699 Film/video and photographic arts, other	0	51	213	639	36	0	0
50.07 Fine arts and art studies	3,668	246	1,309	22,711	3,312	228	0
50.0701 Art, general	9	34	643	11,914	827	21	0
50.0702 Fine/studio arts	3	0	99	4,846	760	4	0
50.0703 Art history, criticism, and conservation	0	0	6	2,437	598	195	0
50.0704 Arts management	0	2	6	227	158	4	0
50.0705 Drawing	2	9	84	230	20	0	0
50.0706 Intermedia	12	15	399	166	17	0	0
50.0708 Painting	0	23	0	722	188	0	0
50.0709 Sculpture	0	8	5	225	61	0	0

Table 12. Earned awards and degrees, by field of study, 1999-2000 — Continued

Classification of Instructional Programs (CIP) codes and titles	Awards, curriculums of under 1 year	1- to 4-year awards	Associate degrees	Bachelor's degrees	Master's degrees	Doctoral degrees	First professional degrees
50.0710 Printmaking	0	8	2	80	35	0	0
50.0711 Ceramics arts and ceramics	0	5	6	113	38	0	0
50.0712 Fiber, textile, and weaving arts	0	0	2	95	38	4	0
50.0713 Metal and jewelry arts	3,642	124	2	94	19	0	0
50.0799 Fine arts and art studies, other	0	18	55	1,562	553	0	0
50.09 Music	369	434	1,248	10,686	3,970	761	0
50.0901 Music, general	30	49	436	5,436	1,310	298	0
50.0902 Music history and literature	0	0	0	88	52	21	0
50.0903 Music-general performance	0	219	90	3,269	1,921	289	0
50.0904 Music theory and composition	0	34	9	349	151	58	0
50.0905 Musicology and ethnomusicology	0	0	0	15	16	4	0
50.0906 Music conducting	0	0	0	5	61	21	0
50.0907 Music-piano and organ performance	0	0	1	79	113	24	0
50.0908 Music-voice and choral/opera performance	0	0	4	189	98	13	0
50.0909 Music business management and merchandising	8	2	60	521	8	0	0
50.0999 Music, other	331	130	648	735	240	33	0
50.99 Visual and performing arts, other	512	100	176	632	434	24	0
51. Health professions and related sciences	72,378	77,256	83,982	79,459	43,038	2,676	36,146
51.01 Chiropractic (D.C., D.C.M.)	0	0	0	0	0	0	3,811
51.02 Communication disorders sciences and services	213	145	661	6,857	5,787	251	0
51.0201 Communication disorders, general	0	0	21	1,806	1,251	32	0
51.0202 Audiology/hearing sciences	0	0	0	161	189	139	0
51.0203 Speech-language pathology	0	0	62	894	1,398	12	0
51.0204 Speech-language pathology and audiology	0	0	6	3,879	2,853	68	0
51.0205 Sign language interpreter	213	145	558	84	7	0	0
51.0299 Communication disorders sciences and services, other	0	0	14	33	89	0	0
51.03 Community health services	160	25	178	959	216	4	0
51.04 Dentistry (D.D.S., D.M.D.)	0	0	0	0	0	0	4,442
51.05 Dental clinical science/graduate dentistry (M.S., Ph.D.)	0	0	10	29	503	27	94
51.06 Dental services	4,791	5,486	5,548	1,101	31	0	0
51.0601 Dental assistant	4,474	4,929	1,049	1	0	0	0
51.0602 Dental hygienist	27	346	4,291	1,086	17	0	0
51.0603 Dental laboratory technician	215	201	195	8	1	0	0
51.0699 Dental services, other	75	10	13	6	13	0	0
51.07 Health and medical administrative services	7,187	4,074	2,492	4,326	4,376	77	0
51.0701 Health system/health services administration	190	148	56	2,378	3,003	62	0
51.0702 Hospital/health facilities administration	2	255	16	963	1,158	2	0
51.0703 Health unit coordinator/ward clerk	605	105	23	0	0	0	0
51.0704 Health unit coordinator/ward supervisor	0	7	6	8	0	0	0
51.0705 Medical office management	3,002	711	309	0	0	0	0
51.0706 Medical records administration	510	350	128	625	7	0	0
51.0707 Medical records technology/technician	712	1,003	1,403	1	8	2	0
51.0708 Medical transcription	906	1,048	232	0	0	0	0
51.0799 Health and medical administrative services, other	1,260	447	319	351	200	11	0
51.08 Health and medical assistants	22,491	19,668	15,820	2,241	1,658	0	0
51.0801 Medical assistant	18,798	16,559	5,409	3	0	0	0
51.0802 Medical laboratory assistant	379	81	28	26	23	0	0
51.0803 Occupational therapy assistant	3	86	2,917	22	0	0	0
51.0804 Ophthalmic medical assistant	46	15	3	0	0	0	0
51.0805 Pharmacy technician/assistant	1,862	1,556	219	0	0	0	0
51.0806 Physical therapy assistant	371	43	4,859	40	0	0	0
51.0807 Physician assistant	48	288	172	2,024	1,623	0	0
51.0808 Veterinarian assistant/animal health technician	326	196	1,910	121	0	0	0
51.0899 Health and medical assistants, other	658	844	303	5	12	0	0
51.09 Health and medical diagnostic and treatment services	10,904	10,531	10,919	1,955	74	2	0
51.0901 Cardiovascular technology/technician	29	810	213	46	0	0	0
51.0902 Electrocardiograph technology/technician	167	42	21	0	0	0	0
51.0903 Electroencephalograph technology/technician	10	14	21	0	0	0	0
51.0904 Emergency medical technology/technician	9,243	2,317	1,152	87	7	0	0
51.0905 Nuclear medical technology/technician	22	118	207	156	0	0	0
51.0906 Perfusion technology/technician	7	4	0	26	14	0	0
51.0907 Medical radiologic technology/technician	539	1,460	5,036	789	11	0	0
51.0908 Respiratory therapy technician	203	1,342	3,094	510	4	0	0
51.0909 Surgical/operating room technician	255	3,238	749	0	0	0	0
51.0910 Diagnostic medical sonography	20	924	340	140	0	0	0
51.0999 Health and medical diagnostic and treatment services, other	409	262	86	201	38	2	0
51.10 Health and medical laboratory technologies	1,820	769	1,777	2,286	501	106	0
51.1001 Blood bank technology/technician	308	13	0	11	0	0	0
51.1002 Cytotechnologist	2	50	1	92	6	0	0
51.1003 Hematology technology/technician	142	58	0	0	0	0	0

Classification of Instructional Programs (CIP) codes and titles	Awards, curriculums of under 1 year	1- to 4-year awards	Associate degrees	Bachelor's degrees	Master's degrees	Doctoral degrees	First professional degrees
51.1004 Medical laboratory technician	282	406	1,642	74	7	0	0
51.1005 Medical technology	0	28	24	1,957	62	2	0
51.1006 Optometric/ophthalmic laboratory technician	284	0	11	0	0	0	0
51.1099 Health and medical laboratory technologies/technicians, other	802	214	99	152	426	104	0
51.11 Health and medical preparatory program	25	2	580	1,548	100	19	0
51.1101 Predentistry studies	0	0	41	141	0	0	0
51.1102 Premedicine studies	0	0	221	666	0	0	0
51.1103 Prepharmacy studies	0	0	69	8	0	0	0
51.1104 Preveterinary studies	0	0	38	221	0	0	0
51.1199 Health and medical preparatory programs, other	25	2	211	512	100	19	0
51.12 Medicine (M.D.)	0	0	0	0	0	0	15,487
51.13 Medical basic sciences	0	4	13	562	510	567	0
51.1301 Medical anatomy	0	0	0	0	13	19	0
51.1302 Medical biochemistry	0	0	0	14	16	76	0
51.1304 Medical physics/biophysics	0	0	0	0	13	9	0
51.1305 Medical cell biology	0	0	0	9	1	25	0
51.1306 Medical genetics	0	0	0	0	39	32	0
51.1307 Medical immunology	0	0	0	0	24	49	0
51.1308 Medical microbiology	0	0	0	101	26	66	0
51.1309 Medical molecular biology	0	4	0	0	8	19	0
51.1310 Medical neurobiology	0	0	0	8	5	31	0
51.1311 Medical nutrition	0	0	0	12	25	0	0
51.1312 Medical pathology	0	0	0	0	13	37	0
51.1313 Medical physiology	0	0	0	0	36	38	0
51.1314 Medical toxicology	0	0	0	11	3	16	0
51.1399 Medical basic sciences, other	0	0	13	407	288	150	0
51.14 Medical clinical sciences (M.S., Ph.D.)	0	0	0	0	79	24	0
51.15 Mental health services	2,560	1,352	2,766	673	616	6	0
51.1501 Alcohol/drug abuse counseling	278	757	830	76	76	0	0
51.1502 Psychiatric/mental health services technician	165	471	1,472	115	14	0	0
51.1503 Clinical and medical social work	1	12	26	130	70	5	0
51.1599 Mental health services, other	2,116	112	438	352	456	1	0
51.16 Nursing	19,319	33,566	41,354	39,614	11,915	469	0
51.1601 Nursing (R.N. training)	357	3,416	40,258	33,530	4,232	243	0
51.1602 Nursing administration (post-R.N.)	0	0	0	306	408	1	0
51.1603 Nursing, adult health (post-R.N.)	0	0	0	137	262	0	0
51.1604 Nursing anesthetist (post-R.N.)	0	0	0	19	595	0	0
51.1605 Nursing, family practice (post-R.N.)	0	2	0	32	1,010	5	0
51.1606 Nursing, maternal/child health (post-R.N.)	0	0	11	0	258	0	0
51.1607 Nursing midwifery (post-R.N.)	0	5	0	108	102	0	0
51.1608 Nursing science (post-R.N.)	0	0	4	1,835	1,317	137	0
51.1609 Nursing, pediatric (post-R.N.)	0	0	0	1	111	0	0
51.1610 Nursing, psychiatric/mental health (post-R.N.)	0	0	0	0	130	0	0
51.1611 Nursing, public health (post-R.N.)	0	0	0	0	290	0	0
51.1612 Nursing, surgical (post-R.N.)	50	0	0	0	97	0	0
51.1613 Practical nurse (L.P.N. training)	1,013	28,369	575	0	0	0	0
51.1614 Nurse assistant/aide	15,847	434	7	0	0	0	0
51.1615 Home health aide	979	80	5	0	0	0	0
51.1699 Nursing, other	1,073	1,260	494	3,646	3,103	83	0
51.17 Optometry (O.D.)	0	0	0	0	0	0	1,383
51.18 Ophthalmic/optometric services	247	109	357	17	90	2	0
51.1801 Opticianry/dispensing optician	164	35	213	0	0	0	0
51.1802 Optical technician/assistant	71	66	109	1	0	0	0
51.1803 Ophthalmic medical technologist	12	6	35	6	5	0	0
51.1899 Ophthalmic/optometric services, other	0	2	0	10	85	2	0
51.19 Osteopathic medicine (D.O.)	0	0	0	0	0	0	2,236
51.20 Pharmacy	24	0	5	3,271	314	256	5,669
51.2001 Pharmacy (B.Pharm., Pharm.D.)	0	0	0	2,926	0	0	5,669
51.2002 Pharmacy administration and pharmaceutics	0	0	0	0	62	21	0
51.2003 Medical pharmacology and pharmaceutical science	0	0	0	150	198	178	0
51.2099 Pharmacy, other	24	0	5	195	54	57	0
51.21 Podiatry (D.P.M., D.P., Pod.D.)	0	0	0	0	0	0	569
51.22 Public health	12	33	95	1,579	4,935	425	0
51.2201 Public health, general	0	32	29	524	2,890	94	0
51.2202 Environmental health	0	0	52	393	283	45	0
51.2203 Epidemiology	0	0	0	6	409	116	0
51.2204 Health and medical biostatistics	0	0	0	12	72	25	0
51.2205 Health physics/radiologic health	0	0	1	13	15	1	0
51.2206 Occupational health and industrial hygiene	12	1	11	85	60	10	0
51.2207 Public health education and promotion	0	0	0	336	447	39	0
51.2299 Public health, other	0	0	2	210	759	95	0
51.23 Rehabilitation/therapeutic services	300	245	784	8,248	9,100	196	0

Classification of Instructional Programs (CIP) codes and titles	Awards, curriculums of under 1 year	1- to 4-year awards	Associate degrees	Bachelor's degrees	Master's degrees	Doctoral degrees	First professional degrees
51.2301 Art therapy	0	0	0	82	233	0	0
51.2302 Dance therapy	0	0	0	2	35	0	0
51.2303 Hypnotherapy	0	122	0	0	0	0	0
51.2304 Movement therapy	0	0	4	0	20	0	0
51.2305 Music therapy	0	4	0	217	41	0	0
51.2306 Occupational therapy	0	8	286	3,902	1,868	8	0
51.2307 Orthotics/prosthetics	0	35	52	25	0	0	0
51.2308 Physical therapy	0	2	283	2,475	5,927	159	0
51.2309 Recreational therapy	35	3	60	299	3	0	0
51.2310 Vocational rehabilitation counseling	4	7	13	187	446	12	0
51.2399 Rehabilitation/therapeutic services, other	261	64	86	1,059	527	17	0
51.24 Veterinary medicine (D.V.M.)	0	0	0	0	0	0	2,251
51.25 Veterinary clinical sciences (M.S., Ph.D.)	0	0	0	0	164	111	0
51.26 Miscellaneous health aides	886	89	48	0	0	0	0
51.27 Miscellaneous health professions	0	34	6	152	1,127	1	202
51.2701 Acupuncture and oriental medicine	0	28	0	71	1,040	0	0
51.2702 Medical dietitian	0	6	6	43	34	0	0
51.2703 Medical illustrating	0	0	0	38	46	1	0
51.2704 Naturopathic medicine	0	0	0	0	0	0	202
51.2705 Psychoanalysis	0	0	0	0	7	0	202
51.99 Health professions and related sciences, other	1,439	1,124	569	4,041	942	133	2
52 Business management and administrative services	47,172	43,987	92,203	253,634	111,205	1,188	0
52.01 Business	7,873	1,693	12,283	24,391	9,540	260	0
52.02 Business administration and management	2,383	2,887	28,462	97,014	69,009	529	0
52.0201 Business administration and management, general	1,624	2,014	24,870	88,793	63,848	508	0
52.0202 Purchasing, procurement, and contracts management	76	0	49	313	552	0	0
52.0203 Logistics and materials management	67	25	86	986	104	0	0
52.0204 Office supervision and management	353	501	1,083	602	54	0	0
52.0205 Operations management and supervision	157	219	710	2,065	1,564	7	0
52.0206 Nonprofit and public management	0	2	8	115	74	0	0
52.0299 Business administration and management, other	106	126	1,656	4,140	2,813	14	0
52.03 Accounting	4,245	6,967	13,558	35,301	5,061	36	0
52.0301 Accounting	1,939	2,865	6,712	34,984	4,984	36	0
52.0302 Accounting technician	1,698	3,615	6,582	35	16	0	0
52.0399 Accounting, other	608	487	264	282	61	0	0
52.04 Administrative and secretarial services	20,559	23,454	16,941	226	68	0	0
52.0401 Administrative assistant/secretarial science, general	6,158	7,936	9,319	90	0	0	0
52.0402 Executive assistant/secretary	608	1,414	2,249	2	0	0	0
52.0403 Legal administrative assistant/secretary	550	1,286	1,244	2	0	0	0
52.0404 Medical administrative assistant/secretary	3,240	3,740	2,405	1	0	0	0
52.0405 Court reporter	22	529	333	42	0	0	0
52.0406 Receptionist	207	89	4	0	0	0	0
52.0407 Information processing/data entry technician	3,645	1,685	807	75	0	0	0
52.0408 General office/clerical and typing services	4,783	3,902	231	3	0	0	0
52.0499 Administrative and secretarial services, other	1,346	2,873	349	11	68	0	0
52.05 Business communications	55	119	23	198	88	0	0
52.06 Business/managerial economics	4	5	19	3,041	191	59	0
52.07 Enterprise management and operation	165	171	231	577	304	0	0
52.0701 Enterprise management and operation, general	161	168	211	560	304	0	0
52.0799 Enterprise management operation, other	4	3	20	17	0	0	0
52.08 Financial management and services	738	203	663	25,532	6,219	43	0
52.0801 Finance, general	13	43	226	23,605	5,206	38	0
52.0802 Actuarial science	0	0	0	225	58	0	0
52.0803 Banking and financial support services	683	140	372	510	311	2	0
52.0804 Financial planning	1	0	4	65	76	0	0
52.0805 Insurance and risk management	37	17	0	431	42	3	0
52.0806 International finance	0	0	0	17	101	0	0
52.0807 Investments and securities	0	0	0	413	340	0	0
52.0899 Financial management and services, other	4	3	61	266	85	0	0
52.09 Hospitality services management	1,684	539	2,855	5,909	376	10	0
52.0901 Hospitality/administration management	32	64	250	1,864	186	3	0
52.0902 Hotel/motel and restaurant management	235	119	1,668	3,165	90	7	0
52.0903 Travel-tourism management	1,371	353	714	316	93	0	0
52.0999 Hospitality services management, other	46	3	223	564	7	0	0
52.10 Human resources management	432	572	504	8,857	5,921	124	0
52.1001 Human resources management	336	133	191	5,019	2,775	23	0
52.1002 Labor/personnel relations and studies	19	436	251	752	559	38	0
52.1003 Organizational behavior studies	0	0	2	1,852	2,276	63	0
52.1099 Human resources management, other	77	3	60	1,234	311	0	0
52.11 International business	97	30	352	4,051	3,249	14	0
52.12 Business information and data processing services	6,821	6,603	13,120	16,479	4,422	14	0

Table 12. Earned awards and degrees, by field of study, 1999-2000 — Continued

Classification of Instructional Programs (CIP) codes and titles		Awards, curriculums of under 1 year	1- to 4-year awards	Associate degrees	Bachelor's degrees	Master's degrees	Doctoral degrees	First professional degrees
52.1201	Management information systems and business data processing, general	1,225	1,770	3,479	14,659	3,520	12	0
52.1202	Business computer programming/programmer	899	733	3,715	62	0	0	0
52.1203	Business systems analysis and design	388	100	1,026	469	45	2	0
52.1204	Business systems networking and telecommunications	2,196	1,574	2,454	1,060	681	0	0
52.1205	Business computer facilities operator	979	628	531	40	0	0	0
52.1299	Business information and data processing services, other	1,134	1,798	1,915	189	176	0	0
52.13	Business quantitative methods and management science	0	4	136	3,195	1,062	33	0
52.1301	Management science	0	4	134	2,285	745	25	0
52.1302	Business statistics	0	0	0	24	19	6	0
52.1399	Business quantitative methods and management science	0	0	2	886	298	2	0
52.14	Marketing management and research	129	141	1,335	25,073	1,591	28	0
52.1401	Business marketing and marketing management	107	114	1,233	23,985	1,257	27	0
52.1402	Marketing research	0	1	0	106	90	0	0
52.1403	International business marketing	21	11	32	84	82	0	0
52.1499	Marketing management and research, other	1	15	70	898	162	1	0
52.15	Real estate	742	89	200	457	214	1	0
52.16	Taxation	984	3	0	1	1,261	0	0
52.99	Business management and administrative services, other	261	507	1,521	3,332	2,629	37	0
95.	Field of study not reported	2,921	1,955	2,464	2,287	1,759	47	209

Appendix. Sources of State and Local Job Outlook Information

State and local job market and career information is available from State Employment Security Agencies. These agencies develop detailed information about local labor markets, such as current and projected employment by occupation and industry, characteristics of the workforce, and changes in State and local area economic activity. Listed below are the Internet addresses of these agencies and addresses and telephone numbers of their directors of research and analysis.

Most States have career information delivery systems (CIDS). Look for these systems in secondary schools, postsecondary institutions, libraries, job training sites, vocational rehabilitation centers, and employment service offices. The public can use the systems' computers, printed material, microfiche, and toll-free hotlines to obtain information on occupations, educational opportunities, student financial aid, apprenticeships, and military careers. Ask counselors for specific locations.

State occupational projections are also available on the Internet at: **http://almis.dws.state.ut.us**

Alabama
Chief, Labor Market Information, Alabama Department of Industrial Relations, 649 Monroe St., Room 422, Montgomery, AL 36130. Phone: (334) 242-8800.
Internet: **http://www.dir.state.al.us/lmi**

Alaska
Chief, Research and Analysis, Alaska Department of Labor and Workforce Development, P.O. Box 25501, Juneau, AK 99802. Phone: (907) 465-4500. Internet: **http://www.labor.state.ak.us**

Arizona
Research Administrator, Arizona Department of Economic Security, Site Code 733A, P.O. Box 6123, Phoenix, AZ 85005. Phone: (602) 542-3871
Internet: **http://www.de.state.az.us/links/economic/webpage**

Arkansas
Robert Mantione, LMI Director, Arkansas Employment Security Department, P.O. Box 2981, Little Rock, AR 72203-2981. Phone: (501) 682-3159. Internet: **http://www.state.ar.us/esd**

California
Chief, Labor Market Information Division, California Employment Development Department, P.O. Box 826880, MIC 57, Sacramento, CA 94280-0001. Phone: (916) 262-2160. Internet: **http://www.calmis.cahwnet.gov**

Colorado
Colorado Department of Labor and Employment, Labor Market Information, 1515 Arapahoe St., Tower 2, Suite 400, Denver, CO 80202-2117. Phone: (303) 318-8850.
Internet: **http://www.coworkforce.com/lmi**

Connecticut
Director, Office of Research and Information, Connecticut Labor Department, 200 Folly Brook Blvd., Wethersfield, CT 06109-1114. Phone: (860) 263-6255.
Internet: **http://www.ctdol.state.ct.us/lmi/index.htm**

Delaware
Office of Occupational and Labor Market Information, Delaware Department of Labor, P.O. Box 9965, Wilmington, DE 19809-0965. Phone: (302) 761-8060. Internet: **http://www.oolmi.net**

District of Columbia
Chief of Labor Market Information, District of Columbia Department of Employment Services, 500 C St. NW., Room 201, Washington, DC 20001. Phone: (202) 724-7213.
Internet: **http://does.dc.gov/info/labor_mkt.shtm**

Florida
Agency for Workforce Innovation, Labor Market Statistics, Commerce Industrial Center Building B, 367 Marpan Lane, Tallahassee, FL 32305. Phone: (850) 488-1048.
Internet: **http://www.labormarketinfo.com**

Georgia
Director, Labor Market Information, Georgia Department of Labor, 148 International Boulevard NE., Atlanta, GA 30303-1751. Phone: (404) 656-3177. Internet: **http://www.dol.state.ga.us/lmi**

Guam
Administrator, Department of Labor, Guam Employment Services, P.O. Box 9970, Tamuning, Guam 96931-9970. Phone: (671) 647-7066. Internet: **http://onestopcareer.gov/gu**

Hawaii
Chief, Research and Statistics Office, Hawaii Department of Labor and Industrial Relations, 830 Punchbowl St., Room 304, Honolulu, HI 96813. Phone: (808) 586-8999.
Internet: **http://dlir.state.hi.us**

Idaho
Bureau Chief, Research and Analysis, Idaho Department of Labor, 317 Main St., Boise, ID 83735-0001. Phone: (208) 332-3570 x3136. Internet: **http://www.sde.state.id.us/cis**

Illinois
Economic Information and Analysis Manager, Illinois Department of Employment Security, 401 South State St., Suite 743, Chicago, IL 60605. Phone: (312) 793-2316.
Internet: **http://www.ioicc.state.il.us/lmi/default.htm**

Indiana
Director, Labor Market Information, Indiana Department of Workforce Development, Indiana Government Center South, E211, 10 North Senate Ave., Indianapolis, IN 46204-2277. Phone: (317) 232-7460. Internet: **http://www.dwd.state.in.us**

Iowa
Division Administrator, Research and Information Services, Iowa Workforce Development, 1000 East Grand Ave., Des Moines, IA 50319-0209. Phone: (800) JOB-IOWA. Internet: **http://www.state.ia.us/iwd**

Kansas
Chief, Labor Market Information Services, Kansas Department of Human Resources, 401 SW Topeka Blvd., Topeka, KS 66603. Phone: (785) 296-5058. Internet: **http://laborstats.hr.state.ks.us**

Kentucky
Manager, LMI Branch, Division of Administration/Financial Management, Department of Employment Services, 275 East Main St., Suite 2-C, Frankfort, KY 40621. Phone: (800) 542-8840. Internet: **http://www.kycwd.org/des/lmi/lmi.htm**

Louisiana
Louisiana Department of Labor, Office of Occupational Information, Research and Statistics Division, P.O. Box 94094, Baton Rouge, LA 70804-9094. Phone: (888) 302-7662. Internet: **http://www.ldol.state.la.us/lmiqm.asp**

Maine
Director, Labor Market Information Services, Maine Department of Labor, 20 Union St., Augusta, ME 04330. Phone: (207) 287-2271. Internet: **http://www.state.me.us/labor/lmis/frdef.htm**

Maryland
Director, Office of Labor Market Analysis and Information, Maryland Department of Labor, Licensing and Regulations, 1100 North Eutaw St., Room 601, Baltimore, MD 21201. Phone: (410) 767-2250. Internet: **http://www.dllr.state.md.us/lmi/index.htm**

Massachusetts
Labor Market Information and Research Director, Massachusetts Division of Employment and Training, 19 Staniford St., 2nd Floor, Boston, MA 02114. Phone: (617) 626-5744. Internet: **http://www.detma.org/lmi**

Michigan
Director, Office of Labor Market Information, Department of Career Development, Employment Service Agency, 7310 Woodward Ave., Room 520, Detroit, MI 48202. Phone: (313) 872-0990. Internet: **http://www.michlmi.org**

Minnesota
Director, BLS Programs, Research and Statistical Office, Minnesota Department of Economic Security, 390 North Robert St., 5th Floor, St. Paul, MN 55104. Phone: (651) 296-4087. Internet: **http://www.mnworkforcecenter.org/lmi**

Mississippi
Labor Market Information Director, Mississippi Employment Security Commission, P.O. Box 1699, Jackson, MS 39215-1699. Phone: (601) 961-7424. Internet: **http://www.mesc.state.ms.us/lmi/index.html**

Missouri
Department of Economic Development, Division of Workforce Development, Labor Market Information Section, P.O. Box 1087, Jefferson City, MO 65102. Phone: (573) 751-3595. Internet: **http://www.works.state.mo.us/lmi**

Montana
Research and Analysis Bureau, Job Services Division, Montana Department of Labor and Industry, P.O. Box 1728, Helena, MT 59624-1728. Phone: (406) 444-2430; within Montana at (800) 633-0229; outside Montana at (800) 541-3904. Internet: **http://rad.dli.state.mt.us**

Nebraska
Labor Market Information Administrator, Nebraska Department of Labor, 550 South 16th St., P.O. Box 94600, Lincoln, NE 68509-4600. Phone: (402) 471-2600. Internet: **http://www.dol.state.ne.us/nelmi.htm**

Nevada
Chief, DETR, Bureau of Research and Analysis, Information Development and Processing Division, 500 East Third St., Carson City, NV 89713-0001. Phone: (775) 684-0450. Internet: **http://detr.state.nv.us/lmi/index.htm**

New Hampshire
Director, Economic and Labor Market Information Bureau, New Hampshire Department of Employment Security, 32 South Main St., Concord, NH 03301. Phone: (603) 228-4123. Internet: **http://www.nhworks.state.nh.us/lmipage.htm**

New Jersey
Assistant Commissioner, Labor Planning and Analysis, New Jersey Department of Labor, P.O. Box 56, 5th Floor, Trenton, NJ 08625-0056. Phone: (609) 292-2643. Internet: **http://www.state.nj.us/labor/lra**

New Mexico
Economic Research and Analysis Bureau, New Mexico Department of Labor, 401 Broadway Blvd. NE., P.O. Box 1928, Albuquerque, NM 87103. Phone: (505) 841-8645. Internet: **http://www3.state.nm.us/dol/dol_lmif.html**

New York
Director, Division of Research and Statistics, New York State Department of Labor, State Campus, Room 403, Albany, NY 12240. Phone: (518) 457-1130. Internet: **http://www.labor.state.ny.us/labor_market/labor_market_info.html**

North Carolina
Director, Labor Market Information, North Carolina Employment Security Commission, P.O. Box 25903, Raleigh, NC 27611. Phone: (919) 733-2936. Internet: **http://www.ncesc.com/lmi/default.asp**

North Dakota
Program Support Area Manager, Job Service North Dakota, 1000 East Divide Ave., P.O. Box 5507, Bismarck, ND 58506-5507. Phone: (701) 328-2868. Internet: **http://www.jobsnd.com**

Ohio
Director, Ohio Department of Job and Family Services, ORAA, LMI Bureau, 4300 Kimberly Pkwy., 3rd Floor, Columbus, OH 43232. Phone: (614) 752-9494. Internet: **http://lmi.state.oh.us**

Oklahoma
Director, Labor Market Information, Economic Research and Analysis Division, Oklahoma Employment Security Commission, P.O. Box 52003, Oklahoma City, OK 73152. Phone: (405) 525-7265. Internet: **http://www.oesc.state.ok.us/lmi/default.htm**

Oregon
Labor Market Information Director, Oregon Employment Department, 875 Union St. NE., Salem, OR 97311. Phone: (503) 947-1212. Internet: **http://olmis.emp.state.or.us**

Pennsylvania
Director, Center for Workforce Information and Analysis, Pennsylvania Department of Labor and Industry, 7th and Forester Streets., Room 220, Labor and Industry Building, Harrisburg, PA 17120-0001. Phone: (877) 4WF-DATA. Internet: **http://www.dli.state.pa.us/workforceinfo**

Puerto Rico
Director, Research and Statistics Division, Puerto Rico Bureau of Employment Security, 505 Munoz Rivera Ave., 17th Floor, Hato Rey, PR 00918. Phone: (787) 754-5385. Internet: **http://www.interempleo.org**

Rhode Island
Director, Labor Market Information, Rhode Island Department of Labor and Training, Building 73, 2nd Floor, 1511 Pontiac Ave., Cranston, RI 02920-4407. Phone: (401) 462-8740. Internet: **http://www.det.state.ri.us/webdev/lmi**

South Carolina
Director, Labor Market Information, South Carolina Employment Security Commission, 631 Hampton St., P.O. Box 995, Columbia, SC 29202. Phone: (803) 737-2660. Internet: **http://www.sces.org/lmi/index.htm**

South Dakota
Director, Labor Market Center, South Dakota Department of Labor, P.O. Box 4730, Aberdeen, SD 57402-4730. Phone: (605) 626-2314. Internet: **http://www.state.sd.us/dol/lmic/index.htm**

Tennessee
Director, Research and Statistics Division, Tennessee Department of Labor and Workforce Development, 500 James Robertson Pkwy., Davy Crockett Tower, 11th Floor, Nashville, TN 37245-1000. Phone: (615) 741-2284. Internet: **http://www.state.tn.us/labor-wdf/outlooks/select.htm**

Texas
Director of Labor Market Information, Texas Workforce Commission, 9001 IH-35 North, Suite 103A, Austin, TX 78753. Phone: (866) 938-4444. Internet: **http://www.texasworkforce.org/lmi/lfs/lfshome**

Utah
Director, Labor Market Information, Utah Department of Workforce Services, 140 East 300 South, P.O. Box 45249, Salt Lake City, UT 84145-0249. Phone: (801) 526-9675. Internet: **http://www.dws.state.ut.us**

Vermont
Chief, Research and Analysis, Vermont Department of Employment and Training, 5 Green Mountain Dr., P.O. Box 488, Montpelier, VT 05601-0488. Phone: (802) 828-4153. Internet: **http://www.det.state.vt.us**

Virgin Islands
Chief, Bureau of Labor Statistics, Virgin Islands Department of Labor, 53A and 54A&B Kronprindsens Gade, Charlotte Amalie, St. Thomas, VI 00802. Phone: (340) 776-3700. Internet: **http//www.vidol.org**

Virginia
Director, Economic Information and Services Division, Virginia Employment Commission, 703 East Main St:, P.O. Box 1358, Richmond, VA 23218-1358. Phone: (804) 786-8223. Internet: **http://www.vec.state.va.us/lbrmkt/lmi.htm**

Washington
Director, Labor Market and Economic Analysis, Employment Security Division, Mail Stop 6000—P.O. Box 9046, Olympia, WA 98507-9046. Phone: (800) 215-1617. Internet: **http://www.wa.gov/esd/lmea**

West Virginia
Director, Research, Information and Analysis, West Virginia Bureau of Employment Programs, 112 California Ave., Charleston, WV 25305-0112. Phone: (304) 558-2660. Internet: **http://www.state.wv.us/bep/lmi/default.htm**

Wisconsin
Chief, LMI Data Development, Wisconsin Department of Workforce Development, 201 East Washington Ave., Room G200, Madison, WI 53702. Phone: (608) 266-2930. Internet: **http://www.dwd.state.wi.us/lmi**

Wyoming
Manager, Research and Planning, Employment Resources Division, Wyoming Department of Employment, P.O. Box 2760, Casper, WY 82602-2760. Phone: (307) 473-3801. Internet: **http://wydoe.state.wy.us**

☆U.S. GOVERNMENT PRINTING OFFICE: 2002- 488-859

ISBN 0-16-051115-1

90000

9 780160 511158